Excel® for Windows®
SmartStart

RALPH DUFFY
NORTH SEATTLE COMMUNITY COLLEGE

Excel® for Windows® 95 SmartStart

Library of Congress Catalog No.: 95-74884

ISBN: 1-57576-032-0

99 98 97 96 4 3 2 1

Interpretation of the printing code: the rightmost double-digit number is the year of the book's printing; the rightmost single-digit number, the number of the book's printing. For example, a printing code of 96-1 shows that the first printing of the book occurred in 1996.

Screens reproduced in this book were created using Collage Plus from Inner Media, Inc., Hollis, NH.

Excel for Windows 95 SmartStart is based on Microsoft Excel Version 7 for Windows 95.

President and Publisher: David P. Ewing

Associate Publisher: Chris Katsaropoulos

Product Marketing Manager: Susan J. Dollman

Dedication

To Michelle, with thanks.

Acquisitions Editor
Diane E. Beausoleil

Managing Editor
Sheila B. Cunningham

Book Designer
Paula Carroll

Development Editor
Jodi Jensen

Production Editor
Sally A. Yuska

Copy Editor
Beth Spencer

Acquisitions Coordinator
Elizabeth D. Brown

Production Team
Mona Brown
Michael Brumitt
Ayanna Lacey
Steph Mineart
SA Springer
Laura Smith
Andrew Stone
Mark Walchle

Indexer
Tim Griffin

Composed in *Stone Serif* and *MCPdigital* by Que Corporation

About the Author

Ralph Duffy holds a B.A. from the University of Michigan and an M.S. from Pennsylvania State University. He has worked as a statistical consultant and programmer/analyst for Pennsylvania State University, the Indiana University School of Medicine, and Purdue University. He is currently an instructor in the Computer Information Systems Department of North Seattle Community College.

Mr. Duffy is also the Director of the IBM Technology Transfer Center in Seattle. This center, in cooperation with Microsoft Corporation, provides training in computer applications for the faculty and staff of colleges throughout the Northwest, including the University of Washington and Seattle University. Mr. Duffy is the author of numerous titles published by Que Education and Training.

Acknowledgments

Que Education and Training is grateful for the assistance provided by Donna Matherly for her review and technical edit of this book.

Trademark Acknowledgments

Preface

Que Education and Training is the educational publishing imprint of Macmillan Computer Publishing, the world's leading computer book publisher. Macmillan Computer Publishing books have taught more than 20 million people how to be productive with their computers.

This expertise in producing high-quality computer tutorial and reference books is evident in every Que Education and Training title we publish. The same tried-and-true authoring and product development process that makes Macmillan Computer Publishing books bestsellers is used to ensure that every Que Education and Training textbook has the most accurate and most up-to-date information. Experienced and respected college instructors write and review every manuscript to provide class-tested pedagogy. Quality-assurance editors check every keystroke and command in Que Education and Training books to ensure that instructions are clear and precise.

Above all, Macmillan Computer Publishing and, in turn, Que Education and Training have years of experience in meeting the learning demands of computer users in business and at home. This "real world" experience means that Que Education and Training textbooks help students understand how the skills they learn will be applied and why these skills are important.

A Smart Start to Learning Excel for Windows 95

Excel for Windows 95 SmartStart provides a hands-on approach to one of the most popular software programs available. The design of the text is flexible enough to meet a wide variety of needs. The text includes both basic and advanced features of Excel for Windows 95. This text can introduce a student to Excel, or it can supplement a student's previous learning. The abundance of step-by-step, hands-on tutorials allows the student to learn either independently or within a large lab setting.

Before presenting the step-by-step tutorials, *Excel for Windows 95 SmartStart* explains the purpose and practical use of each feature. Within this context, students quickly learn how to use Excel for Windows 95. The explanations and many tutorials enable students to remember how to apply the particular skill and to transfer their knowledge easily to Windows 95 applications. This approach ensures that students will use their skills in a practical manner.

Organization

Excel for Windows 95 SmartStart uses a logical, simple-to-complex organization. Features that are easy to use and understand are presented first. The student can quickly master basic features and develop a framework for learning more complicated features. In addition, features that students can use to improve efficiency as they are learning are introduced very early in the text.

Each chapter begins with an introduction explaining why the features in that chapter are used. Learning objectives are listed after the introduction and then repeated at the appropriate points within the chapter.

Each chapter contains an abundance of hands-on tutorials, tables, and screen illustrations to facilitate learning. Each chapter ends with a summary to help the student absorb and remember the chapter skills. The end-of-chapter exercises include objective questions and hands-on projects to help students check and apply their skills.

Distinctive Features

Excel for Windows 95 SmartStart provides many distinctive features to ensure students success, including the following:

- For convenience and easy reference, key terms are defined in the margin where a new term is first used.
- Each tutorial consists of concise, clear steps. These steps are highlighted in the book design for ease of use and later reference.
- Notes, shortcuts, and other helpful hints provide additional information to enhance learning.
- "If you have problems..." sections act as a teaching assistant in the lab by anticipating where common student errors occur and offering practical assistance.
- Each project is realistic and designed to appeal to a wide variety of business skills and interests.
- The numerous end-of-chapter exercises focus on developing and applying critical thinking skills—not on rote memorization.
- Continuing projects are provided throughout the text. The continuing projects help learners "pull the pieces together."
- An alphabetical index helps users quickly locate information.

To the Student

Although this *SmartStart* provides a step-by-step approach, it is much more than a button-pushing book. In response to your requests, we have included a short explanation of the purpose for each feature. Our focus is on teaching you to use Windows 95 effectively rather than on simply listing its features. We want to make certain that you remember how to apply your knowledge of Windows 95 long after you have taken this course.

You will not spend a great deal of time simply typing documents. We have provided your instructor with a data disk containing example information for many of the hands-on projects. You can then spend your time completing interesting projects with real-life scenarios.

To the Instructor

The Instructor's Manual, available on disk, includes a Curriculum Guide to help you plan class sessions and assignments. Each chapter in the Instructor's Manual disk contains teaching tips, answers to "Checking Your Skills" questions, transparency masters, and test questions and answers. The manual also offers advice on what to teach when time is short or when the students have a specific need. Additional project ideas and suggestions also are included.

The Instructor's Manual disk also includes the student data files needed for completing the tutorials.

This Instructor's Manual disk (ISBN 1-57576-043-8) is available to the adopters of *Excel for Windows 95 SmartStart*, upon written request. Please submit your request on school letterhead to your local representative or to S. Dollman, Macmillan Computer Publishing, 201 W. 103rd Street, Indianapolis, IN 46290-1097.

Look for the following additional SmartStarts:

Access 2 for Windows SmartStart	1-56529-874-8
dBASE 5.0 for Windows SmartStart	0-7897-0439-0
Excel 5 for Windows SmartStart	1-56529-794-6
Lotus 1-2-3 for Windows Release 5 SmartStart	0-7897-0009-3
Novell NetWare SmartStart	1-56529-411-4
Paradox 5 for Windows SmartStart	0-7897-0011-5
PowerPoint 4 for Windows SmartStart	1-56529-795-4
Quattro Pro 6 for Windows SmartStart	0-7897-0007-7
Quattro Pro DOS 4.0 SmartStart	1-56529-408-4
Windows 3.1 SmartStart, 2/e	0-7897-0010-7
Windows 95 SmartStart	0-7897-0428-5
Word 6 for Windows SmartStart	1-56529-796-2
WordPerfect 6 for Windows SmartStart, 2/e	0-7897-0008-5
WordPerfect for Windows SmartStart	1-56529-403-3
Works for DOS 3.0 SmartStart	1-56529-395-9
Works for Windows 3.0 SmartStart	1-56529-394-0

For more information call:

1-800-428-5331

Contents at a Glance

Table of Contents

Introduction

Welcome to *Excel for Windows 95 SmartStart*. Whether you are new to Excel or upgrading from an earlier version of Excel, this SmartStart tutorial is one of the fastest and easiest ways to get started and become productive.

If you are experienced with Windows 95, you may be familiar with many of the concepts used in Excel for Windows 95. If you are new to Windows 95, you will discover that Windows 95 is a much easier and more intuitive operating environment than the traditional character-based environment.

All aspects of Excel for Windows 95 contain improvements, including enhanced analytical capabilities, greater flexibility with database management, increased charting options, and the capability to automate tasks and customize Excel with Visual Basic macros. Excel for Windows 95 also includes many new features designed to enhance its presentation capabilities. All Excel features focus on ease of use and increased productivity—which is why Excel is considered the spreadsheet of choice by many users.

Who Should Use This Book?

Excel for Windows 95 SmartStart is a tutorial developed with easy-to-follow, step-by-step instructions. Because *Excel for Windows 95 SmartStart* concisely covers only the most important concepts, your time on the learning curve is greatly reduced. Each chapter begins with a set of objectives. You learn by following the hands-on tutorials in each chapter. Exercises and questions at the end of each chapter give you a chance to practice what you have learned and to check your understanding of the objectives.

If you are a new spreadsheet user, *Excel for Windows 95 SmartStart* will help you become productive quickly. If you are an experienced computer user who is new to the Windows 95 environment, *Excel for Windows 95 SmartStart* will give you a head start on learning other Windows applications, such as Microsoft Word for Windows 95, Microsoft PowerPoint, Aldus PageMaker, or any of the many Windows applications you might use.

How This Book Is Organized

Each chapter of this book follows the same format. A chapter overview comes first, where chapter objectives are listed. Next, procedures are presented in tutorial steps to guide you through the required actions. In most cases, illustrations show how the screen should appear during and after a certain action. Each tutorial is set off on the page by a different color background. Key terms are defined in the margin when they are used for the first time in the chapter. Chapters include questions that check your mastery of the chapter objectives and end with chapter review questions and continuing projects in which you apply the skills learned in the chapter. Special "If you have problems..." boxes point out possible trouble spots and give you simple solutions to these difficulties.

The early chapters provide an understanding of Excel worksheet basics. The rest of the chapters discuss more advanced features, including functions, charting, database management, macros, and linking and consolidating worksheets.

Chapter 1, "Learning Excel Workbook and Worksheet Basics," explains the main components of Excel. The information includes how to start Excel and reviews the basics of the screen, menus, keyboard, and commands. You learn how to enter data, move around the worksheet, access commands, and save and print a workbook.

Chapter 2, "Building a Worksheet," covers defining ranges; moving, copying, and clearing cell contents; inserting and deleting cells, columns, and rows; and changing column width and row height.

Chapter 3, "Formatting Worksheets," shows you how to use Excel's various formatting commands to enhance the appearance of your worksheets. This chapter also explains how to check the spelling in a worksheet and introduces Excel's on-line Help and tutorials.

Chapter 4, "Using Functions," describes many of Excel's built-in functions, explains the types of functions used for a variety of calculations, and demonstrates how to enter functions in a worksheet.

Chapter 5, "Managing Workbooks and Printing Worksheets," explains how to name, move, copy, and delete a workbook's sheets. Then you learn how to use the Zoom and Page Preview commands and how to set up a worksheet for printing.

Chapter 6, "Charting Data," teaches you how to create a chart; change chart types; and enhance, format, modify, and print charts.

Chapter 7, "Managing Data," explains what an Excel database (List) is and tells you how to build an Excel database. Then you learn how to add data to the database, view the data, delete records, and sort records. This chapter also covers searching for records in a database and using the AutoFilter.

Chapter 8, "Using Excel Macros to Automate Repetitive Tasks," shows you how to create a macro using the Macro Recorder, run a macro, create a button to run a macro, and how to delete a macro you no longer need.

Chapter 9, "Linking Worksheets and Creating Summary Reports," explains links between worksheets and shows how to create, change, and restore links between two Excel worksheets. Then you learn how to link an Excel worksheet with a document in another Windows application. Creating summary reports with subtotals and consolidated reports is also demonstrated.

Chapter 10, "What If Analysis and Scenario Manager," shows you how to set up one- and two-input tables, introduces forecasting worksheets, and explains how to use the Scenario Manager.

Appendix A, "Working with Windows 95," gives you the basics for working with Microsoft Windows 95 and any Windows 95 application.

Finally, the Glossary provides an alphabetized list of all the key terms defined in the text.

Where to Find More Help

After you have gained a solid foundation in using Excel from this SmartStart, you may want to explore some of the more advanced features in Excel for Windows 95. These features include auditing worksheets, adding notes and pictures to worksheets, importing and exporting text data, doing advanced charting, using lookup functions, drawing with Excel, and accessing external databases.

Que Corporation has a complete line of Excel books designed to meet the needs of all computer users. Other Excel books include *Special Edition Using Excel for Windows 95*, *Excel for Windows 95 Visual Quick Reference*, and *The Big Basics Book for Excel for Windows 95*.

System Requirements for Running Excel for Windows 95

To install and run Excel for Windows 95, your computer and software should meet or exceed the following requirements:

Hardware Requirements

- IBM or compatible computer with a hard disk and an 80386 or higher processor
- At least 4M of conventional RAM memory (8M recommended)
- At least 35M hard disk space for minimum installation (actual requirements will vary based on features you choose to install)
- VGA or higher resolution graphics card
- 3 1/2-inch high-density disk drive
- A printer (optional)

Software Requirements

- Windows 95

Conventions Used in This Book

This book uses a number of conventions to help you learn the program quickly.

Step-by-step tutorials are given a light, screened background to set them off from the rest of the text. Information that you are asked to type is printed in **boldface and teal** in the tutorials and in **boldface** elsewhere. Menu letters you type to activate a command appear in **boldface and teal** in tutorials, review exercises, and projects—**V**iew—and in boldface elsewhere—**V**iew. Keys you press are shown as keyboard icons—↵Enter—and in teal icons in tutorials, review exercises, and projects—↵Enter. Keys you press together are joined by a plus sign—Alt+F2.

Exact quotations of words that appear on-screen are spelled as they appear on-screen and printed in a `special typeface`.

CHAPTER 1

Excel Workbook and Worksheet Basics

One of the most valuable computer programs for businesses is the spreadsheet. Spreadsheet programs are used in the financial and scientific analysis of numeric data. Spreadsheet programs perform calculations, illustrate relationships in data by displaying charts, and can also help organize data. Microsoft Excel for Windows 95 is a popular and powerful spreadsheet program developed for users of all skill levels. Excel is easy for beginners to learn and use; yet it provides powerful features for programmers and high-level users. Using Excel for Windows 95 has become an essential skill for many office workers and managers.

Cell
The intersection of a column and a row in a spreadsheet.

In Excel, you work with electronic worksheets that contain numbers, formulas, and text. An electronic worksheet is organized in lettered columns and numbered rows. The intersection of a row and column is called a *cell*. You enter data into cells, and Excel uses this data when it performs calculations. Typical uses of electronic worksheets include the calculation of budgets, expense accounts, and accounting problems. Excel worksheets are also used for business plans, financial analysis, list management, and data analysis. Because relationships within large volumes of numeric data can be confusing, Excel also has the capability of creating graphs, or charts, from worksheet data. Related Excel worksheets and charts are stored in the same disk file, called a workbook.

In this chapter, you learn the worksheet basics—how to move around in the rows and columns of the worksheet and then to enter data, formulas, and functions into a blank worksheet. As you work on a project, you learn to use commands, print, and work with the individual worksheets in a workbook. In addition, you become familiar with commands that open, close, name, save, and delete a workbook. Finally, you learn to exit Excel.

Note: *If you have never used Windows 95, you need to read Appendix A, "Working with Windows 95." Appendix A provides basic information about working in Windows 95.*

Objectives

By the time you have finished this chapter, you will have learned to

1. Start Excel
2. Become Comfortable with the Excel Screen
3. Understand Excel's Toolbar Buttons
4. Move around in a Worksheet
5. Enter and Edit Text, Numbers, and Formulas
6. Name and Save a Workbook File
7. Print a Worksheet
8. Open and Close a File
9. Exit Excel

Objective 1: Start Excel

Excel icon
A small picture representing the Excel program displayed when you select the Start, Programs command on the Windows 95 desktop.

You must have Windows 95 loaded on your machine before you can start Excel for Windows 95. If Windows 95 is running on your computer, you will see the Windows 95 desktop on your screen. If Windows 95 is not running, your instructor can explain how to start Windows 95.

After Windows 95 is loaded, the Windows 95 desktop appears (if you are unfamiliar with Windows 95, refer to Appendix A).

Note: *As users become more familiar with Excel, they may prefer to use keyboard commands and shortcuts to save time.*

Starting Excel with the Mouse

The best way to learn the basics of Excel is to dive in and start exploring. This section explains how to start Excel using the mouse. Follow these steps:

1. Make sure that Windows 95 is running on your computer and that the desktop is displayed.
2. Click the Start button at the lower left corner of the desktop (the button is in the taskbar).
3. Move the mouse pointer to **P**rograms in the Windows 95 menu.

   The programs available on your computer are displayed in the **P**rograms submenu. If Microsoft Excel is not in the menu, move the mouse pointer to the folder that contains Excel (check with your instructor).

4 Click Microsoft Excel to open the Excel program window (see figure 1.1). A Microsoft Excel button appears in the taskbar at the bottom of your screen.

1

Objective 2: Become Comfortable with the Excel Screen

When you start Excel, do not be overwhelmed by the many details on the screen. You don't have to learn everything at once. This chapter is simply an orientation. In this book, you learn about Excel one step at a time. See figure 1.1 and table 1.1 for an overview of the major components of the Excel screen.

Note: *Your screen may not look exactly like the screens in this book.*

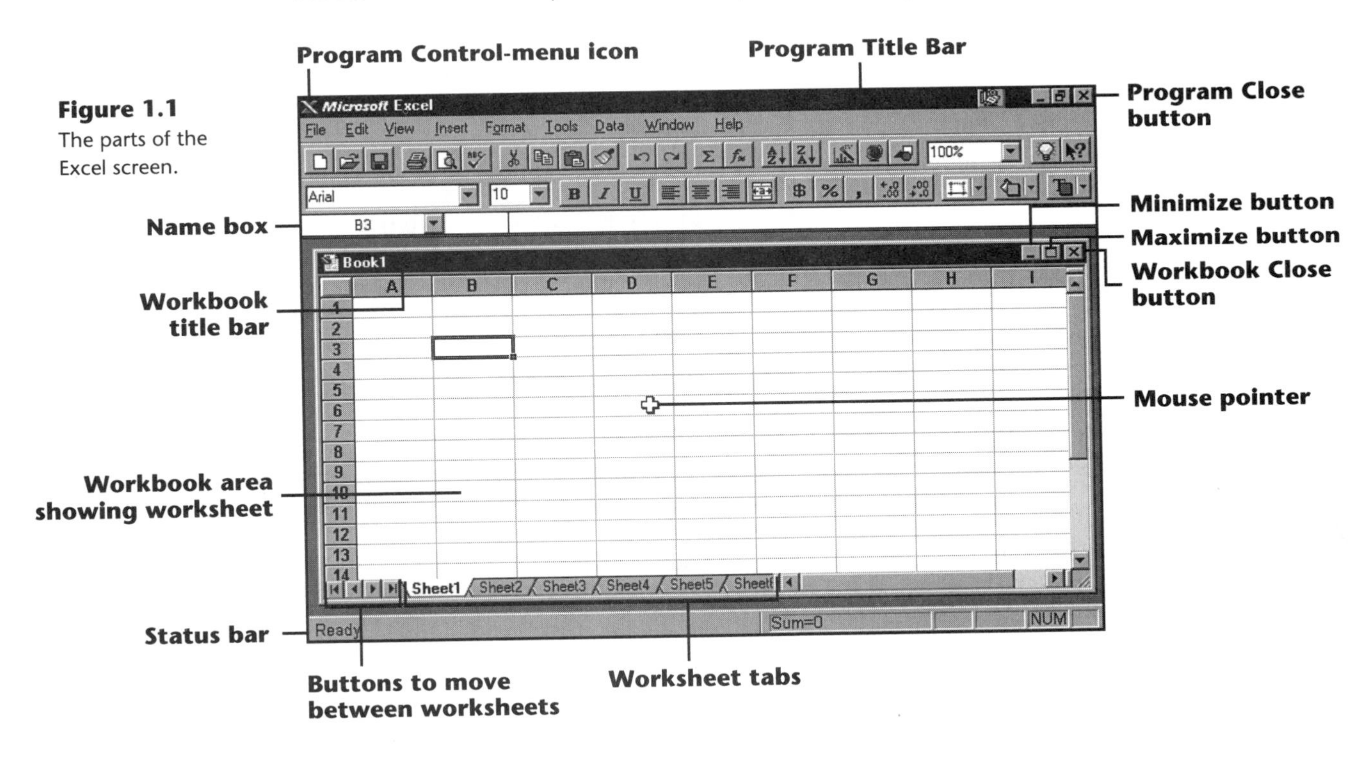

Figure 1.1
The parts of the Excel screen.

Table 1.1 contains a brief description of each screen component. More detail about certain components is covered later in this chapter.

Table 1.1 The Excel Screen

Component	Description
Program window	The outer window, in which Excel runs.
Document window	The inner window containing the workbook; enclosed by numbered row headings and lettered column headings.
Program Control menu icon	A hyphen inside a gray box in the upper left corner of the program window; used to close the program window.
Document Control menu icon	A hyphen inside a gray box in the upper left corner of the document window; used to close the document window.
Title bar	Top portion of the window listing the program or document name.
Minimize button	In the upper right corner of the window (looks like a minus sign); reduces the program window or the document window to a small picture.
Maximize button	In the upper right corner of the window (looks like a box); expands the program window to fit the entire screen; expands the document window to fill the program window.
Restore button	In the upper right corner of the window (looks like two overlapping boxes); replaces the Maximize button when the window is maximized; restores the window to the size between minimized and maximized positions.
Menu bar	Located directly below the title bar. Each menu contains a list of commands; the list drops down when the menu is activated.
Standard toolbar	Located between the menu bar and the formula bar; contains buttons represented by icon buttons for quick, graphical access to commands.
Formatting toolbar	Contains buttons that enable you to change and enhance the appearance of your worksheets; located below the standard toolbar.
Formula bar	Located immediately above the document window; displays cell contents and is used to edit cell contents.
Cell reference area	Located at the left end of the formula bar; contains the address of the active cell.
Scroll bars	Located along the right side and bottom of the document window; used to move the screen display horizontally or vertically.
Worksheet tabs	Located at the bottom of the worksheet area. The highlighted tab tells you which worksheet you are using; also used to move among worksheets.
Status bar	Located at the very bottom of the program window; displays a prompt line to tell you what a command will do or what to do next to complete the execution of the command. The status bar displays the word Ready when Excel will accept data entered into the worksheet.

Learning the Parts of the Program Window

Toolbar
An area of the Excel screen containing a series of icon buttons used to access commands and other features.

The program window is the outer window, with `Microsoft Excel` and the name of the open workbook displayed in the title bar. This window contains the menu bar, formula bar, *toolbars*, and any open document windows, but does not contain scroll bars. To minimize, maximize, restore, or close the program window, use the sizing icons in the upper right corner of the window. When minimized, the window disappears but the Microsoft Excel button remains in the taskbar. You can restore the program to its previous position and size by clicking the Microsoft Excel button in the taskbar.

The Menu Bar

The Excel program window has a *menu bar* that displays nine menus. The **F**ile, **E**dit, **V**iew, **I**nsert, F**o**rmat, **T**ools, **D**ata, **W**indow, and **H**elp menus are listed across the menu bar. When selected, each menu displays a list of commands (see figure 1.2). You access a menu by using the mouse or the keyboard. You learn how to use menus later in the chapter.

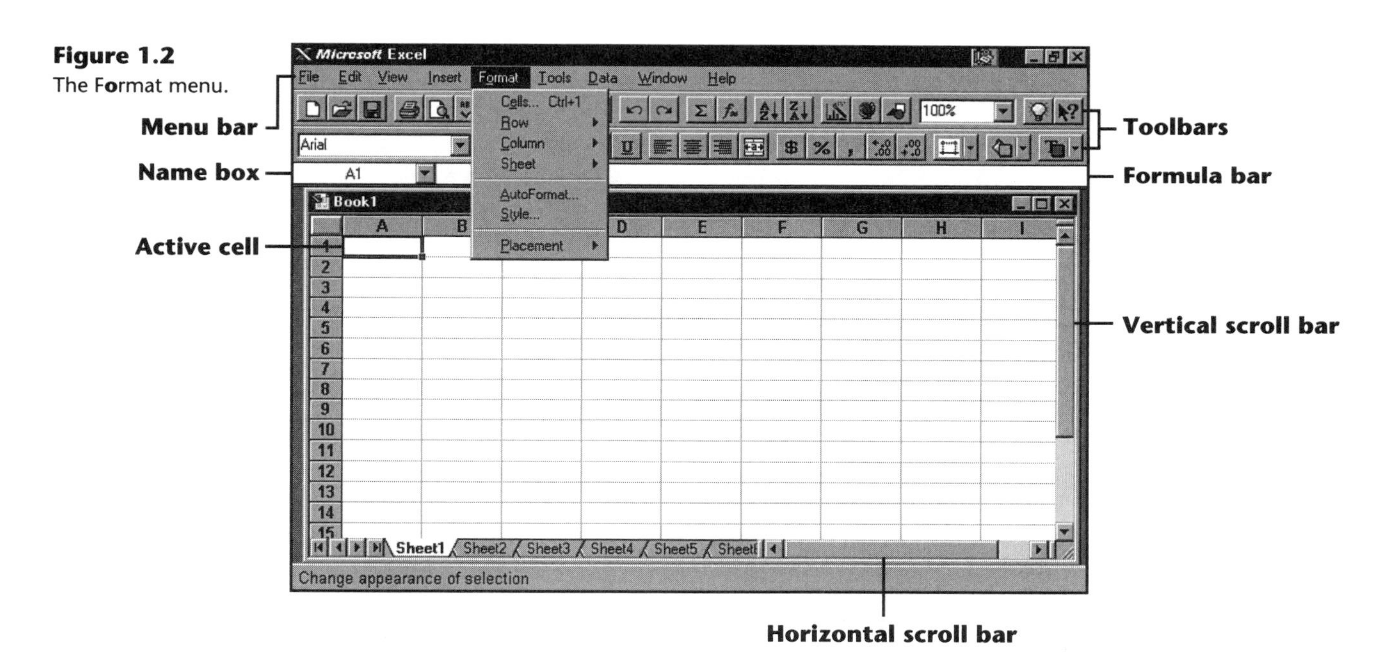

Figure 1.2
The Format menu.

The Toolbars

A toolbar is a strip of icon buttons displayed across the top part of the Excel program window just below the menu bar. Excel's Standard and Formatting toolbars are designed to provide easy access to common commands, such as automatic summation, borders, printing, formatting, and styles.

The Formula Bar

Active cell
The worksheet cell receiving the data you type surrounded by a thick border.

The *formula bar* is located directly above the column headings in a worksheet (refer to figure 1.1). The address of the *active cell* is displayed at the left end of the formula bar. The formula bar becomes active when you enter data into a cell. When the formula bar is active, a button with a red X (the Cancel button) and a button with a green check mark (the Confirm button) appear to the left of the area displaying the entered data. You click the X button to cancel the entry, and you click the check mark button to accept the entry into the cell. The button to the right of the check mark button activates the Function Wizard, explained in Chapter 4. The formula bar displays the formula (calculation) or data contained in the active cell, and the cell itself displays the number that results from calculating the formula (see figure 1.3).

Figure 1.3
The activated formula bar.

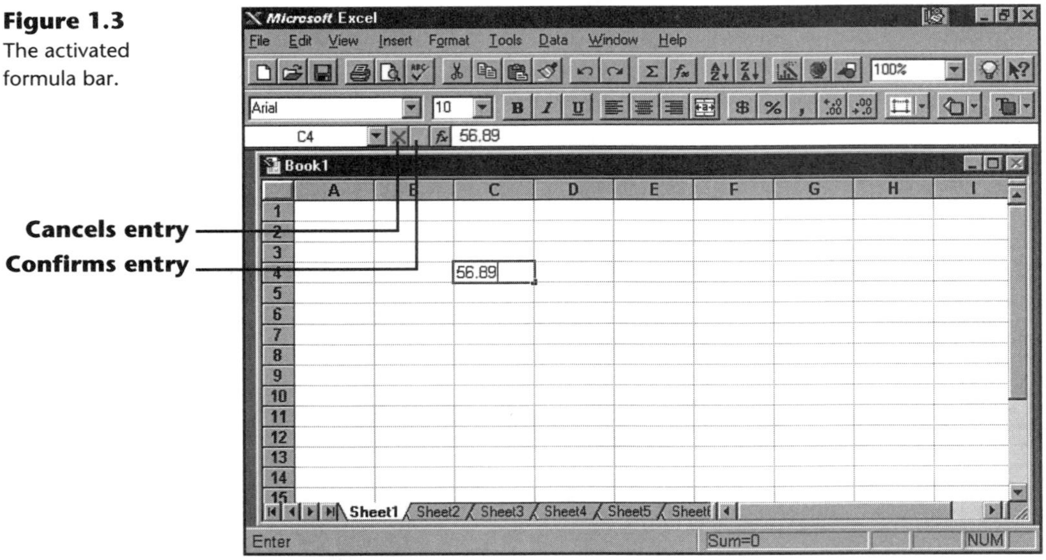

Cancels entry

Confirms entry

The Document Window

Workbook
A set of worksheet pages provided by Excel. Related charts and worksheets are kept in one workbook. Workbooks are stored as disk files.

The document window is the inner window within the program window. The title bar of the document window contains the name of your document (*workbook*). If you have not saved your workbook on disk, Excel assigns a name to the document window. Excel assigns Book1, for example, to a new, unnamed workbook.

You can manipulate the document window in three ways. You can minimize or maximize the document window, or you can restore the document window to its previous size. If the window is maximized, the document window title appears in the title bar of the program window (see figure 1.4). Most people maximize the document window to see as much as possible of a worksheet.

To restore a maximized window, click the restore sizing button in the upper right corner of the document window.

The Worksheet Area

Worksheet
The grid of rows and columns into which you enter text, numbers, and formulas.

A *worksheet* is a grid with labeled columns and rows. Columns are labeled with letters across the top of the worksheet; rows are labeled with numbers down the left side of the worksheet. The intersection of a column and a row is called a *cell*. An Excel worksheet contains 256 columns and 16,384 rows, which makes a grid of more than 4 million cells available for entering text, numbers, or calculations. Usually, you use only relatively few rows and columns, those in the upper left corner of a worksheet. A new workbook comes with 16 worksheets; worksheets can be added or deleted.

Figure 1.4
The maximized document window.

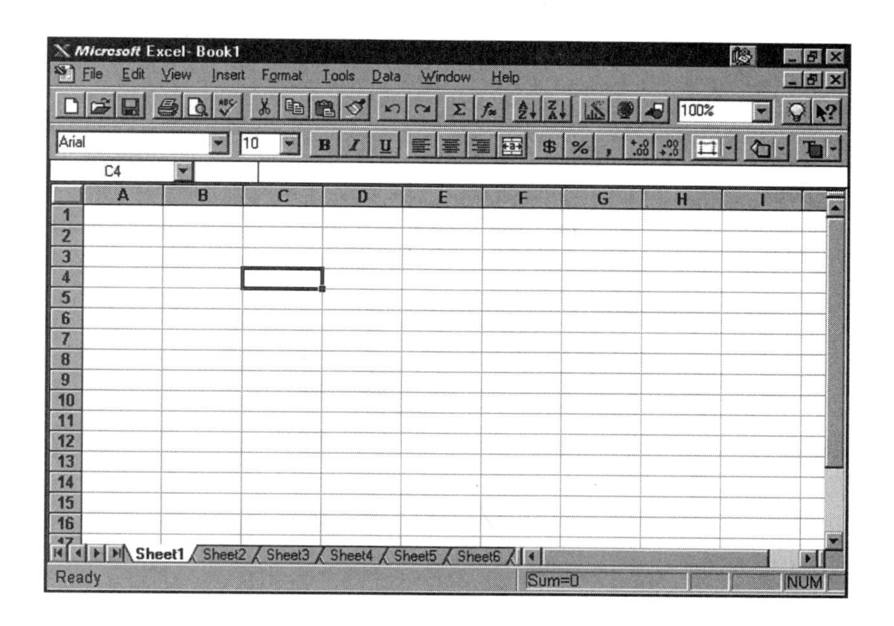

Cell address
Location of a cell based on the intersection of a column and row.

When referring to a particular worksheet cell, you use the *cell address*, which is determined by the column and row intersection. Cell B6, for example, refers to the cell at the intersection of column B and row 6.

Objective 3: Understand Excel's Toolbar Buttons

Dialog box
An on-screen box in Windows 95 programs requesting information and input.

Excel displays the Standard and Formatting toolbars across the top of the screen. A toolbar is a group of buttons, or icons, representing commonly used menu commands. Buttons offer more efficient methods of executing Excel commands. For example, to boldface an entry, click the Bold button on the Formatting toolbar rather than choose the F**o**rmat, C**e**lls command, click the Font tab, select the Bold option in the *dialog box*, and then choose OK.

If you place the mouse pointer on a button in a toolbar and *don't* click, Excel displays a ToolTip—a small label that displays the name of the button. Placing the mouse pointer on a button also causes information on the button to be displayed in the status bar. You can use both the ToolTip and the status bar to learn more about the toolbar buttons.

Table 1.2 lists the functions of the buttons on each toolbar. These buttons are explained in later chapters as you need to use them.

Table 1.2 The Toolbar Buttons

Icon	Button Name	Purpose
Standard Toolbar		
	New Workbook	Opens a new workbook.
	Open File	Displays the dialog box for opening an existing file.

(continues)

Table 1.2 Continued

Icon	Button Name	Purpose
	Save File	Saves the active file; displays the File Save As dialog box if the file has no name.
	Print	Begins printing the active document.
	Print Preview	Displays the current worksheet as it will appear when printed.
	Spelling Check	Performs a spelling check on the current worksheet.
	Cut	Cuts selection and places it in the Clipboard.
	Copy	Copies selection and places it in the Clipboard.
	Paste	Places the contents of the Clipboard into the worksheet at the active cell.
	Format Painter	Copies and pastes cell formats only.
	Undo	Undoes your last action or command.
	Repeat	Repeats last action or command.
	AutoSum	Inserts the SUM function and adds numbers directly above or to the left of the active cell.
	Function Wizard	Aids in the creation of functions.
	Sort Ascending	Arranges selected rows from the smallest to the largest value.
	Sort Descending	Arranges selected rows from the largest to the smallest value.
	ChartWizard	Aids in the construction of a chart.
	Map	Creates a map of your data.
	Drawing	Shows or hides the Drawing toolbar.
100%	Zoom Control	Increases or decreases the visible worksheet area.
	TipWizard	Shows or hides helpful Excel tips.
	Help	Provides information on a command or screen region.
Formatting Toolbar		
B	Bold	Boldfaces selected text.
I	Italic	Italicizes selected text.

Icon	Button Name	Purpose
	Underline	Underlines selected text.
	Align Left	Left-aligns text.
	Center	Centers text.
	Align Right	Right-aligns text.
	Center Across	Centers text across selected columns.
	Currency Style	Adds a dollar sign, commas, a decimal point, and two decimal places to selected cells.
	Percent Style	Applies percent style to cells.
	Comma Style	Applies to selected cells a style like currency but without the dollar sign.
	Increase Decimal	Adds one decimal place to selection.
	Decrease Decimal	Removes one decimal place from selection.
	Borders	Applies most recently used border style to the selected cell or range of cells.
	Color	Colors background and fills pattern of selection.
	Font Color	Colors the characters in the selection.

Exploring the Toolbars

To use the Help button to see the function of a button on the toolbar, follow these steps:

1. Click the Maximize button to maximize the program window.
2. Place the mouse pointer on the Help button at the far right of the Standard toolbar, and click the left mouse button. The mouse pointer should now have a large black question mark attached to it.
3. Place the mouse pointer on the Bold button (the button displaying a B in the Formatting toolbar), and click the left mouse button.
4. Read the information in the Help note that appears in the document window.
5. Click the Help note to make it disappear.
6. Use this same technique with the Help button if you want to learn the functions of all the buttons on the toolbar.

Objective 4: Move around in a Worksheet

When you start Excel, a blank worksheet appears in the document window (see figure 1.5). This worksheet is the first of 16 blank worksheets in a workbook titled Book1. Excel automatically assigns the name Book1 to the workbook until you save the workbook in a disk file and give it a file name. The worksheet is the document that Excel uses for storing and manipulating data.

Figure 1.5
The Excel worksheet.

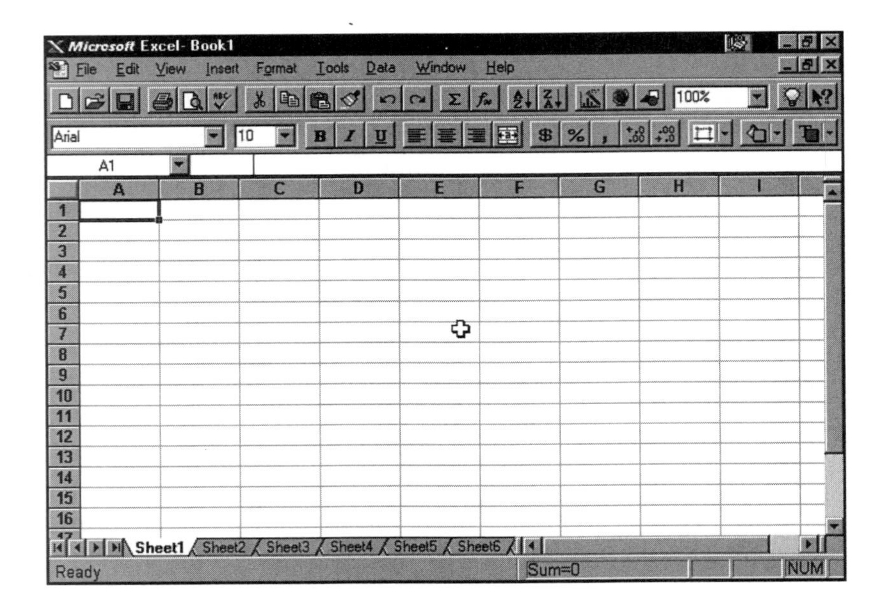

In a new worksheet, the cell at the intersection of column A and row 1 is outlined with a border darker than the other cells' borders. The darker border indicates that cell A1 is the active cell. If you start typing, data appears in this cell. To enter data into another cell, you must activate that cell. You activate another cell in the worksheet by clicking the cell or by using the mouse or the arrow keys to move the cell pointer to the cell. Moving to different locations in a worksheet is the first skill you should master.

Cell pointer
A cross-shaped white marker; the shape the mouse pointer takes when it is on the worksheet.

You can easily accomplish many tasks in Excel with a mouse. If you are using a mouse to move in a worksheet, you can make a cell active by placing the *cell pointer*, a white cross, on the cell and clicking the left mouse button once. Using the keyboard, you can press the arrow keys, PgUp or PgDn, to move to another cell and activate that cell. The keys used for moving to new locations are listed in table 1.3.

Table 1.3 Moving among Cells with the Keyboard

Key(s)	Description
←, →, ↑, ↓	Moves one cell to the left, right, up, or down, respectively; activates the new cell.
Home	Moves to column A of the active row.

Key(s)	Description
Ctrl+Home	Moves to cell A1, the home cell; activates the home cell.
PgUp	Moves up one screen.
PgDn	Moves down one screen.

You also can use the F5 key to move to a specific cell. When you press F5, the Go To dialog box appears (see figure 1.6).

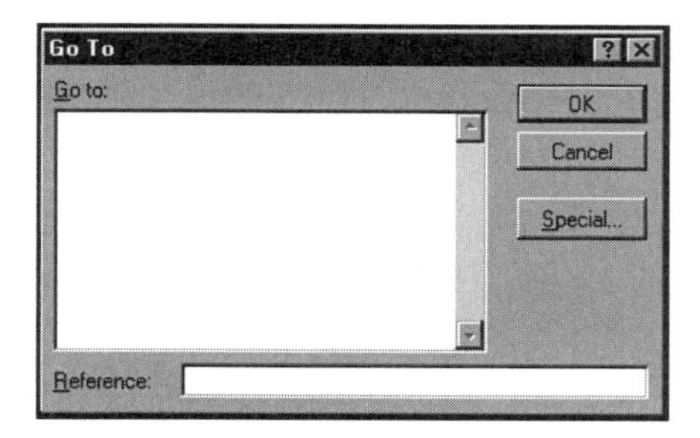

Figure 1.6
The Go To dialog box.

When the Go To dialog box appears, type in the **R**eference text box the address of the cell you want activated, and then press ←Enter. If, for example, you want to move to the cell in column D, row 5, type **D5**, and then press ←Enter or choose OK. Cell D5 becomes active.

Changing the Active Cell Using the Mouse

To activate cell E10, make sure that you have started Excel; then follow these steps:

1. Place the cell pointer on cell E10.
2. Click the left mouse button. A dark border appears indicating that cell E10 is the active cell.

You can enter data more efficiently into a worksheet if you keep your hands on the keyboard and use the movement keys on the keyboard. You practice using the keyboard in the next tutorial.

Changing the Active Cell Using the Keyboard

To change cell C7 to the active cell, follow these steps:

1. From cell E10, press ← twice.
2. Press ↑ three times.

To go directly to cell H16, follow these steps:

1. Press F5.

Changing the Active Cell Using the Keyboard (continued)

2. When the Go To dialog box appears, type **H16**, and press Enter. Cell H16 should be activated.

3. To return to the upper left corner of your worksheet, press Ctrl+Home.

Using the Mouse Pointer

With the mouse, you can efficiently perform a variety of actions. The mouse pointer's shape indicates what you can do with the mouse. The shape changes as the mouse pointer is moved to different areas of the Excel windows. Table 1.4 lists the various shapes.

Table 1.4 Mouse Pointer Shapes

Pointer Shape	Location(s)	To Use
	Menu, scroll bar, toolbar	Select by moving the tip of the arrow on a name or icon and then clicking.
	Text boxes, formula bar	Repositions the flashing cursor (insertion point) within editable text. To move the insertion-point location, move the I-beam to the new desired location, and click.
	Appears during placement, resizing, or drawing of placement command objects	Select object and drag across sheet or move to square handle on object and drag to resize.
	Appears between column headings	Drag to change column width.
	Appears between row headings	Drag to change row height.
	Appears on window edge	Drag to change position of window edge.
	Window corners	Drag to reposition two window edges at one time.
	Inside worksheet	Click to select cells in worksheet.
	Split bar at ends of scroll bar	Drag to split window into two views.
	Print Preview	Select workbook area for closer view.
	Help window, macro buttons	Click for help or to run macro.
	Appears at corner of selected cells	Drag to contiguous cells to copy cell contents to the contiguous cells.
	Appears at corner of selected cell(s) when you press Ctrl	Drag to copy and increment to contiguous cells.
	Appears after you click the Help button	Click any part of the Excel screen to get help information about that area.

Pointer Shape	Location(s)	To Use
	Appears when you are specifying where you want Excel to display a chart	Drag to select the desired height and width of the chart.
	Appears when you are resizing an object	Drag to resize the object.
	Appears when you are resizing a control	Drag to place the control where you want it.
	Appears at the edge of selected object	Drag to move the object.
	Any screen	Means "Please wait."

Objective 5: Enter and Edit Text, Numbers, and Formulas

You can enter text—such as a row or column heading—and numbers into a worksheet cell. The headings show what the numbers represent. Some worksheet cells contain (store) numbers. These numbers are data that you enter, and they change only when you enter a different number into the cell. In other cells, you place formulas that use the data cells to produce and display calculated results. The value displayed in a formula cell depends on the numbers you type in the data cells. The power of using a worksheet for financial reports, income statements, budget forecasts, and other business programs comes from Excel's automatic recalculation of formulas when you change data in the worksheet.

Understanding Formulas

Formula bar
Area near the top of the Excel screen where you enter and edit data.

Formulas can calculate data using numbers or the addresses of other cells. A *formula* starts with an equal sign (=) and uses mathematical symbols to indicate what type of operation the formula will perform and cell addresses to identify the location of the data the formula calculates. As you create the formula, it is displayed in an area called the *formula bar* (see figure 1.7). The numerical results, however, are displayed in the cell itself.

After you enter a formula, Excel automatically performs the calculation. If you change a number stored in a cell address used in a formula, Excel automatically recalculates the results of the formula. The use of a formula enables you to test outcomes by using different numbers in the cells referenced in the formula. For example, if a formula in cell C5 includes cell B10 and you type a new number in cell B10, the cell containing the formula (C5) automatically recalculates and displays the new result.

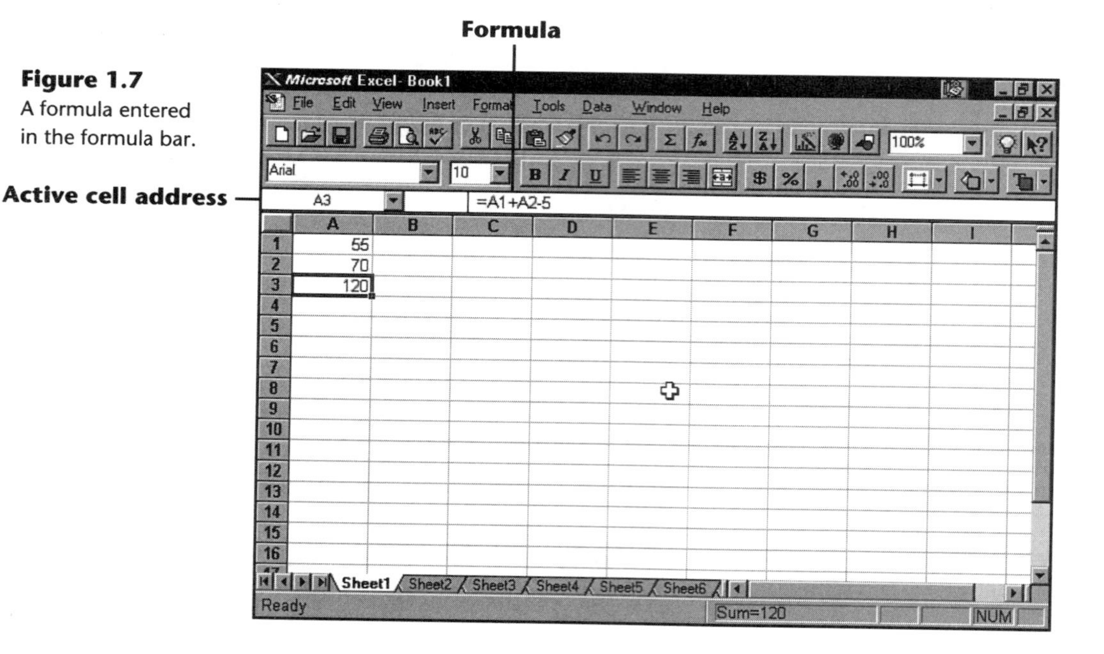

Figure 1.7
A formula entered in the formula bar.

Entering a Formula

To enter a formula in the active cell, first type = (an equal sign). Next, type the formula. If, for example, three numbers have been entered into cells B1, B2, and B3, and you want to display the total in cell B4, you type the formula =B1+B2+B3 in cell B4. Both the active cell and the formula bar display the formula as you enter it. Do not type spaces in the formula.

Because the entry in cell B4 starts with an equal sign, Excel recognizes the entry as a formula. After the formula is complete and you press ↵Enter, cell B4 displays the result of the formula. The formula bar shows the formula whenever cell B4 is activated. In the first review exercise at the end of this chapter, you set up a business worksheet. In the following set of tutorials, you practice the skills you need for this project.

Entering Text and Numbers into Cells and Adding the Numbers

To enter numbers into the top three rows of column B and then add them, follow these steps:

1. Make cell A1 the active cell, and type **BUDGET**.
2. Make cell B1 the active cell, and type **5**.
3. Make cell B2 the active cell, and type **8**.

4. Make cell B3 the active cell, and type **9**.
5. Make cell B4 the active cell, and type the formula **=B1+B2+B3**.
6. Press ↵Enter.
7. Make cell B1 the active cell, type **200**, and then press ↵Enter. This entry replaces the old contents of cell B1. Notice that the result in cell B4 changes because cell B1 changed.
8. Make cell A4 the active cell, and type the label **SUM** = for your result.
9. Press ↵Enter.
10. Make cell A12 the active cell, and type **MY FIRST EXCEL WORKSHEET**.
11. Press ↵Enter.

You will use this worksheet in the next tutorial.

Unfortunately, errors may occur when you are typing cell addresses in a formula. To avoid making typing errors, you may choose to build a formula by selecting cells (pointing to the cells you want Excel to use) rather than typing cell addresses. Use either the mouse or the keyboard to select cells for use in a formula.

Building a Formula by Using the Mouse to Select Cells

Suppose that you want in cell D9 a formula that subtracts the number in cell B2 from the total in cell B4. To build the formula with the mouse, follow these steps:

1. Type an equal sign (=) in cell D9 to start the formula.
2. Click cell B4 to add that cell address to the formula in the formula bar.
3. Type a minus sign (–).
4. Click cell B2 to insert that cell address into the formula.
5. Press ↵Enter to complete the formula entry. The complete formula is entered in cell D9, with the result displayed in that cell and the formula displayed in the formula bar when D9 is the active cell (see figure 1.8).

You will use this worksheet in the next tutorial.

(continues)

Building a Formula by Using the Mouse to Select Cells (continued)

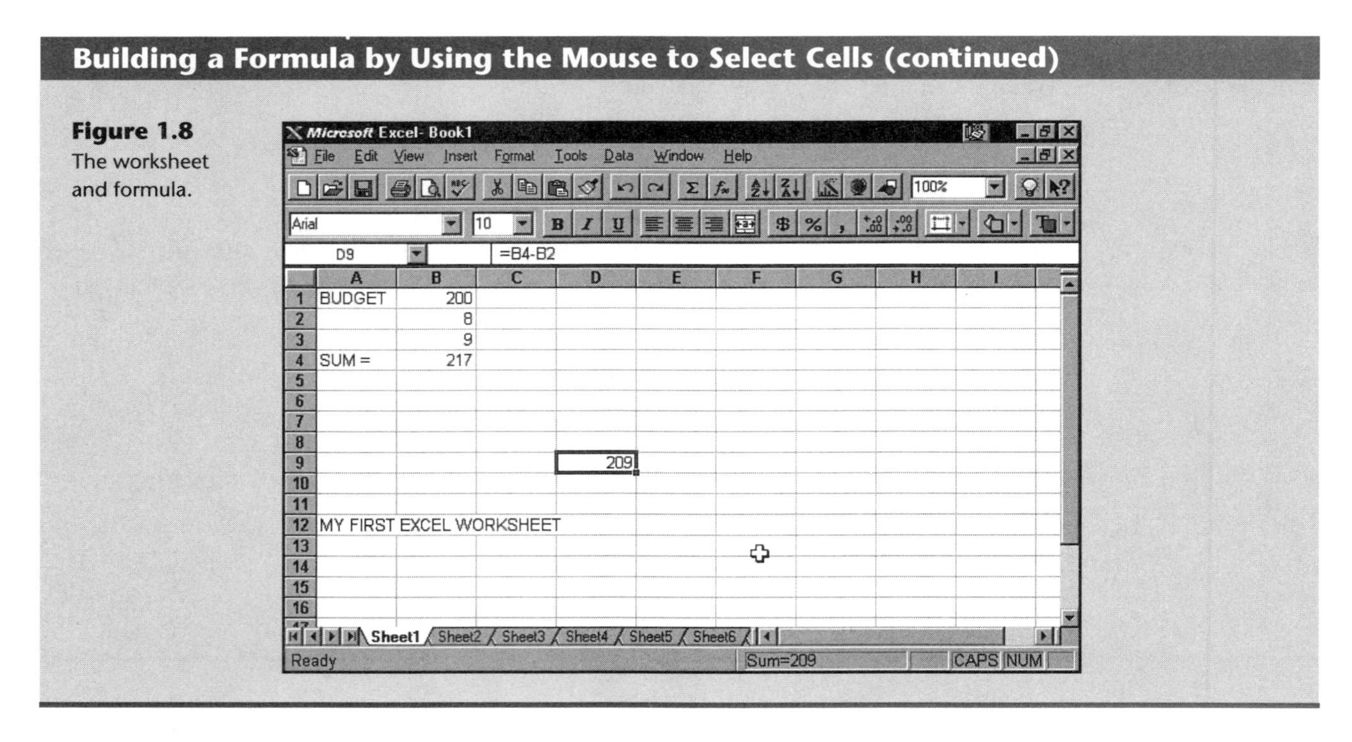

Figure 1.8 The worksheet and formula.

Using Mathematical Operators in Formulas

The following mathematical operators are used in calculations:

+	Addition
–	Subtraction
*	Multiplication
/	Division
^	Exponentiation

Order of precedence
The order mathematicians have established for performing arithmetical operations in a formula.

Errors will occur in your worksheet if you do not remember the *order of precedence*—the mathematically defined order of calculations. Excel always follows the correct order of precedence. The order of precedence for mathematical operations is

^	Exponentiation
*, /	Multiplication, division
+, –	Addition, subtraction

Exponentiation occurs before multiplication or division in a formula, and multiplication and division occur before addition or subtraction. If a formula includes mathematical operators that are at the same level of precedence, calculations are done from left to right. For example, if a formula includes only addition and subtraction, and the addition operation appears in the formula to the left of the subtraction, Excel performs addition first. The computer always performs exponentiation first, no matter where it appears in a formula.

To alter the normal order of precedence, use parentheses around one or more mathematical operations in the formula. Any operations enclosed in parentheses are evaluated first; then the order of precedence is followed.

Editing Formulas, Text, and Data

When you are setting up a worksheet, you sometimes need to make a change to the formula, number, or text in a cell. To replace a cell's contents, activate the cell containing the data you want to replace. Enter the new data in the selected cell. The new data replaces any old data in the cell.

Cursor
A blinking line in the formula bar, indicating the point of insertion.

To edit (rather than replace) the contents of a cell, first activate that cell. Next, activate the formula bar by pressing F2 or by using the mouse. To activate the formula bar using the mouse, move the mouse pointer to the formula bar. The mouse pointer becomes an I-beam. Position the I-beam in the formula bar, and click the left mouse button. A blinking bar appears in the formula bar indicating the location of the insertion cursor. To move this cursor, use the arrow keys. Pressing ←Backspace deletes characters to the left of the cursor. Pressing Del removes characters to the right of the cursor. Pressing Ctrl+Del deletes to the end of the line. The status bar shows that you are in Edit mode rather than Ready or Enter mode.

After activating the cell into which you want to enter data, you can type text, numbers, or formulas in that cell. As you enter data, the data appears in both the active cell and the formula bar. The cell address of the active cell appears in the left end of the formula bar. A Cancel button, Enter button, and Function Wizard button all appear at the left of the formula bar (see figure 1.9).

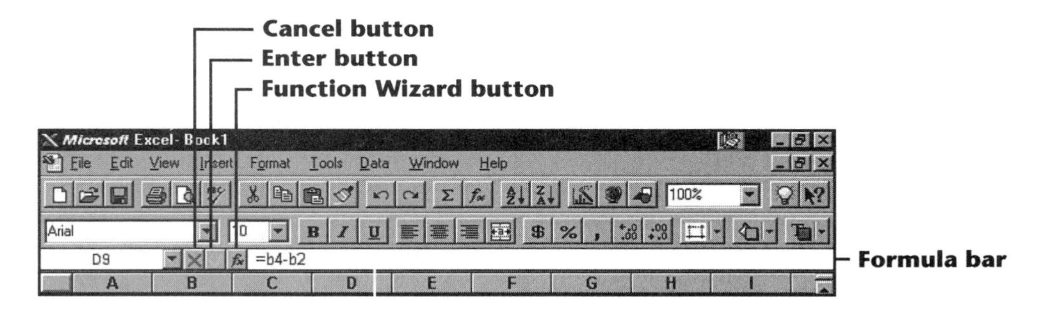

Figure 1.9
The Excel formula bar.

Caution
Excel retains only the last action or command you have performed, so you must choose the Undo command immediately after you choose a command or perform an action.

In the formula bar, typed data appears to the right of the three buttons. To accept your entry into the active cell, click the check mark button, or press ←Enter. To reject your entry, click the X button, or press Esc.

Using the Edit Undo Command

Excel has a built-in safety net that enables you to reverse many commands or actions. In the **E**dit menu, the **U**ndo command reverses the last command chosen or the last action performed. To undo a command or action, choose the **U**ndo command from the **E**dit menu or use the Undo button on the Standard toolbar.

Although the **U**ndo command can reverse many actions, it is not available for all commands. For example, if you choose the **F**ile, **C**lose command and close a file, the **E**dit menu displays the dimmed command `Can't Undo`.

To reverse the **U**ndo command, open the **E**dit menu, and choose the **R**epeat command. This step is necessary only if you undo a change that you want to keep.

Using the Edit Undo Command

To practice undoing an action, follow these steps:

1. Make cell B3 the active cell.
2. Type **123**, and press Enter. `123` appears in cell B3.
3. Click **E**dit in the menu bar, and then click **U**ndo Entry in the drop-down **E**dit menu. The contents of cell B3 should have reverted to what they were before you entered 123.

You will use this worksheet in the next tutorial.

In the next tutorial, you edit a formula that you have already entered in a cell.

Editing the Contents of a Cell

Make sure that the worksheet you have been working in is on-screen. Edit the formula (=B1+B2+B3) in cell B4 so that you first double the contents of cell B3 and then perform the addition. Follow these steps:

1. Make cell B4 the active cell, and press F2.

   The blinking insertion cursor appears at the end of the formula in the formula bar.

2. Type ***2** at the end of the formula in the formula bar; then press Enter. This formula multiplies B3 by 2 and then adds the result to the sum of B1 and B2.

You will use this worksheet in the next tutorial.

Remember that in the new formula (=B1+B2+B3*2) multiplication has a higher order of precedence and is performed before any addition.

Correcting Mistakes in Formulas

The purpose of this tutorial is to show you how to enter a formula and correct mistakes in a formula and to illustrate the importance of the order of precedence. To find the average of the numbers you entered in the worksheet, follow these steps:

1. Use the worksheet you have created, which has `200` in cell B1, `8` in cell B2, and `9` in cell B3.

2. Make cell B5 the active cell, type **=B1+B2+B3/3**, and press Enter.

   This formula *apparently* instructs Excel to find the average by adding the three numbers and then dividing by 3.

   Notice that cell B5 obviously does not contain the average because Excel follows the established order of precedence and divides B3 by 3 before the addition occurs. You must use parentheses to cause the addition to occur before the division.

   To correct the formula, you must place parentheses around the addition operation so that the formula is =(B1+B2+B3)/3.

3. Double-click cell B5 to begin editing the formula.

4. Use the left-arrow key to move the insertion point to the right of the = sign, and then type **(**.

5. Use the right-arrow key to move the insertion point to the left of the `/`, and then type **)**.

6. Press Enter.

Now the parentheses force the addition to be completed before the division. Always check your worksheet's formulas to be sure that they are working the way you intended. You will use this worksheet in the next tutorial.

Editing and Formatting Commands

Every Windows 95 program has a menu bar directly below the program's title bar. (Appendix A, "Working with Windows 95," reviews the use of Windows 95 menus.) Excel's menu bar has nine menus, starting with the **F**ile menu on the left and ending with the **H**elp menu on the right. In Excel, you can quickly access some of the more commonly used Edit and Format commands by using a shortcut menu. Edit commands—such as Cut, Copy, Paste, Clear Contents, Insert, and Delete—and Format commands—such as Number, Alignment, Font, Border, and Patterns—appear on a shortcut menu when you click the right mouse button (see figure 1.10).

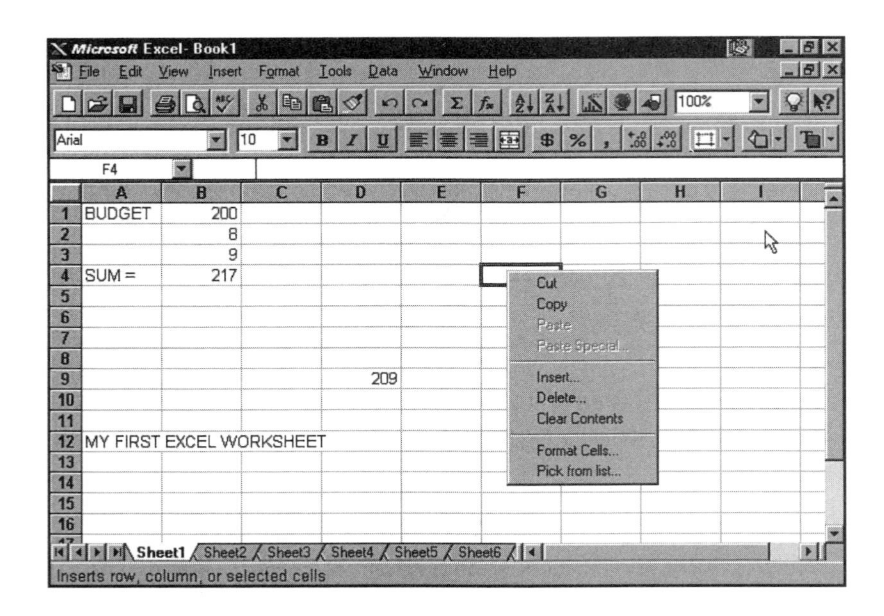

Figure 1.10
The Edit shortcut menu.

Using a Worksheet Command

In this tutorial, you use the Format command to change the way numbers are displayed in cell B1 of the worksheet you have created. To use the Format command, follow these steps:

1. Select the cell you want to format by placing the cell pointer on cell B1 and clicking the left mouse button.

2. Place the mouse pointer on Format in the menu bar, and click the left mouse button. The Format menu drops down (see figure 1.11).

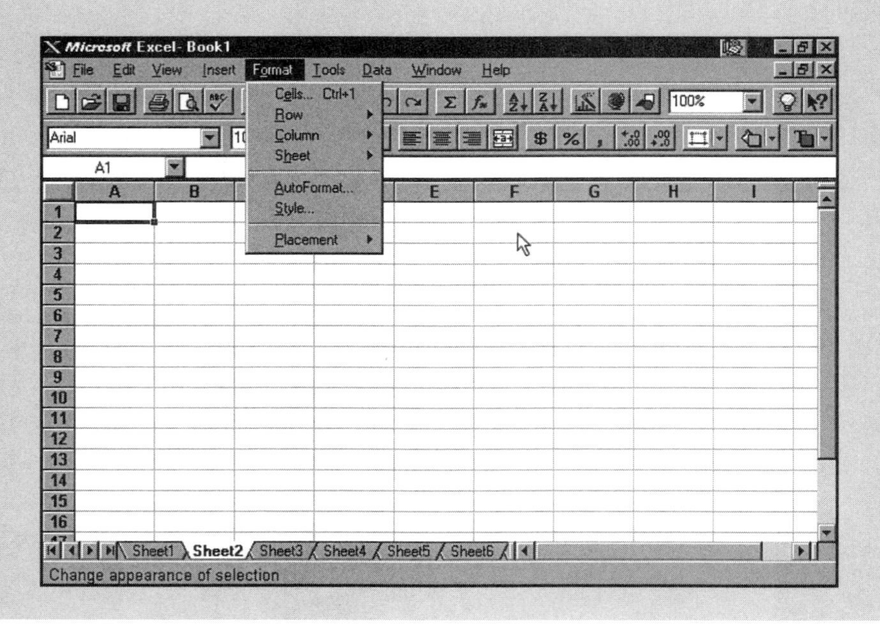

Figure 1.11
The Format menu.

3. Choose Cells by placing the mouse pointer on this option and then clicking the left mouse button. The Format Cells dialog box appears (see figure 1.12).

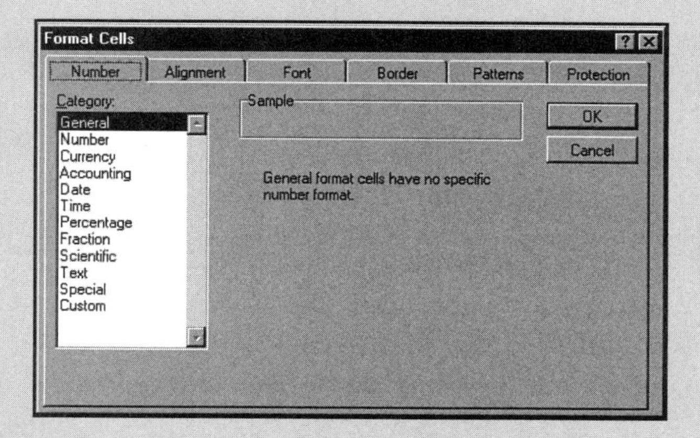

Figure 1.12 The Format Cells dialog box.

1

4. Place the mouse pointer on Number in the Category list box; then click the left mouse button.

The Format Cells dialog box now shows a sample of how the value entered in cell B1 will appear when using the number format (see Figure 1.13).

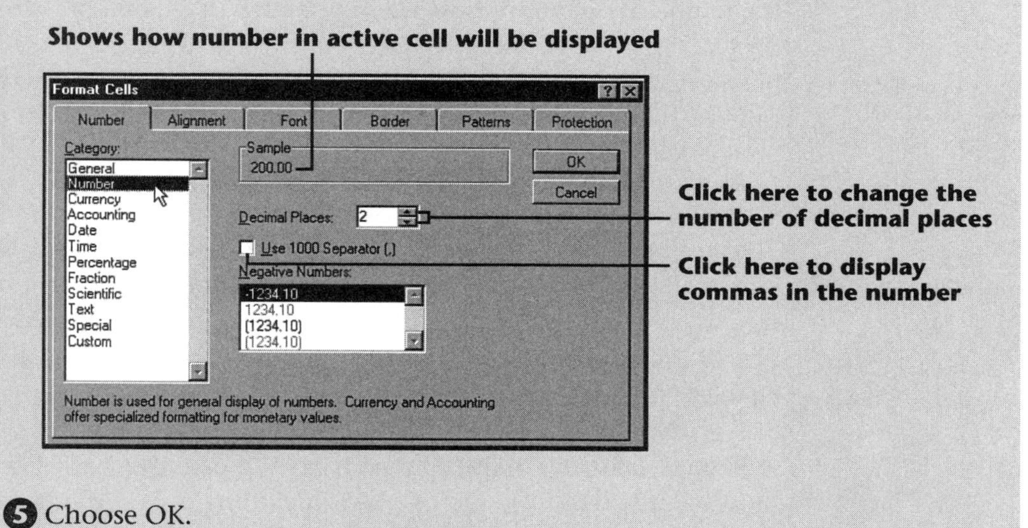

Figure 1.13 The Format Cells dialog box showing a sample of the entered value.

5. Choose OK.

The number in cell B1 should now display two decimal places. You will use this worksheet in the next tutorial.

Using a Toolbar Button

In this tutorial, you use the Currency style button in the Formatting toolbar to change the way numbers are displayed in cell B2 of the worksheet. Follow these steps:

1. Make cell B2 the active cell.
2. Place the mouse pointer on the Currency style button (the button with the $).
3. Click the left mouse button.

The number in cell B2 is now displayed as currency. You will use this worksheet in the next tutorial.

Objective 6: Name and Save a Workbook File

RAM
Random-access memory; a temporary memory area in a computer.

File
The area on a disk where workbooks are saved.

Some of the most frequently used Excel commands involve files. When you are working with a worksheet in a workbook, the data you enter or edit is actually stored in a temporary memory area of your computer called *RAM* (random-access memory). If a power outage or computer failure occurs while you are working, the temporary memory is wiped out, taking all entered or edited data with it. To avoid losing your work, save it frequently onto a disk. Also, save your workbook before exiting Excel. Items saved on disk are stored in a permanent memory area called a *file*. Each file must have a unique name. When you need to use a workbook already on disk, you must open the workbook's file.

Naming and Saving a Workbook File

Your internal hard drive or floppy disk permanently stores data. To place a file in a permanent storage area, you must issue a command to save the file and indicate on which disk drive (A:, B:, or C:) you want the file saved. When saving a file for the first time, you must give the workbook a file name. The file name enables you (and Excel) to identify your file in the permanent storage area on disk. When saving a new workbook, give it a name different than the other workbooks already on disk. As mentioned previously, each file name in a folder must be unique. The complete path, including drive letter, folder path, and file name can contain up to 218 characters. In addition, file names cannot include any of the following: forward slash (/), backslash (\), greater than sign (>), less than sign (<). asterisk (*), question mark (?), quotation mark ("), pipe symbol (|), colon (:), or semicolon (;).

Understanding the File Save Command

To save a new workbook in Excel, you open the **F**ile menu and choose the **S**ave command, or you click the Save button on the toolbar. The Save As dialog box appears on-screen when you are saving a file for the first time or when you choose the **F**ile, Save **A**s command (see figure 1.14).

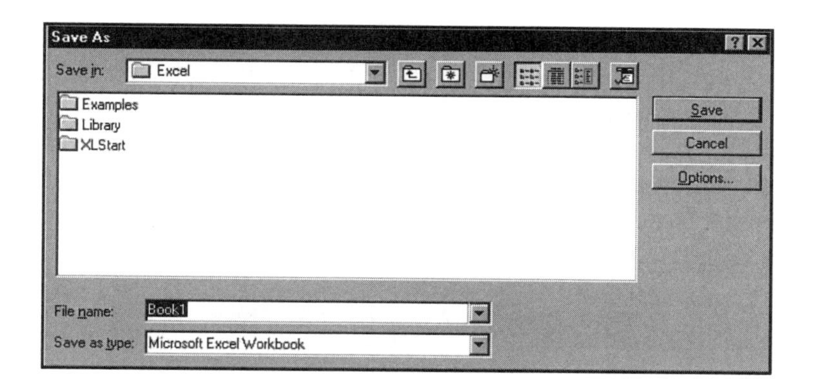

Figure 1.14
The Save As dialog box.

1

In the File **n**ame text box, type a name that will help you identify the workbook in the future.

You can also save a file to another drive and folder. Select the drive and folder from the Save **i**n drop-down list. When you choose the **F**ile, **S**ave command to save changes to a file already saved and named, the File Save As dialog box does not appear. The **F**ile, **S**ave command overwrites the named file with the changes made.

Saving a Workbook File

In this tutorial, you save your worksheet in a file named My file. You will use this worksheet in the next tutorial.

If you are saving files on your own disk, make sure that you have a formatted disk in the proper drive (A: or B:). Then follow these steps:

1. Open the **F**ile menu by clicking the menu name.
2. From the **F**ile drop-down menu, click the **S**ave command. The Save As dialog box appears (refer to figure 1.14).
3. Type **My file** in the File **n**ame text box.
4. If you are saving to the hard drive (usually designated the C: drive), choose OK.

   If you are saving your file on a floppy disk, click the arrow to the right of the Save **i**n drop-down list. Select your disk drive by moving the mouse pointer to the designated drive and/or folder and clicking the left mouse button. Then choose OK. Your workbook is now saved on disk.

The worksheet is saved on disk in the workbook named My file. The document window title bar should now display the name `My file`.

Using the File Save As Command

Sometimes you may want to keep different versions of a worksheet. For example, if you need to build a worksheet for this month's budget, many of the formulas will be the same as those in last month's budget worksheet. You can work most efficiently by starting with last month's worksheet. In such situations, when you want to refer to a previous version of a document and keep the original, you will want to have two copies of the document: one containing the changes made and one without changes. The **F**ile, **S**ave As command enables you to keep the original document and assign another file name when you save the changed document. The Save As dialog box looks like the dialog box that appears when an unnamed document is saved (see figure 1.15).

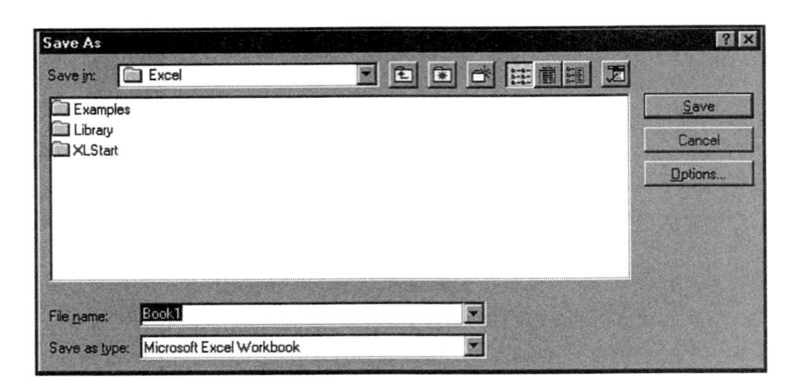

Figure 1.15
The Save As dialog box.

Saving a File with the File Save As Command

In this tutorial, you save your workbook in a second file named My file2. Follow these steps:

1. Open the **F**ile menu by clicking the menu name.
2. From the **F**ile drop-down menu, click Save **A**s. The Save As dialog box appears (refer to figure 1.15).
3. Type **My file2** in the File **n**ame text box.
4. If you are saving your file on a floppy disk, select the letter of the proper drive from the Save **i**n drop-down list.
5. Choose OK to save the workbook as My file2.
6. Check to see that the document title bar now displays the name My file2.

You will use this worksheet in the next tutorial.

Your workbook has been saved in two separate files—once as My file and once as My file2.

Objective 7: Print a Worksheet

When you are building your worksheet or making changes to it, the worksheet must be in the computer's internal memory. When the worksheet is in internal memory and on-screen, you can print it.

Note: *To print, a worksheet must contain data.*

If your worksheet has data in more columns than can print on one page, the column(s) on the right side will be printed on the second page.

Printing a Worksheet

In this tutorial, you print the first worksheet in the My file workbook. (If My file is not on-screen, use the **F**ile, **O**pen command to open My file —see Objective 8.) If your computer is not connected to a printer, you cannot complete this tutorial. (Refer to your instructor in this case.) Follow these steps:

1. Make sure that your printer is turned on.
2. Click the Print button on the Standard toolbar. The worksheet begins printing.

If you do not have a printer attached to your computer, you can get an idea of what a printout will look like by choosing **F**ile, Print Pre**v**iew.

Objective 8: Open and Close a File

You have learned how to name and save a file on disk. In this section, you learn how to retrieve a file stored on disk and how to close a workbook.

Opening and Closing a File

A workbook file must be open before any of its worksheets can be used.

To open a workbook file, click the **F**ile menu, and choose the **O**pen command, or click the Open button on the toolbar. The Open dialog box appears (see figure 1.16).

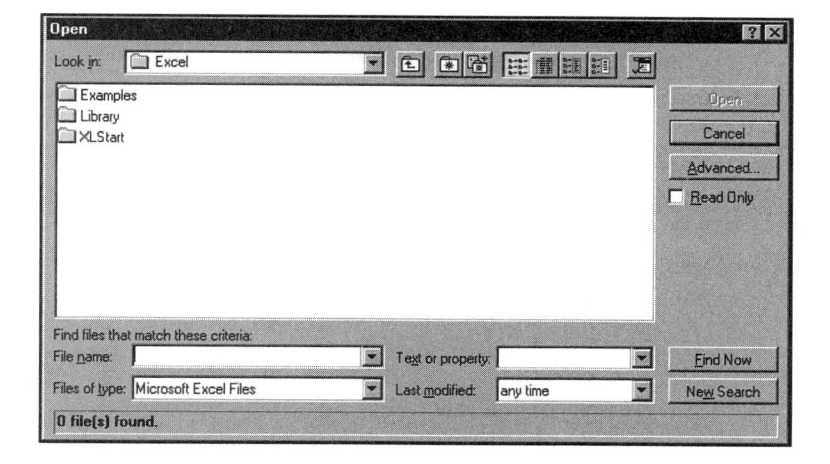

Figure 1.16 The Open dialog box.

Using the Options in the Open Dialog Box

The Open dialog box enables you to open a workbook; you can specify its file name, its folder, and the drive on which it is stored. The File **n**ame text box appears when the Open dialog box is displayed. Open a file by typing the file name in the text box and then choosing OK or pressing Enter.

The Open dialog box displays an alphabetical list of all Excel files in the current folder, and the current drive and folder are also displayed in the Look **i**n list box. To select a file with the mouse, move the mouse pointer to the file name; then double-click the left mouse button.

The Look **i**n list box displays all available folders, enabling you to locate a file in another folder. To change to another folder with the mouse, move the mouse pointer to the folder name; then double-click the left mouse button, or select the folder name and choose OK. (To view choices not visible in the list box, use the scroll bar.)

The Look **i**n list box has a downward pointing arrow button at its right end. To switch drives, place the mouse pointer on the arrow button and click the left mouse button. Then click the drive name in the drop-down list.

Using the Close Command

When you finish working on a worksheet, close its workbook file. Open the **F**ile menu, and choose the **C**lose command. If you have not saved changes made to the file, Excel prompts you to save before closing the workbook (see figure 1.17).

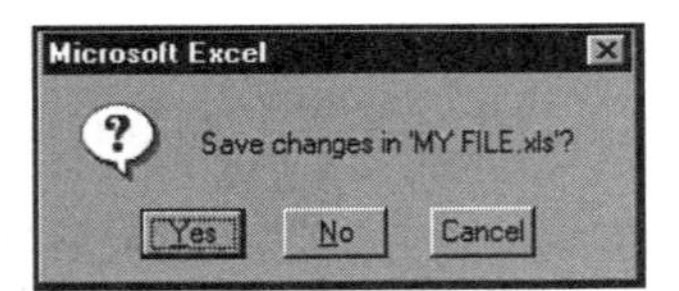

Figure 1.17
The Excel prompt for saving a file.

To close the workbook and save changes, choose **Y**es. To close the workbook and not save your changes, choose **N**o. To close the dialog box and keep the workbook open, choose Cancel. If you saved all changes before choosing **F**ile, **C**lose, you do not need to save again because the window closes without prompting you to save.

Closing a Workbook

In this tutorial, you close the active workbook My file2. Follow these steps:

1. Open the **F**ile menu, and choose the **C**lose command.
2. If the Save Changes dialog box appears on-screen, choose the **Y**es button to save any changes made since you last saved the worksheet. Choose the **N**o button to close the worksheet without saving changes made since you last saved. Either choice can be used in this tutorial. The workbook area disappears from the screen, and menu choices are limited to **F**ile and **H**elp.

Notice how your screen changes when no workbook is open (see figure 1.18).

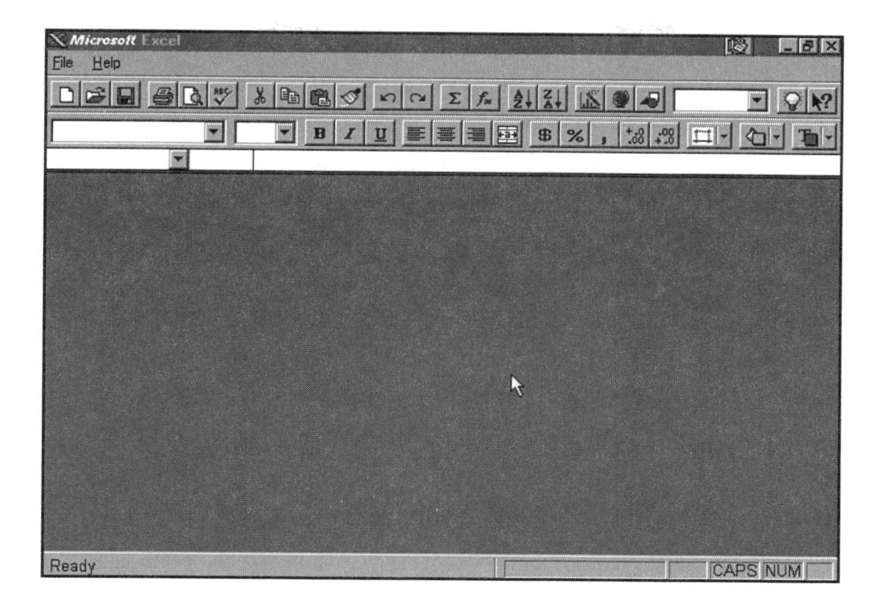

Figure 1.18
The Excel screen when no workbooks are open.

1

Opening a Workbook File

In this tutorial, open the disk file containing the workbook My file. You need to remember on which disk drive (A:, B:, or C:) and in which folder, you saved the file in the preceding tutorial. Follow these steps:

1. Open the **F**ile menu, and choose the **O**pen command. The Open dialog box appears (refer again to figure 1.16).

2. Check to see that the drive and folder listed in the Look **i**n list box in the upper left corner of the dialog box shows the correct drive and folder. If not, click the button with the black triangle to the right of the Look **i**n list box; then click the letter of the correct drive. Also check that the Look **i**n list shows the correct folder. If not, select the correct folder by clicking its name in the Look **i**n list.

3. Names of the workbook files in the folder on the disk appear in the center of the Open dialog box. Move the mouse pointer to the file name MYFILE.XLS; then double-click the left mouse button. The My file workbook should open in the document window, and the title bar should display `My file`.

You can now use the worksheets in My file.

Objective 9: Exit Excel

At the beginning of this chapter, you learned to start Excel. This section shows you how to exit, or quit, the Excel program. You can exit Excel in the following ways:

- Open the **F**ile menu, and choose E**x**it.
- Click the program Control menu icon, and choose **C**lose.
- Double-click the program Control menu icon.
- Press Alt+F4.

If you have forgotten to save any open documents, Excel prompts you with a dialog box (refer to figure 1.17). Choose **Y**es to save any changes made to the document(s). Choose **N**o to lose the changes. After Excel closes, you return to the Windows 95 desktop.

Exiting Excel

In this tutorial, use the Control menu to quit Excel. Follow these steps:

1. Place the mouse pointer on the Program Control-menu icon (represented by a "W" with a page of text, located in the upper left corner of the Excel window).
2. Click the left mouse button.
3. Choose **C**lose from the Control menu by placing the mouse pointer on the command, and clicking the left mouse button.

You exit Excel and return to the Windows 95 desktop.

Chapter Summary

This chapter covers many concepts crucial for using Excel, including starting and exiting Excel. You have learned to move around in a worksheet; to enter and edit data and formulas; to use toolbar buttons, menus, and dialog boxes; and to print worksheets. Additionally, you have learned procedures for opening, saving, naming, and closing workbook files.

If you feel comfortable with the information in this chapter, you are ready to learn more about building Excel worksheets. In Chapter 2, you learn to use worksheet ranges, change column widths and row heights, move cells, copy cells, and insert and delete columns and rows.

Checking Your Skills

True/False

For each of the following, circle *T* or *F* to indicate whether the statement is true or false.

T F **1.** The active cell in an Excel worksheet is outlined with a border that is darker than the other cells' borders.

T F **2.** To insert the formula-bar entry into the active cell, you can click the Cancel button in the formula bar or press ↵Enter.

T F **3.** If you turn off your computer, your Excel worksheet will be lost unless you have saved it in a disk file.

T F **4.** To close a workbook file, you must exit from Excel.

T F **5.** To choose a command from a menu with the mouse, point to the command, and click the left mouse button.

T F **6.** The Excel screen displays the toolbar across the bottom of the screen.

T F **7.** Excel worksheet column headings are labeled with numbers.

T F **8.** In an Excel worksheet, the intersection of a column and a row is called a field.

T F **9.** Before entering data into a worksheet, you must type the address of the cell in which the data will be stored.

T F **10.** The formula bar is located directly above the worksheet's column headings.

Multiple Choice

In the blank provided, write the letter of the correct answer for each of the following.

_____ **1.** The function key that enables you to go directly to a particular cell in the worksheet is _______.

a. F1

b. F2

c. F5

d. none of the above

_____ **2.** To view an area of your worksheet not on-screen, you can use the _______.

a. Minimize icon

b. scroll bar

c. =

d. **R**ange command

_____ **3.** To change (edit) the contents of the active cell, you first press _______.

a. F8

b. F3

c. F2

d. F9

_____ **4.** When you save your workbook on disk, the workbook is saved in a(n) _______.

a. file

b. active cell

c. range

d. extension

_____ **5.** To move to the cell A1, press _______.

a. Ctrl+Home

b. Home

c. Home+Home

d. PgUp

_____ **6.** Excel assumes that the content of a cell is a formula if the entry starts with _______.

a. =

b. !

c. *

d. ^

_____ **7.** An Excel worksheet can consist of a maximum of _______ columns.

a. 100

b. 200

c. 300

d. 400

_____ **8.** To move to column A of the active row, press _______.

a. Ctrl+Home

b. Home

c. Alt+Home

d. PgUp

_____ **9.** The cell address of the active cell appears in the _______.

a. toolbar

b. status bar

c. formula bar

d. menu bar

____ **10.** The symbol used for multiplication in an Excel formula is _______.

a. x

b. ( )

c. >

d. *

Completion

In the blank provided, write the correct answer for each of the following.

1. To save a file to the A drive, select a: from the _______________ drop-down list in the Save As dialog box.

2. To open a workbook you saved on disk, choose the _______________ command from the **F**ile menu.

3. The formula used to multiply the contents of cell D5 by the contents of cell E2 is _______________.

4. The formula used to add the contents of cell A3 to the contents of cell B3 and divide the sum by 4 is _______________.

5. The order in which arithmetic operations are performed by Excel is _______________.

6. Scrolling does not change the _______________ cell.

7. To activate a cell, place the cell pointer over the cell and _______________.

8. A new workbook contains _______________ worksheets.

9. A new workbook comes with _______________ worksheets.

10. The _______________ window is the outer window with Microsoft Excel in the title bar.

Applying Your Skills

Review Exercises

Exercise 1: Entering, Saving, and Printing a Worksheet

This exercise reviews some of the information covered in the chapter and helps bring it all together. In this exercise, you enter and save your first Excel workbook, shown in figure 1.19. Read all the steps before you begin.

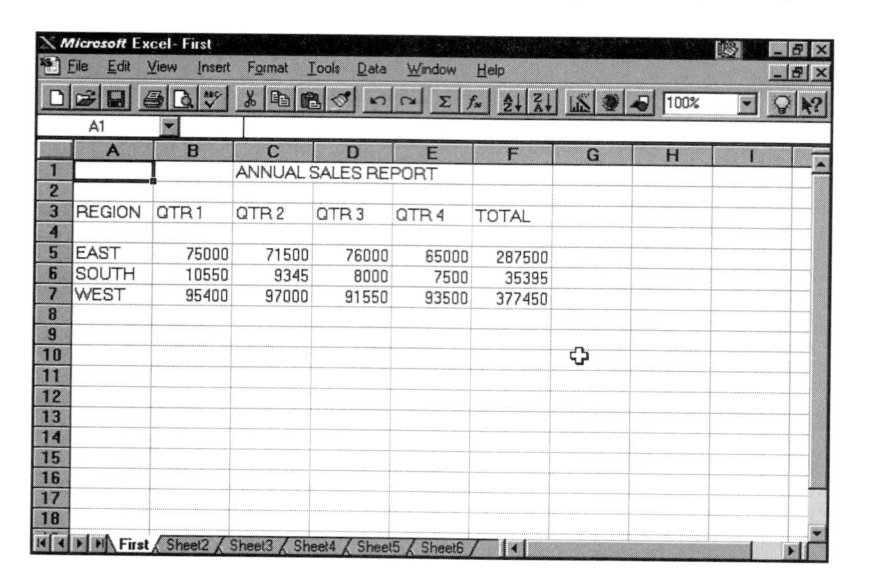

Figure 1.19
The First workbook.

1. Start Excel by using the Start, Programs command. If you plan to save your worksheet on a floppy disk, make sure that a formatted disk is in your disk drive.

2. Activate cell C1 by clicking it with the left mouse button. Type **ANNUAL SALES REPORT**. Then press Enter.

   Note: *If you make a mistake typing in a cell or selecting from a menu, press* Esc *to start again.*

3. Activate cell A3. Type **REGION** in cell A3, **QTR1** in cell B3, **QTR2** in cell C3, **QTR3** in cell D3, **QTR4** in cell E3, and **TOTAL** in cell F3. Press Enter after each entry.

4. Activate cell A5. Type **EAST** in cell A5, **SOUTH** in cell A6, and **WEST** in cell A7. Press Enter after each entry.

5. Activate cell B5. Type **75000** in cell B5, and press Enter.

6. Fill in the remaining sales figures for quarters 1 through 4 by activating the correct cell, typing the number, and pressing Enter.

   Do not enter numbers in the TOTAL column; in the next steps, you will insert formulas into that column so that changes in quarterly sales are reflected in the new total.

7. Now enter the formulas that calculate total sales for each region. Make cell F5 the active cell, enter the formula **=B5+C5+D5+E5**, and press Enter.

8. Enter the formula **=B6+C6+D6+E6** in cell F6, and press Enter. Enter the formula **=B7+C7+D7+E7** in cell F7, and press Enter.

   Now your worksheet should look like the one in figure 1.19.

9. Next, save your worksheet's workbook. Do this either by clicking the Save button on the toolbar or by opening the **F**ile menu near the top of your screen, and choosing the **S**ave command.

10. A dialog box should appear. Type **First** as the name of your file.

    Note: *Be sure to use the Save **i**n drop-down list to identify the drive and folder where you want the file to be stored.*

11. Click OK. Your worksheet has been saved in a workbook file named FIRST, on the drive and folder you selected. This name will appear in the document window title bar. You could exit from Excel now, and your worksheet would not be lost.

12. If your computer is attached to a printer, print your worksheet by clicking the Print button on the Standard toolbar. Exit from Excel.

Exercise 2: Modifying an Existing Worksheet

In this exercise, you add totals and averages to your FIRST workbook.

1. Start Excel. (If you plan to save your workbook on a floppy disk, make sure that a formatted disk is inserted into the proper drive.) Retrieve the FIRST workbook from your disk.

2. Enter **TOTAL** in cell A9 of Sheet1. In cell B9, enter the formula to calculate total sales for QTR 1. Enter the formulas to calculate the respective total sales in cells C9 through F9.

3. Change the contents of cell C5 to **100**. Do cells F5, C9, and F9 change? Should any other cells change when you change the contents of C5?

4. In cell G3, enter **AVERAGE**, and in cell A11, enter **AVERAGE**. In cell B11, enter the formula to calculate the average sales for QTR 1. In cell G5, enter the formula to calculate the average sales for the EAST.

5. Fill in the appropriate cells in column G and in row 11 so that the proper averages are calculated. Do the averages change when the quarterly sales figures are changed?

6. Print the worksheet, and save it in a workbook named **Second**. Exit from Excel, if you like.

Exercise 3: Using the Formatting Toolbar

In this exercise, you use the Formatting toolbar to make formatting changes to the SECOND workbook.

1. Open the workbook you created in Review Exercise 2.
2. Use the Bold and the Underline buttons on the Formatting toolbar to format the contents of cell C1.
3. Use the buttons on the Formatting toolbar to make the contents of cells A3, A9, and G3 boldface and centered in their cells.
4. Print the worksheet.
5. Close the worksheet without saving changes.
6. Exit from Excel.

Exercise 4: Indicating Which Cells Contain Formulas

A good way to indicate which cells in your worksheet contain formulas is to format the formula cells to boldface.

1. Open the workbook you created in Review Exercise 2. To indicate that a cell in the worksheet contains a formula, format to boldface each cell that contains a formula.
2. Save the workbook in a file whose name is your initials; print the worksheet. You can exit from Excel, if you like.

Continuing Projects

Project 1: Building a Payroll Worksheet

Worksheets are often used for payroll calculations. In this project, you set up a payroll for your hypothetical company.

Set up a worksheet to calculate a weekly payroll. The title should use your company's name and four column headings: EMPLOYEE, HOURS, RATE, and PAY. Employee's last name only should be in column A (and B if the name is long). Hours worked should be entered in column C. Enter the names, hours, and rates for five employees.

No overtime is allowed. PAY is calculated by multiplying HOURS times RATE. Your worksheet should contain a formula to compute the total amount of the payroll for this pay period (one week). Display this amount in Currency style and in boldface. Your worksheet should also calculate the average number of employee hours worked and the average amount an employee is paid. Display the average pay in Currency style and in boldface. Include labels in your spreadsheet to identify the totals and averages. Save this worksheet in a workbook file named **Payroll**. Print the worksheet.

Change the hours worked and the rate of pay for the first employee; then verify that the formulas automatically recalculate the new totals and averages correctly.

Project 2: Tracking Hours in a Worksheet

Worksheets are often used to keep track of employee hours worked and to produce productivity statistics. In this project, you set up a worksheet to maintain this information for yourself.

Set up your own worksheet to enter the hours you work each day during a typical week. Be honest. In your worksheet, also include formulas that calculate total number of hours worked during the week and average daily number of hours worked. Make sure that you include labels like TOTAL for any calculations in your worksheet.

Give the worksheet's workbook a name, and save it on your disk. If you have a printer attached to your computer, you can print your worksheet. Verify that when you change the value for the number of hours worked on Wednesday, your weekly total and daily average automatically change to reflect the new value.

Project 3: Keeping a Record of the Mileage of Vehicles in a Motor Pool

A small company's marketing department contains six automobiles. Assume that you need to maintain a record of the vehicles' mileage for insurance, maintenance, and depreciation purposes. Set up a worksheet in which the miles driven for each day of the week (M–F) can be recorded for each vehicle.

The worksheet should show daily totals for miles driven and weekly totals for each of the six individual vehicles. Also show average number of miles per day each vehicle traveled. Make the cells with formulas boldface. Save the workbook as **Template**. Enter sample numbers for each vehicle for every day of the week, check the results of your formulas, and print the worksheet.

CHAPTER 2

Building a Worksheet

Chapter 1 covers a variety of topics, including moving around in a worksheet, entering data, saving files, using menus and toolbars, and printing a worksheet. Now that you are familiar with some basic concepts, you are ready to learn more about setting up worksheets. The topics covered in this chapter include defining ranges; moving, copying, and clearing cell contents; inserting and deleting cells, columns, and rows; and changing column width and row height.

Objectives

By the time you have finished this chapter, you will have learned to

1. Start a New Workbook
2. Work with Ranges
3. Move Cell Contents
4. Copy Cell Contents
5. Clear, Delete, and Insert Cells
6. Insert and Delete Columns and Rows
7. Change Column Width and Row Height

Objective 1: Start a New Workbook

When you start Excel, you always have an empty workbook in your document window. If you want to start building a new worksheet in your workbook, Excel is ready for you to begin. In Chapter 1, you learned how to save a workbook on disk and how to retrieve it later to continue working on it. At times, however, you may want to save a finished workbook and then clear it out from the document window to begin a new workbook. You could exit Excel and then start again to get a new workbook. But for a more efficient way to start a new workbook, use the **F**ile, **N**ew command or use the New Workbook button on the toolbar.

If you have another workbook open, Excel keeps the other workbook open in RAM and gives your new workbook a temporary title—Book1, Book2, Book3, and so on, depending on how many new workbooks have already been opened when you issue the **F**ile, **N**ew command.

Using the File, New Command

To use the **F**ile, **N**ew command, make sure that Excel is running. Then follow these steps:

1. Click the **F**ile menu and choose **N**ew.

   The New dialog box appears.

2. Click OK and maximize the document window.

   Your screen should now look like figure 2.1. Notice that the new workbook is named Book2.

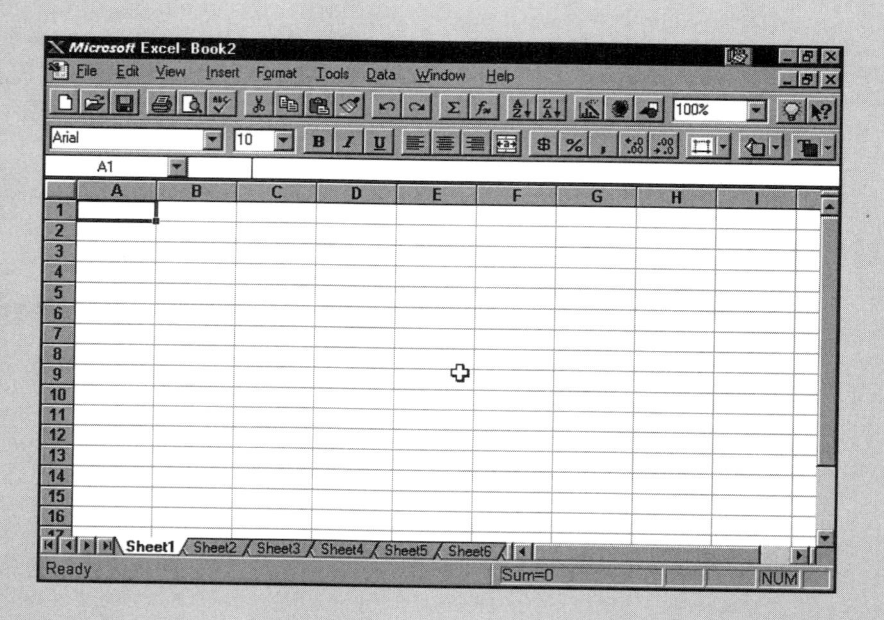

Figure 2.1 The result of choosing the **F**ile, **N**ew command.

The opposite of the **F**ile, **N**ew command is the **F**ile, **C**lose command, introduced in Chapter 1. **F**ile, **C**lose does not take you out of Excel, but gives you a blank (empty) workbook window. Before you can work on a worksheet, you must choose **F**ile, **N**ew to open a new workbook or choose **F**ile, **O**pen to open an existing workbook. When your workbook window is empty, only the **F**ile and **H**elp menus are available.

The File, Close Command

First, make sure that you have saved on disk any workbooks that you do not want to lose. To use the **F**ile, **C**lose command, follow these steps:

1. Choose **F**ile, **C**lose until you see a blank workbook window.

2. When your workbook window is empty, retrieve the First worksheet from your disk by choosing the **F**ile, **O**pen command.

Objective 2: Work with Ranges

Range
One or more blocks of cells that can be formatted, moved, copied, or referred to as a unit.

Sometimes you will need to perform actions on a block of cells in your worksheet. A group of cells that you define is called a *range*. While building a worksheet, you save time by applying a command to a group of cells rather than to individual cells. For example, if you want to format the cell contents of several cells, select all the cells; then apply the F**o**rmat command. Any command or action you can apply to one cell, you can usually apply to a range. Excel F**o**rmat commands are commonly applied to a range (see figure 2.2).

Figure 2.2
A selected range formatted to display currency.

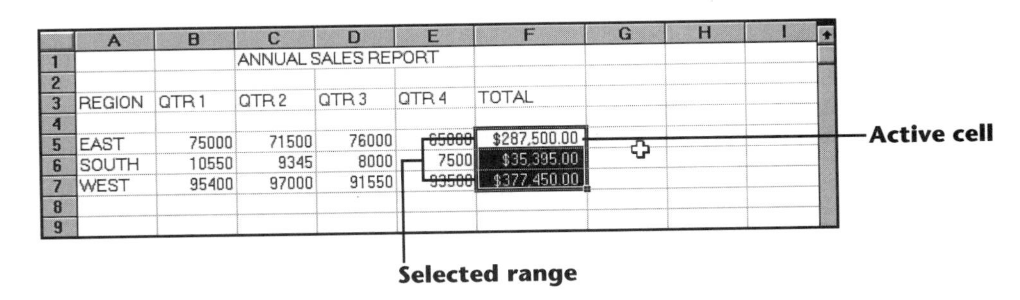

Excel refers to a range of cells by the address of the upper left cell in the block followed by a colon and then the address of the lower right cell in the block. If you are selecting only the cells in one row, the first cell address is the left cell in the row followed by a colon and then the address of the last cell in the row. Likewise, if you are selecting only the cells in one column, the first cell address in the range is the top cell in the column followed by a colon and then the address of the bottom cell in the column.

When a range is selected, the cells in the selected range are surrounded by a gray border. The first cell of the selection is the active cell and has a white background; the rest of the selected range is dark (refer again to figure 2.2).

Selecting a Range of Adjacent Cells Using the Mouse

Open the First worksheet (created in Chapter 1) if it is not already on-screen. Use this worksheet for all the tutorials in this chapter. In this tutorial, you select the range of cells from cell A5 to cell A7. Follow these steps:

1. Place the cell pointer on cell A5; then press and hold down the left mouse button.
2. Drag the cell pointer to cell A7, and release the mouse button. The thick cell border and darkened cells indicate that the range of cells in the block A5 to A7 are selected.
3. To deselect the range, click any cell outside the range (for example, cell F6).

A range is usually one solid rectangular block of adjacent cells in the work-sheet. You can also define as one range several blocks of cells in separate parts of the worksheet. These multiple nonadjoining ranges can be very useful, as you will learn later in this chapter and in Chapter 6, where you chart data. Figure 2.3 shows two nonadjoining ranges selected at the same time.

Figure 2.3
Two selected nonadjoining ranges.

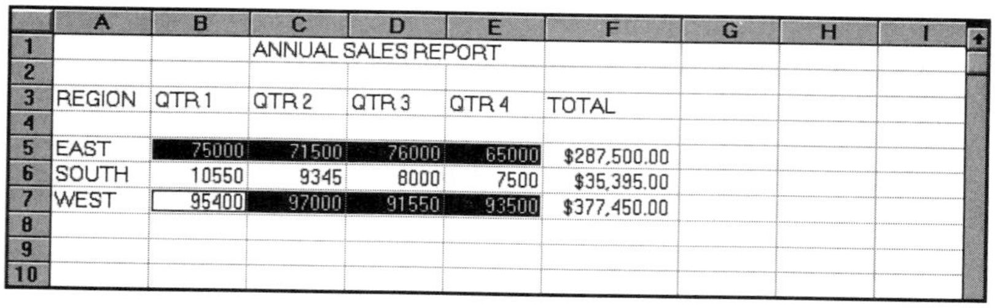

	A	B	C	D	E	F	G	H	I
1			ANNUAL SALES REPORT						
2									
3	REGION	QTR 1	QTR 2	QTR 3	QTR 4	TOTAL			
4									
5	EAST	75000	71500	76000	65000	$287,500.00			
6	SOUTH	10550	9345	8000	7500	$35,395.00			
7	WEST	95400	97000	91550	93500	$377,450.00			
8									
9									
10									

Selecting a Range of Nonadjoining Cells Using the Mouse

In this tutorial, you select a range of cells in two separate blocks—from cell B3 to cell F3 and from cell B7 to cell F7. Use the First worksheet, and follow these steps:

1. Place the cell pointer on cell B3; press and hold down the left mouse button as you drag the cell pointer to cell F3; then release the mouse button.
2. Place the cell pointer on cell B7; press and hold down Ctrl. Then press the left mouse button, and drag the cell pointer to cell F7. Release the mouse button and Ctrl. The thick cell borders and darkened cells indicate that the ranges of cells in blocks B3 to F3 and B7 to F7 are selected.
3. To deselect the range, click any cell outside the range (for example, cell A1).

A range can be any size. You can also select a range using the keyboard. You hold down Shift and use the arrow keys to select the cells.

After selecting a range, use the buttons on the Formatting toolbar just as you use them to apply formats (such as Currency) to a cell. (Refer to Objective 3 in Chapter 1 for information about using the toolbars.)

Formatting a Range

In this tutorial, you select a range in the First worksheet and make the contents of the cells in the range boldface. Follow these steps:

1. Select cells A3 through F3 by dragging the cell pointer along row 3 over these cells.
2. Click the Bold button on the Formatting toolbar. This button looks like a large letter B.

   The text in cells A3 through F3 appears in boldface.
3. Click a cell outside the range to deselect the range.

Understanding Range Names

Range name
A meaningful name that you give to a cell or range of cells.

Assigning a meaningful name to a range of cells is useful when you are building a formula. You can use this name in formulas and in dialog boxes. All range names defined for a workbook are listed in the name box at the left end of the formula bar. Named ranges can make calculations easier to create and understand. This section teaches you to use a name to refer to a range of cells. When you save a workbook on disk, all the worksheet *range names* are also saved on disk; they are available whenever you open the file. You do not need to rename a range every time you open your workbook.

Range names must start with a letter or an underscore, but after the initial character, you can use any character except a space or a hyphen. Instead of the space, use an underscore (_) or a period. To name a range, you first select the range; then use the **I**nsert, **N**ame, **D**efine command. In the following tutorial, you assign the name TOTALS to the range of cells from cell F5 to F7.

2

Naming a Range

To name the range of cells from F5 to F7, follow these steps:

1. Using the mouse or the keyboard, select the block of cells F5 to F7.
2. From the **I**nsert menu, choose **N**ame; then choose **D**efine.

   The Define Name dialog box opens (see figure 2.4). Excel sometimes suggests an appropriate name.

Figure 2.4
The Define Name dialog box.

3. Type the name **TOTALS** in the Names in **W**orkbook text box.
4. Choose OK to leave the dialog box.
5. Save the worksheet as **First**.

In Chapter 3, you learn how to use this named range in a function.

Objective 3: Move Cell Contents

Drag and Drop
A mouse procedure enabling you to move or copy data.

At some point, almost any worksheet will require modifications. For example, you may insert data into several cells and then decide to place that data elsewhere in the worksheet. Rather than delete the data and enter it again, you can move the data to the new location. In Excel, you can move data to a new location in two ways. One method, *Drag and Drop*, uses the mouse pointer to move data. Cut and Paste, the other method, uses the **E**dit, Cu**t** command to move selected data to the Windows Clipboard and then uses the **E**dit, **P**aste command to extract data from the Clipboard and place that data in a new location. If you make a mistake while editing your worksheet, choose the **E**dit, **U**ndo command before continuing.

Moving Cell Contents Using Drag and Drop

The Drag and Drop method enables you to move or copy data using the mouse. First, you select the data that you want to move. Then, you drag it to the new location and drop it there by releasing the mouse button.

Paste area
The new location in the worksheet where selected data will be moved or copied.

If the *paste area* (the new location for the data) is located in an area of the worksheet not visible on-screen, drag the selection to the edge of the window. Excel starts scrolling through the worksheet. Release the mouse button when the gray outline is in the correct location. The selected data drops into the new location.

In this chapter, you are using the First worksheet to practice. Because you are practicing skills, don't worry about disrupting the worksheet's layout. You have a copy of the First worksheet on disk.

Using Drag and Drop

In this tutorial, you use the Drag and Drop method to move the data in column F to column H in the First worksheet. Follow these steps:

1. Select rows 3 through 7 of column F.
2. Place the mouse pointer on the right edge of the highlighted data. The mouse pointer should change to an arrow.
3. Hold down the left mouse button, and drag to the new location (column H, rows 3 through 7).

   As you drag, a gray outline of the selection moves with the pointer. A border equal in size to the selection outlines the cell or area where the selection (the paste area) will appear (see figure 2.5).

Figure 2.5 The outline where the selection will appear.

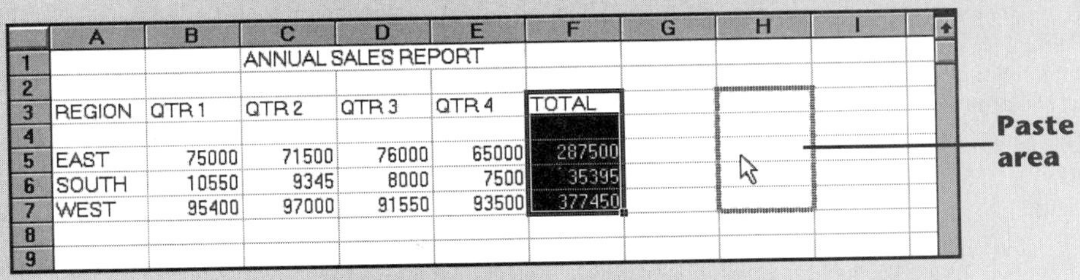

	A	B	C	D	E	F	G	H	I
1			ANNUAL SALES REPORT						
2									
3	REGION	QTR 1	QTR 2	QTR 3	QTR 4	TOTAL			
4									
5	EAST	75000	71500	76000	65000	287500			
6	SOUTH	10550	9345	8000	7500	35395			
7	WEST	95400	97000	91550	93500	377450			
8									
9									

Paste area

❹ Release the mouse button to drop the selected data into the new location.

Understanding the Clipboard

Clipboard
A temporary storage area for data you cut or copy.

Excel and all other Windows applications use the Clipboard for moving and copying data. The Clipboard is a section of computer memory that stores information temporarily so that you can move or copy it. Because the Clipboard is in RAM memory (volatile), information placed on the Clipboard is lost when you turn off the computer. Basic facts about the Clipboard are as follows:

Your computer contains only one Clipboard for temporary storage.

You can place only one item on the Clipboard at a time.

You can place text or graphics on the Clipboard.

The **E**dit, **C**opy and **E**dit, Cu**t** commands (and the Cut and Copy buttons on the Standard toolbar) place information on the Clipboard.

The **E**dit, **P**aste command (and the Paste button on the Standard toolbar) extracts information from the Clipboard.

With the Clipboard, you can copy worksheet cells, formulas, and charts to locations within the same worksheet, to other worksheets, and to other applications. The Clipboard helps you build worksheets, ensure accuracy, and share information.

After you cut or copy information to the Clipboard, you can place that information in another location on the same worksheet, on another worksheet, or in another Windows application that supports the Clipboard. The **E**dit, **P**aste command extracts information that is on the Clipboard and places it into the selected location. Information that you have copied to the Clipboard stays on the Clipboard until you use the Cu**t** or **C**opy command again, or until you turn off your computer.

Although you can access the Clipboard to see what is on it, you will seldom need to because you will have just cut or copied the selection into the Clipboard. For more information on how to access the Clipboard, refer to your Windows documentation or on-line Help in Excel.

Moving Cell Contents Using Cut and Paste

Marquee
Moving dashes outlining the area cut or copied to the Clipboard.

The Cut and Paste method uses the Clipboard to store temporary information that you want to move to another location. The **E**dit, Cu**t** command enables you to place selected data on the Clipboard. Using the **E**dit, **P**aste command, you can paste information placed on the Clipboard to another location. To place information on the Clipboard, you first select the data you want moved. Then open the **E**dit menu, and choose Cu**t**. A *marquee*, small moving dashes ("the marching ants"), outlines the data placed on the Clipboard.

Select a single cell in the upper left corner of the paste area rather than the whole paste range. If you select more than one cell, the range you select must be exactly the same size as the range on the Clipboard. If the ranges are different sizes, a dialog box appears. Choose OK, or press Enter, to clear the dialog box.

Using Cut and Paste to Move Data

In this tutorial, you use the Cut and Paste method to move the data in rows 3 through 7 of column H back to the old location in column F of the First worksheet file; follow these steps:

1. Select rows 3 through 7 of column H.
2. Open the **E**dit menu, and choose Cu**t**. The marquee appears around the data.
3. Activate cell F3, the first cell in which you want the data to appear. Press Enter, or open the **E**dit menu and choose **P**aste. The selected data disappears from column H and appears in cells F3 through F7.

You can also cut and paste selections by using the Cut and the Paste buttons on the Standard toolbar.

Objective 4: Copy Cell Contents

You can copy cell contents using one of three methods: Drag and Drop, AutoFill, or Copy and Paste. With the Drag and Drop method, you use the mouse pointer to copy cell contents. With the *AutoFill* method, you use the mouse pointer and fill handle to copy cell contents to cells adjacent to the data you want to copy. With the Copy and Paste method, you use the Clipboard to store contents you want to copy to another location. Steps for each procedure are described in the following text.

Copying with Drag and Drop

In this tutorial, you use the Drag and Drop method to copy the data in column A to column H in the First worksheet. Follow these steps:

1. Select the data in cells A3 through A7.
2. Position the mouse pointer on the right border (but not the lower right corner) of the selected data. The mouse pointer should change to an arrow.
3. Hold down the left mouse button, and press Ctrl. A plus sign appears next to the mouse pointer. The status line displays the prompt `Drag to copy cell contents.`
4. Drag to column H, where you want to place the copied data.

   A border outlines the area where the copied data will appear.
5. Release the mouse button first; then release Ctrl to drop the copied data into the outlined area.

If you have problems... If the paste area is located in an area of the worksheet not visible on-screen, drag the selection to the edge of the window. Excel will start scrolling through the worksheet. Release the mouse button first, and then release Ctrl to drop the copied data into the outlined area.

Copying Cell Contents Using AutoFill

Fill handle
The black square at the lower right corner of a selected cell or range.

AutoFill is a method that enables you to copy cell contents to adjacent cells. You use the *fill handle*, the black square in the lower right corner of a selected cell or range (see figure 2.6). When you use AutoFill to copy data from one location to an adjacent cell or range of cells, a border outlines the area where the copied data will appear.

Figure 2.6
A selected range with fill handle.

	A	B	C	D	E	F	G	H	I
1			ANNUAL SALES REPORT						
2									
3	REGION	QTR 1	QTR 2	QTR 3	QTR 4	TOTAL			
4									
5	EAST	75000	71500	76000	65000	287500			
6	SOUTH	10550	9345	8000	7500	35395			
7	WEST	95400	97000	91550	93500	377450			
8									
9									
10									

Fill handle

Copying with AutoFill

In this tutorial, you use AutoFill to copy the data in cells H3 through H7 to column I in the First worksheet. Follow these steps:

1. Select the data in cells H3 through H7.
2. Position the mouse pointer on the fill handle at the lower right corner of the selected border. The mouse pointer changes to a black cross.
3. Drag the fill handle to the right to copy the selected data to the adjacent cells in column I.
4. Release the mouse button. The data should appear in column I.

If you have problems... If the selected cells contain data, that data is replaced with the contents of the active cell. If you inadvertently replace existing data, open the **E**dit menu, and choose the **U**ndo Fill command immediately after you perform the fill to reverse the action.

Filling a Range with a Numerical Series

In addition to copying a selected single row or column, AutoFill also enables you to create a series of numbers based on data you have already entered into the worksheet. For example, when you enter the numbers 5 and 10 into consecutive cells within a single row or column, Excel can determine that this series consists of increments of 5. Using AutoFill, you can extend this series to 15, 20, 25, 30, and so on, by selecting the range you want to fill and dragging the fill handle. The selected cells in a column determine the increments of the series (see figure 2.7). Excel assumes that if you select a series, you want the series extended rather than the numbers copied.

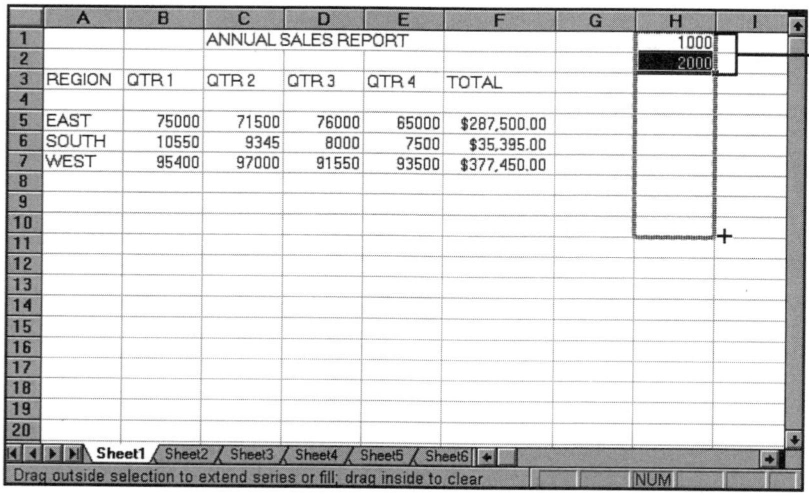

	A	B	C	D	E	F	G	H	I
1			ANNUAL SALES REPORT					1000	
2								2000	
3	REGION	QTR 1	QTR 2	QTR 3	QTR 4	TOTAL			
4									
5	EAST	75000	71500	76000	65000	$287,500.00			
6	SOUTH	10550	9345	8000	7500	$35,395.00			
7	WEST	95400	97000	91550	93500	$377,450.00			

Sheet1 Sheet2 Sheet3 Sheet4 Sheet5 Sheet6

Drag outside selection to extend series or fill; drag inside to clear NUM

The selected series

Figure 2.7
Using the fill handle to fill a series.

When you release the mouse button. The selected cells fill with numbers in the series (see figure 2.8).

	A	B	C	D	E	F	G	H	I
1			ANNUAL SALES REPORT					1000	
2								2000	
3	REGION	QTR 1	QTR 2	QTR 3	QTR 4	TOTAL		3000	
4								4000	
5	EAST	75000	71500	76000	65000	$287,500.00		5000	
6	SOUTH	10550	9345	8000	7500	$35,395.00		6000	
7	WEST	95400	97000	91550	93500	$377,450.00		7000	
8								8000	
9								9000	
10								10000	
11									

Figure 2.8
The completed data series.

Filling a Range with a Data Series

In this tutorial, you fill cells A12 through I12 in the First worksheet with a data series. Follow these steps:

1. Enter the number **1** in cell A12, and the number **3** in cell B12. Then select these two cells by dragging over them with the mouse.
2. Position the mouse pointer on the fill handle located in the lower right corner of cell B12. The mouse pointer changes to a black cross.
3. Because the range you are filling is a row, press the left mouse button, and drag the fill handle to the adjacent cells to the right of your selection until you reach cell I12.
4. Release the mouse button. Row 12 should fill with a data series.

Copying Cell Contents Using Copy and Paste

Copying cell contents is similar to moving cell contents; however, you use the **E**dit, **C**opy command. You can use the **E**dit, **P**aste command to paste the same information repeatedly. The **E**dit, **P**aste command is available as long as the marquee outlines the copied data. When you paste the copied data by pressing Enter, the marquee that outlines the copied data disappears, and the **E**dit, **P**aste command appears dimmed, indicating that the command is no longer available. The marquee also disappears if you press Enter without choosing the command or if you begin to enter data into a cell.

Copying Cells Using Cut and Paste

In this tutorial, you copy the number series in row 12 to row 14 in the First worksheet, using Cut and Paste. Follow these steps:

1. Select the data in cells A12 through I12.
2. Open the **E**dit menu, and choose **C**opy. A marquee outlines the data copied to the Clipboard.

(continues)

Copying Cells Using Cut and Paste (continued)

3. Activate the cells in which you want the data to appear (cells A14 to I14). Then press Enter, or open the **E**dit menu and choose **P**aste. A copy of the selected data appears in the new location, and the original data remains in the original location.

   A shortcut is to click only the first cell (A14) of the new location and then paste.

4. If you used the **E**dit, **P**aste command, you may want to remove the marquee from the worksheet by pressing Enter.

If you have problems... If you inadvertently paste over a formula or other important cell contents, use the **E**dit, **U**ndo Paste command *immediately* after pasting to reverse the procedure.

Copying Formulas to Multiple Cells

The capability to enter a formula and copy that formula down the rows in a column or across columns can save considerable time. For example, if you need to total rows 5 through 8 of column C and display the result in cell C10, you enter the formula =C5+C6+C7+C8 into cell C10. If you also need to calculate the totals for rows 5 through 8 of columns D, E, and F, you can copy the formula in cell C10 to cells D10, E10, and F10. Excel adjusts the formula when it is copied so that the formula totals the proper columns. For example, when the formula in cell C10 is copied to cell E10, the formula is =E5+E6+E7+E8. The cell addresses in the formula are adjusted relative to their new location.

If you copy numbers or text in a worksheet, they are not changed when they are copied unless you are copying a series of numbers. In most cases, you will want formulas to change when they are copied. Only if you use absolute cell references (discussed in the "Understanding Absolute, Relative, and Mixed Cell References" section) will formulas and functions remain the same when they are copied. The formulas and functions change in a very logical and useful way that will become clear when you look at some examples. First, you need to understand some general guidelines for copying cells in a worksheet.

If you copy the contents of a single cell, you can select multiple cells as a location for the copy. Then you can paste the copied data from the single cell into several cells. If you copy more than a single cell, the paste area you select must equal the area of the copied data. To avoid the problem of unequal copy and paste areas, select a single cell for pasting. When you select a single cell for pasting, the **E**dit, **P**aste command pastes the data automatically into an area equal to the copied area. When you select a single cell for pasting, however, you may inadvertently paste over existing data. If you do paste over existing data, you can use the **E**dit, **U**ndo Paste command immediately after pasting to reverse the action.

In Excel, you can easily copy a formula from a single cell to multiple cells. In many worksheets, data is organized in a consistent format with formulas built to calculate the data. You may, for example, have several columns of data with a formula in the last column that adds the numbers in each column. In figure 2.9, the formula bar displays in cell F5 a formula that adds the values in columns B through E in row 5. The corresponding formulas in cells F6 and F7 should be the same as the formula in cell F5 except that the row numbers should be different. In this kind of situation, copying the formula from F5 is more efficient than retyping the formula in F6 and F7.

Figure 2.9
A case where copying a formula is efficient.

=B5+C5+D5+E5

	A	B	C	D	E	F	G	H	I
1			ANNUAL SALES REPORT						
2									
3	REGION	QTR 1	QTR 2	QTR 3	QTR 4	TOTAL			
4									
5	EAST	75000	71500	76000	65000	$287,500.00			
6	SOUTH	10550	9345	8000	7500				
7	WEST	95400	97000	91550	93500				
8									
9									

Although summing a range of numbers is not too difficult, some formulas are very long and complicated. Suppose that you need to enter a long, complex formula repeatedly. Rather than entering the formula manually each time, you can use the **E**dit, **C**opy command to copy a formula to other cells and save a considerable amount of time.

Understanding Absolute, Relative, and Mixed Cell References

You have learned how to copy a formula to other cells. When you paste a formula or function, Excel takes the cell address in the copied formula and changes the cell address *relative* to the location of the pasted formula. If, for example, a formula in cell B11 displays =B3-B9 and this formula is copied and pasted to cells C11 through F11, the formula in cell C11 displays `=C3-C9`, cell D11 displays `=D3-D9`, and so on. The copied formula adjusts to the location in which it is pasted.

Relative cell reference
A cell reference that adjusts to its new location when copied or moved.

Cell references that adjust to a pasted location are referred to as *relative cell references*. As you enter formulas, Excel assumes that you want cell addresses to contain relative references.

In some cases, however, you will not want relative cell references. For example, you may have a formula that refers to a single value in another cell, and regardless of where the formula is pasted, you want to refer to that value in that particular cell. If you want a cell reference to remain the same wherever you paste the copied formula, change the cell address from a relative reference to an absolute cell reference.

Absolute cell reference
A cell reference that remains the same when copied or moved.

An absolute cell address is indicated by a dollar sign ($) preceding the column letter and a dollar sign ($) preceding the row number of the cell address. For example, $B$3 is an *absolute cell reference*. To make a cell reference (a cell address) absolute, enter a dollar sign ($) to the left of the column letter and a dollar sign ($) to the left of the row number of the cell address in the formula bar. You can use F4 to add the dollar signs rapidly.

If the formula in cell B11 displays `=$B$3-B9` and this formula is copied to other cells, the formula adjusts B9 relative to the location in which it is pasted. However, regardless of where the formula is pasted, the first part of the formula always refers to the value in cell B3. In figure 2.10, the formula copied to cell C11 contains an absolute cell reference that always refers to the value in cell B3.

Figure 2.10
A formula containing an absolute cell reference.

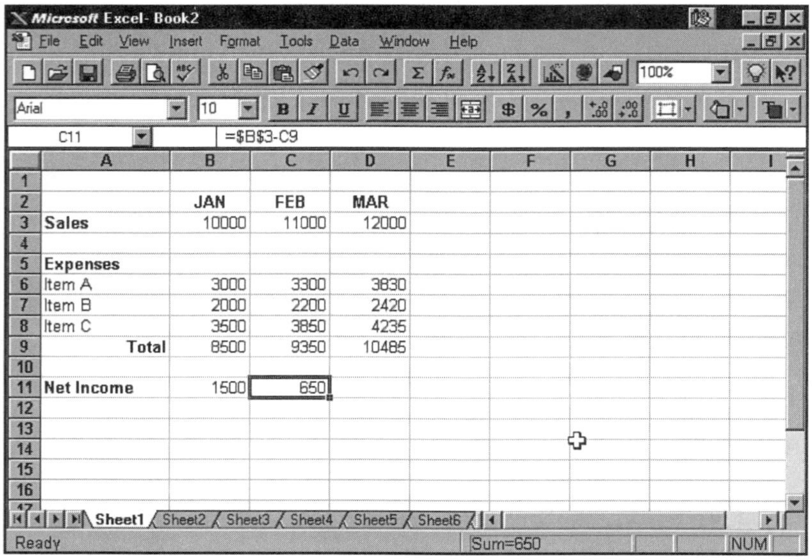

Mixed cell address
A single cell address that contains a relative and an absolute reference.

In most cases, you will want a formula to contain either relative or absolute cell references. Sometimes, however, you will want the column reference of a cell address to remain the same (absolute reference) and the row reference to adjust to the relative position of the formula; or you will want the column to adjust and the row to remain the same. A *mixed cell address* enables you to have this flexibility.

To mix cell references, place a dollar sign ($) in front of one address component and not the other. If you want the column reference to remain the same regardless of where the formula is copied, for example, place a dollar sign ($) in front of the column letter. If you want the row number to adjust depending on the row in which the copied formula is pasted, do not place a dollar sign in front of the row number of the cell address. The formula =$B3-D9, for example, is a mixed cell address. The column B reference is absolute; the row reference is relative.

Table 2.1 shows the types of cell references.

Table 2.1 Types of Cell References

Cell Reference	Description
A1	Relative cell reference. The formula adjusts to the relative location when copied or moved.
$A$1	Absolute cell reference. The formula refers to this cell always, regardless of where the formula is copied or moved.
A$1	Mixed cell reference. The formula always refers to row 1. The column adjusts to the relative location when copied or moved.
$A1	Mixed cell reference. The formula always refers to column A. The row adjusts to the relative location when copied or moved.

Copying Formulas with Relative Cell Addresses

In this tutorial, you copy a formula with relative cell addresses in the First worksheet. Follow these steps:

1. Make sure that cell B9 is the active cell. Enter the formula **=B5+B6+B7** in cell B9.
2. With B9 the active cell, open the **E**dit menu, and choose **C**opy. A marquee appears around cell B9.
3. Select the range of cells C9, D9, and E9, the cells you want to contain the formula.
4. Open the **E**dit menu, and choose **P**aste. To turn off the marquee around cell B9, press ↵Enter.

Note that the formula in cell B9, not the result, was copied and adjusted so that each column total is correct.

Copying Formulas with Absolute Cell Addresses

In this tutorial, you copy a formula with absolute cell addresses in the First worksheet. Follow these steps:

1. Enter the formula **=$B$5+$B$6+$B$7** in cell B8.
2. Make sure that the formula calculates the correct total.
3. Use the same Copy and Paste technique you used in the preceding tutorial to copy the formula in cell B8 to cells C10, D10, and E10.
4. How are the formulas in C10, D10, and E10 different from the formula in cell B8?
5. How are the formulas in C10, D10, and E10 different from the formulas in C9, D9, and E9?

Objective 5: Clear, Delete, and Insert Cells

Excel provides one command for deleting cell contents and another command for deleting the cells themselves: **E**dit, Cle**a**r and **E**dit, **D**elete. Although the two commands sound as if they perform similar functions, they do not. You use the **E**dit, Cle**a**r command to clear the contents of a cell, including formatting, formulas, and notes. When you clear a cell, the cell contents are removed, but the cell remains in the worksheet. You use the **E**dit, **D**elete command to actually remove the cell from the worksheet. The **E**dit, **D**elete command prompts you to move the surrounding cells to fill the space occupied by the deleted cell.

The two commands are often confused because Del on the keyboard is assigned to the **E**dit, Cle**a**r command. When you press Del, the content of the range is cleared, but the cells remain.

Clearing Cell Contents

The **E**dit, Cle**a**r command deletes the contents of the selected cell(s) and leaves the cell(s) in the worksheet. When you choose the **E**dit, Cle**a**r command, you use the Clear submenu to select what you want deleted from the cell(s). The Clear submenu provides the following four options:

All	Clears everything from the selected cells including formatting, formulas, and cell notes.
Formats	Removes formatting only from the selected cells.
Contents	Clears formulas from the selected cells.
Notes	Clears only notes attached to the selected cells.

Clearing a Cell or Range

To clear a cell or range, use the First worksheet, and follow these steps:

1. Select the cell or range you want to clear. For example, select cells A12 through I12.
2. Open the **E**dit menu, and choose Cle**a**r. The Clear menu appears.
3. Select **A**ll.
4. If you just removed something from your worksheet you didn't want to lose, choose **U**ndo Clear from the **E**dit menu.

Deleting Cells

When you delete cells from the worksheet using the **E**dit, **D**elete command, Excel removes the cells and prompts you to move surrounding cells to fill the space of the deleted cells. The Delete dialog box appears when you select **E**dit, **D**elete.

You can use the Delete dialog box to select how you want the surrounding cells to fill the space of the deleted cells. The Delete dialog box provides the following four options:

Shift Cells **L**eft	Shifts surrounding cells to the left.
Shift Cells **U**p	Shifts surrounding cells up.
Entire **R**ow	Shifts the entire row up.
Entire **C**olumn	Shifts the entire column to the left.

2

Deleting a Cell or Range

To delete a cell or range, use the First worksheet, and follow these steps:

1. Select the cell or range you want to delete. For this example, select cells A14 through I14.
2. Open the Edit menu, and choose Delete. The Delete dialog box appears (see figure 2.11).

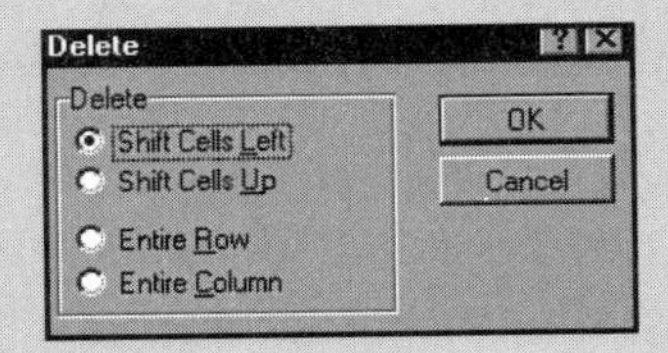

Figure 2.11 The Delete dialog box.

3. Choose the option in the dialog box that represents the direction you want to move the surrounding cells. Select Shift Cells Up by clicking the option button to the left of the option.
4. Choose OK, or press Enter. Based on the option selected, surrounding cells shift to fill the deleted space.

If you do not want the surrounding cells to fill the deleted cells, choose Edit, Clear.

Inserting Cells

Inserting cells into a worksheet is the reverse of deleting cells. The **I**nsert, **C**ells command prompts you to move surrounding cells to make space in the worksheet for the new cells, and then inserts the blank cells.

Inserting a Cell or Range

To insert a cell or range, use the First worksheet, and follow these steps:

1. Select the cell or range where you want blank cells to appear. Select cell B5.
2. Open the Insert menu, and choose the Cells command. The Insert dialog box appears (see figure 2.12).

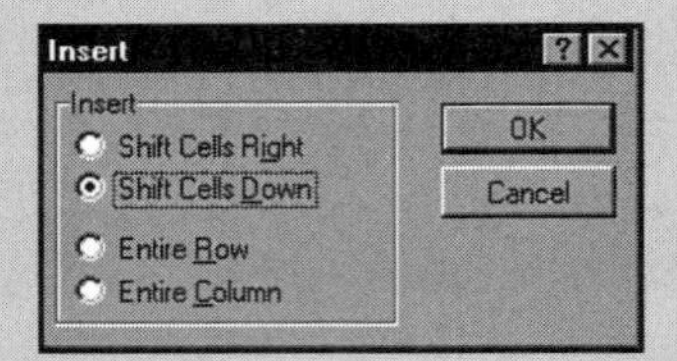

Figure 2.12
The Insert dialog box.

3. Make room for the additional cells by selecting the option in the dialog box that represents the direction you want to move the selected and surrounding cells. Click the button to the left of the Shift Cells Right option.
4. Choose OK, or press Enter. Based on the selected range, blank cells appear, and the selected cells and surrounding cells move according to the direction indicated in the Insert dialog box.
5. If you just inserted cells you don't want in the worksheet, choose Undo from the Edit menu.

Objective 6: Insert and Delete Columns and Rows

You have learned to modify worksheets by inserting and deleting cells. Sometimes you will want to insert and delete columns and rows. If you want to create additional space in the middle of a worksheet, you can insert a column or row that runs, respectively, through the entire length or width of the worksheet. If you have a column or row that is no longer necessary, you can delete the entire column or row rather than delete the cells.

Inserting a Row

To insert a row, use the First worksheet, and follow these steps:

1. Select row 6 by clicking the row heading 6, at the left of your worksheet.

   The heading of a row is the number at the left of the row.

2. Open the Insert menu, and choose Rows to insert a blank row above the selected row.

   An empty row 6 is inserted, and old rows 6 and higher are renumbered and moved down one position in the worksheet.

Click a cell outside the selected row to deselect the row.

When you delete a row or column, you do not delete the row or column *heading*, so the worksheet looks as if the row or column is still in the worksheet. The **D**elete command pulls out the original data from the selection and moves in the data from the neighboring row or column to replace the deleted data. Pressing Del does not delete the selected row or column; it clears all data from the selection without moving in replacement data.

Deleting a Column

To practice the deletion of a column from the First worksheet, follow these steps:

1. Select the column you want to delete by clicking its heading; click the column B heading. The heading of a column is the letter of the column.

2. From the **E**dit menu, choose **D**elete.

   The old column B data is removed from the worksheet and is replaced by the data in the old column C. All the other data is "bumped" over one column to the left.

Click a cell outside the selected column to deselect the column.

Insert menu commands and **E**dit, **D**elete are extremely useful; however, these commands can cause problems if you are not careful. Remember that when you are inserting or deleting a column or row, the entire length or width of the worksheet is affected by the change. You may have formulas or data in cells in another section of the worksheet that you cannot see; these cells may be affected by an insertion or deletion. If a formula refers to a cell that is deleted, the cell containing the formula displays the #REF! error value. To undo a deletion, open the **E**dit menu, and choose **U**ndo Delete immediately after making the deletion. This command reverses the action.

The **I**nsert menu commands are a little more adaptable than the **E**dit, **D**elete command. Formulas adjust to cell address changes when you insert a column or row; however, the command can disorganize areas of the worksheet. Always double-check your worksheet to verify worksheet results when using the **I**nsert menu commands or the **E**dit, **D**elete command.

In the preceding tutorials, you inserted and deleted one row and column at a time. To insert or delete multiple adjacent rows or columns, you simply select the multiple row or column headings and then issue the **I**nsert or **D**elete command.

Objective 7: Change Column Width and Row Height

One of the most frequently used worksheet commands is the command used to adjust the width of a column. Text is often cut off because the column is not wide enough to display the entire contents of the cell. If a cell cannot display an entire number or date, the cell fills with #########, or the number is displayed in scientific notation. After you widen the column sufficiently, the number or date appears in the cell. You can adjust the column width using the mouse or the keyboard. Most people like to experiment with different column widths to see which looks best. If, however, you know exactly how wide you want a column to be, you can use the Column command in the Format menu. You can select multiple columns by dragging over the column headings with the mouse.

Changing Column Width

In this tutorial, you increase the width of column B in the First worksheet. Follow these steps:

1. Position the mouse pointer on the right border of the heading at the top of column B. When positioned properly, the mouse pointer changes to a black double-headed horizontal arrow with a vertical bar in the middle.
2. Press and hold down the left mouse button, and drag to the right to increase the column width. A light gray outline indicates the column width.
3. Move the mouse back and forth. Notice that a Width indicator appears in the area just above the column A heading. Move the mouse so that the black double-headed arrow is in the middle of column D, and then release the mouse button.

Using the Best Fit Column Width Command

Best Fit
A command that automatically adjusts the column width or row height to the widest cell in the column.

The *Best Fit* column width command enables you to adjust the column width automatically to the widest cell in the column. To access the Best Fit command using the mouse, you position the mouse pointer on the right border of the column heading. When positioned properly, the mouse pointer changes to a black double-headed horizontal arrow with a vertical bar in the middle. Double-click with the left mouse button. The column adjusts to the widest cell contents in the column.

Adjusting Row Height

Adjusting the height of a row works much the same as adjusting the width of a column. You can adjust the row height using the mouse or the keyboard. You select multiple rows by dragging over the row heading numbers.

Increasing Row Height

In this tutorial, you increase the height of row 3 in the First worksheet. Follow these steps:

1. Place the mouse pointer on the border between the row 3 heading (at the left end of row 3) and the row 4 heading. When positioned properly, the

mouse pointer changes into a black double-headed vertical arrow with a horizontal bar in the middle.

2. Hold down the left mouse button, and drag the arrow down and then up. A light gray outline indicates the column width. Notice that a Height indicator appears in the area just above the column A heading.

3. Move the mouse down, and then release the mouse button when the double-headed arrow is in the middle of row 8.

When you need to set a column or row to an exact width, you use the Format command.

Adjusting the Column Width by Using the Format Columns Command

To set the width of column A to exactly 27, use the First worksheet, and follow these steps:

1. Select column A by clicking the column A heading.

2. Choose F**o**rmat, **C**olumn, **W**idth.

   The Column Width dialog box appears (see figure 2.13).

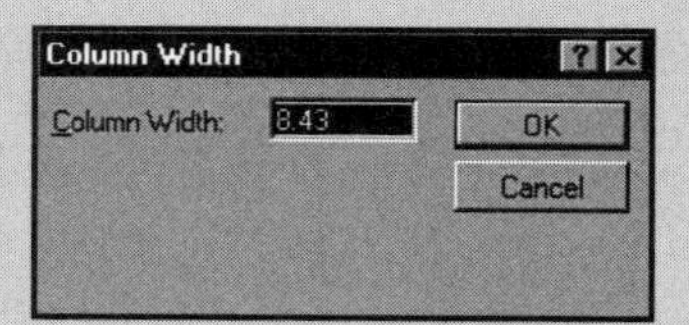

Figure 2.13 The Column Width dialog box.

3. Type the column width you want; type **27**.

4. Click OK, or press Enter.

The width of column A is set to exactly 27.

Chapter Summary

This chapter covers many important worksheet features that are necessary for setting up ranges and moving or copying data. You have also learned step-by-step procedures for inserting and deleting cells, rows, and columns. Additionally, you have learned to adjust column width and row height.

Checking Your Skills

True/False

For each of the following, circle *T* or *F* to indicate whether the statement is true or false.

T F **1.** A range in a worksheet can be given a meaningful name.

T F **2.** To copy a range using the Drag and Drop technique, you use the mouse and the Shift key.

T F **3.** Relative cell references remain unchanged when a formula is copied to a new location.

T F **4.** In Excel, the width of a column can be increased, but the height of a row cannot be changed.

T F **5.** If a cell's width is too narrow to display a number, Excel displays question marks in the cell.

T F **6.** A range can be any size.

T F **7.** Columns cannot be deleted from a worksheet.

T F **8.** Rows cannot be inserted into a worksheet.

T F **9.** The **E**dit, Cu**t** command enables you to place selected data on the Clipboard.

T F **10.** The **E**dit, **P**aste command places the contents of the Clipboard in your worksheet.

Multiple Choice

In the blank provided, write the letter of the correct answer for each of the following.

_____ **1.** When placed on the AutoFill fill handle, the mouse pointer becomes a ________.

a. double-headed arrow

b. white cross

c. black cross

d. dark rectangle

_____ **2.** Which of the following characters is used to make a cell address absolute in a formula?

a. *

b. $

c. #

d. none of the above

_____ **3.** To automatically adjust the column width to the widest cell contents in the column, place the mouse pointer on the right border of the column heading, and _______.

a. click

b. double-click

c. press Ctrl

d. press ↵Enter

_____ **4.** When you paste data into a cell, any data already in the cell is _______ the data you paste.

a. replaced by

b. added to

c. subtracted from

d. none of the above

_____ **5.** The moving dashes around a cell that appear when **E**dit, **C**opy is chosen are called the _______.

a. AutoFill

b. clipping

c. highlight

d. marquee

_____ **6.** Which of the following is a relative cell address?

a. $D$5

b. %D5

c. A0

d. none of the above

_____ **7.** To adjust the height of a row, place the mouse pointer on the _______ border of the row heading.

a. top

b. bottom

c. left

d. right

_____ **8.** If you delete a cell that is used in a formula, the cell containing the formula displays _______.

a. ?

b. ###

c. #REF!

d. none of the above

_____ **9.** The command that enables you to insert blank cells into a worksheet is _______.

a. **E**dit, **I**nsert

b. **O**ptions, **I**nsert

c. both a and b

d. none of the above

____ **10.** If a number is too large to be displayed in a cell, a series of _______ is displayed in the cell.

a. Error!

b. ?

c. *

d. #

Completion

In the blank provided, write the correct answer for each of the following.

1. The _______________ command from the _______________ menu will undo an editing change in a worksheet.

2. A _______________ is a group of cells in the worksheet.

3. The _______________ is a temporary storage area containing data you can place in a worksheet using the **E**dit, **P**aste command.

4. When you use the Copy and Paste method to copy the contents of more than a single cell, the _______________ area you select must be only one cell or must be the same size as the area of the copied data.

5. The **E**dit, _______________ command removes cells from the worksheet and prompts you to move the surrounding cells.

6. Moving dashes _______________ the area you cut or copy to the Clipboard.

7. To clear the contents of the active cell, you press the _______________ key.

8. A _______________ cell reference is adjusted when a formula is copied to a new location in the worksheet.

9. Excel offers ______________ different ways to copy cell contents from one location in a worksheet to another location.

10. The ______________ commands in the **E**dit menu enable you to copy the contents of the active cell to adjacent cells without using the Clipboard.

Applying Your Skills

Review Exercises

Exercise 1: Entering and Modifying a Worksheet

1. Enter the Performance Report worksheet, shown in figure 2.14. Set the width of column A to 20. Use the Best Fit feature to adjust the width of columns B, C, and D. Save this worksheet on your disk in the workbook **C2sp1**.

Figure 2.14
The C2sp1 worksheet.

QUARTERLY PERFORMANCE REPORT			(in thousands)
	Actual	Estimated	Variance
Costs			
Direct materials	$823.57	$ 615.00	$ 208.57
Direct labor	$517.79	$ 450.00	$ 67.79
Overhead:			
Variable:			
Supplies	$ 75.00	$ 72.00	$ 3.00
Power	$ 40.00	$ 45.00	$ (5.00)
Fixed:			
Supervision	$112.55	$ 95.00	$ 17.55
Depreciation	$150.00	$ 150.00	$ -
Rent	$ 30.00	$ 30.00	$ -
TOTAL =			

2. The cells in columns B and C contain data values. The Variance is found by using a formula that subtracts the budget estimate from the actual expenditure. Set the format of all the cells that contain numbers to currency.

3. Delete row 1. Insert a new item, **Indirect labor (Actual = 225.00, Estimated = 179.00)**, in a new row between Supplies and Power, and enter the formula to calculate the Variance for this item.

4. Make the row that contains the column headings twice as high as the other rows. Select the heading names as a range, and make them boldface. Enter formulas to calculate the total Actual cost and total Estimated cost. Give the range containing the data in the Variance column a name. Enter a formula that calculates the total Variance.

5. Save the worksheet in the workbook file C2sp1. Print the worksheet. Then choose **F**ile, **C**lose to close all your open workbooks.

Exercise 2: Creating a Sales Order Worksheet

1. Enter the worksheet shown in figure 2.15. Do not change the default width of column A, but set the width of column B to 9. Use the Best Fit feature to set the column width for columns C, D, and E.

Figure 2.15
The C2sp2 worksheet.

	A	B	C	D	E	F	G
1							
2	CUSTOMER NUMBER 138					SALES REP:	Schreiver
3							
4	ITEM	QUANTITY	DESCRIPTION	PRICE	AMOUNT		
5	1	5	Cordless Phone	$299.99	$1,499.95		
6	2	2	Headset Phone	$139.99	$ 279.98		
7	3	4	Answering Machine	$127.99	$ 511.96		
8	4	1	Fax/Phone	$250.00	$ 250.00		
9	5	3	Personal Pager	$ 97.50	$ 292.50		
10							
11				Subtotal	$2,834.39		
12							
13				Tax	$ 198.41		
14							
15				TOTAL =	$3,032.80		

2. Format the cells in columns D and E to currency. Quantity and Price are data values. The Amount equals Quantity times Price. The tax rate is 7 percent. Enter a formula to calculate the Subtotal.

3. Save this worksheet in a workbook named **C2sp2**; print the worksheet.

4. Insert a row containing the following data:

ITEM	QUANTITY	DESCRIPTION	PRICE
6	2	Three Station Intercom	$100.00

5. Calculate the AMOUNT for this item, and verify that the Subtotal is correct. Save and print the new worksheet.

Exercise 3: Creating a Worksheet of Invoices

1. Enter the worksheet shown in figure 2.16. Enter the formula to calculate the amount owed in cell G4; then use AutoFill to copy the formulas down the BALANCE column. Save your work on disk in a file named **C2sp3**, and then print it.

Figure 2.16
The C2sp3 worksheet.

	A	B	C	D	E	F	G
1	INVOICE	INVOICE	CUST.		AMOUNT	TOTAL	
2	NUMBER	DATE	NUMBER	CUSTOMER NAME	DUE	PAID	BALANCE
3							
4	1830	11/23/94	110	CAMPBELL	782.56	400.56	382
5	1831	11/24/94	17	CAPON	947.28	100.25	847.03
6	1832	11/24/94	83	CLARK & CO.	281.95	281.95	0
7	1833	11/25/94	64	DAUM & CHARNLEY	847.53	300.95	546.58
8							
9							

2. Insert a DATE DUE column between the CUSTOMER NAME and the AMOUNT DUE columns. Verify that the formulas in the BALANCE column are adjusted properly. Fill in any date you like. Save the workbook using the same file name. Print the worksheet.

2

Exercise 4: Copying and Moving Columns and Rows

1. Using the worksheet you created in Review Exercise 3, practice using the copy and move techniques and column and row insertion and deletion to move the contents of the rows and columns to different locations in the worksheet.

2. When you have totally rearranged the order of the columns and the order of the rows, print the result, but don't save your work on disk.

Exercise 5: Creating a Worksheet to Set Up a Daily Schedule

1. In this review exercise, you practice using AutoFill to set up a series. B2:F2 should contain the days of the week (MONDAY through FRIDAY). A3:A24 should contain the hours in the working day from 7:30 to 6:00 in half-hour increments. Enter only the first two days of the week in columns B and C, and use AutoFill to fill in the rest. Enter 7:30 in cell A3 and 8:00 in cell A4, and use AutoFill to fill in the remaining times.

2. Save the worksheet as **C2sp5**. Then print it.

3. Modify the worksheet so that it displays `7:30 - 12:30` (for the A.M. hours) and `1:00 - 6:00` (for the P.M. hours). Save and print the file.

Continuing Projects

Project 1: The NSCC Quarterly Report

To help a struggling new business, you are asked to set up an Excel worksheet to help the owner understand her cash flow. The completed worksheet is shown in figure 2.17.

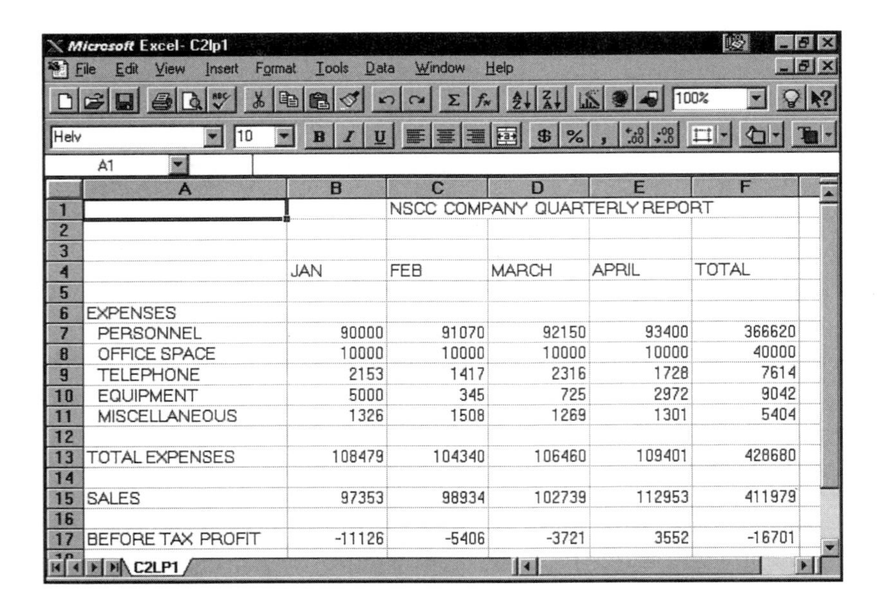

Microsoft Excel- C2lp1

File Edit View Insert Format Tools Data Window Help

	A	B	C	D	E	F
1			NSCC COMPANY QUARTERLY REPORT			
2						
3						
4		JAN	FEB	MARCH	APRIL	TOTAL
5						
6	EXPENSES					
7	PERSONNEL	90000	91070	92150	93400	366620
8	OFFICE SPACE	10000	10000	10000	10000	40000
9	TELEPHONE	2153	1417	2316	1728	7614
10	EQUIPMENT	5000	345	725	2972	9042
11	MISCELLANEOUS	1326	1508	1269	1301	5404
12						
13	TOTAL EXPENSES	108479	104340	106460	109401	428680
14						
15	SALES	97353	98934	102739	112953	411979
16						
17	BEFORE TAX PROFIT	-11126	-5406	-3721	3552	-16701

C2LP1

Figure 2.17 The NSCC Quarterly Report worksheet.

The expense figures for January through April are actual numbers, as are the sales figures for these months. However, cells F7 through F11, F13, F15, and F17 must all contain formulas (not just numbers) because the owner wants to continue to use the worksheet in the future. For the same reason, cells B13 through F13 and B17 through F17 should contain formulas. Remember, Profit = Sales – Expenses.

1. Create the worksheet shown in figure 2.17.
2. Save the worksheet in the workbook file **C2lp1** (you will use it in later continuing projects), and then print it.

Project 2: International Investment Analysis

The worksheet you will complete for this project is used for investment analysis. The completed worksheet is shown in figure 2.18. At this point, the worksheet is in a rough form. In later chapters, you will spruce it up and make some additions. No formulas or functions are in the worksheet yet.

Figure 2.18 The investment analysis worksheet you will use later.

	A	B	C	D	E	F	G	H
1								PERCENT
2								RETURN
3					(Mil.)		(Mil.)	ON
4				(Mil.)	NET	(Mil.)	MARKET	INVESTED
5	COMPANY	INDUSTRY	COUNTRY	SALES	INCOME	ASSETS	VALUE	CAPITAL
6								
7	Solvey	Retail	Australia	11293	273	4262	3939	12.1
8	Kesko	Diversified	Brazil	6242	715	11684	9554	9.6
9	CNX	Automobile	Germany	12579	268	12059	2180	10.8
10	Dumez	Electronic	Italy	4283	66	2786	994	7.2
11	Nobunaga	Steel	Japan	11709	294	16036	8630	4.7
12	Nordlund	Optical	Norway	5476	291	5991	1438	9.7
13	Olnza	Machine	Spain	7602	1174	14114	14640	13.9
14	Lucus & Smith	Aerospace	U. K.	8272	160	8964	5415	7.3

Simply type the numbers, and save the worksheet in the workbook file C2lp2.

Project 3: A List of Sales Offices

1. Enter the list of information shown in figure 2.19.
2. Save this workbook as **C2lp3** for use in projects later in this book, and then print the worksheet.

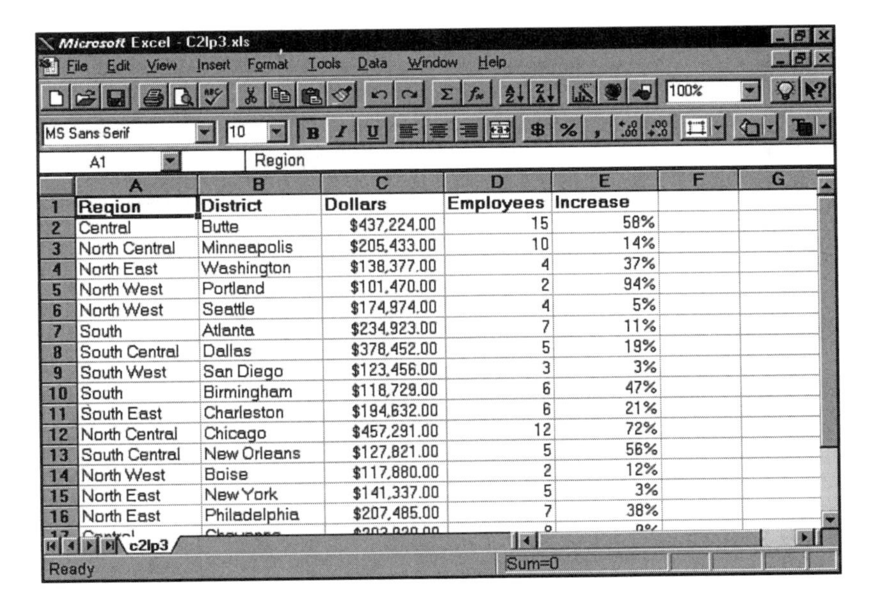

Region	District	Dollars	Employees	Increase
Central	Butte	$437,224.00	15	58%
North Central	Minneapolis	$205,433.00	10	14%
North East	Washington	$138,377.00	4	37%
North West	Portland	$101,470.00	2	94%
North West	Seattle	$174,974.00	4	5%
South	Atlanta	$234,923.00	7	11%
South Central	Dallas	$378,452.00	5	19%
South West	San Diego	$123,456.00	3	3%
South	Birmingham	$118,729.00	6	47%
South East	Charleston	$194,632.00	6	21%
North Central	Chicago	$457,291.00	12	72%
South Central	New Orleans	$127,821.00	5	56%
North West	Boise	$117,880.00	2	12%
North East	New York	$141,337.00	5	3%
North East	Philadelphia	$207,485.00	7	38%

Figure 2.19
The list worksheet you will use later.

CHAPTER 3

Formatting Worksheets

Formatting The process of changing the appearance of text, numbers, or cells in your worksheet.

In Chapter 2, you learned how to build a simple worksheet. In this chapter, you learn how to move between the worksheets in a workbook, use Excel's built-in help, and make changes to the appearance of your worksheet. The appearance and layout of a worksheet can increase its usefulness and effectiveness. This chapter also shows you how to improve the appearance of your worksheet by *formatting*. When you format a part of a worksheet, you change the appearance of that element. For example, you can format the text or numbers in a cell to appear in boldface, italic, and color, and in a larger size type. Additional formatting is available for numbers so that they can be displayed as currency (with dollar signs), as percentages (with percent signs), or as dates.

Specifically, this chapter covers formatting numbers and text, aligning cell contents (including centering text over multiple columns and making text read vertically or horizontally), using automatic range format, changing fonts, and enhancing cells with borders and patterns. The chapter also covers the Formatting toolbar and concludes with a topic vital to the professional appearance of your worksheet—spell checking.

Because so many possibilities exist for formatting, you also learn about Excel's Help facility in this chapter. You can use Help to answer your questions and aid you when you are lost—in this chapter and throughout this book. The Help facility contains information about all aspects of Excel, not just formatting. This chapter teaches you to use Help efficiently.

Objectives

By the time you have finished this chapter, you will have learned to

1. Move among the Worksheets in a Workbook
2. Use Excel's On-Line Help

3. Apply Formats to Numbers
4. Change Fonts
5. Align Cell Contents
6. Format Cells with Borders and Color
7. Check Spelling in the Worksheet

Objective 1: Move among the Worksheets in a Workbook

In Excel, most of your work will involve the use of worksheets. As you have learned, worksheets are contained in workbooks. At the bottom of each worksheet window is a tab that identifies that worksheet. After you have opened a workbook, you can go directly to a worksheet by clicking its tab. In a later chapter, you learn how to add new worksheets and charts to the workbook, how to give meaningful names to a worksheet's tab, and how to remove a worksheet from a workbook.

In Excel, you can see at the bottom of your screen the tabs for only a few of the worksheets in your workbook. However, you can scroll a different set of tabs into view. To see the tabs for other sheets, you click the scroll arrow buttons to the left of the worksheet tab area (see figure 3.1). The two outermost arrow buttons, the ones with the arrow and the vertical line, scroll to the first or the last tab in the workbook. The two innermost arrow buttons (the ones without the line) scroll one tab in the direction of the arrow.

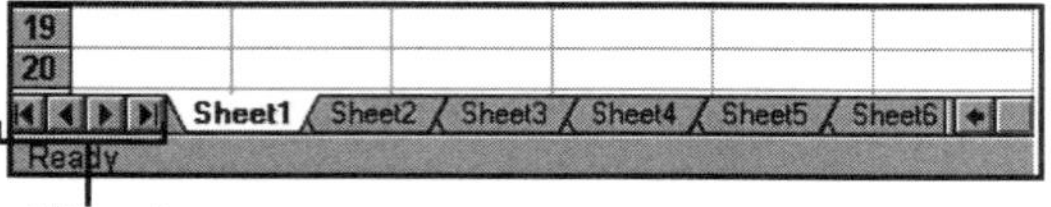

Figure 3.1
The tab scrolling buttons.

Moving among Worksheets

In this tutorial, you move between the worksheets in a workbook. Make sure that the workbook My File is open; then follow these steps:

1. Place the mouse pointer on the tab labeled Sheet4, and click the left mouse button.
2. Type **This is Sheet 4** in cell A1 of this worksheet, and press Enter.
3. Click the tab for Sheet1. Notice that it is just as you left it.
4. Click the tab for Sheet4. You can see that Sheet1 and Sheet4 are two separate worksheets.

5. Click the right-arrow button several times. Notice that the sheet names change as you scroll to the right. Next, click the right-arrow button with the vertical line to display the last sheet name in the workbook.

6. Click the left-arrow button several times. Notice that the sheet names change as you scroll to the left. Then click the left-arrow button with the vertical line to return to the Sheet1 tab to display the first sheet name in the workbook.

   The worksheet tabs and arrow buttons enable you to move quickly among the worksheets in a workbook.

7. Close My File without saving changes.

Objective 2: Use Excel's On-Line Help

Excel contains an indispensable feature that will help you learn about the program: the on-line Help. This section explains how to use this feature. In addition to the on-line Help feature, Excel displays helpful information in the status bar at the bottom of the screen. This bar is especially useful when you want to see what a menu choice does without actually making the choice. The status bar also displays information about a toolbar button when you place the mouse pointer on that button. Get in the habit of glancing down at the status bar when you try something new in Excel; you will find that this practice makes learning Excel much easier. Notice that placing your mouse pointer on a button in a toolbar for a second or two causes the name of the button to appear in a small box. More extensive help on toolbar buttons is available if you click the Help button at the far right of the Standard toolbar. When you do this, a dark question mark will attach itself to your mouse pointer. Now, when you click a button in a toolbar, the button won't perform an action; instead, an explanation of the button will be displayed. To turn the help feature off, click the Help button again and the button appears to pop out.

Another useful feature is Excel's TipWizard. To display the TipWizard, click the TipWizard button. This button, located at the right of the Standard toolbar, contains a light bulb. When the button has been clicked, TipWizard is "on" and will give you tips in a tip box that appears above the formula bar near the top of the screen. Tips are information about more efficient ways to accomplish a task you are working on. To turn off the TipWizard, click the TipWizard button again. Excel's Help has more information on using the TipWizard.

Using On-Line Help

Excel comes with a complete on-line Help system designed to assist users with commands and other topics. This section of the chapter provides you with an overview of how to use Excel's on-line Help system: how to search for help with a specific topic, how to use the Answer Wizard, and how to print a Help topic.

You access the Help system by selecting an option from the **H**elp menu (see figure 3.2). The first menu choice, Microsoft Excel **H**elp Topics, displays the Help Topics tabbed dialog box (see figure 3.3). The tabs in this dialog box provide four different methods (Contents, Index, Find, and Answer Wizard) that you can use to ask Excel for help. The Contents tab is like the Table of Contents in a book; it provides an overview of the 23 major categories of help available. The Index tab is like the index in the back of a book; it provides an alphabetical list of the detailed help that is available. The Find tab enables you to type a word that you need help with, and then lists any help topics that are related to the word you typed.

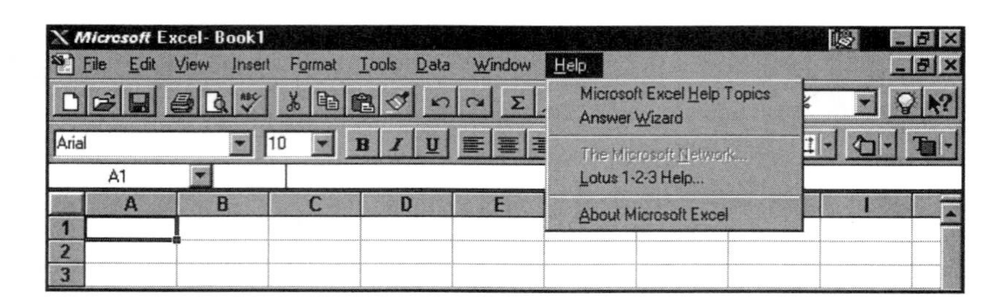

Figure 3.2
The **H**elp menu.

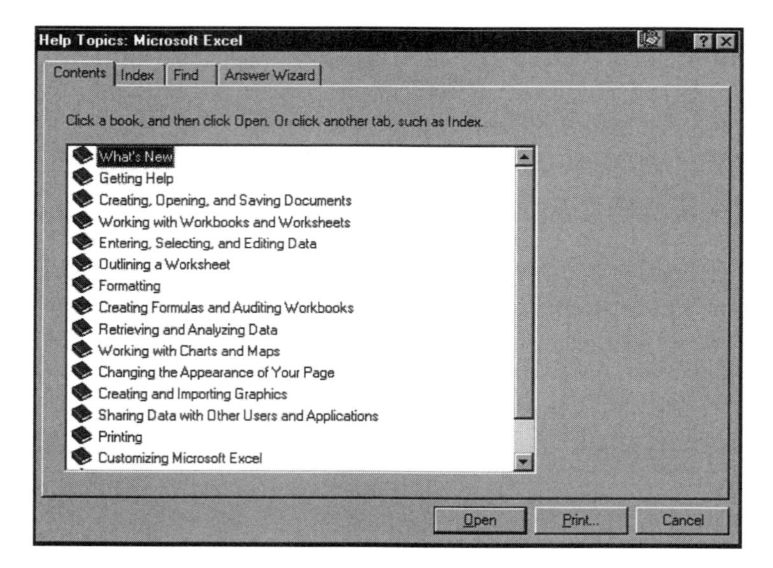

Figure 3.3
The Microsoft Excel **H**elp Topics tabbed dialog box.

When you use the Answer Wizard tab to provide help, you type your question and the Answer Wizard tries to provide an answer. The second choice in the **H**elp menu, Answer **W**izard, takes you directly to the Answer Wizard tab in the Help Topics tabbed dialog box. Try using the Help available via Contents, Index, and the Answer Wizard.

Using Help Contents

If you have not started Excel, do so now; then follow these steps:

1. Open the **H**elp menu, and choose Microsoft Excel **H**elp Topics.
2. Click the Contents tab.

3. Click the Getting Help Topic and then click the **O**pen button.
4. Click the Getting assistance while you work topic.
5. Click the **D**isplay button.

   The Getting assistance while you work help screen appears (see figure 3.4). In this, and in similar Excel help screens (windows), you click a label (like Answer Wizard or Screen Tips) and a yellow note box that contains an explanation appears. You read the explanation and then click the yellow note box to make it disappear.

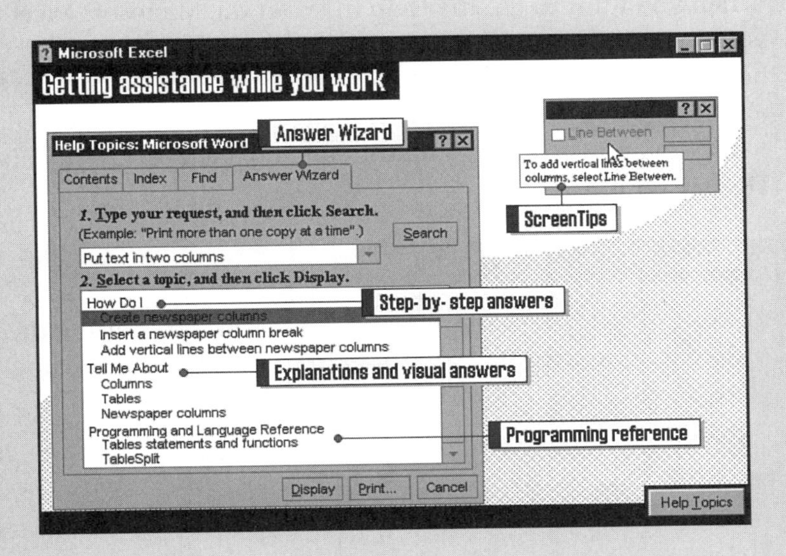

Figure 3.4 The Getting assistance while you work screen.

6. Click the Answer Wizard label; a yellow note box appears (see figure 3.5). Read the information in the note box providing help on the Answer Wizard. Then click the note box to dismiss it.

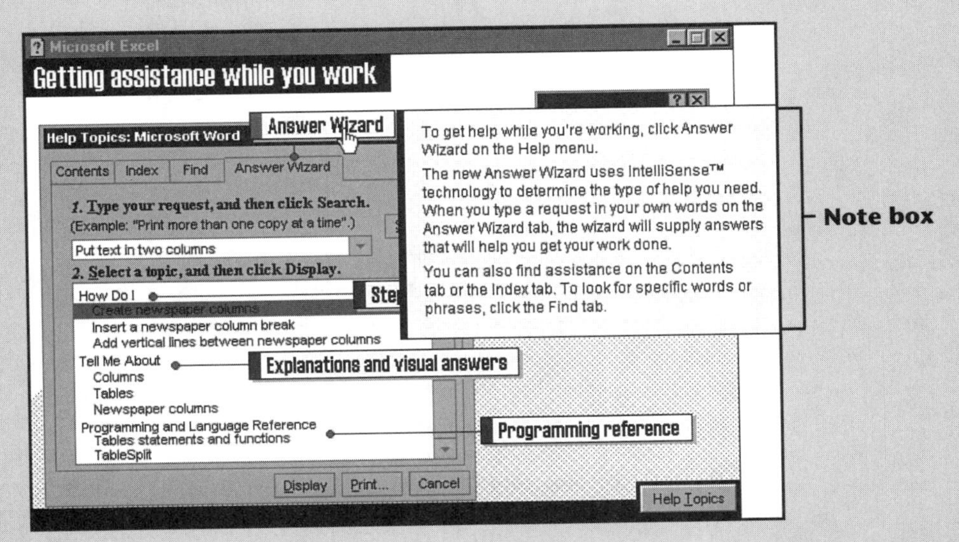

Figure 3.5 The Note Box associated with the Answer Wizard label.

(continues)

Using Help Contents (continued)

7. Click (one at a time) the Step-by-step answers, the Explanations and visual answers, and the Screen Tips labels. After you have read an explanation in a note box, dismiss it by clicking the note box.

8. Click the Help **T**opics button in the lower right corner of the Getting assistance while you work Help window to return to the Microsoft Excel Help Topics tabbed dialog box.

When you want to use the Help Index in the Microsoft Excel tabbed dialog box, you first click the Index tab. Then you press Tab (or click in the topmost text box) and type the word you want to look up. The bottom text box will display all the available Help topics that relate to the word you typed. To see more information on an entry in the bottom text box, click the entry and then click the **D**isplay button.

Using the Help Index

In this tutorial, you learn to search for a Help topic, using the Index tab. First, make sure that the Microsoft Excel Help Topics tabbed dialog box is displayed on your screen. Then follow these steps:

1. Click the Index tab to display it in the dialog box (see figure 3.6).

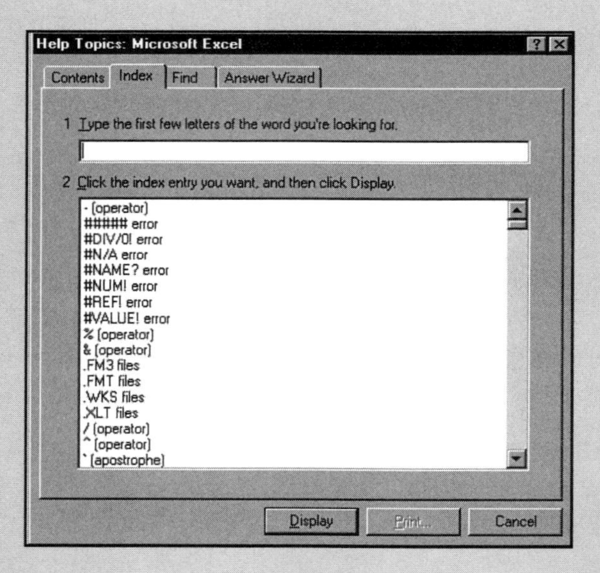

Figure 3.6 The Index tab in the Microsoft Excel tabbed dialog box.

2. Click in the Type the first few letters of the word you're looking for text box and type **formatting**.

3. Click the **D**isplay button.

4. In the Topics Found text box, click the Basic formatting topic.

5. Click the **D**isplay button.

   The Basic Formatting Help screen appears.

6. Click and read the information on the five different topics (the labeled topics).

7. Click the Help **T**opics button at the lower right corner of the Basic formatting window to return to the Help Topics tabbed dialog box.

The Answer Wizard

To display the Answer Wizard, click the Answer Wizard tab in the Microsoft Excel Help Topics tabbed dialog box. Or you can display the Answer Wizard by choosing Answer **W**izard in the **H**elp menu. Then type a question for the Answer Wizard and click the **S**earch button to see a listing of the relevant Help topics. The list will appear in the lower text box. Click a topic to select it and then click the **D**isplay button. When you are working on a worksheet, press F1 to immediately display the Answer Wizard.

Using the Answer Wizard

Make sure that the Microsoft Excel Help Topics tabbed dialog box is displayed on your screen. Then do the following:

1. Click the Answer Wizard tab in the Microsoft Excel Help Topics tabbed dialog box. The Answer Wizard appears (see figure 3.7).

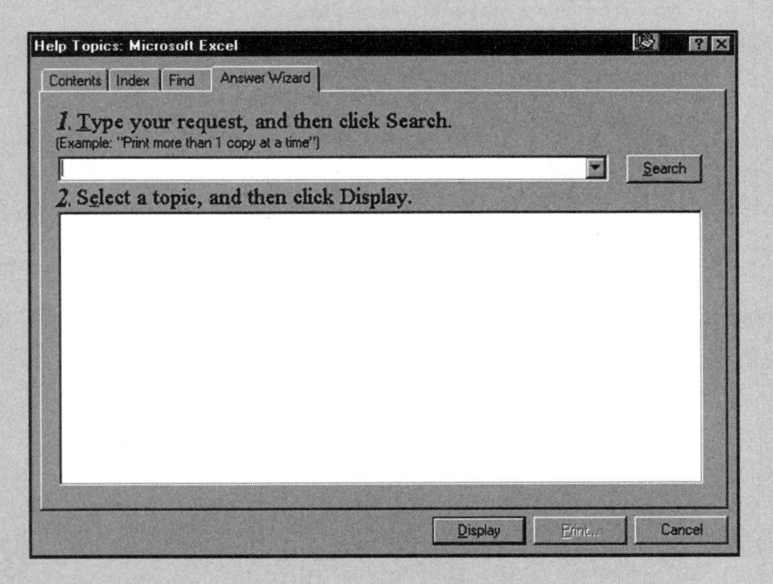

Figure 3.7
The Answer Wizard tab in the Microsoft Excel tabbed dialog box.

2. Type **How do I print a worksheet.**

3. Click the **S**earch button.

(continues)

Using the Answer Wizard (continued)

4. In the bottom text box, click the Troubleshoot printing topic and then click the **D**isplay button.

   The Troubleshoot printing Help box appears (see figure 3.8). This Help box displays the six Help subtopics for troubleshooting printing. To obtain help on a topic, you click it with your mouse.

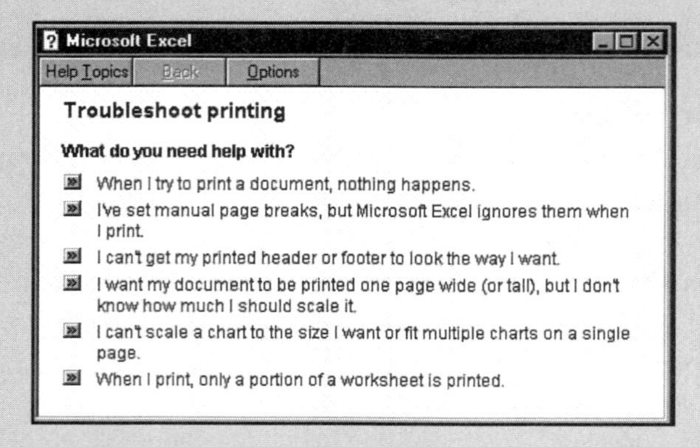

Figure 3.8
The Trouble-shoot printing Help box.

5. Click the When I try to print a document, nothing happens topic.

   The Help information under this subtopic appears in a Help window (see figure 3.9).

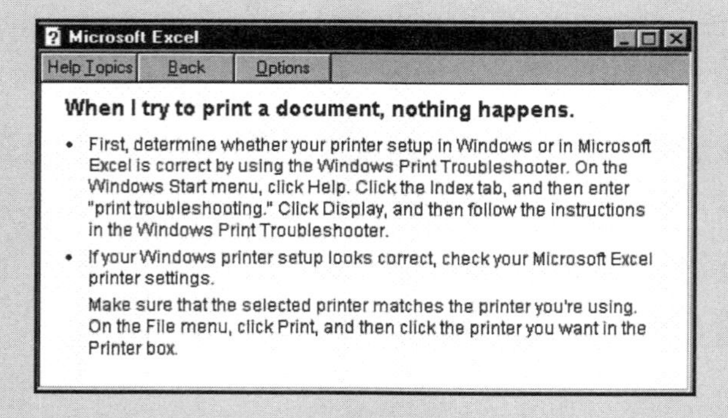

Figure 3.9
The When I try to print a document, nothing happens Help Window.

Note: *Clicking the Help Topics button returns you to the Microsoft Excel Help Topics tabbed dialog box.*

Clicking the **B**ack button (when it is enabled) returns you to the previous Help window (the Troubleshooting printing Help window in this example).

Clicking the **O**ptions button displays the Options menu (see figure 3.10). The two most useful choices in this menu are **P**rint Topic (which gives you a hard copy of the Help topic information) and **K**eep Help on Top. Help on top means that the Help topic window will stay open (float) above your worksheet so that you can read the Help topic instructions as you work on your worksheet.

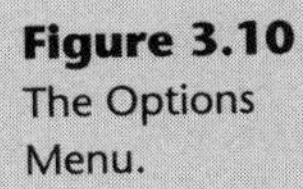

Figure 3.10
The Options Menu.

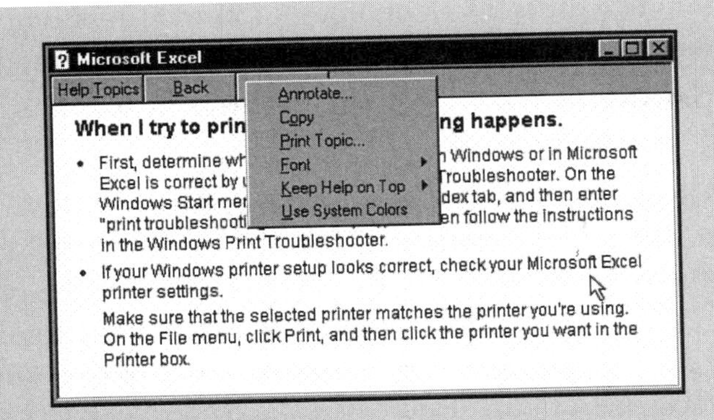

6. Click the Close button at the upper right of the When I try to print a document, nothing happens Help window to leave Excel Help and return to your worksheet.

You will find that Help is available in most of Excel's dialog boxes. This help, which is specific to the particular dialog box, is accessed by clicking the Help button in the dialog box (see figure 3.11). When you click this button, a question mark appears next to the mouse pointer. When you click an item or part of the dialog box, helpful information about that item will be displayed.

Figure 3.11
The Help button in a dialog box.

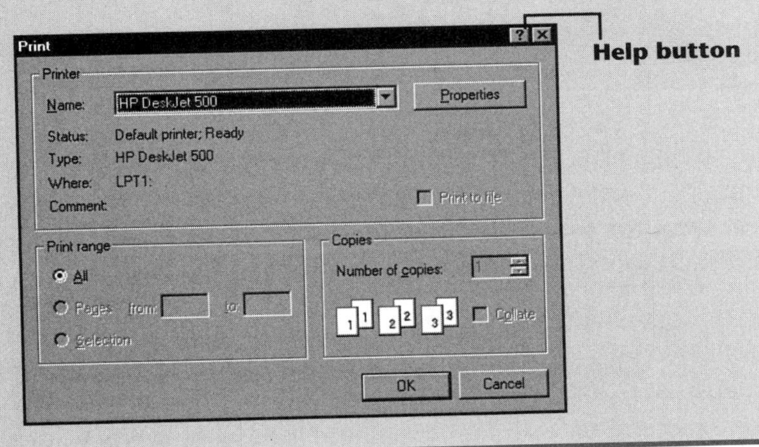

Help button

Objective 3: Apply Formats to Numbers

Predefined formats
Standardized formats that come with Excel.

Because numbers are the most common items on a worksheet, Excel offers a variety of *predefined formats* for numbers. You may want a number to appear with two decimals in some places and with no decimals in other places on the same worksheet. You may also want to display negative numbers in red or in parentheses. Often you may want to display currency symbols or the percent sign without having to type the symbol every time you enter a number.

While you are entering numbers, you don't need to be concerned about how they look. After you have completed your entries, you can apply formatting to numbers and change the way they look on-screen or in print. Remember, formatting affects only the way a number is *displayed* or *printed*. Formatting does not change the value of the number stored in a cell and used in calculations.

Excel offers you two different techniques for formatting numbers. You can use the Format menu or the Formatting toolbar. The most commonly used formatting can be done using the toolbar. The complete selection of formatting capabilities, however, is available only through the Format menu.

Understanding the Format Cells Dialog Box

When you use the Format, Cells command, the Format Cells tabbed dialog box appears (see figure 3.12). This *tabbed dialog box* with six tabbed cards is really six dialog boxes in one; the commands all relate to changing some characteristic of the selected cell(s). A tabbed dialog box is like a card index. You click a tab to move that tabbed card to the front of the dialog box so that you can use it to format the cell or the contents of the cell.

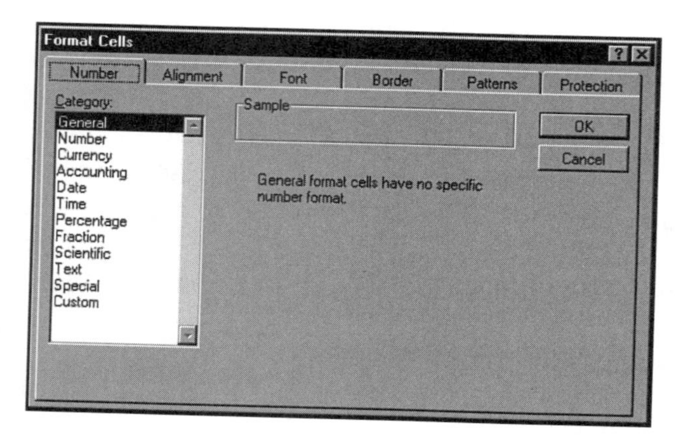

Figure 3.12
The Format Cells tabbed dialog box.

In the Numbers tab, the **C**ategory list shows the types of numeric formats. When appropriate, a list of predefined number formats for the selected category appears in the Type list box on the right side of the dialog box. The General format is the default format for numbers.

Each Custom formatting type consists of a format for positive numbers (on the left), followed by a semicolon, and then the format for negative numbers. Symbols such as #, 0, and . (period) are used in the codes. Think of the formatting code as a pattern, or layout guide, that tells Excel how you want a number displayed. The # indicates an available space where a number can print. The 0 indicates where a zero will be displayed if the value in the cell does not contain a digit at that position. The period indicates where the decimal point will be placed. Excel places the value in the cell in the formatting code's layout; adding commas, decimal points, currency symbols, and zeros, and rounding numbers as necessary. Although these codes seem strange at first, the codes will become obvious to you as you use them.

Note: *Throughout the rest of this chapter, you will work on a series of tutorials that show you how to format the First workbook. If possible, work through all the tutorials, keeping the First workbook open at the end of each tutorial. If you need to take a break, however, save the First workbook temporarily as Ch3tutr; then, when you resume work, open Ch3tutr and continue working.*

Formatting Numbers Using the Format Menu

In this tutorial, you format the number in cell B5 using the Format menu. Follow these steps:

1. Open the First workbook you created in Review Exercise 1 at the end of Chapter 1.

   You need to increase the width of columns A through F to 12; you can see the width displayed in the left end of the formula bar.

2. Click the column A heading, and drag over the column headings so that columns A through F are selected.

3. Choose the Format, Column, Width command, and set the width to 12.

4. If you have added any formulas, clear them so that your worksheet looks like figure 3.13.

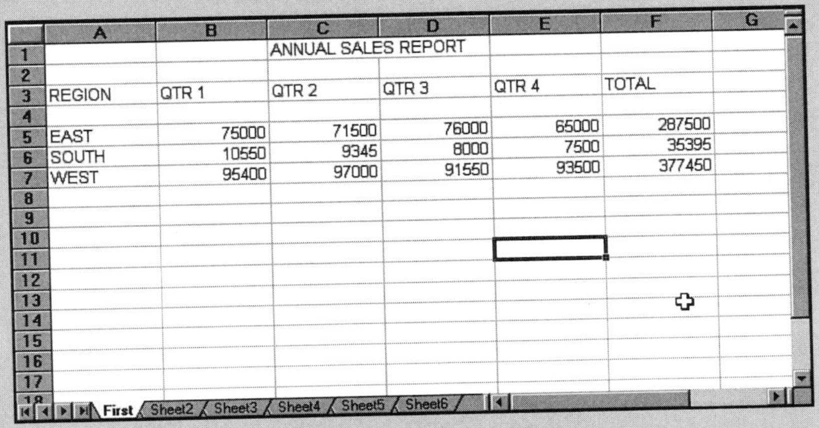

	A	B	C	D	E	F	G
1			ANNUAL SALES REPORT				
2							
3	REGION	QTR 1	QTR 2	QTR 3	QTR 4	TOTAL	
4							
5	EAST	75000	71500	76000	65000	287500	
6	SOUTH	10550	9345	8000	7500	35395	
7	WEST	95400	97000	91550	93500	377450	

First / Sheet2 / Sheet3 / Sheet4 / Sheet5 / Sheet6

Figure 3.13
The First workbook with wider columns.

5. Save the First workbook with the wide columns before you continue with this tutorial.

6. Activate cell B5.

7. From the Format menu, choose Cells. The Format Cells dialog box appears.

8. Click the Number tab near the top of the dialog box if the Number tab is not active. The Number tab in this dialog box displays a list of predefined number formats (see figure 3.14).

(continues)

Formatting Numbers Using the Format Menu (continued)

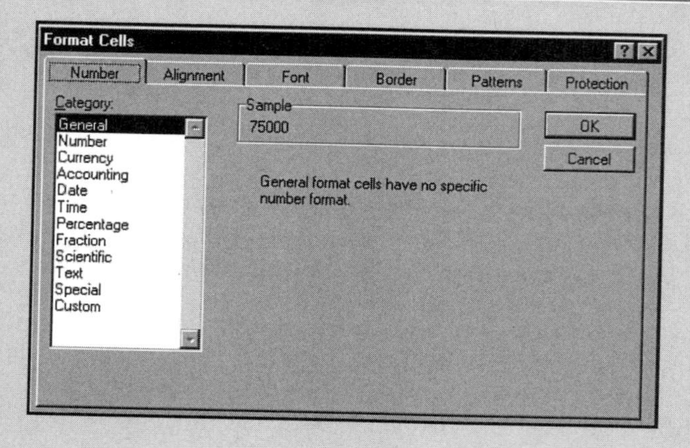

Figure 3.14
The Format Cells dialog box with the Number tab active (at the front).

❾ Click the Number category from the **C**ategory drop-down list.

Your screen should now look similar to figure 3.15. Notice that the value in cell B5 is displayed in the Sample area.

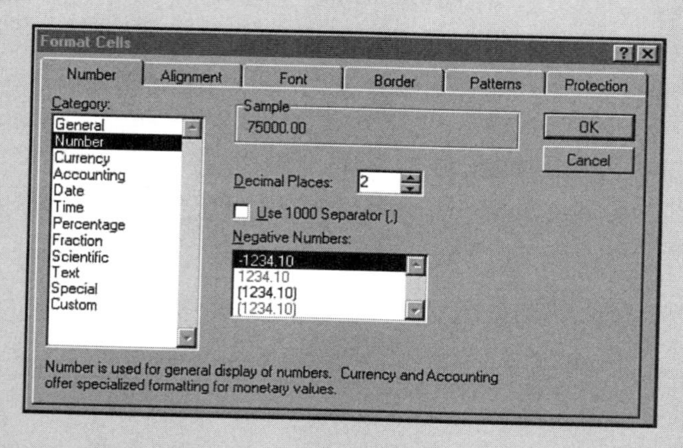

Figure 3.15
The Number tab of the Format Cells dialog box after a format has been chosen.

❿ Click OK. Your screen should now look like figure 3.16.

	A	B	C	D	E	F	G
1			ANNUAL SALES REPORT				
2							
3	REGION	QTR 1	QTR 2	QTR 3	QTR 4	TOTAL	
4							
5	EAST	75000.00	71500	76000	65000	287500	
6	SOUTH	10550	9345	8000	7500	35395	
7	WEST	95400	97000	91550	93500	377450	
8							

Figure 3.16
Cell B5 with the new format.

⓫ Make sure that B5 is activated; then choose F**o**rmat, C**e**lls. Click the Number tab if it is not at the front of the dialog box.

⓬ Choose Currency from the **C**ategory list.

Notice that the Sample area displays `$75,000.00`.

⓭ Click OK.

Applying Number Formats Using the Formatting Toolbar

You can quickly apply commonly used predefined number formats, such as Currency, Comma, and Percent, with the buttons on the Formatting toolbar. Your choice of formats, however, is more limited than in the F**o**rmat menu. You can also use the Increase or Decrease Decimal buttons to change the number of decimal places (see figure 3.17).

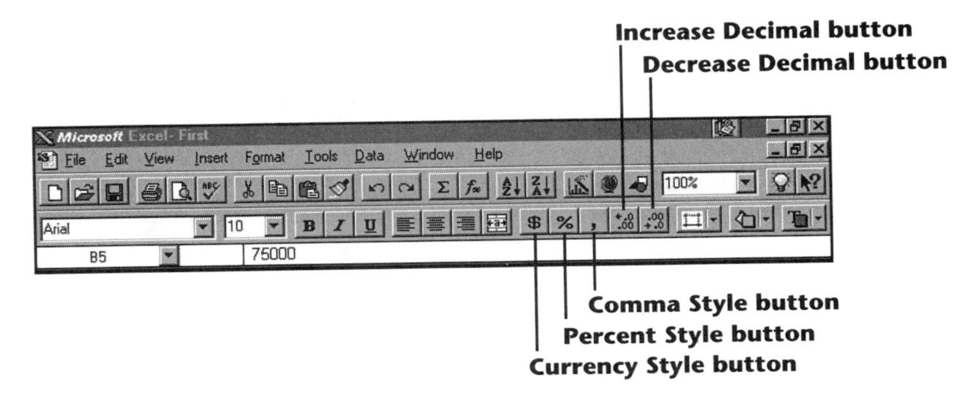

Figure 3.17 The number formatting buttons on the Formatting toolbar.

Style A combination of formatting commands (such as alignment, borders, font, and number formatting).

Each of the five formatting buttons applies a specific *style*. This default style, set by Excel when it is installed, is usually the one you want to use. But you can change the style associated with a formatting button by selecting the F**o**rmat menu's **S**tyle command. The Style dialog box appears (see figure 3.18). Press F1 for an explanation of how to change styles. You can name and save your own combinations so that you can apply them more efficiently. Use the default styles in this text.

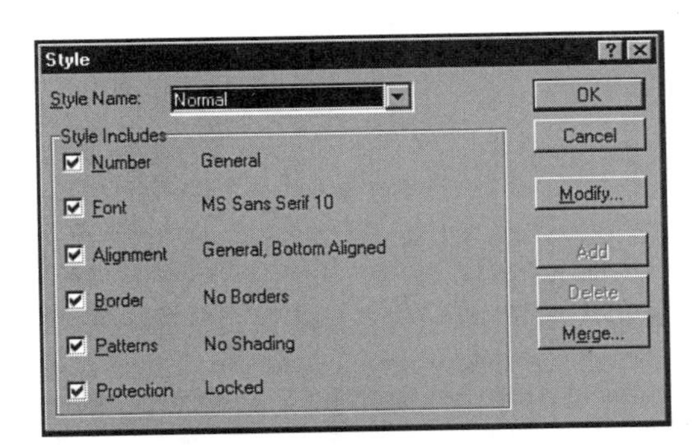

Figure 3.18 The Style dialog box.

Formatting Numbers Using the Formatting Toolbar

In this tutorial, you use the formatting buttons to apply a number format to a range of cells. Follow these steps:

1. Select the range B5:E7 by dragging over the cells.

Note: *The notation B5:E7 means "the range of cells from B5 through E7."*

(continues)

Formatting Numbers Using the Formatting Toolbar (continued)

2. Select the Comma (,) format button on the Formatting toolbar. The numbers are displayed with a comma and two decimal places.

3. Click the Increase Decimal button once. Notice that the numbers in the selected cells now have three decimal places.

4. Click the Decrease Decimal button three times, and notice the effect on the numbers in the selected cells.

5. Notice the effect on the numbers in the selected cells when you click the Percent (%) button; then click the Currency ($) button. The actual value in the cell does not change—only the way the number is displayed.

Now your worksheet should look like figure 3.19.

	A	B	C	D	E	F	G
1			ANNUAL SALES REPORT				
2							
3	REGION	QTR 1	QTR 2	QTR 3	QTR 4	TOTAL	
4							
5	EAST	$75,000.00	$71,500.00	$76,000.00	$65,000.00	287500	
6	SOUTH	$10,550.00	$9,345.00	$8,000.00	$7,500.00	35395	
7	WEST	$95,400.00	$97,000.00	$91,550.00	$93,500.00	377450	
8							
9							

Figure 3.19
The worksheet with the new formats applied.

Changing Date and Time Formats

If you enter 1-1-96 into a cell, Excel assumes that you are entering a date. The cell, therefore, displays the number in a date format. (The default date format is 1/1/96.) If you enter 9:45, Excel assumes that you are referring to a time and displays a time format. To change to another date or time format, you can use the Format, Cells command. The procedure for changing a date or time format is the same as changing a number format. The date and time formats are separate categories of number formats. When you select the Date category in the Category list of the Format Cells Numbers tab dialog box, the date format codes appear.

Changing a Date Format

To change a date format, follow these steps:

1. In cell F1, enter the date **9-10-96**. The date is displayed in the default format.

2. Make sure that cell F1 is activated.

3. Choose Cells from the Format menu.

4. Because Excel recognizes that the number in cell F1 is a date, the format codes for the Date category are displayed.

5. In the Type list, select the sixth format: 04-Mar-95.

   Notice how the date is displayed in the Sample area.

6. Click OK.

The date in cell F1 should now be displayed as `10-Sep-96`.

Objective 4: Change Fonts

Font
A typeface, a group of characters with the same characteristics.

Point
One point equals 1/72 inch. In Excel, font size and row height are measured in points. The larger the point size, the larger the font size.

Excel for Windows 95 enables you to use as many as 256 different fonts on a worksheet. You can also italicize, underline, boldface, and change the size of a font (measured in points). Excel offers two ways for you to change a font or change the appearance of a font. You can use buttons on the Formatting toolbar, or you can use the Format Cells command. In the Format Cells Font tabbed dialog box, you can select a font, choose a size for the selected font, and apply a style. The list of fonts available depends on the type of printer you are using.

If you want to increase or decrease the size of the font in a cell without actually changing the font, use the Font Size box at the left end of the Formatting toolbar. Clicking the Font Size drop-down list button displays a list of font sizes from which you can choose. You can change a font by selecting a cell, a range, or the entire worksheet. To select the entire worksheet, click in the area where the column and row headings intersect—in the upper left corner of the worksheet above row 1 and to the left of column A.

Changing the Font Size from the Toolbar

To change the font size of the headings in the First workbook, follow these steps:

1. Select the range of cells A3:F3.

2. Click the Font Size drop-down list button (see figure 3.20). A list of font sizes (in points) is displayed; the larger the number, the bigger the font.

Figure 3.20
The Font box, the Font Size box, and the Color buttons.

3. Click 18.

   The font size of the headings is increased to 18 points.

4. Click the Font Size drop-down list button, and click 10 to change the font back to the default size.

3

You use the Font box on the Formatting toolbar to change the font of selected cells in a worksheet. To see a list of the fonts available for you to use, click the Font Size drop-down list button.

Changing the Font Using the Font Box

To change the font used in the column headings, follow these steps:

1. Select the cells in the range A3:F3.
2. Click the Font box drop-down list button at the far left of the Formatting toolbar.

   Your screen should look similar to figure 3.21, although the available fonts may differ, depending on the fonts installed on your computer.

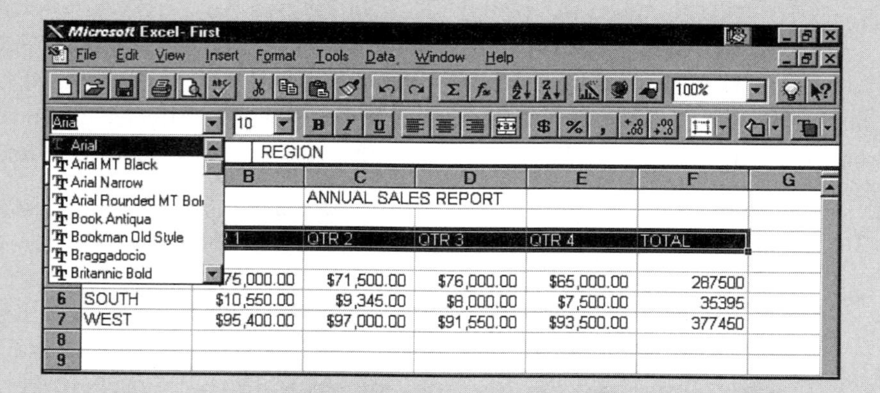

Figure 3.21 The Fonts box drop-down list.

3. Click the Terminal font, if available. If Terminal is not available, click Roman. The font used in the headings should change.
4. Click the Font box drop-down list button to display the list of fonts.
5. Click the MS Sans Serif font to return to the default font.
6. Click the Color button drop-down list button at the right of the Formatting toolbar, and try changing the color of the font.

You can use the Format, Cells command to control fonts, size, and styles. In the Format Cells Font tabbed dialog box, you can select a font, choose a size for the selected font, and apply a style. The list of fonts available depends on the type of printer that you are using.

Changing the Font Using the Format, Cells Command

In this tutorial, you change the font in a range of cells. Follow these steps:

1. Select the range A5:A7.
2. Choose Format, Cells.

❸ Click the Font tab in the Format Cells dialog box.

Your screen should now look like figure 3.22.

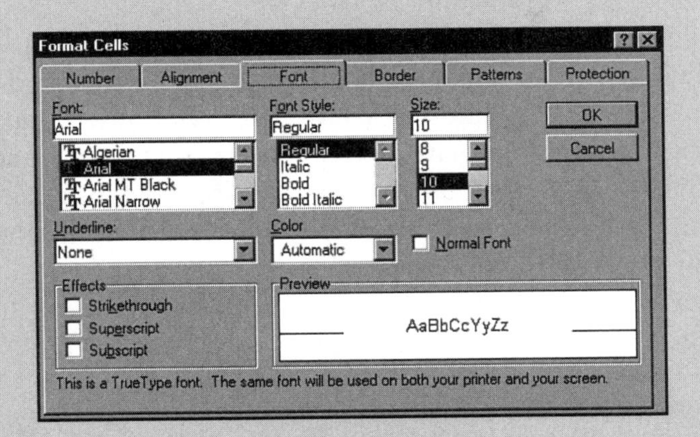

Figure 3.22 The Format Cells dialog box with the Font tab active.

❹ Use the scroll bar in the Font area to scroll down to Terminal (or Roman).

❺ Click Terminal (or Roman).

❻ In the Font Style area, click Bold Italic.

❼ In the Color list, click the drop-down arrow button. A palette of colors appears.

❽ Click the blue square in the middle of the top row of the palette.

Note: *The Preview area of the dialog box shows you what your font will look like.*

❾ Click OK.

❿ Click cell A1 to deselect the range of cells and see the formatting.

⓫ Select the range A3:F3.

⓬ Again, choose Format, Cells.

⓭ In the Color area of the dialog box, click the drop-down list button.

⓮ Click the red square in the top row of the color palette.

⓯ Click OK.

⓰ Click cell A1 to deselect the range of cells.

If you have a color printer, you can print your worksheet in color; otherwise, you can print only in black and white.

Using the Bold, Italic, and Underline Buttons on the Toolbar

The Formatting toolbar in Excel for Windows 95 contains buttons that represent commonly used formatting commands, such as Bold, Italic, and Underline (see figure 3.23).

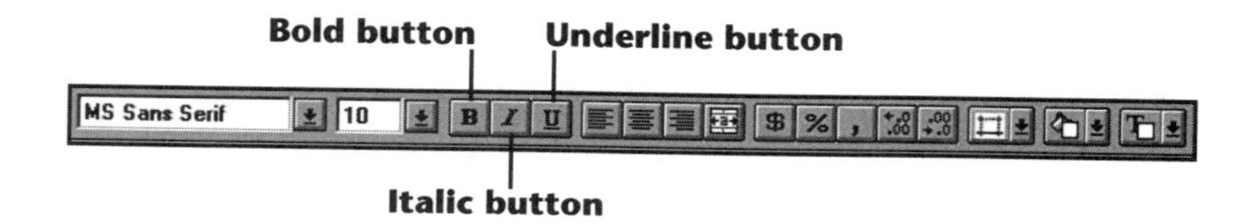

Figure 3.23 The Formatting toolbar.

As you have seen, you can apply boldface or italic formatting to text or numbers using the Format Cells Font dialog box. You can, however, accomplish this task much faster using the Formatting toolbar. When you click one of the buttons shown in figure 3.23, the button changes color and looks as if it has been "clicked in." If you select a cell that has already been formatted in Bold, Italic, or Underline, the corresponding button looks "clicked in" to indicate this fact. If you decide that you don't want the formatting, select the cell, and "click out" the button. The formatting of the text or number in the cell is turned off.

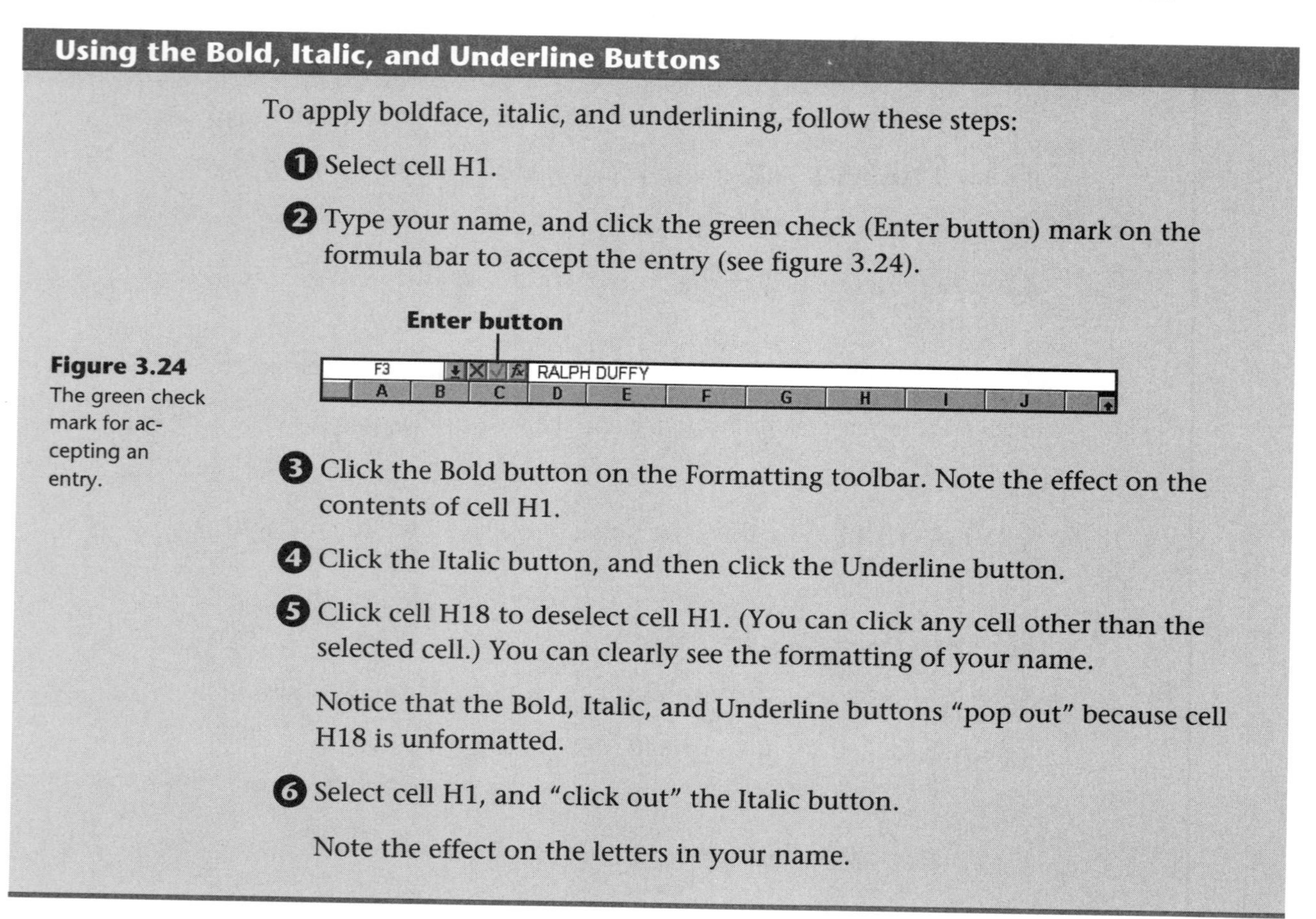

Using the Bold, Italic, and Underline Buttons

To apply boldface, italic, and underlining, follow these steps:

1. Select cell H1.
2. Type your name, and click the green check (Enter button) mark on the formula bar to accept the entry (see figure 3.24).

Figure 3.24 The green check mark for accepting an entry.

3. Click the Bold button on the Formatting toolbar. Note the effect on the contents of cell H1.
4. Click the Italic button, and then click the Underline button.
5. Click cell H18 to deselect cell H1. (You can click any cell other than the selected cell.) You can clearly see the formatting of your name.

   Notice that the Bold, Italic, and Underline buttons "pop out" because cell H18 is unformatted.
6. Select cell H1, and "click out" the Italic button.

   Note the effect on the letters in your name.

Objective 5: Align Cell Contents

Sometimes, you may want to change the arrangement of numbers or text within a cell. You can format numbers and text so that they are left-aligned, right-aligned, or centered in a cell. You can also format long text entries to wrap within a cell, or you can center text across a range of columns. To wrap text within a cell causes a long string of text to appear on multiple lines within a cell.

The height of the cell increases as you type so that it can contain the lines of text. You can also align text so that it is vertical in a cell (first letter of the text at the top of the cell, last letter at the bottom of the cell).

Unless you change the alignment, Excel left-aligns text and right-aligns numbers in a cell. This default alignment is called the General alignment. You can apply alignment formatting, such as left, center, and right, to selected cells using the alignment buttons in the middle of the Formatting toolbar (see figure 3.25). The Format Cells Alignment tab dialog box also enables you to wrap text, choose horizontal or vertical alignment, and choose orientation options for vertical text. The Formatting toolbar and the F**o**rmat, C**e**lls Alignment command's dialog box are outlined in the text and tutorials that follow.

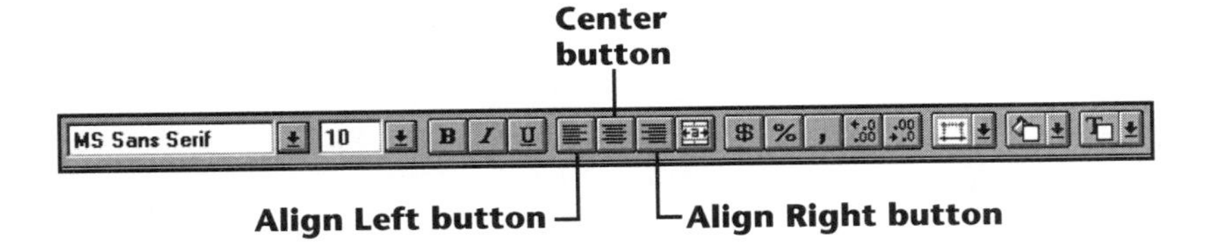

Figure 3.25 The Alignment buttons.

Aligning Text Using the Formatting Toolbar

In this tutorial, you use the Formatting toolbar to align text in a range in the First workbook. Follow these steps:

1. Select the range B3:F3 by dragging over the cells with the cell pointer.
2. Click the Align Right button on the Formatting toolbar to apply alignment formatting to the selection.

   Notice how the text in the selection has moved to the right in each cell. Then watch for the effects of the following steps.
3. Click the Center button.
4. Click the Align Left button.

You can also use the Format Cells dialog box to align text in a selected cell or cells.

Aligning Data and Text Using the Format, Cells Command

To align data or text using the F**o**rmat, C**e**lls command, follow these steps:

1. Select the cell or range in which you want to align data or text. Select A3:F7.
2. Open the F**o**rmat menu, and choose the C**e**lls command. When the Format Cells dialog box appears, click the Alignment tab.

(continues)

Aligning Data and Text Using the Format, Cells Command (continued)

Your screen should now look like figure 3.26.

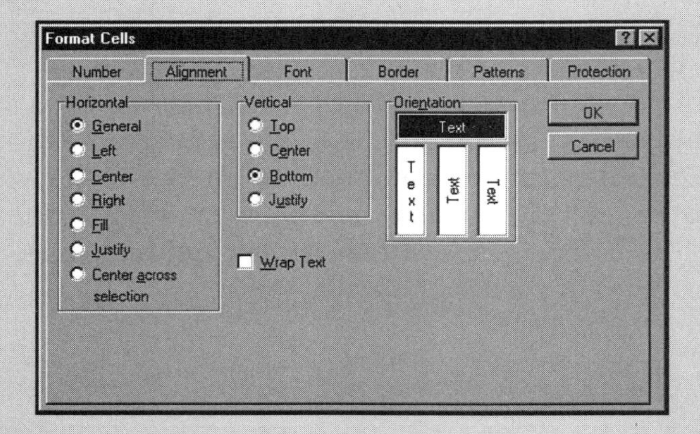

Figure 3.26
The Format Cells dialog box with the Alignment tab displayed.

The Alignment tab of the Format Cells dialog box offers a number of options.

General, the default Horizontal alignment, aligns text to the left and numbers to the right. Left, Center, and Right, respectively, left-align, center, and right-align text or numbers. Fill repeats the contents of the selected cell until it is full. Justify, which can be used only with two or more lines of wrapped text, aligns wrapped text within a cell on both the left and the right.

Bottom is the default Vertical alignment.

The Wrap Text check box makes wide text entries wrap into multiple lines within the cell. Center across selection enables you to select a range of cells and center the contents of the leftmost cell within the range. This option is useful to center headings across the top of your worksheet.

3. Try using several of these options. Choose OK, or press Enter to see the effect of a change on your worksheet.

In the following tutorial, you right-align text in a range in the First workbook, using the Format Cells Alignment tabbed dialog box.

Aligning Text Using the Format, Cells Alignment Command

To right-align selected text, follow these steps:

1. Select the range A5:A7.
2. Choose Format, Cells. The Format Cells dialog box appears.
3. Click the Alignment tab (refer to figure 3.26). In the Horizontal section, choose the Right option button.
4. Choose OK, or press Enter. The text is right-aligned.

If you have used a word processing program, you are probably familiar with word wrap. This option in Excel enables you to display a long line of text on multiple lines inside a cell.

Wrapping Text Using the Format, Cells Alignment Command

In this tutorial, you wrap a string of text within a cell. Follow these steps:

1. Select cell A9, and type **This is the first Excel worksheet I created.**

   Press Enter to enter the text into the cell. Notice that the text extends across other cells.

2. Make cell A9 the active cell.

3. Choose the F**o**rmat, C**e**lls command. The Format Cells dialog box appears. Click the Alignment tab if it isn't in front (refer to figure 3.26).

4. Click the **W**rap Text check box so that a check mark appears in it.

5. Choose OK, or press Enter.

Row 9 increases in height, enabling all the text to be displayed in cell A9 (see figure 3.27).

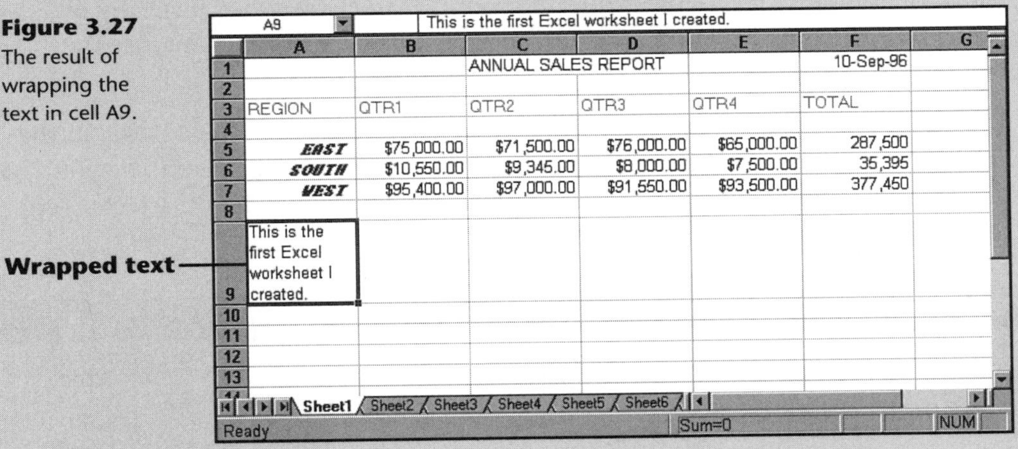

A9 | This is the first Excel worksheet I created.

	A	B	C	D	E	F	G
1			ANNUAL SALES REPORT			10-Sep-96	
2							
3	REGION	QTR1	QTR2	QTR3	QTR4	TOTAL	
4							
5	EAST	$75,000.00	$71,500.00	$76,000.00	$65,000.00	287,500	
6	SOUTH	$10,550.00	$9,345.00	$8,000.00	$7,500.00	35,395	
7	WEST	$95,400.00	$97,000.00	$91,550.00	$93,500.00	377,450	
8							
9	This is the first Excel worksheet I created.						
10							
11							
12							
13							

Sheet1 Sheet2 Sheet3 Sheet4 Sheet5 Sheet6

Ready Sum=0 NUM

Wrapped text

Figure 3.27
The result of wrapping the text in cell A9.

Sometimes, you may want to center the title on a worksheet. You can easily accomplish this task using Excel's text-centering capability.

You can center text from one cell horizontally over a selected range of columns using either the Center **a**cross selection option button in the Format Cells Alignment dialog box or the Center Across Columns button on the Formatting toolbar (see figure 3.28). The text from the leftmost cell in the selection is centered across all selected blank cells to the right. (Selected cells defining the range of columns must be blank.)

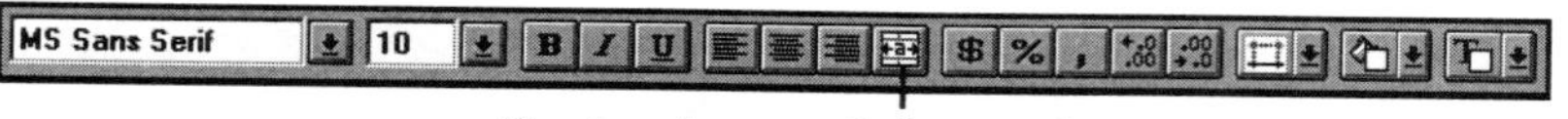

Figure 3.28
Center Across Columns button centers selected text across columns.

Centering Text across Multiple Columns Using the Toolbar

In this tutorial, you use the toolbar and the First workbook to center text stored in cell B2 over columns B through E. Follow these steps:

1. Select cell B2, and type **CASHMAN, INC**.

   Press Enter to enter the text into the cell.

2. Select cell B2, and select columns B through E (the range of columns you plan to center the text across) by dragging over the columns with the cell pointer.

3. Click the Center Across Columns button on the toolbar.

The text is centered across the four columns.

Caution
Remember, the text to be aligned must be in the leftmost column, and the columns to the right must be blank.

Excel for Windows 95 enables you to format text to align either vertically or horizontally. When aligning text vertically, you usually need to increase the height of the row.

To format text vertically, you use the Format Cells Alignment dialog box. In the Orie**n**tation section of this dialog box, you select the vertical orientation you want by clicking one of the boxes containing the word `Text`. If you select a vertical orientation, you must also select a specific vertical alignment.

Aligning Text Vertically

In this tutorial, you format text to be displayed vertically. Follow these steps:

1. Select cell F3.

2. Choose the F**o**rmat, C**e**lls command; then click the Alignment tab. The Alignment dialog box appears (refer again to figure 3.26).

3. In the Vertical section of the dialog box, select the C**e**nter option.

4. In the Orientation section in the dialog box, click the far left rectangle.

5. Choose OK, or press Enter.

   Your screen should now look like figure 3.29.

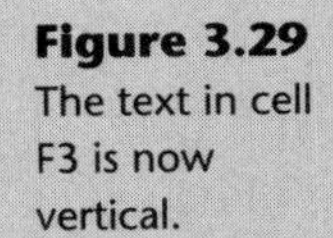

Figure 3.29
The text in cell F3 is now vertical.

	A	B	C	D	E	F	G
1			ANNUAL SALES REPORT			10-Sep-96	
2			CASHMAN, INC.				
3	REGION	QTR1	QTR2	QTR3	QTR4	TOTAL	
4							
5	EAST	$75,000.00	$71,500.00	$76,000.00	$65,000.00	287,500	
6	SOUTH	$10,550.00	$9,345.00	$8,000.00	$7,500.00	35,395	
7	WEST	$95,400.00	$97,000.00	$91,550.00	$93,500.00	377,450	
8							
9	This is the first Excel worksheet I created.						

To adjust the column width or row height for vertical text, follow the steps for the AutoFit Selection feature covered in Chapter 2. You can also use the Row or Column command in the Format menu.

Objective 6: Format Cells with Borders and Color

So far, most of this chapter has covered formatting numbers or text (the *contents* of cells). This section deals specifically with applying formats to *cells* themselves. Formatting cells includes adding a border around a cell or range of cells, filling a cell with a color or pattern, and using a combination of predefined formats (automatic formatting) to format a range or the entire worksheet.

To place borders around a cell or to place a single or double underline below a series of numbers, you use the Format Cells Border dialog box or the Borders button on the Formatting toolbar (see figure 3.30).

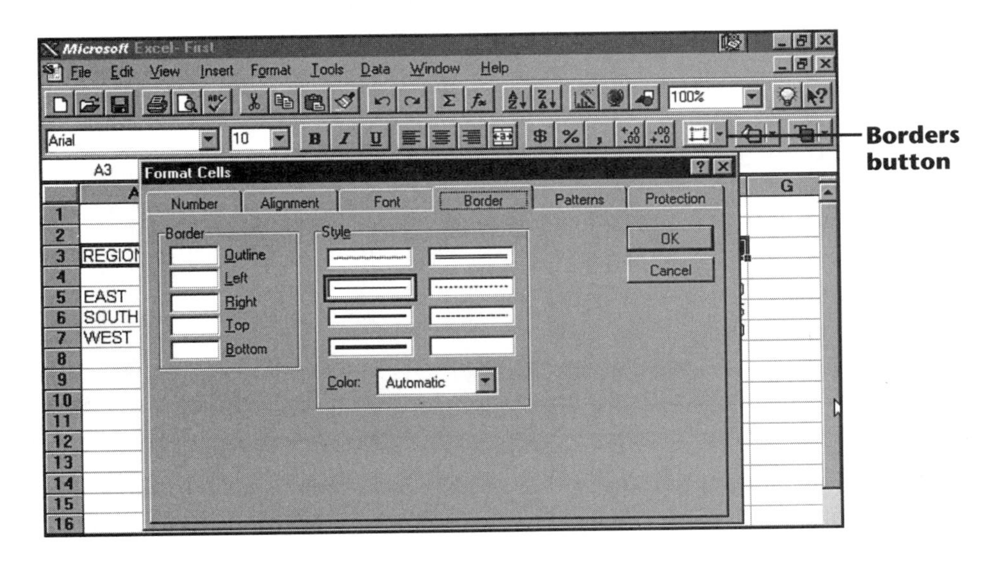

Figure 3.30
The Format Cells Border dialog box and the Borders button on the Formatting toolbar.

To apply a border to a cell or selected range, you choose the placement of the border by selecting **O**utline, **L**eft, **R**ight, **T**op, or **B**ottom in the Border box. The **O**utline option puts a border around the outer edges of the selection. The **L**eft, **R**ight, **T**op, and **B**ottom options put a border along the specified edge of each cell in the selection. From the Styl**e** area, you can select the type of border you want. To change the color of the border, you click the **C**olor drop-down list button to display the list of colors.

Applying Bottom Borders to a Cell Using the Format Cells Dialog Box

To complete the tutorials in this section, make sure that the First workbook is open. In this tutorial, you use the Format Cells tabbed dialog box to apply a bottom border to selected cells. Follow these steps:

1. Select the cells containing the column headings: cells A3:F3.
2. Choose the F**o**rmat, C**e**lls command, and click the Borders tab in the Format Cells dialog box (refer to figure 3.30).
3. In the Border section at the left of the dialog box, click **B**ottom.
4. In the Styl**e** section of the dialog box, click the thickest black line—the selection just above the word **C**olor. A thick black line appears to the left of the **B**ottom choice in the Border selection area.
5. Click OK.

   A thick black border appears below the entries in A3:F3.
6. Click cell A1 to deselect cells A3:F3 so that you can see the effect of the cell formatting you applied.

Your screen should now look like figure 3.31.

	A	B	C	D	E	F	G
1			ANNUAL SALES REPORT			10-Sep-96	
2			CASHMAN, INC.				
3	REGION	QTR1	QTR2	QTR3	QTR4	TOTAL	
4							
5	EAST	$75,000.00	$71,500.00	$76,000.00	$65,000.00	287,500	
6	SOUTH	$10,550.00	$9,345.00	$8,000.00	$7,500.00	35,395	
7	WEST	$95,400.00	$97,000.00	$91,550.00	$93,500.00	377,450	
8							
9	This is the first Excel worksheet I created.						

Figure 3.31 The cells A3:F3 are now formatted with a bottom border.

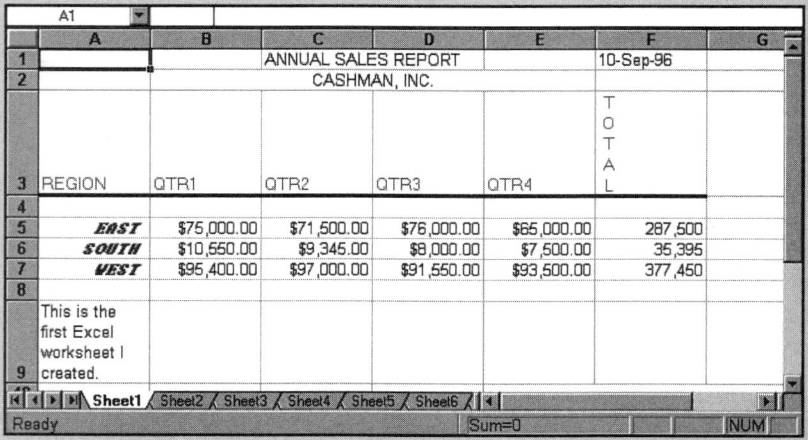

You can apply frequently used borders, such as an outline around a selected cell or range, using the Borders button on the Formatting toolbar. The Borders button always applies either Excel's default border (a bottom border) or the most recent border you selected from the palette of borders. As you click selections from the palette, the Borders button changes to show which kind of border it will apply.

Using the Borders Button

To use the Borders button to put a border around the range A5:A7, follow these steps:

1. Select cells A5:A7.
2. Click the Borders button drop-down arrow (refer to figure 3.30).

   A palette of borders appears (see figure 3.32).

Figure 3.32 The palette of borders that can be applied using the Borders button.

3. Click the square in the lower right corner of the palette—the square with thick borders on all four sides of the selection.
4. Click cell A1.

Notice that the range A5:A7 is now surrounded by a thick border. Notice also that the Borders button has changed; now you can simply click the button without having to select the thick borders.

Using the Format Cells Patterns Dialog Box

In addition to adding borders to cells, you can enhance a cell with patterns and colors. The Format Cells Patterns dialog box enables you to choose colors as well as a pattern from the **P**attern drop-down list (see figure 3.33).

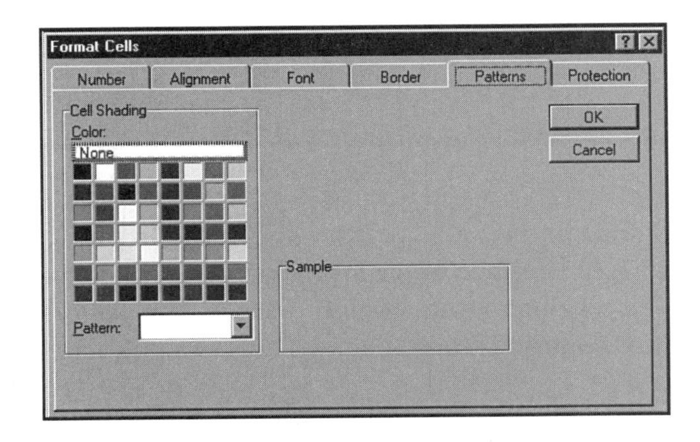

Figure 3.33 The Patterns dialog box.

In the Cell Shading section of the dialog box is a palette of colors; click the one you want to use in the selected cell(s). The Sample box in the lower middle of the dialog box shows you what the formatting looks like. If you click the drop-down arrow next to **P**attern in the Patterns dialog box, you can select from a palette of patterns in black and white or color.

Tip

If you don't like the formatting you have chosen after it has been applied, choose the **E**dit, **U**ndo Format Cells command before proceeding with another command. If you like the formatting and want to apply the same formatting to another area, select the new area, and choose **E**dit, **R**epeat Format Cells immediately after the formatting has been applied.

Using Color and Patterns in a Range of Cells

Close the copy of the First workbook that you have been using, but don't save the changes. Open the First workbook you have stored on disk. In this tutorial, you apply color to a range and a pattern to a second range. Follow these steps:

1. Select cells A3:F3.
2. Choose F**o**rmat, C**e**lls, and click the Patterns tab.
3. Click the light blue square in the top row of the color palette.
4. Click OK.
5. Click outside the selected cells to see the color.
6. Select cells D20:E23.
7. Choose F**o**rmat, C**e**lls, and click the Patterns tab.
8. Click the **P**attern drop-down arrow.
9. Click the square with the vertical black-and-white bars in the second row of the palette.
10. Click OK; then click outside the selection to see the result.

If you aren't sure which colors and formats work well together, Excel's AutoFormat feature eliminates much of the work for you. AutoFormat enables you to select from 16 predefined range formats. These formats are a combination of number formats, cell alignments, column widths, row heights, fonts, borders, and other formatting options. You can apply automatic formatting using the F**o**rmat menu.

Using the Format, AutoFormat Command

In this tutorial, you format a range in the First workbook using the Format, AutoFormat command. Follow these steps:

1. Select the range A1:F7. You most often will apply the formatting to your entire work area.
2. Open the Format menu, and choose the AutoFormat command. The AutoFormat dialog box appears (see figure 3.34).

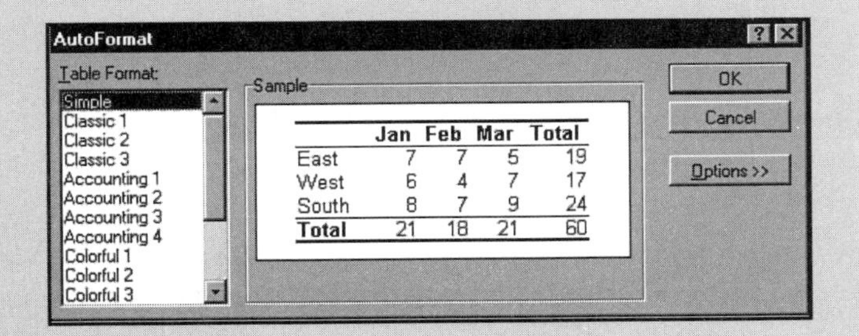

Figure 3.34
The selected format displayed in the Sample box of the AutoFormat dialog box.

3. Select Accounting 1 from the Table Format list box. In the Sample box, Excel displays the selected format.
4. Choose OK, or press Enter.
5. Click a cell outside the range to see the change.

If you don't like a change, choose Edit, Undo AutoFormat.

3

Objective 7: Check Spelling in the Worksheet

Spell Check
A feature enabling you to check for misspelled words, unusual capitalization, and repeated words.

The spelling function in Excel enables you to check for spelling errors and correct worksheets, macro sheets, and charts. Excel provides two ways for you to perform a spelling check: You can click the Spelling button on the Standard toolbar, or you can choose the **Spelling** command in the **Tools** menu. Excel displays misspelled words, repeated words in a single cell, and words that do not display a normal pattern of capitalization. You can spell check the entire worksheet, a chart, a single word, or a defined range. If you do not select a word or range of words, Excel checks the spelling for all text in the worksheet, including headers, footers, footnotes, annotations, and hidden text.

To use the spell checker, you follow these general steps:

1. Select cell A1 to begin spell checking from the beginning of the worksheet. Spell checking starts from the point of the active cell and moves forward to the end of the worksheet.

2. Open the **T**ools menu, and choose the **S**pelling command. Excel begins checking for misspelled words, repeated words, and unusual capitalization. The Spelling dialog box appears if a word is misspelled (see figure 3.35).

Figure 3.35
The Spelling dialog box.

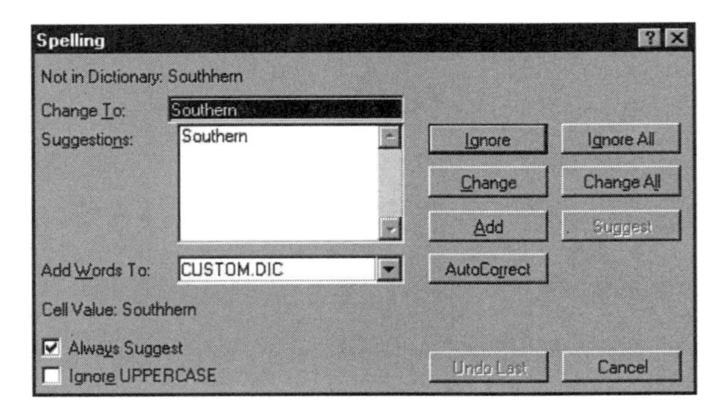

Each time a word appears in the dialog box, you can choose to ignore the word, ignore all identical words found throughout the worksheet, change the word, change all identical words found throughout the worksheet, or add the word to a dictionary.

3. To substitute the misspelled word with the word suggested in the Change **T**o text box, choose the **C**hange button. To change all examples of the same word found throughout the entire worksheet, choose the Change A**l**l button.

4. To use a different correction, select a word from the Suggestio**n**s list box, and choose the **C**hange or Change A**l**l button. If Excel cannot suggest an alternative word, the misspelled word appears in the Change **T**o text box. You can ignore the word by choosing the **I**gnore button, or you can type a new word in the Change **T**o text box and then choose the **C**hange button.

   To leave a word unchanged, choose the **I**gnore button. To leave the word unchanged throughout the entire worksheet, select I**g**nore All.

   To delete a repeated word, click the **D**elete button. Excel removes the repeated word and the unnecessary spaces between the remaining words.

   To add a word to the dictionary, click the **A**dd button.

   This choice adds the new word to the list of correctly spelled words in the spelling check dictionary.

   To clear the dialog box, choose OK, or press Esc.

Caution
Make sure that a word is spelled correctly before you add it to the dictionary.

5. If you did not begin the spell check with cell A1 as the active cell, a dialog box prompts you to continue spell checking from the beginning. Choose **Y**es to continue checking from the beginning of the worksheet to the point where the spell checking began.

If no misspellings are found, Excel displays a box informing you that the spelling check is completed.

Note: *If a misspelled word is entered in all uppercase letters, Excel does not identify it as misspelled. To be spell checked, a word must be all lowercase or have only the first letter (or first few letters) capitalized.*

Spell Checking Your Worksheet

In this tutorial, you use the spell checker on the First workbook. You begin by entering a misspelled word that the spell checker can find. Follow these steps:

1. To enter a misspelled word, make cell F3 the active cell, type **Totl**, and press Enter. Make C3 the active cell, type **Qtr 2**, and press Enter.
2. Select cell A1 to begin spell checking from the beginning of the worksheet.
3. Open the Tools menu, and choose the Spelling command.
4. When the spell checker questions the word `Qtr`, click the Ignore button.
5. When the spell checker finds `Totl` misspelled, scroll down the Suggestions list box until Total appears. Click Total to select it. `Total` appears in the Change To text box.
6. To replace the misspelled word with *Total*, click the Change button.
7. Close, without saving the file.

You can also spell check your worksheet using the Spelling button. First, select the cell where you want the spelling check to start. Next, click the Spelling button. The Spelling dialog box appears.

Chapter Summary

This chapter covers the commands and features that enable you to improve the appearance of your worksheets. You have learned about number formats, including date and time formats. You learned how to format using the AutoFormat feature, center text over columns, align text vertically and horizontally, change fonts, and apply justification. You also learned about the **S**tyle command on the F**o**rmat menu. Finally, you learned how to check for misspellings in your worksheet.

The next chapter introduces you to Excel's Function Wizard. This feature enables you to access a list of approximately 200 built-in functions. Chapter 4, "Using Functions," explains what a function is, lists the various types of functions, and tells you what some of the built-in functions do.

Checking Your Skills

True/False

For each of the following, circle *T* or *F* to indicate whether the statement is true or false.

T F **1.** If you want dollar signs or commas to appear in the numbers in your worksheet, you must type them as you enter each number into a cell.

T F **2.** More than three different number formats are available in Excel.

T F **3.** If you type 7-10-95 in a cell, Excel will subtract the three numbers.

T F **4.** A button on the Standard toolbar enables you to italicize text in a worksheet.

T F **5.** You can underline the contents of a cell using the Border command located in the Format Cells dialog box.

T F **6.** Formatting affects only the way a number is displayed or printed.

T F **7.** You can use the Excel spell checker to check charts and worksheets for misspellings.

T F **8.** The F**o**rmat, **C**enter command enables you to select long text entries and spread the text over a selected area.

T F **9.** You can use the F**o**rmat, C**e**lls command to control fonts, size, and styles.

T F **10.** The F**o**rmat, C**e**lls Borders tab can be used to underline the contents of cells.

Multiple Choice

In the blank provided, write the letter of the correct answer for each of the following.

_____ **1.** The spell checker is accessed from the _______ menu.

a. **H**elp

b. F**o**rmat

c. **T**ools

d. **O**ptions

_____ **2.** Which of the following refers to the range of cells from A5 to E5?

a. A5-E5

b. A5:E5

c. A5>E5

d. none of the above

_____ **3.** Which alignment is the Excel default for numbers in cells?

a. left

b. center

c. right

d. wrap

_____ **4.** Which term is used to refer to the size and shape of characters in the worksheet?

a. font

b. scale

c. fill

d. pixel

_____ **5.** Which alignment is the Excel default for text in cells?

a. left

b. center

c. right

d. wrap

_____ **6.** To _______ text within a cell causes a long string of text to appear on multiple lines within a cell.

a. align

b. justify

c. wrap

d. locate

_____ **7.** To center text from one cell horizontally over a selected range of columns, use the ___________ command.

a. Center Across Selection

b. Center

c. Align

d. All justification

_____ **8.** In the spell checker, which of the following buttons replaces a misspelled word in a worksheet?

a. Add

b. Change

c. Replace

d. Select

_____ 9. Which of the following formatting tools is found on the Formatting toolbar?

a. Bold

b. Center

c. Italic

d. all the above

_____ 10. Which of the following can be done to the contents of a cell using the Format, Cells command?

a. applying double underlining

b. using a color in a cell

c. placing an outline around a cell

d. all the above

Completion

In the blank provided, write the correct answer for each of the following.

1. To display text vertically, you first choose the ______________ command in the Format menu.
2. To move to another worksheet in a workbook, you click the ______________.
3. You can use the ______________ button on the Formatting toolbar to center text in a cell.
4. You can change the appearance of text, numbers, or cells in a worksheet using a(n) ______________ command.
5. ______________ alignment is the Excel default for numbers in a cell.
6. ______________ alignment is the Excel default for text in a cell.
7. The ______________ of a character refers to the character's size and shape.
8. You can underline the contents of a cell using one of the buttons on the ______________ toolbar.
9. The ______________ command enables you to format text so that it is vertical.
10. The Spell Checker is accessed from the ______________ menu.

Applying Your Skills

Review Exercises

Exercise 1: Using the Format AutoFormat Command

Open the Performance Report workbook, C2sp1, you built in Review Exercise 1 in Chapter 2. Use the AutoFormat command to apply the Classic 2 format to your worksheet. Print the worksheet.

Then use the AutoFormat command to apply the Colorful 2 format to your worksheet. Print the worksheet, then close without saving the workbook.

Exercise 2: Using the Format Tools and Format Border Command

1. Open the workbook C2sp2 that you created in Review Exercise 2 in Chapter 2. Use the Font Size button to increase the size of the font of the column headings.
2. Use the Bold button to make the headings boldface; then underline the column headings with a thick blue line.
3. Click the Font Size button twice to reduce the size of the column headings. Then center the headings over each column.
4. Use the Format, Cells command to format all the numbers with two decimal places.
5. Use the spell checker to check for misspellings in the worksheet. Are names always identified as possible misspellings? Print your worksheet.
6. Close without saving changes to the workbook.

Exercise 3: Exploring AutoFormats

Open the First workbook that you created in Chapter 1. In cells B8:E8, use AutoSum to sum the sales for each of the four quarters. Then use AutoFormat to see which of the available formats looks best on this worksheet. Print your results. Close without saving the workbook.

Exercise 4: Using the Borders Tool

Open the First workbook that you created in Chapter 1. Use the Borders button to place a double-line border under cells C1:E1. Then change the font color to red. Print the worksheet. Close without saving the workbook.

Exercise 5: Experimenting with Fonts and Styles

Open the First workbook that you created in Chapter 1. Select cells A3:F3. Try a variety of fonts, font styles, and font sizes. Print the result that you think looks best. Close without saving the workbook.

Continuing Projects

Project 1: Preparing a Worksheet for a Presentation

Open the NSCC Company Quarterly Report workbook, C2lp1, which you created in Continuing Project 1 at the end of Chapter 2. Do not use the AutoFormat feature in this project. Change the font and size of the text in the title. Try to center the title between the left and right edges of the worksheet.

Place borders around the column headings, and select a pattern to use inside the cells of the column headings. Change the format so that thick vertical lines are displayed between the cells in rows 4 through 17.

Format all numbers in the worksheet as currency with two decimal places. Display negative numbers in red. Place the date in cell A1. Save the workbook as **C3lp1**, and print the worksheet.

Project 2: Completing the International Investments Worksheet

Open the financial workbook, C2lp2, you created in Continuing Project 2 at the end of Chapter 2. Insert three rows at the top of the worksheet, and enter the title **CONSOLIDATED UNIVERSAL AMALGAMATED HOLDING COMPANY** in cell A1. Center this title across columns A through F.

Align the `(Mil.)` column headings vertically in their cells. Apply the Accounting 2 AutoFormat to the worksheet; then spell check the worksheet. Save the workbook as **C3lp2**, and print the worksheet.

Project 3: Creating a Worksheet and Formatting It

Enter the worksheet shown in figure 3.36, adjusting the column widths on your worksheet to approximate those shown. Center the contents of rows 1 and 2 of columns A through F. Use the appropriate date format in column B, and center the dates. Center the number of shares in C4 through C7.

	A	B	C	D	E	F	G
1		DATE	NUMBER OF	1994	1995		
2	COMPANY	PURCHASED	SHARES	VALUE	VALUE	INCREASE	
3							
4	PG&E	13-Feb-90	100	$200,000.00	$179,000.00	-10.50%	
5	RED INC.	20-Apr-90	350	$87,000.00	$87,500.00	0.57%	
6	ACME CORP.	3-Jan-91	500	$352,000.00	$400,000.00	13.64%	
7	G & H CO.	25-May-92	200	$70,000.00	$34,000.00	-51.43%	
8							
9							
10							
11							
12							
13							
14							
15							
16							

c3lp3

Ready Sum=0 NUM

Figure 3.36
The sample worksheet.

The formulas in column F subtract the 1994 value from the 1995 value and divide the difference by the 1994 value. (Don't forget about the mathematical order of precedence.) The numbers in column F should be formatted with the appropriate percent format and centered. Place a thick border around cells A1:F2. Print the worksheet. Save the worksheet as **C3lp3**.

CHAPTER 4

Using Functions

Excel provides nearly 200 built-in functions. A *function* is a predefined formula that performs calculations on the data in your worksheet. Knowledge of these functions empowers you as a worksheet user and helps you work more efficiently.

Using an Excel function in your worksheet is often much easier and more efficient than writing a formula yourself. With a function, you do not have to enter mathematical operators as you do in a formula. As you build a worksheet, you usually find that Excel has functions to save you time and effort. You can use a function by itself in a cell, as part of a formula, or in another function.

When you work with only a few cells, building a mathematical or financial formula by typing the formula and selecting cells may not seem difficult. If you need to total 50 cells, however, typing the correct formula to perform this calculation would take a great deal of time, and one typing error would make the formula incorrect. Using the SUM function makes accurately totaling a column or row of 50—or 500—cells easy.

This chapter explains what a function is, illustrates some types of functions, and demonstrates how to enter a function. The types of functions included in Excel range from functions that accomplish relatively simple tasks, such as SUM or AVERAGE functions or DATE and TIME functions, to functions that perform complex financial and statistical calculations. After completing a few of the tutorials in this chapter, you will become comfortable using functions and excited about the possibilities they offer for creating powerful worksheets.

Objectives

By the time you have finished this chapter, you will have learned to

1. Understand What a Function Is
2. View the List of Functions Available in Excel
3. Enter Functions into a Worksheet
4. Use the AutoSum Button
5. Use the Function Wizard
6. Recognize the Types of Functions

Objective 1: Understand What a Function Is

Function
A predefined formula consisting of a name and one or more arguments.

Argument
The number(s), cell(s), or named range(s) that a function uses in its calculations.

A *function* is a formula predefined by Excel and consisting of the equal sign (=), the function's name and, inside parentheses, the argument. The SUM function, for example, adds the numbers in selected cells. The selected cells make up the argument portion of the function. The *argument* of a function can be a single cell, a range of cells, a named range, or a number. Some functions require a single argument; others require multiple arguments. Multiple arguments are separated by commas. The formula bar in figure 4.1 displays a simple SUM function that adds a list of numbers.

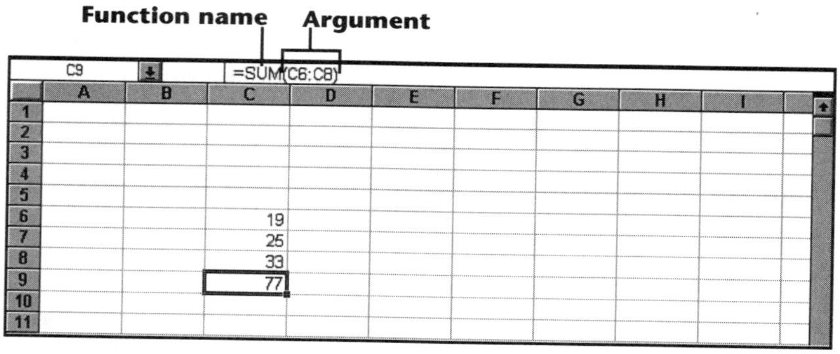

Function name **Argument**

C9 =SUM(C6:C8)

	A	B	C	D	E	F	G	H	I
1									
2									
3									
4									
5									
6			19						
7			25						
8			33						
9			77						
10									
11									

Figure 4.1
The SUM function in the formula bar.

The argument in the function is the range of cells C6 through C8. The result of this function is the sum of the values in cells C6 through C8. As with a formula, the result of a function appears in the cell that contains the function (cell C9), and the function appears in the formula bar when the cell is active. The function in figure 4.1 contains one argument. Other functions, however, may contain several arguments, and some functions have no arguments.

Objective 2: View the List of Functions Available in Excel

A complete list of all the functions in Excel and an explanation of how to use them is available through the **H**elp menu. This menu shows you commonly used functions and instructions on how to obtain help with using functions. Later in this chapter, the kinds of Excel functions are covered in more detail.

Viewing a List of the Available Excel Functions

Make sure that you have started Excel; then follow these steps:

1. From the **H**elp menu, choose Microsoft Excel **H**elp Topics.
2. Click the Index tab in the Help topics tabbed dialog box.
3. In the text box, type **functions**.
4. In the list box, double-click worksheet function index.

   The list of function categories appears (see figure 4.2).

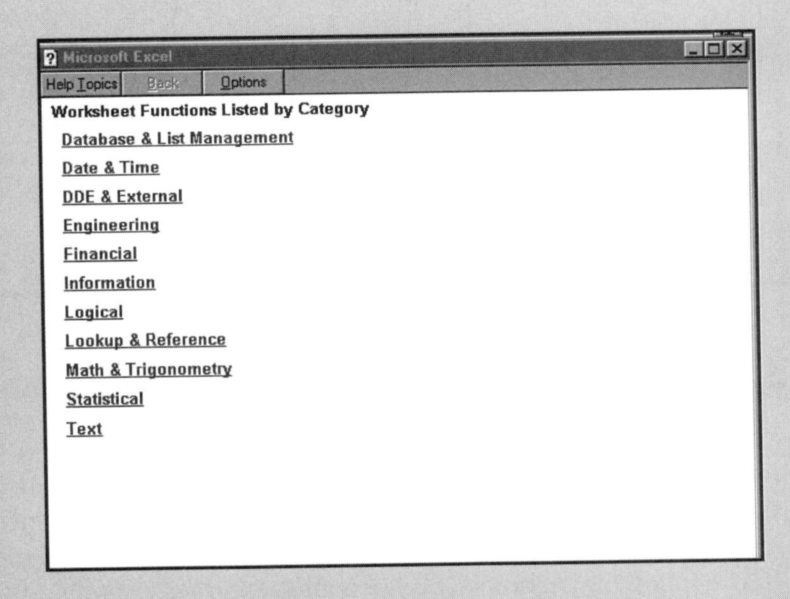

Figure 4.2 The list of function categories.

(continues)

Viewing a List of the Available Excel Functions (continued)

5. Click Date & Time.

   The alphabetical list of Date & Time functions appears (see figure 4.3).

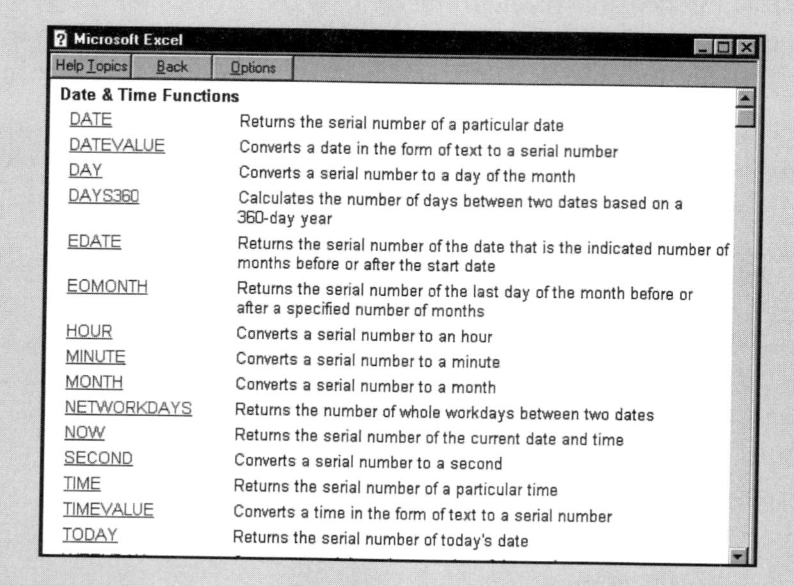

Figure 4.3
The alphabetical list of Date & Time functions.

6. Click the green DAYS360 function name to see a help screen on this function.

7. Exit from Help by clicking the Close button in the upper right corner of the worksheet window.

Objective 3: Enter Functions into a Worksheet

You can always enter a function into an active cell in one of two ways: type the function and argument(s), or use the Function Wizard. Because the SUM function is probably the most frequently used function, a third method (the AutoSum button) is often available when you want to enter the SUM function. In the following sections, you learn all these ways to enter a function.

Entering a Function by Typing

You can type both the function name and the argument(s). Remember that, as previously mentioned, the argument(s) of a function can refer to a range. If, for example, you are using the SUM function to add a group of numbers, you could select the range you want to sum. When a range is selected, the range address appears in parentheses in the formula bar. The cell address of the first cell in the range is followed by a colon and the cell address of the last cell in the range.

Using the SUM Function

In many of the tutorials in this chapter, you use the international investment analysis worksheet you completed in Continuing Project 2 at the end of Chapter 2; the workbook name is C2lp2. Open this workbook, and compare it with the worksheet in figure 4.4. If you used different rows and columns in your worksheet, move your work so that you can use the same rows and columns used in the following tutorials.

Figure 4.4
The C2lp2 workbook.

	A	B	C	D	E	F	G	H
1								PERCENT
2								RETURN
3					(Mil.)		(Mil.)	ON
4				(Mil.)	NET	(Mil.)	MARKET	INVESTED
5	COMPANY	INDUSTRY	COUNTRY	SALES	INCOME	ASSETS	VALUE	CAPITAL
6								
7	Solvey	Retail	Australia	11293	273	4262	3939	12.1
8	Kesko	Diversified	Brazil	6242	715	11684	9554	9.6
9	CNX	Automobile	Germany	12579	268	12059	2180	10.8
10	Dumez	Electronic	Italy	4283	66	2786	994	7.2
11	Nobunaga	Steel	Japan	11709	294	16036	8630	4.7
12	Nordlund	Optical	Norway	5476	291	5991	1438	9.7
13	Olnza	Machine	Spain	7602	1174	14114	14640	13.9
14	Lucus & Smith	Aerospace	U. K.	8272	160	8964	5415	7.3
15								

To use the SUM function to add the entries in cells D7:D14, follow these steps:

1. Activate cell D16.
2. Type **=SUM(D7:D14)** (in either upper- or lowercase letters with no spaces in the formula), and press Enter.

   The total sales figure is now displayed in cell D16.
3. Click cell D16. The SUM function is displayed in the formula bar.

The AVERAGE function is another commonly used function. In the next tutorial, you learn how to use the AVERAGE function.

Using the AVERAGE Function

To find the average (the mean) of the sales for the companies, follow these steps:

1. Make cell D17 the active cell.
2. Type **=AVERAGE(D7:D14)**, and press Enter.

The average sales appear in cell D17.

You can also indicate to Excel the range of cells used as the argument by clicking and dragging over the cells. As a shortcut, you do not have to type the final parenthesis.

4

Entering a Function Argument by Clicking and Dragging

To enter a function by clicking and dragging, follow these steps:

1. Activate cell E17.
2. Type **=AVERAGE(**.
3. Place your mouse pointer on cell E7. Press and hold down the left mouse button, and drag the mouse pointer to cell E14. Release the mouse button.

   Notice that the range is selected and is now the argument of the function displayed in the formula bar and in cell E17.
4. Press ↵Enter to complete the function.

The average Net Income appears in cell E17.

If you have problems... When you enter a function, one of the most common errors is leaving out a comma between arguments. Another common mistake is inserting spaces into the function. Do not put spaces anywhere in the function.

If you need to edit a function, select the function in the worksheet, then activate the formula bar by pressing F2 or clicking the formula bar. Use normal editing procedures to make insertions or deletions. In some cases, if you have an error in your function, a message dialog box appears. The message prompts you to correct the error. Choose OK or press ↵Enter to clear the error message dialog box. The part of the function causing the error is selected in the formula bar. You can then determine what the error is. Check for such mistakes as missing commas, too many commas, or blank spaces in the selected area.

Using Named Ranges in Functions

Using a named range as the argument of a function is especially efficient. This practice also makes a calculation easier to understand if a coworker uses your worksheet or if you are modifying a worksheet that you created months ago. Which of the three following examples is easier to understand?

=F7+F8+F9+F10+F11+F12+F13+F14

=SUM(F7:F14)

=SUM(ASSETS)

Using a Named Range in a Function

In Chapter 2, you learned how to name a range and created a range named TOTALS. When you saved the First workbook before continuing with the tutorials in Chapter 2, the range name information was saved with the worksheet. Once you have named a range in a worksheet, when you save your workbook, you also save the range name. In the following tutorials, you first name a range and then use that range in a SUM function and an AVERAGE function.

Naming a Range to Use in a Function

To name the range of cells from F7 to F14 in C2LP2, follow these steps:

1. Using the mouse or the keyboard, select the range of cells F7 to F14.
2. From the **I**nsert menu, choose **N**ame, and then choose **D**efine.

   The Define Name dialog box opens (see figure 4.5). Excel sometimes suggests a name it "thinks" is appropriate.

Figure 4.5 The Define Name dialog box.

3. Type **ASSETS** in the Names in **W**orkbook text box.
4. Choose OK to leave the dialog box.

Now that you have assigned a name to the range, you can use the named range as the argument in a function. You do this in the next tutorial.

Using the Named Range in a SUM and an AVERAGE Function

After you have given the name ASSETS to the range F7:F14, to find the sum and average of the assets for the companies, follow these steps:

1. Activate cell F20.
2. Type **=SUM(ASSETS)**, and press Enter.

   The total assets appear in cell F20.

3. Activate cell F21.
4. Type **=AVERAGE(ASSETS)**, and press Enter.

The average assets appear in cell F21.

The Standard toolbar and the Formula bar contain many parts that relate to functions and named ranges (see figure 4.6 and table 4.1).

4

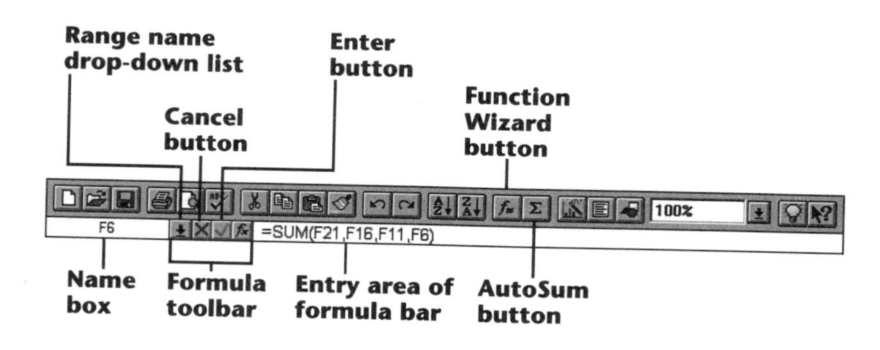

Figure 4.6 Standard toolbar and formula bar buttons that relate to functions.

Table 4.1 Standard Toolbar and Formula Bar Elements for Creating Functions

Name	Description
Standard Toolbar	
AutoSum	Enables you to total a range, and places the SUM function in a cell or cells.
Function Wizard	Guides you through the process of creating any function.
Formula Bar	
Name box	Shows cell reference or name of active cell.
Range Name drop-down list	Displays a list of named cells or ranges.
Cancel box	Click to cancel the function.
Enter box	Click to enter the function into the cell.
Function Wizard	Works like the Function Wizard on the Standard toolbar.
Entry area	Displays formula function as you create or edit it.

Objective 4: Use the AutoSum Button

AutoSum button A button on the Standard toolbar, an efficient way to total rows or columns in your worksheet.

Although you can write a formula or SUM function to total a column or a row of your worksheet, clicking the *AutoSum button* is usually more efficient. AutoSum attempts to generate the SUM function based on the data you have entered into your worksheet. You can use the AutoSum button efficiently only when the cell containing the total is at the bottom of a column of numbers or at the end of a row of numbers. Using AutoSum is almost always faster than writing a formula.

Using the AutoSum Button

In this tutorial, you use the AutoSum button to total a column of numbers. First, clear all functions from cells D15:H22 so that you can easily see what is happening in your worksheet. Then follow these steps:

1. Activate cell D15.

2. Click the AutoSum button, located in the middle of the Standard toolbar—it has the Greek letter sigma on it (refer to figure 4.6).

   `=SUM(D7:D14)` appears in the formula bar (see figure 4.7).

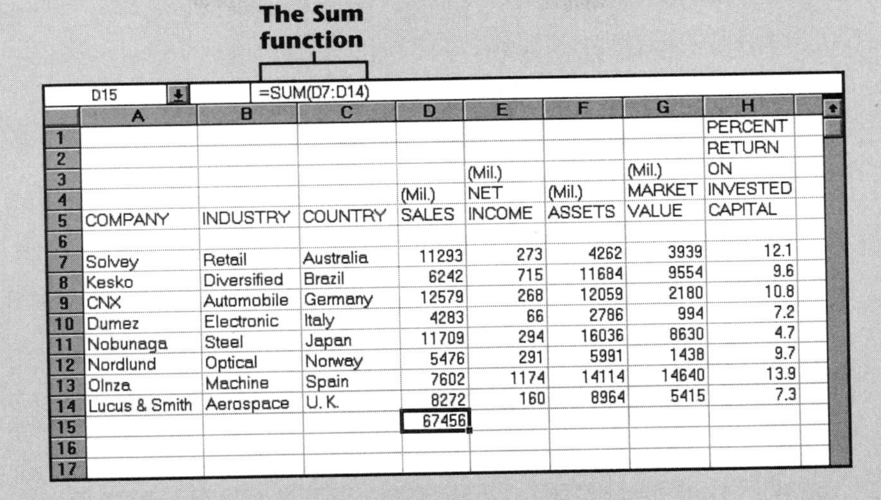

D15 =SUM(D7:D14)

	A	B	C	D	E	F	G	H
1								PERCENT
2								RETURN
3					(Mil.)		(Mil.)	ON
4				(Mil.)	NET	(Mil.)	MARKET	INVESTED
5	COMPANY	INDUSTRY	COUNTRY	SALES	INCOME	ASSETS	VALUE	CAPITAL
6								
7	Solvey	Retail	Australia	11293	273	4262	3939	12.1
8	Kesko	Diversified	Brazil	6242	715	11684	9554	9.6
9	CNX	Automobile	Germany	12579	268	12059	2180	10.8
10	Dumez	Electronic	Italy	4283	66	2786	994	7.2
11	Nobunaga	Steel	Japan	11709	294	16036	8630	4.7
12	Nordlund	Optical	Norway	5476	291	5991	1438	9.7
13	Olnza	Machine	Spain	7602	1174	14114	14640	13.9
14	Lucus & Smith	Aerospace	U. K.	8272	160	8964	5415	7.3
15				67456				
16								
17								

Figure 4.7 AutoSum produces this function.

3. Press Enter to indicate that you want this calculation entered into cell D15.

The total of the numbers should appear in cell D15.

If your worksheet has a blank row at the foot of each column and you select a range of columns and then click the AutoSum button, a SUM function for each column is placed in the empty cell at the foot of each column.

Using the AutoSum Button on a Range of Columns

To automatically enter SUM functions for the values in columns E, F, G, and H, follow these steps:

1. Select the range E7:H14.
2. Click the AutoSum button.
3. Verify that Excel has placed the appropriate SUM functions in cells E15, F15, G15, and H15.
4. Delete the SUM functions in cells E15, F15, G15, and H15 to prepare for the next tutorial.

You can also use the AutoSum button to sum one or more rows. You need a blank column at the end of the rows, and you need to include the blank column in the selection. In the next tutorial, you use the AutoSum button to enter sum formulas for the rows and the columns at the same time.

Using the AutoSum Button to Sum Rows and Columns

To automatically create SUM functions for the rows and columns of a selection, follow these steps:

1. Select the range of cells E7:I15.

   Be sure to include the blank row 15 and the blank column I in the selection.

2. Click the AutoSum button.

Your screen should look like figure 4.8. Note that the correct SUM functions for both the columns and the rows have been entered in the correct positions. AutoSum gives you one way to "work smarter—not harder" in Excel.

Figure 4.8
The worksheet with the functions to sum the rows and columns.

	D	E	F	G	H	I	J	K	L
1					PERCENT				
2					RETURN				
3		(Mil.)		(Mil.)	ON				
4	(Mil.)	NET	(Mil.)	MARKET	INVESTED				
5	SALES	INCOME	ASSETS	VALUE	CAPITAL				
6									
7	11293	273	4262	3939	12.1	8486.1			
8	6242	715	11684	9554	9.6	21962.6			
9	12579	268	12059	2180	10.8	14517.8			
10	4283	66	2786	994	7.2	3853.2			
11	11709	294	16036	8630	4.7	24964.7			
12	5476	291	5991	1438	9.7	7729.7			
13	7602	1174	14114	14640	13.9	29941.9			
14	8272	160	8964	5415	7.3	14546.3			
15	67456	3241	75896	46790	75.3	126002.3			
16									
17									

Objective 5: Use the Function Wizard

Function Wizard
A sequence of dialog boxes that aid in the entry of functions in your worksheet.

So far in this chapter, you have entered functions by typing them or using the AutoSum button for the SUM function. Now you learn how to enter functions using the *Function Wizard*. The Function Wizard is a series of dialog boxes that help you build your function. This button is probably the fastest and most accurate way of entering functions—especially the functions with multiple arguments or function names that are hard to remember.

You can access the Function Wizard by choosing the **F**unction command from the **I**nsert menu or by clicking the Function Wizard button. This button is found on the formula bar (when it is active) and next to the AutoSum button on the Standard toolbar (refer to figure 4.6). The Function Wizard is designed to help you quickly find and select the appropriate function from the list of functions in Excel. Another role of the Function Wizard is to guide you through the steps of entering a function and to supply the correct arguments for the function.

The Function Wizard has two dialog boxes: Step 1 of 2 and Step 2 of 2. In the Step 1 dialog box, the left-hand list, the Function **C**ategory list, lists the function categories, discussed later in this chapter (see figure 4.9). The Function **C**ategory list also includes the categories Most Recently Used and All.

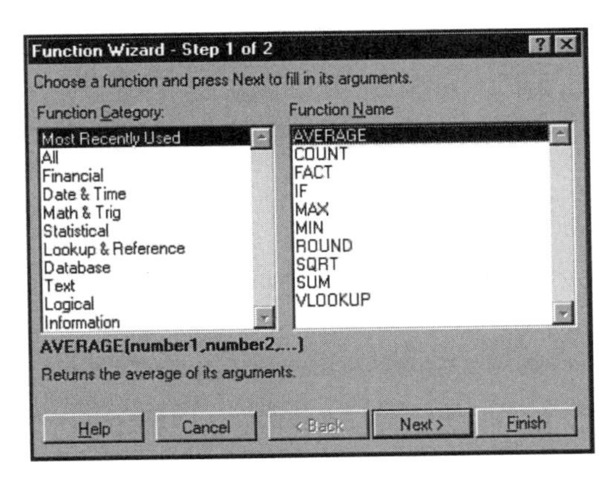

Figure 4.9
The Function Wizard Step 1 of 2 dialog box.

The Most Recently Used category is the collection of your recently used functions. The All category provides an alphabetical list of all the functions available in Excel.

When you click a function name, the area near the bottom of the dialog box displays a short description of what the function does and a list of its arguments. Below the description is a row of five buttons. These buttons appear in both the Function Wizard dialog boxes and are used for the following purposes:

- **H**elp provides help on using the Function Wizard.
- Cancel closes the Function Wizard dialog box without entering anything into the formula bar or selected cell and returns you to the worksheet.
- <**B**ack moves from the second Function Wizard dialog box to the first dialog box; unavailable in the Step 1 dialog box.
- Next> moves to the second screen of the Function Wizard after you have selected the name of the function you want inserted into the formula bar or selected cell.
- **F**inish inserts the function into the formula bar. If no arguments are entered, Excel inserts the argument names as placeholders in the formula.

The contents of the Step 2 dialog box change according to the function you select in the Step 1 dialog box. Figure 4.10 shows the Step 2 dialog box as it appears when you select the PMT function in the Step 1 dialog box.

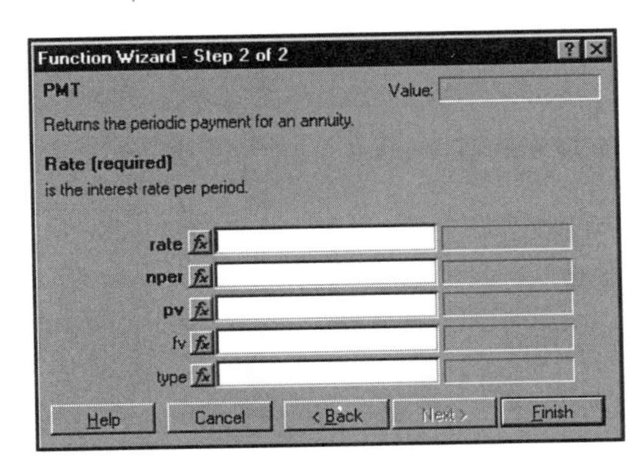

Figure 4.10
The Function Wizard Step 2 of 2 dialog box.

For functions with multiple argument values, the argument values you must enter (required arguments) are in boldface type in the dialog box. The optional argument values are in normal type. In figure 4.10, `rate` (periodic interest rate), `nper` (term), and `pv` (present value) are the argument values you must supply; *`fv`* (future value) and *`type`* are optional argument values.

Caution
Make sure that the selected cell does not currently contain a function. Otherwise, you will get the Edit Function dialog box.

If you click in the text box to the right of an argument, Excel explains the argument in the dialog box. This function is covered in a tutorial later in this chapter. After you have entered values for each of the required argument values, the calculated result for the function appears in the value box at the top of the Step 2 dialog box.

Note: *In this book, required arguments are printed in a special font:* `number1`. *Optional arguments are printed in an italic special font:* *`number1`*.

Building a SUM Function Using the Function Wizard

In this tutorial, you use the Function Wizard to enter the SUM function, with which you are already familiar, into cell D20. You cannot use the AutoSum button in this situation because it attempts to include in the sum any numbers in cells D15 through D19, and these cells may not contain sales figures.

To enter a SUM function using the Function Wizard, follow these steps:

1. Click cell D20 to activate it.
2. Click the Function Wizard button.

   The Step 1 dialog box appears (refer to figure 4.9).
3. The SUM function is in the Math and Trig category; click Math and Trig in the Function **C**ategory list.
4. In the Function **N**ame list, scroll down the list until SUM appears.
5. Click SUM in the Function **N**ame list.

   Your screen should now look like figure 4.11.

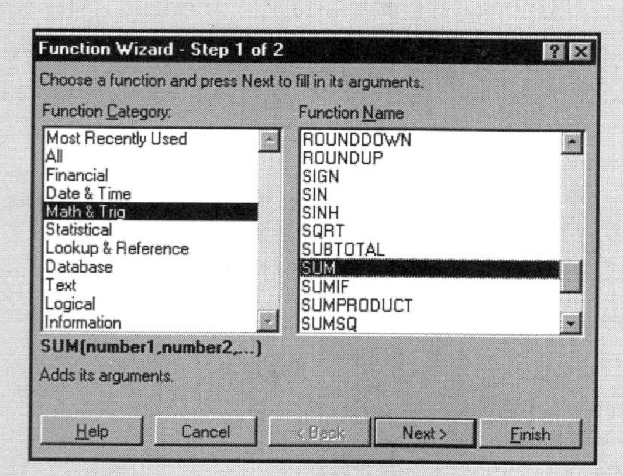

Figure 4.11
The Step 1 dialog box with the SUM function selected.

6. Click the Next> button.

   The Step 2 dialog box appears (see figure 4.12).

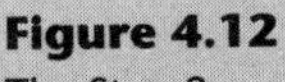

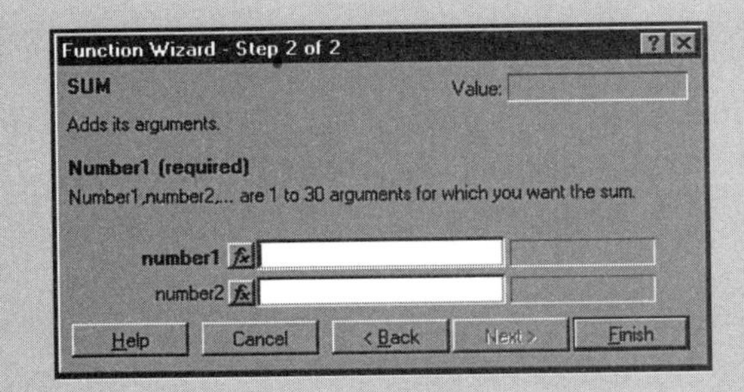

Figure 4.12 The Step 2 dialog box with the SUM function selected.

7. In the argument edit box to the right of number1, type **D7:D14**.

   You must enter values or cell references for each required argument before the function will work properly. Note that 67456, the sum of the values currently in that range, appears in the Value box (in the upper right corner of the dialog box).

8. Click the **F**inish button to enter the SUM function into cell D20.

4

Now that you see how the Function Wizard works, in the next section you use it to enter some new functions.

Objective 6: Recognize the Types of Functions

This section gives a brief description of some of the most commonly used worksheet functions and lists the arguments for each function.

Table 4.2 lists the types of arguments and their descriptions.

Table 4.2 Function Argument Types

Argument Type	Description
Value	A number or cell reference containing a value.
Logical	Result is TRUE or FALSE.
Number	A number or numeric formula.
Text	Nonnumeric data; text must be enclosed in quotation marks.
Array	A range of values treated as a single group.
Serial number	A date and time.
Reference	A cell or range address.

Excel has nearly 200 built-in functions. Most of these functions are grouped (for easy access) into one of the following categories:

Database & List Management

Date & Time

DDE & External

- Engineering
- Financial
- Information
- Logical
- Lookup & Reference
- Math & Trigonometry
- Statistical
- Text

A complete listing of all the functions, and a short explanation of each function, is available under the Worksheet Functions topic in Excel's Help. If you need more information on the function, click the function's name in the list. You are then given an explanation of the function and examples of its use.

Understanding Database Functions

The database functions are a group of functions that refer to areas of a worksheet that are organized as a database. Most of the functions provide summary statistics such as averages, counts, sums, and standard deviations on Excel databases. In Chapter 7 of this book, you learn about Excel databases.

Understanding Date and Time Functions

Serial number
A date expressed as a number. Days are numbered from the beginning of the twentieth century.

Caution
In order for the NOW function to show the correct date and time, your computer must have the time and date set properly.

To keep track of the date and time, Excel counts the number of days that have passed since the beginning of the twentieth century. Excel uses a date serial number that starts with January 1, 1900, as day 1. All days from this date forward are numbered sequentially. For example, 1/25/1900 is the date serial number 25, and so on. If you use a date function to find the serial number for July 4, 1991, the serial number returned is 33423 (the number of days that have passed since January 1, 1900). Excel includes date functions for converting the day, month, year, and time to serial numbers and functions to convert a serial number to the actual date or time.

The date and time cell formats discussed in Chapter 3 are designed to be used with the date and time functions so that you can decide the appearance of dates and times in your worksheet. When a date function is used in a cell, the cell's format is automatically changed from General, the default, to a date format. To see the actual serial number of a date, you use the DATE function in a cell and then change the format of the cell back to General.

The functions TODAY and NOW enable you to use the current date or the current date and time, respectively. The NOW function is useful for documents that must always include the current date and time. Some of the date and time functions are listed in table 4.3.

Table 4.3 Some Commonly Used Date and Time Functions

Function	Description
DATE(year,month,day)	Returns specified date.
DATEVALUE(date_text)	Returns date text as a serial number.
DAY(serial_number)	Returns day, as an integer from 1 to 31, corresponding to serial number.
DAYS360(start_date,end_date)	Returns number of days between two dates.
HOUR(serial_number)	Returns hour, as an integer from 0 to 23, corresponding to serial number.
NETWORKDAYS (start_date,end_date,holidays)	Returns the number of whole working days between start_date and end_date; working days exclude weekends and any dates identified in holidays.
NOW( )	Returns serial number of current date and time.
TIME(hour,minute,second)	Returns serial number of time specified by hour, minute, and second.
TODAY( )	Returns serial number of current date.
YEAR(serial_number)	Returns year corresponding to serial number.

Note: *For a complete listing of Excel functions, see Help.*

Entering a Date Function into a Cell

Close the international investments analysis worksheet without saving the changes. Start a new workbook to use for the next four tutorials.

To enter a date function into a cell, follow these steps:

1. Activate cell A1.
2. Click the Function Wizard. The Step 1 of 2 dialog box appears.
3. In the Function Category list, click Date & Time.
4. In the Function Name list, click NOW.
5. Click the Next> button. You see the Step 2 of 2 dialog box (see figure 4.13). The NOW function has no arguments.

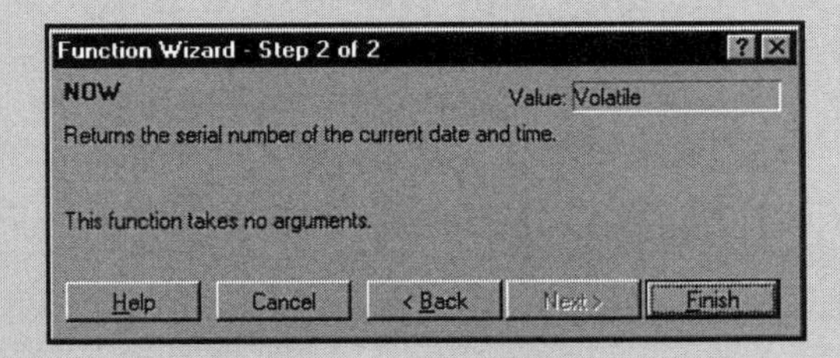

Figure 4.13 Step 2 of 2 dialog box for the NOW function.

(continues)

Entering a Date Function into a Cell (continued)

6. Click the Finish button.

   Cell A1 is not wide enough to display the date and time so a series of # are displayed in the cell.

7. Widen column A to a width of 15. The date and time are displayed.

8. Change the format of cell A1 to Number. The number you see is the serial number of the date and time.

9. Change the format of cell A1 back to the date and time format. You should see the date and time as it is displayed in figure 4.14.

Figure 4.14
The date and time displayed in a worksheet.

A1	=NOW()	
A	B	C
11/27/95 10:05		

Keep this workbook open for the next tutorial.

Understanding Financial Functions

Annuity calculations
Calculations based on a series of equal payments over a specified time.

Excel has built-in financial functions to calculate payments on a loan, depreciation, present and future values, internal rate of returns, net present value, and other *annuity calculations*. An annuity function performs a calculation based on a series of even payments over a specified time. You don't have to understand higher finance to use these functions—you just "fill in the blanks." The factors involved in solving most annuity problems are PV (present value) or FV (future value), NPER (number of periods), PMT (payment each period), and RATE (periodic interest rate). These factors are all available as functions in Excel.

The arguments for the PMT function are `nper`, `rate`, `pv`, *`fv`*, and *`type`*; *`type`* and *`fv`* (future value) are optional arguments. The number of periods in the argument is 360, which is the total number of months for the loan. The periodic interest rate is the annual interest rate divided by 12; the interest rate must be in months because the payments are in months. The present value is the amount of the loan. Because this payment is an outflow of cash, the result always appears in the cell as a negative number.

Table 4.4 summarizes some of Excel's financial functions.

Table 4.4 Some Commonly Used Financial Functions

Function	Description
ACCRINT(issue,first_interest, settlement,coupon, par, frequency, basis)	Accrued interest for a security that pays periodic interest.

Function	Description
ACCRINTM(issue,settlement,rate,par,basis)	Accrued interest for a security that pays interest at maturity.
CUMPRINC(rate,nper,pv,start_period,end_period,type)	Cumulative principal paid on a loan between start_period and end_period.
DISC(settlement,maturity,pr,redemption,basis)	Discount rate for a security.
EFFECT(nominal_rate,nper)	Effective annual interest rate.
FV(rate,nper,pmt,pv,type)	Future value of an investment.
FVSCHEDULE(principal,schedule)	Future value of an initial principal after applying a series of compound interest rates.
IRR(values,guess)	Internal rate of return for list of values.
NPV(rate,value1,value2,...)	Net present value for list of values.
PV(rate,nper,pmt,fv,type)	Present value of an investment.
SLN(cost,salvage,life)	Straight-line method of depreciation.

Entering a Financial Function into a Cell

In this tutorial, you use the PMT function in a new worksheet. Assume that you borrow $15,000 at 9 percent for 3 years to buy a new car. What will your monthly payments be? Move to a new worksheet in your workbook. Then follow these steps:

1. Make sure that the width of column A is 15. Activate cell A3.
2. Click the Function Wizard. The Step 1 of 2 dialog box appears (refer to figure 4.9).
3. In the Function Category list, click Financial.
4. In the Function Name list, click PMT.
5. Click the Next> button. The Step 2 of 2 dialog box appears (refer to figure 4.10).
6. In the rate argument edit box, type **0.09/12** (to convert annual to monthly interest rate), and press Tab to move to the next argument edit box. Do not press Enter.
7. In the nper argument edit box, type **36** (the number of payment periods), and press Tab to move to the next argument edit box.
8. In the pv argument edit box, type **15000** (the amount of the car loan).

   Your Function Wizard Step 2 of 2 dialog box should look like figure 4.15.

(continues)

Entering a Financial Function into a Cell

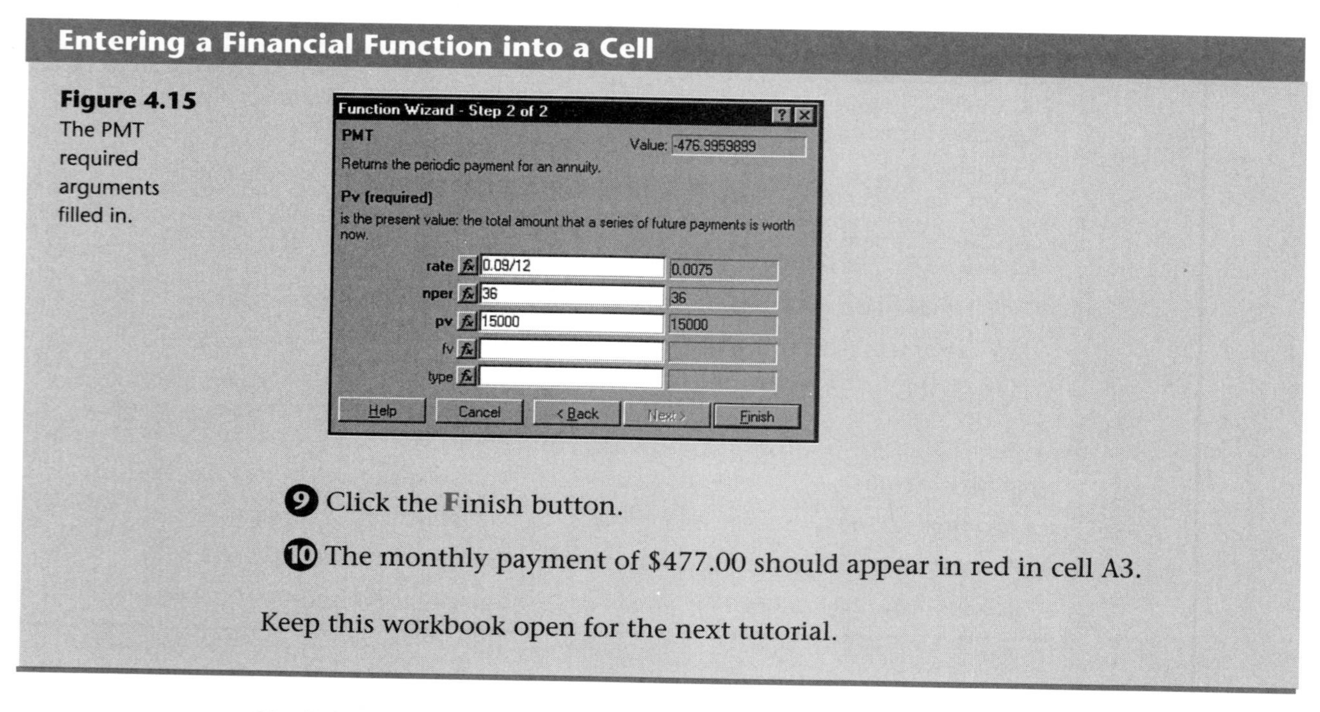

Figure 4.15
The PMT required arguments filled in.

9. Click the Finish button.
10. The monthly payment of $477.00 should appear in red in cell A3.

Keep this workbook open for the next tutorial.

Understanding Information Functions

You can use Excel's information functions to analyze cells, columns, rows, ranges, and areas. These parts of a worksheet may need to be analyzed before you perform a calculation, function, or macro.

The IS functions enable you to test the type of entry in a cell or range; the functions return a logical value of TRUE or FALSE. If a cell meets the condition of the function, the value of the cell is TRUE. If the cell does not meet the function condition, the value is FALSE. For example, if you want to determine whether a cell is blank, you can use the ISBLANK function. If the cell is blank, the value is TRUE; otherwise, the value of the cell is FALSE. The IS functions are generally used with IF functions to establish the contents of a cell or range. In figure 4.16, the two functions are combined to establish whether cell D10 contains text. The IF and ISTEXT functions are entered as a combined function in cell A1.

A1 =IF(ISTEXT(D10),"Cell D10 contains text","Cell D10 does not contain text")

	A	B	C	D	E	F	G	H
1	Cell D10 contains text							
2								
3	($477.00)							
4								
5								
6								
7								
8								
9								
10				hello				
11								

Figure 4.16
The IF and ISTEXT functions used together in cell A1.

The IF function includes arguments to define `value_if_true` and `value_if_false`. The `value_if_true` argument is defined as the message `Cell D10 contains text.` The `value_if_false` argument is defined as the message `Cell D10 does not contain text.` If the result of the function in cell A1 is true, cell A1 displays the message `Cell D10 contains text`. If the result of the function in cell A1 is false, cell A1 displays the message `Cell D10 does not contain text`. You must enter text arguments in quotation marks.

Understanding Logical Functions

Excel's logical functions are used frequently for testing conditions and making decisions. The IF function enables you to set conditions. You can combine the IF function with other logical functions, such as AND and OR, to test for multiple conditions. Logical functions are listed and described in table 4.5.

Table 4.5 Logical Functions

Function	Description
AND(`logical1`,*`logical2`*,...)	Returns TRUE if every argument is TRUE.
IF(`logical_test`,`value_if_true`, *`value_if_false`*)	Returns value_if_true if test is TRUE; returns value_if_false if logical value is FALSE.
NOT(*`logical`*)	Reverses TRUE and FALSE logicals.
OR(*`logical1`*,*`logical2`*,...)	Returns true if any argument is TRUE.

Using the IF Function

To use the IF function to see whether the numbers in two cells are equal, move to an empty worksheet, and follow these steps:

1. Enter **5** in cell A1, and **10** in cell B1.
2. In cell D1, enter the IF function **=IF(A1=B1,"THE NUMBERS ARE EQUAL", "THE NUMBERS ARE NOT EQUAL")**.

   This function displays the message `THE NUMBERS ARE EQUAL` in cell D1 if the numbers are equal. If the numbers are not equal, the function displays the other message (`THE NUMBERS ARE NOT EQUAL`) in cell D1.
3. Enter the number **5** in cell B1, and note the result.
4. Edit the IF function in cell D1 so that the function is now =IF(A1=B1,A1-B1,A1*B1).
5. Enter the number **6** in cell A1, and note the result.

Keep this workbook open for the next tutorial.

Understanding Lookup and Reference Functions

Array
A rectangular range of values or formulas treated as one group.

Lookup functions are used to retrieve a value or cell reference from a table or an *array* in your worksheet. Examples of lookup functions include LOOKUP, MATCH, and various INDEX functions. Table 4.6 lists some of the lookup functions.

Table 4.6 Lookup and Reference Functions

Function	Description
HLOOKUP(lookup_value,table_array, row_index_num)	Looks across the top row of range until value is met.
LOOKUP(lookup_value,array)	Value in array selected by lookup value.
VLOOKUP(lookup_value,table_array, col_index_num)	Looks down the first column of range until value is found.

Understanding Math and Trig Functions

Excel's built-in mathematical functions enable you to perform standard arithmetic operations. Other mathematical functions enable you to round and truncate numbers. These types of mathematical functions are the basis for using mathematical functions in building a worksheet.

Excel also includes several trigonometric functions, used primarily to build complex scientific and engineering formulas, and matrix functions, used primarily for solving complex problems that involve several unknown variables in an array, a rectangular range of values or formulas treated as a single group.

You can use three mathematical functions to round a number to certain specifications. The INT function rounds a number to the nearest integer. The TRUNC function shortens a number to its next lower integer, and the ROUND function rounds a number up or down. Some of the commonly used built-in mathematical functions are listed in table 4.7.

Table 4.7 Some Commonly Used Math and Trig Functions

Function	Description
ABS(number)	Absolute value of number.
INT(number)	Number rounded down to the nearest integer.
RAND( )	Random number between 0 and 1.
ROUND(number,num_digits)	Rounds number to specified number of digits.
SQRT(number)	Square root of number.
SUM(number1,*number2,...*)	Total of arguments.
TRUNC(number,num_digits)	Changes number to an integer by truncating the decimal portion.

Entering a Math and Trig Function in a Cell

In this tutorial, you determine the square root of a number. Move to an empty worksheet in your workbook, and then follow these steps:

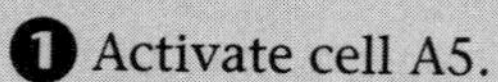

1. Activate cell A5.

(continues)

Entering a Math and Trig Function in a Cell (continued)

2. Click the Function Wizard. You see the Step 1 of the Function Wizard dialog box.
3. In the Function Category list, click Math and Trig.
4. Scroll down to SQRT in the Function Name list, and then click SQRT.
5. Click the Next> button to display the Step 2 of the Function Wizard dialog box.
6. Type the number **68** as the argument of the function.
7. Click the Finish button, or press Enter.

The square root of 68 appears in cell A5.

Close the workbook that you have used in the previous tutorials, and do not save the workbook on your disk.

4

Understanding Statistical Functions

Excel includes a comprehensive set of statistical functions. These functions enable you to find the average, minimum, maximum, standard deviation, or variance of a group of values in your worksheet. Many commonly used statistical tests, such as the T-test, Chi-Squared, and F-test, are available as functions. Other statistical functions include the TREND, LINEST, LOGEST, and GROWTH functions. You can use these functions to calculate lines and curves that fit data. Table 4.8 lists some of the most commonly used statistical functions built into Excel.

Table 4.8 Statistical Functions

Function	Description
AVERAGE(number1,*number2*,...)	Returns average of defined range.
COUNT(value1,*value2*,...)	Returns total of nonblank cells in range.
MAX(number1,*number2*,...)	Returns largest number in defined range.
MEDIAN(number1,*number2*,...)	Returns middle value in defined range.
MIN(number1,*number2*,...)	Returns smallest number in defined range.
MODE(number1,*number2*,...)	Returns the most frequently occurring value in a range of data.
STDEV(number1,*number2*,...)	Returns standard deviation for a sample.
VAR(number1,*number2*,...)	Returns variance for a sample.

Entering a Statistical Function into a Cell

In this tutorial, you enter a statistical function into the international investments worksheet that you were using earlier in this chapter. Close the worksheet you used in the three previous tutorials, and open the C2lp2 workbook. Then follow these steps:

1. Activate cell H18.
2. Type **=MAX(H7:H14)**, and press ↵Enter. This function finds the largest value in the range.

Keep this workbook open for the next tutorial.

In a small worksheet, the usefulness of functions like MAX and MIN may not be obvious. In a worksheet with hundreds or thousands of entries, these functions are essential.

Understanding Text Functions

Excel includes a number of built-in text functions that help you find or edit text in a cell or range. Several of these functions are listed in table 4.9.

Table 4.9 Text Functions

Function	Description
LOWER(text)	Changes text to all lowercase characters.
PROPER(text)	Changes text to lowercase with the first character capitalized.
TEXT(value,format_text)	Converts number value to formatted text value.
UPPER(text)	Changes text to all uppercase characters.
VALUE(text)	Converts text to numbers.

Entering a Text Function into a Cell

In this tutorial, you enter a text function into a cell. Make sure that the international investments worksheet is open. Follow these steps:

1. Activate cell A6.
2. Type **=LOWER(A5)**, and press ↵Enter.

Because cell A5 contains COMPANY, cell A6 contains the same text in lowercase letters.

Close the workbook, but do not save the changes on your disk.

Chapter Summary

In this chapter, you have been introduced to functions. You have learned what a function is, what an argument is, and how you use functions to improve accuracy and efficiency in formulas. You have also learned how to use AutoSum and the Function Wizard.

This chapter provides several tables outlining the different types of functions, giving the required and optional arguments, and summarizing what each function does. Excel's Help contains a complete reference for all Excel functions.

Chapter 5, "Managing Workbooks and Printing Worksheets," deals with various aspects of printing. The chapter introduces you to the Excel commands for setting up the printer, previewing a document before printing, and adjusting margins and columns in Preview mode. You learn how to define a print area, define titles to be printed on every page, change the printer orientation, and create headers and footers for a document.

Checking Your Skills

True/False

For each of the following, circle *T* or *F* to indicate whether the statement is true or false.

T F **1.** When you use a function, you do not have to enter mathematical operators as you do in a formula.

T F **2.** Arguments are the number(s), cell(s), or named range(s) that a function uses in its calculations.

T F **3.** A properly entered function begins with =.

T F **4.** If multiple arguments are used in a function, they must be separated by semicolons.

T F **5.** All functions require an argument.

T F **6.** Spaces cannot be included in a function.

T F **7.** A function cannot be used inside a formula or another function.

T F **8.** Functions can be entered into a cell only by using the Function Wizard.

T F **9.** Functions can be edited in the formula bar.

T F **10.** The serial number for a day begins with January 1 of the current year.

Multiple Choice

In the blank provided, write the letter of the correct answer for each of the following.

_____ **1.** Which of the following is *not* a category of functions available in Excel?

- **a.** Date and Time
- **b.** Statistical
- **c.** Financial
- **d.** Graphics

_____ **2.** Day number 1 in Excel is _______.

- **a.** 1/1/1900
- **b.** today's date
- **c.** January 1 of the current year
- **d.** none of the above

_____ **3.** In Excel, a date expressed as a number is a(n) _______.

- **a.** argument
- **b.** parameter
- **c.** array number
- **d.** serial number

_____ **4.** Which of the following can be used as an argument in a function?

- **a.** a cell
- **b.** a range
- **c.** a number
- **d.** all the above

_____ **5.** Which function returns the serial number of today's date?

- **a.** SERIAL
- **b.** DAY
- **c.** DATEVALUE
- **d.** none of the above

_____ **6.** Which function returns the current date and time?

a. TIMEVALUE

b. TODAY

c. NOW

d. none of the above

_____ **7.** Excel stores dates as _______.

a. functions

b. text

c. serial numbers

d. all the above

_____ **8.** Which of the following functions converts a number to an integer by cutting off the decimal portion?

a. INTER

b. ABS

c. TRUNC

d. all the above

_____ **9.** Which function returns the serial number of today's date?

a. DATE

b. DAY

c. DATEVALUE

d. none of the above

_____ **10.** Which function could be used to calculate your monthly payments for a new car?

a. COST

b. IRR

c. PMT

d. RATE

Completion

In the blank provided, write the correct answer for each of the following.

1. A _______________ is a predefined formula.

2. In a function, the _______________ appears inside parentheses.

3. The _______________ function tells you the number of days between two dates.

4. The function that rounds a number to a specified number of digits is the _______________ function.

5. A complete explanation of all the functions available in Excel is found in Excel's _______________.

6. The _______________ number of a date is the number of days from the beginning of this century.

7. The _______________ function can be used to calculate the monthly payments on a home loan.

8. The _______________ function finds the largest number in a range of numbers.

9. The _______________ function returns the most frequently occurring number in a range of numbers.

10. The _______________ function returns the average of a range of numbers.

Applying Your Skills

Review Exercises

Exercise 1: Using Time and Date Functions

Open the First workbook you created in Chapter 1, and place today's date (only) in cell G1. Widen column G if necessary. Place the time of day (only hours and minutes) in cell H1. Print the worksheet. Keep the worksheet open for the next exercise.

Exercise 2: Calculating the Average

In cell G5 of the First workbook, use a statistical function to calculate the average quarterly sales for the EAST region. Print the worksheet; close the worksheet without saving changes.

Exercise 3: Calculating Monthly Payments

Use the PMT function to calculate the monthly payments for borrowing $200,000 at 10% for 30 years. Print the worksheet; close without saving the worksheet.

Exercise 4: Using the Date and Time Formats

Open the C2lp2 workbook workbook you created in Chapter 2. In cell A1, place a function to display the day's date. In cell A2, place a function to display the time. Then explore the effects of using the various date and time formats on these cells. Save your worksheet as C4sp4, and print your worksheet.

Exercise 5: Using Statistical Functions

Open the C2lp2 workbook workbook you created in Chapter 2. In row 16 of the worksheet, use the Function Wizard to display the average SALES, NET INCOME,

ASSETS, MARKET VALUE, and PERCENT RETURN. In rows 17 and 18, use the Function Wizard to display, respectively, the lowest and the highest values for SALES, NET INCOME, ASSETS, MARKET VALUE, and PERCENT RETURN. Save the worksheet as **C4sp5** and print the worksheet.

Continuing Projects

Project 1: Using Date and Serial Numbers

In an empty worksheet, use the serial number of today's date and the date formats to calculate what the dates will be 30, 60, and 90 days from today. (*Tip:* You can add numbers to a date serial number.) Print today's date and the dates 30, 60, and 90 days from today. Calculate the total number of days from the day you were born until today. (*Tip:* Serial numbers of dates can be subtracted.) Print the worksheet; save the workbook in a file named **C4lp1**.

Project 2: Using Statistical Functions

Enter the worksheet shown in figure 4.17, and save it on your disk as **C4lp2**.

Figure 4.17
Enter this worksheet for Continuing Project 2.

COMPANY	$ MIL. 1994 SALES	% CHANGE FROM 1993	RETURN ON COMMON EQUITY	PRICE - EARNINGS RATIO
Wachovia - Crestar	2330.8	61	10.6	11
PNB Contintal	1021.5	-14	11.9	7
First United Mining	3127	7	22.1	18
Cabot & Dexter	2960	-6	-10.4	10
National Chemicals	8399	15	15.7	14
Republic	934.57	3	19.4	18
First Southern	1170.41	9	6.7	26
Meridian Central	2968	-4	11.6	24
Signet & Murry	3995	-25	3	11
Wells Union	9827.57	2	13.9	12
Citicore	243.49	8	11.6	10
Becker Industries	2040	3	12.5	5
Ridalantic	837	6	15.6	9
Endicott Industrial	708.4	4	12.7	13
Clark	1175.11	7	11.4	22
Campbell & Capon	432.8	-57	-12.7	-1.3
Hwang Chemicals	7398.4	17	11.2	15

Use statistical functions to determine the average, standard deviation, median, smallest value, and largest value for the SALES data. Perform the same calculations for the data in the % CHANGE FROM 1993 column, for the data in the RETURN ON COMMON EQUITY column, and for the data in the PRICE - EARNINGS RATIO column. (*Tip*: You can copy functions just as you copy formulas.) Label each statistic clearly. Save and print the worksheet.

Project 3: Using the IF function

Assume that the company you work for needs a worksheet to calculate the pay for its temporary employees and consultants.

The company policy is that these employees are paid at their hourly rate for all hours they work in a week up to 40. If the employee works more than 40 hours in a week, he or she is paid for the first 40 hours at the regular hourly rate; for all hours past 40, employees are paid 1.5 times their hourly rate.

The C4lp3 worksheet shows an example (see figure 4.18).

Figure 4.18
A completed payroll worksheet.

	A	B	C	D	E	F	G	H
1		HOURS	HOURLY	TOTAL				
2	EMPLOYEE NAME	WORKED	RATE	PAY				
3								
4	CHARNLEY	40	$ 50.00	$2,000.00				
5	DAUM	10	$ 150.00	$1,500.00				
6	MITCHELL	60	$ 12.50	$ 875.00				
7	WILCOX	41	$ 15.00	$ 622.50				
8								

Your job is to set up a worksheet that uses the IF function to test whether hours worked are greater than 40 and that calculates the correct total pay. Enter the sample data shown in figure 4.18, and add your name, hours worked, and hourly rate as row 8. Print your worksheet and save the file as **C4lp3**.

Use a function to display the date in cell A1. Then increase the width of column D to double the width shown in C4lp3. From the **T**ools menu, choose **O**ptions and click the View tab. Click the Fo**r**mulas check box in the Windows Options area of the dialog box, and click OK.

Print the worksheet again. This time your IF function (rather than the result of the IF function) should print.

Chapter 5

Managing Workbooks and Printing Worksheets

Header
Text, date, page numbering, and formatting in the top margin of each page of a document.

Footer
Text, date, page numbering, and formatting in the bottom margin of each page of a document.

Organizing and printing the worksheets in Excel for Windows 95 workbooks are valuable skills. In the first section of this chapter, you learn how to organize your worksheets: to name, move, copy, insert, and delete a workbook's sheets. Next, you learn how to use Excel's **Z**oom command to view your worksheet at different degrees of magnification. By zooming out, you reduce the image of your worksheet so that you can see more of it on your screen. By zooming in, you magnify an area of the worksheet so that you can format it precisely.

Controlling the way your worksheets and charts are printed is also an important skill in Excel. By completing the tutorials in the last sections of this chapter, you learn to print professional-looking worksheets. You will learn how to set up a page for printing, preview your printout on-screen, define a print area, use *headers* and *footers*, and choose where the page breaks will occur in a large spreadsheet.

Objectives

By the time you have finished this chapter, you will have learned to

1. Rename Worksheets
2. Move and Copy Worksheets within Workbooks
3. Insert and Delete Worksheets in a Workbook
4. Use the Zoom Command
5. Set Up the Page
6. Add Headers and Footers
7. Use Print Preview

8. Break a Worksheet into Pages by Inserting Manual Page Breaks
9. Print Worksheets

Objective 1: Rename Worksheets

Sheet1, Sheet2, or Sheet3 are not useful worksheet names because you cannot tell from the name what is in the worksheet. Names have not been a problem for you so far because you have generally used only the first worksheet in a workbook and you have named the workbook file so that you know which worksheet is in the workbook. But you will find that grouping and organizing your sheets and charts into workbooks is helpful—even necessary. Meaningful names on the sheet tabs will be invaluable when you want to find a piece of information quickly.

A workbook can contain one sheet or as many as 255 sheets. When you start a new workbook, Excel (by default) provides 16 blank worksheets named Sheet1 through Sheet16. You can use these blank sheets for one of three different purposes: as worksheets, charts, or Visual Basic modules. If you like, you can add more sheets or delete sheets in the workbook. You are already familiar with worksheets. You learn about charts in Chapter 6 and about Visual Basic modules (sometimes called macros) in Chapter 8.

When you have more than just a few sheets in a workbook, you will need to start using tab (sheet) names that indicate both the type—worksheet, chart, or macro—and the contents of the sheet. Tab names can be up to 31 characters long, and the tab of the active worksheet is always shown in boldface type.

Renaming a Sheet Tab

In this tutorial, you change the names of several worksheet tabs. Because the worksheets are empty, the tab names cannot be descriptive of the contents of the sheet. But you are practicing skills now that you will put to use later.

Open the workbook C2sp2, which you created in Review Exercise 2 at the end of Chapter 2. The worksheet containing the order information has the tab name Sheet1. To change to a more meaningful tab name, follow these steps:

1. Click the Sheet1 tab to make this worksheet the active worksheet.

2. Click the Sheet1 tab with the *right mouse button*.

   Right-clicking displays a shortcut menu of sheet commands (see figure 5.1). You can also access these commands from the menu bar, but you will find that using the shortcut menu is more efficient.

Figure 5.1 The shortcut menu of sheet commands.

Note: *In this book, when you should click with the right mouse button, you will be told to right-click; otherwise, click with the left mouse button.*

3. Click (with the left mouse button) the Rename command in the shortcut menu.

   The Rename Sheet dialog box appears (see figure 5.2).

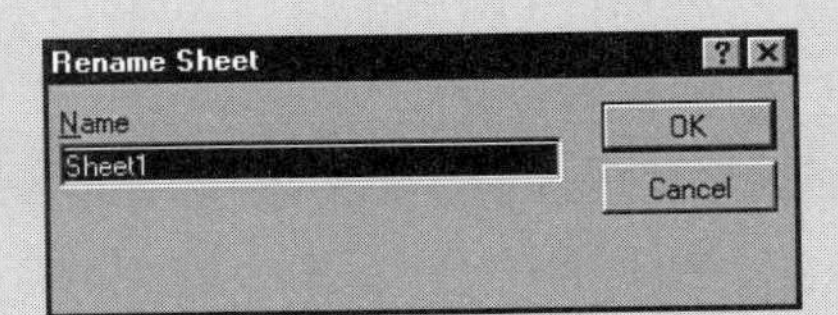

Figure 5.2 The Rename Sheet dialog box.

4. Type **Customer 138 Order**, and press Enter.

   Now your worksheet tab will indicate the contents of the worksheet (see figure 5.3). You can use up to 31 characters (including spaces) in a sheet name.

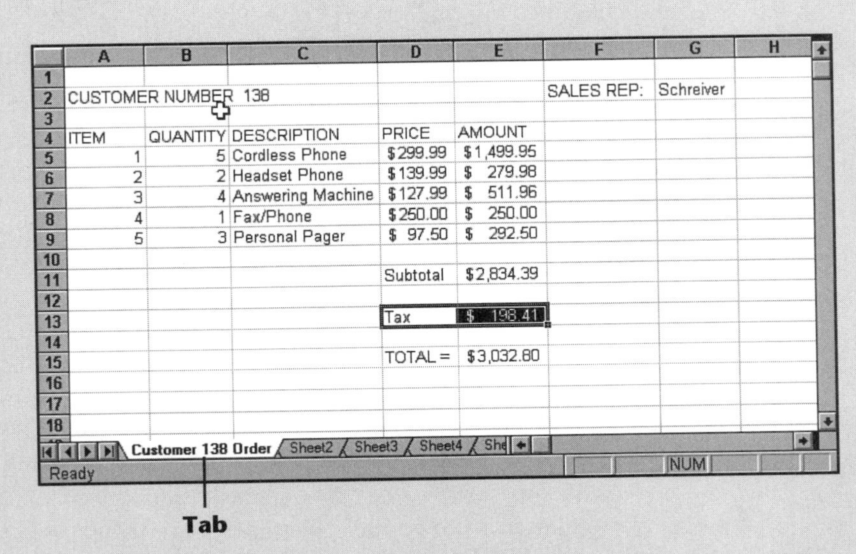

	A	B	C	D	E	F	G	H
1								
2	CUSTOMER NUMBER		138			SALES REP:	Schreiver	
3								
4	ITEM	QUANTITY	DESCRIPTION	PRICE	AMOUNT			
5	1	5	Cordless Phone	$299.99	$1,499.95			
6	2	2	Headset Phone	$139.99	$ 279.98			
7	3	4	Answering Machine	$127.99	$ 511.96			
8	4	1	Fax/Phone	$250.00	$ 250.00			
9	5	3	Personal Pager	$ 97.50	$ 292.50			
10								
11				Subtotal	$2,834.39			
12								
13				Tax	$ 198.41			
14								
15				TOTAL =	$3,032.80			
16								
17								
18								

Figure 5.3 The Customer 138 Order worksheet with the new tab name.

Keep this workbook open for the following tutorial.

Objective 2: Move and Copy Worksheets within Workbooks

An Excel workbook is used in much the same way that you use an indexed three-ring notebook or a file folder. You place in the notebook or folder the papers that belong together. For example, in one notebook, you may place all the sheets that contain work done in one fiscal year or in the first quarter of a year. You might also organize your worksheets according to the project, the vendor, or funding source.

In your workbooks, just as in your system of notebooks or files, you will need to move and copy worksheets and charts (you learn about charts in Chapter 6). At this point in learning Excel, you have not created enough worksheets to feel the need to organize them or to move copies of a worksheet from one workbook into another workbook. The tutorials in this section, therefore, simply show you how to move and copy worksheets—without a logical reason to do so. But as you use Excel, you will often encounter situations where you will need the skills you develop by completing the following tutorials.

Moving a Sheet within a Workbook

In this tutorial, you move the Customer 138 Order worksheet and place it between Sheet4 and Sheet5 in the same workbook. Follow these steps:

1. If the Customer 138 Order sheet is not the active sheet, click its tab.
2. *Right-click* the Customer 138 Order tab to open the Sheet shortcut menu.
3. Click the Move or Copy command in the shortcut menu.

   The Move or Copy dialog box appears (see figure 5.4). You can set the options in this box to control whether a sheet is moved or copied and whether the sheet is placed in a different workbook when it is moved or copied. You will use these options in later tutorials.

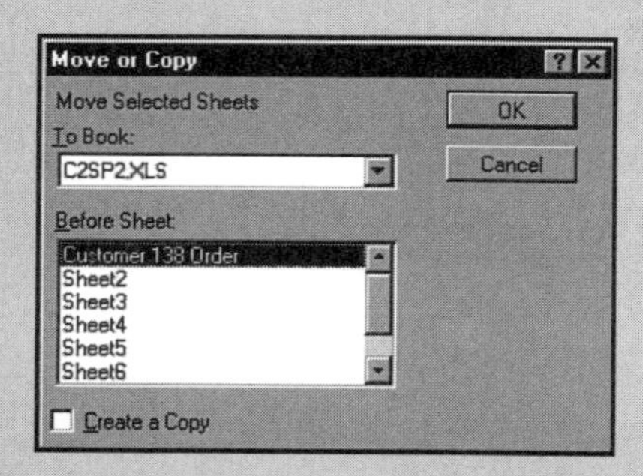

Figure 5.4 The Move or Copy dialog box.

4. You want to move the active sheet and place it between Sheet4 and Sheet5. Click Sheet5 in the Before Sheet list in the Move or Copy dialog box (see figure 5.5).

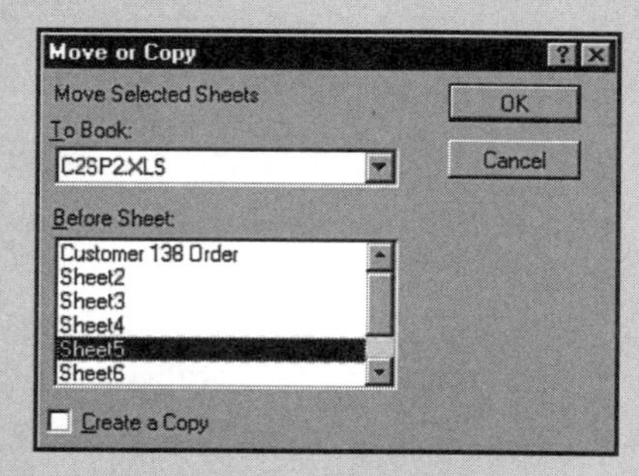

Figure 5.5 Indicating that the insertion is before Sheet5.

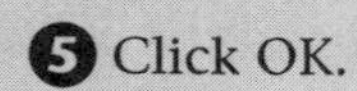

5. Click OK.

The order worksheet has been moved to its new position (see figure 5.6).

Figure 5.6
The worksheet in its new location.

	A	B	C	D	E	F	G	H
1								
2	CUSTOMER NUMBER 138					SALES REP:	Schreiver	
3								
4	ITEM	QUANTITY	DESCRIPTION	PRICE	AMOUNT			
5	1	5	Cordless Phone	$299.99	$1,499.95			
6	2	2	Headset Phone	$139.99	$ 279.98			
7	3	4	Answering Machine	$127.99	$ 511.96			
8	4	1	Fax/Phone	$250.00	$ 250.00			
9	5	3	Personal Pager	$ 97.50	$ 292.50			
10								
11				Subtotal	$2,834.39			
12								
13				Tax	$ 198.41			
14								
15				TOTAL =	$3,032.80			
16								
17								
18								

Sheet2 / Sheet3 / Sheet4 / Customer 138 Order / Sh
Ready NUM

Keep this workbook open for the following tutorial.

At times, you will want more than one copy of a worksheet—perhaps to record the figures at different times. You can copy a worksheet to a different location in your workbook using the Sheet shortcut menu.

5

Copying a Sheet within a Workbook

In this tutorial, you copy the Customer 138 Order worksheet and place the copy between Sheet9 and Sheet10 in the same workbook. Follow these steps:

1. If the Customer 138 Order sheet is not the active sheet, click its tab.
2. Right-click the Customer 138 Order tab to open the Sheet shortcut menu.
3. Click the Move or Copy command in the shortcut menu.

   The Move or Copy dialog box appears.
4. Click the **C**reate a Copy check box in the lower left corner of the Move or Copy dialog box. You want to copy the active sheet and place the copy between Sheet9 and Sheet10 in the same workbook.
5. Move the scroll bar slider box in the scroll bar of the **B**efore Sheet list until Sheet10 appears in the list.
6. Click Sheet10 in the **B**efore Sheet list in the Move or Copy dialog box.
7. Click OK.

   The Order worksheet has been copied to its new position (see figure 5.7).

(continues)

Copying a Sheet within a Workbook (continued)

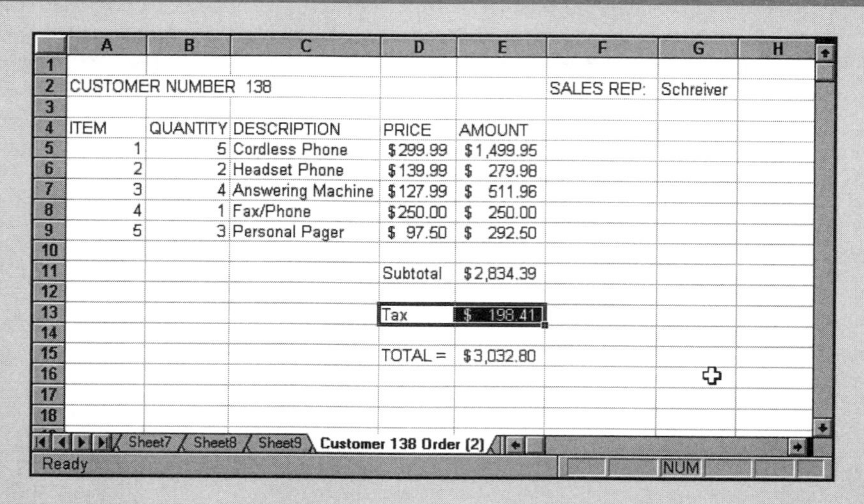

	A	B	C	D	E	F	G	H
1								
2	CUSTOMER NUMBER 138					SALES REP:	Schreiver	
3								
4	ITEM	QUANTITY	DESCRIPTION	PRICE	AMOUNT			
5	1	5	Cordless Phone	$299.99	$1,499.95			
6	2	2	Headset Phone	$139.99	$ 279.98			
7	3	4	Answering Machine	$127.99	$ 511.96			
8	4	1	Fax/Phone	$250.00	$ 250.00			
9	5	3	Personal Pager	$ 97.50	$ 292.50			
10								
11				Subtotal	$2,834.39			
12								
13				Tax	$ 198.41			
14								
15				TOTAL =	$3,032.80			
16								
17								
18								

Figure 5.7
The copy in the workbook.

This worksheet now appears twice in the workbook. Notice that Excel automatically names the copy Customer 138 Order (2) so that you are not confused by the duplicate names.

Keep this workbook open for the following tutorial.

Moving and Copying between Two Workbooks

Frequently, you will want to reuse all or part of a worksheet that you already have rather than to build a new worksheet from scratch. You can keep the layout and formulas from the old worksheet, but clear out all the old data. By using the **C**opy command, you can copy within the same workbook. But what if you have already set up a good worksheet to keep track of project expenses during the last quarter of 1993, and want to copy the sheet with all its headings, formats, and calculations into the workbook for 1994?

In the following tutorials, you learn how to move and copy worksheets to different workbooks. To make this move or copy, you must have both the workbook that is the *source* of the sheet and the workbook that is the *destination* for the sheet open at the same time. Use the **F**ile, **O**pen command to open a second workbook without closing the first workbook. You also need to move back and forth between the two open workbooks. Excel displays the names of the four most recently used worksheets near the bottom of the **F**ile menu.

Remember, Excel displays only one workbook at a time even though several workbooks are open. You move between the open workbooks by clicking the name (at the bottom of the **F**ile menu) of the workbook you want to see on-screen. When several workbooks are open, you can tell which workbook is currently displayed because its name is shown in the window's title bar. A workbook does not have to be on-screen if you want to copy or move a worksheet to it; however, it must be open.

Moving a Sheet to Another Workbook

In this tutorial, you first open a new worksheet. Then you move the Customer 138 Order sheet to the new workbook. You do not need to create a new workbook if you want to move the worksheet to an existing workbook. You are creating a new workbook here so that you have a workbook to practice with and you won't lose data if you make a mistake. If you have named a workbook (and saved it on disk), you can move between workbooks by using the listed files at the bottom of the **F**ile menu. You can also move to any open workbook, even if it has not been named and saved, by using the list of open workbooks at the bottom of the **W**indow menu. In the following tutorial, you use the list of the four most recently opened workbooks at the bottom of the **F**ile menu.

To open the destination workbook (the practice workbook) and then move a sheet from the open source workbook (C2sp2), follow these steps:

1. Click the New Workbook button to open a new workbook. Then save the workbook, and name it **Test**.

   Now you have an open destination workbook for the worksheet that you will remove from the C2sp2 workbook.

2. Switch to the C2sp2 workbook by clicking **F**ile in the menu bar. Then click C2sp2 at the bottom of the **F**ile menu (see figure 5.8).

Figure 5.8 The list of workbooks in the **F**ile menu.

Your C2sp2 workbook is now on-screen. Your Test workbook, however, is also still open.

3. Click the Customer 138 Order (2) tab if it is not active.

4. Right-click the Customer 138 Order (2) tab, and then choose Move or Copy from the shortcut menu.

(continues)

5

Moving a Sheet to Another Workbook (continued)

5. Click the To Book drop-down list button to display the names of the workbooks you have open and that can be used as destination workbooks (see figure 5.9).

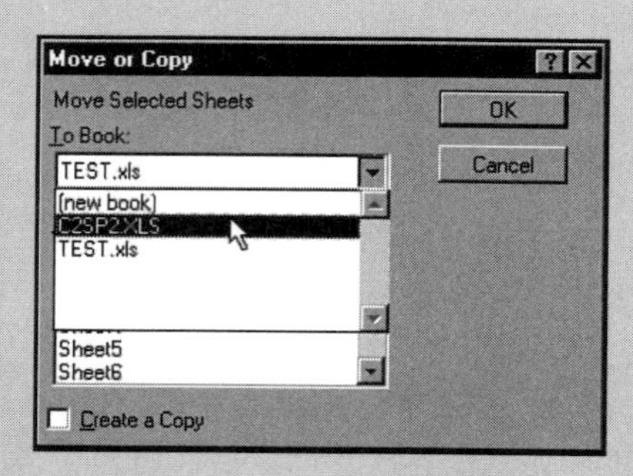

Figure 5.9
The To Book list.

6. Click TEST.xls.
7. In the Before Sheet list, click Sheet3.
8. Click the OK button.

   Excel displays the worksheet in its new location between Sheet2 and Sheet3 of Test (see figure 5.10).

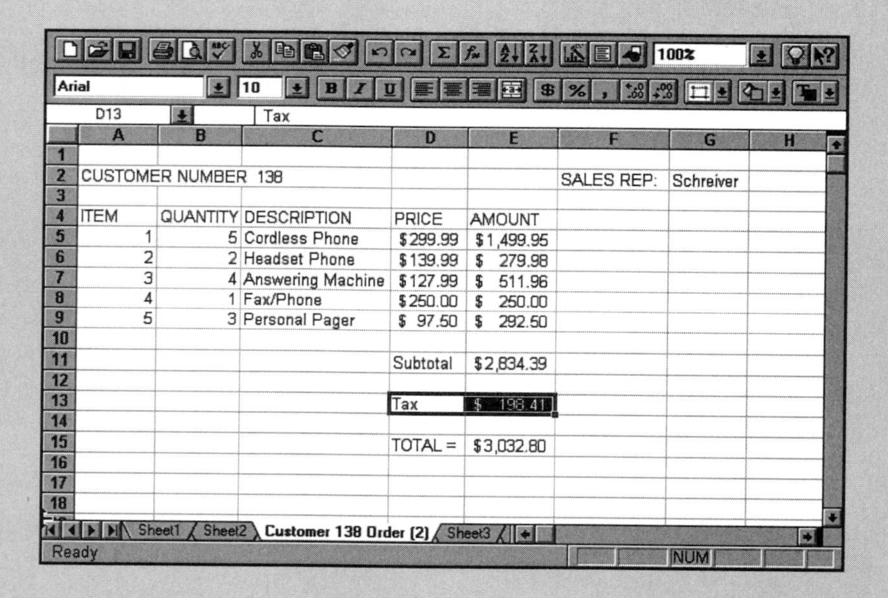

Figure 5.10
The worksheet in its new location.

9. Close the Test workbook, and save the changes.
10. Check to see whether the worksheet Customer 138 Order (2) is still in the workbook C2sp2.

In the next tutorial, you copy a sheet from C2sp2 into a new workbook; the copied worksheet will be the only worksheet in the new workbook.

Copying a Sheet to Another Workbook

To copy a sheet to another (new and empty) workbook, follow these steps:

1. In cell A1 of Sheet2 in the C2sp2 workbook, type **THIS IS FROM C2sp2**, and press Enter.
2. Right-click the Sheet2 tab, and then choose Move or Copy from the shortcut menu.
3. Click the To Book drop-down list button to display the names of the workbooks you have open and available as destination workbooks.

   Notice that the Test workbook is not available because it is not open; you closed it in step 9 of the preceding tutorial.
4. Click (new book) in the To Book list.

   Notice that the Before Sheet list is empty. The sheet you copy will be the only sheet in the new book.
5. Click the Create a Copy check box so that it has a check mark in it.
6. Click OK.

   The new workbook is displayed. If you want to keep it, you need to name and save it on your disk.
7. Check to see whether Sheet2 is still in the workbook C2sp2. Click File, and choose C2sp2.

Keep this workbook open for the following tutorial.

5

Objective 3: Insert and Delete Worksheets in a Workbook

Just as you sometimes need to insert a blank piece of paper into a three-ring notebook, you sometimes need to insert a blank sheet into an Excel workbook. You also need to remove old or unused sheets from a notebook or file, and you will need to do the same in an Excel workbook. In the following tutorials, you insert a blank sheet into a workbook and delete sheets from a workbook.

Again, this task is not necessitated by the work you are doing in the workbook. Rather, you are learning and practicing useful skills that will make you a more efficient and productive user of Excel.

Adding a Sheet to a Workbook

If the workbook C2sp2 is not open, open it now. To add a new sheet to this workbook, follow these steps:

1. Click the Sheet3 tab to make it active.
2. Right-click the Sheet3 tab.
3. Choose Insert from the Sheet shortcut menu.
4. The Insert dialog box appears (see figure 5.11).

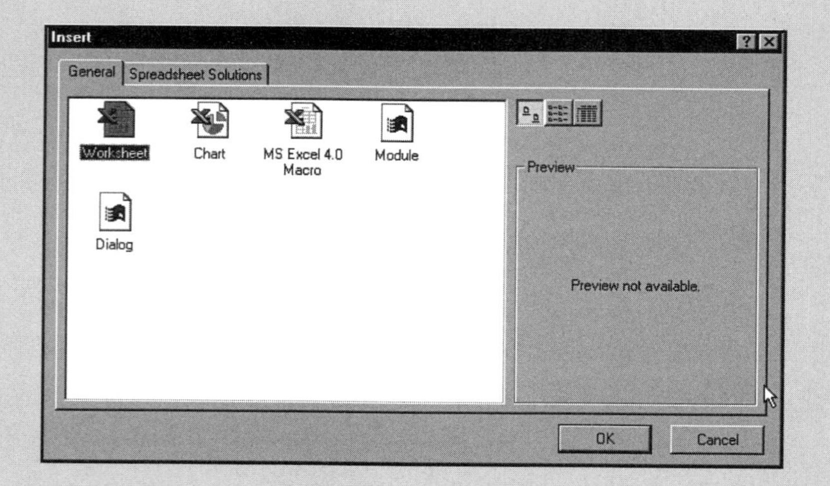

Figure 5.11
The Insert dialog box.

5. You want to insert a new worksheet. Click OK. The new worksheet is inserted into the workbook (see figure 5.12).

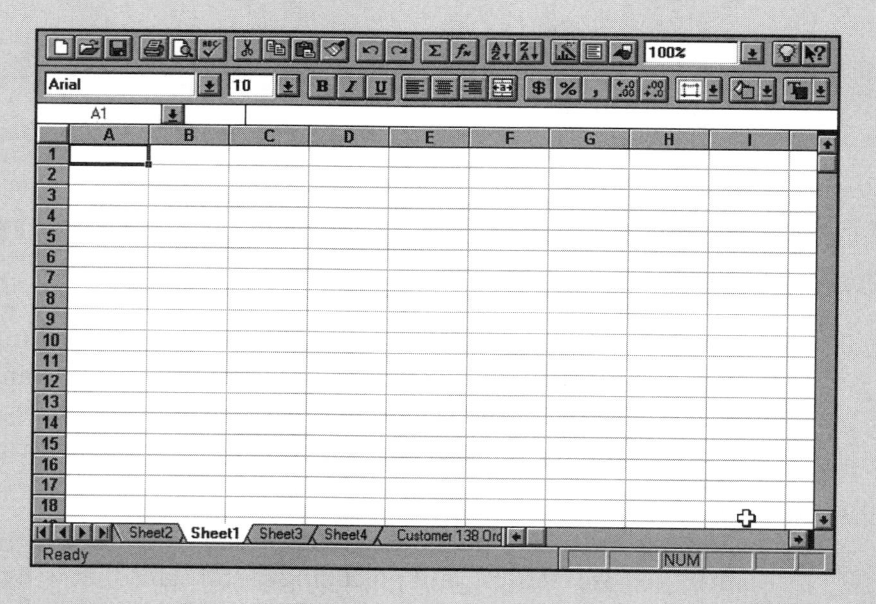

Figure 5.12
The worksheet in its new location.

Keep this workbook open for the following tutorial.

In Excel for Windows 95, you can also easily delete a sheet from a workbook. In the following tutorial, you learn how to delete a sheet.

Deleting a Sheet from a Workbook

To delete Sheet3 from your worksheet, follow these steps:

1. Click the Sheet3 tab to make it active.
2. Right-click the Sheet3 tab.
3. From the shortcut menu, choose Delete.
4. The Delete warning box appears (see figure 5.13).

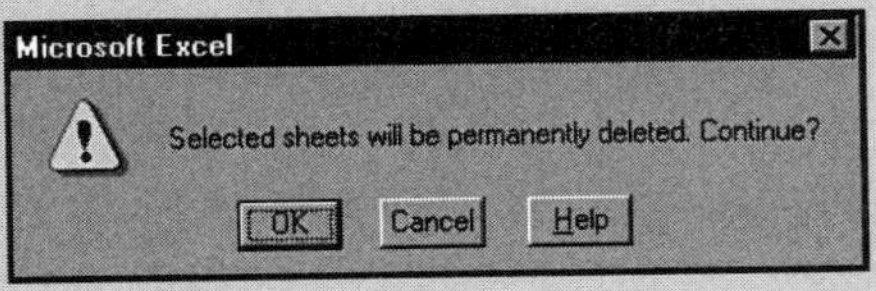

Figure 5.13 The Delete warning box.

Microsoft Excel

Selected sheets will be permanently deleted. Continue?

OK | Cancel | Help

5. Click OK.

   Sheet3 is deleted.

Keep this workbook open for the following tutorial.

You can also delete multiple adjacent sheets from your workbook. You delete several sheets in the following tutorial.

Deleting Adjacent Sheets from a Workbook

To delete Sheets 6 through 9 from the workbook, follow these steps:

1. Click the Sheet6 tab. Then press and hold down Shift, and click the Sheet9 tab.

   Sheets 6 through 9 are selected.
2. Right-click the Sheet9 tab.
3. From the shortcut menu, choose Delete.
4. The Delete warning box appears.
5. Click OK.

   Sheets 6 through 9 are deleted.

Keep this workbook open for the following tutorial.

You use a similar technique to delete nonadjacent worksheets from your workbook. This technique is illustrated in the following tutorial.

Deleting Nonadjacent Sheets from a Workbook

To delete Sheets 10, 12, and 14 from the workbook, follow these steps:

1. Click the Sheet10 tab. Then press and hold down Ctrl, and click the Sheet12 tab and the Sheet14 tab.

   Sheets 10, 12, and 14 are selected.

2. Right-click the Sheet14 tab.
3. From the shortcut menu, choose Delete.
4. The Delete warning box appears.
5. Click OK.

   Sheets 10, 12, and 14 are deleted.

You can close and save your workbook now.

Objective 4: Use the Zoom Command

Excel's **Z**oom command in the **V**iew menu enables you to select varied degrees of magnification or reduction in which to view your worksheet. The Zoom Control Box button at the right side of the Standard toolbar is another—quicker—way to zoom. The zoom reduction capability is useful when you want to "move back" to see more of a worksheet on-screen. Magnifying ("moving closer to") an area of the worksheet enables you to see details and polish your formatting before you print. You can view the worksheet in size increments varying from 10 percent to 400 percent of the normal size. The **Z**oom command does not affect the way your worksheet prints; the command affects only what you see on your screen. Excel provides five preset **Z**oom levels. Table 5.1 describes the **V**iew, **Z**oom options.

Table 5.1 View Zoom Options

Option	Description
20**0**%	Magnifies view to 200 percent.
100%	Displays normal view.
75%	Reduces view to 75 percent.
50%	Reduces view to 50 percent.
25%	Reduces view to 25 percent.
Fit Selection	Calculates Zoom factor so that all cells fit in current window size.
Custom %	Enables you to choose precise levels of magnification or reduction between 10% and 400%.

Using the View Zoom Command

For the remaining tutorials in this chapter, open the financial worksheet (C2lp2) that you saved in Continuing Project 2 at the end of Chapter 2.

In this tutorial, you use the **View, Zoom** command to see more of the worksheet.

1. Open the **View** menu, and choose the **Zoom** command. The Zoom dialog box appears (see figure 5.14).

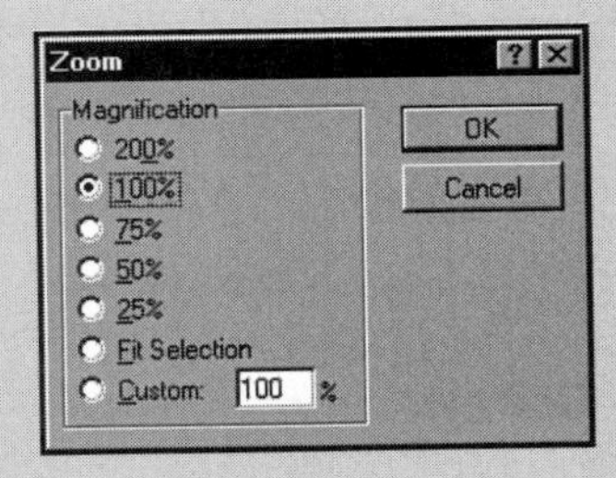

Figure 5.14 The Zoom dialog box.

2. Choose the **50%** Zoom option.
3. Click OK, or press Enter.
4. Return to the standard Zoom size by opening the **View** menu and choosing the **Zoom** command. Choose the **100%** option. Choose OK, or press Enter.

5

You can "zoom in" on an area of your worksheet so that you can see it in more detail. This feature is useful for people who cannot clearly see the numbers and text displayed at Excel's standard size.

Using the View Zoom Command to Magnify

In this tutorial, you increase the magnification of an area on the C2lp2 worksheet. Follow these steps:

1. Make cell A8 the active cell.
2. Open the **View** menu, and choose the **Zoom** command. The Zoom dialog box appears (refer to figure 5.14).
3. Choose the 20**0**% Zoom option.
4. Choose OK, or press Enter.
5. Return to the standard Zoom size by opening the **View** menu and choosing the **Zoom** command. Choose the **100%** option. Choose OK, or press Enter.

You can also zoom by using the Zoom Control box on the Standard toolbar. Many users find that this method is more convenient.

Using the Zoom Control Box

To use the Zoom Control box on the right side of the Standard toolbar, follow these steps:

1. Click the downward-pointing arrow button next to the magnification percent displayed in the Zoom Control box on the Standard toolbar.
2. In the list, click 25%.
3. Notice that you can see more rows and columns in your worksheet.
4. Click the downward-pointing arrow button next to the magnification percent displayed in the Zoom Control box.
5. In the list, click 100% to return to the standard view of your worksheet.

Keep this workbook open for the following tutorial.

Objective 5: Set Up the Page

Sometimes, you may want to change certain print settings for only a single document. Excel's **F**ile, Page Set**u**p command enables you to change printer settings that affect only the active document. When you choose the **F**ile, Page Set**u**p command, the Page Setup tabbed dialog box appears (see figure 5.15). You use the options in this tabbed dialog box to control the way the document appears on the page.

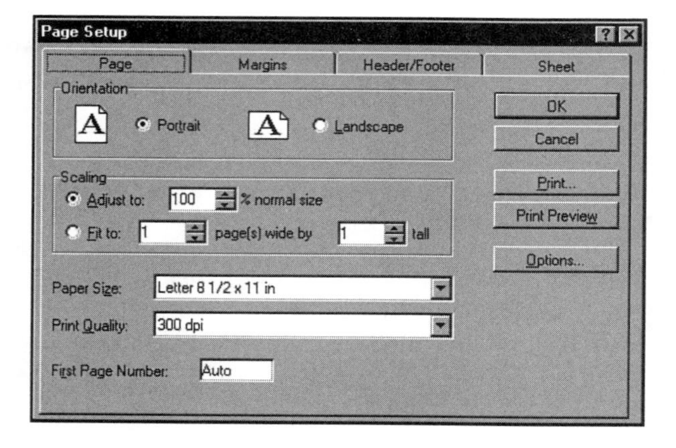

Figure 5.15
The Page Setup dialog box with the Page tab in front.

Gridlines
The intersecting horizontal and vertical lines on a worksheet.

The **F**ile, Page Set**u**p command also provides capabilities for adding headers and footers to a document, changing margins, turning on or off worksheet gridlines, choosing page order, and positioning spreadsheet data on the page. The Scaling options function only on printers that are capable of scaling and will not be covered in this text. For more information on the **F**ile, Page Set**u**p command, see *Special Edition Using Excel for Windows 95*, from Que Corporation.

The Page Setup dialog box contains four tabs: Page, Margins, Header/Footer, and Sheet. To access the options on a tab, click the tab to bring it to the front. Excel's

Help contains detailed information on these options. This book gives an overview of the most frequently used options.

Table 5.2 outlines the options that the **F**ile, Page Set**u**p command provides in the four Page Setup tabs in the Page Setup dialog box.

Table 5.2 Important Page Setup Dialog Box Options

Option	Description
Page Tab	
Orientation	Por**t**rait prints worksheet columns vertically down the length of the paper. **L**andscape rotates the worksheet and prints it "sideways" on the page so that more columns can fit on one page. Use **L**andscape when you have few rows but many columns of data in your worksheet and need to fit all the columns on one page.
Paper Si**z**e	Specifies size of paper, appropriate for letter, legal, executive, or envelope (A4) sizes.
Fi**r**st Page Number:	If pages are numbered in the header or footer, this option controls the starting page number. Generally, you will start numbering on the first page and leave this setting at Auto.
Margins Tab	
Left, **R**ight, **T**op, **B**ottom	Controls amount of space between left, right, top, and bottom edges of the paper and the printed document.
Center on Page	Centers the document horizontally between left and right margins or vertically between top and bottom margins.
Header/Footer Tab	
Custom Header button	Displays the Header dialog box, in which you can alter the default header.
C**u**stom Footer button	Displays the Footer dialog box, in which you can alter the default footer.
Sheet Tab	
Page Order	Changes the page numbering and printing sequence on your worksheet. **D**own, then Across prints down rows page by page, then returns to top of the next set of columns and prints down page by page. Acro**s**s, then Down prints and numbers a group of rows across columns to the right until all data is printed page by page, then goes down to the next set of rows and prints across.
Gridlines	Turns worksheet gridlines on or off for printing.
Black & White Cells	If color formats were used in cells and text boxes, but you have a black-and-white printer, use this option. The colors are removed when printing to a noncolor printer.
Row & Co**l**umn Headings	Turns row number headings and column letter headings on or off for printing.

The **P**rint and Print Previe**w** buttons appear in all the Page Setup tabbed dialog boxes. Clicking the **P**rint button displays the Print dialog box so that you can immediately print your worksheet. The Print Previe**w** button displays (in a Preview window) your worksheet as it will look when printed. To leave the Preview window, click the Close button at the top of the screen. You can try the Print Preview button on your own, or you can wait until previewing is covered in detail later in this chapter.

Using the Page Setup Command to Change Settings

In this tutorial, you change the default page print settings in the C2lp2 worksheet. Follow these steps:

1. Print the C2lp2 worksheet. The worksheet will print according to the default page setup settings.
2. Open the File menu, and choose the Page Setup command. The Page Setup tabbed dialog box appears. Click the Page tab if it is not at the front of the dialog box so that the rows print down the length of the page.
3. Choose the Landscape option in the Orientation section of the Page dialog box so that the rows print down the length of the page.
4. Click the Sheet tab.
5. Click the Row & Column Headings option. (A check mark should appear.)
6. Click the Gridlines check box to turn off this setting. (The check mark should disappear.)
7. Click the Print button; the Print dialog box appears.
8. Click OK to print the worksheet with the new Page Setup settings.
9. Compare the first (default) printout with the second printout to see the effect of the changes.

Keep this workbook open for the following tutorial.

Default settings Predefined settings for printing all Excel documents.

Sometimes you will find that the original (*default*) *settings* are better than your altered settings for printing a document. In the following tutorial, you learn how to return to the default settings.

Using the Page Setup Command to Return to the Default Settings

In this tutorial, you return to the default settings in the C2lp2 worksheet. Follow these steps:

1. Open the File menu, and choose the Page Setup command. The Page Setup tabbed dialog box appears. Click the Page tab if it is not at the front of the dialog box.
2. Choose the Portrait option in the Orientation section of the Page Setup dialog box so that the data columns print down the page.

3. Click the Sheet tab.
4. Click the Row & Column Headings check box to turn off this setting. (The check mark should disappear.)
5. In the Sheet tab, click the Gridlines option. (A check mark should appear.)
6. Click the Print button, and the Print dialog box appears.
7. Click OK to print the worksheet with these Page Setup settings.

Keep this workbook open for the following tutorial.

Defining the Print Area

Print area
Section of worksheet defined to be printed.

To print only a part of a worksheet, you must define that portion as a print area. If you select nonadjoining sections of your worksheet and define the multiple sections as a single print area, Excel prints each nonadjoining area on a separate page. If you do not define a print area, Excel assumes that you want to define the entire worksheet as the print area.

Defining a Print Area

In this tutorial, you define a print area (B1:D8) that is a range in the C2lp2 worksheet. Follow these steps:

1. Open the File menu, and choose the Page Setup command. The Page Setup tabbed dialog box appears.
2. Click the Sheet tab if it is not at the front of the dialog box.
3. Click in the Print Area text box, and type the **B1:D8** as the range to print.
4. Click OK.
5. Print the worksheet. Only the range you defined as the print area prints.

Keep this workbook open for the following tutorial.

You may find that you need to remove a print area that you have set up. In the next tutorial, you learn how to do this.

Removing a Print Area

In this tutorial, you remove the print area that you have set in the C2lp2 worksheet. Follow these steps:

1. Open the File menu, and choose the Page Setup command. The Page Setup tabbed dialog box appears.

(continues)

Removing a Print Area (continued)

2. Click the Sheet tab if it is not at the front of the dialog box.
3. Click and drag over B1$D$8 (to select it) in the Print Area text box, and press Del.
4. Click OK.
5. Print the worksheet. The entire worksheet will print.

Keep this workbook open for the following tutorial.

Sometimes, you will need to print areas of the worksheet that are not adjacent. The next tutorial explains how to do this.

Defining a Print Area That Contains Nonadjacent Cell Ranges

In this tutorial, you define a print area that consists of two nonadjacent ranges in the C2lp2 worksheet. Follow these steps:

1. Open the **F**ile menu, and choose the Page Set**u**p command. The Page Setup tabbed dialog box appears.
2. Click the Sheet tab if it is not at the front of the dialog box.
3. Click in the Print Area text box, and type **A1:A8,D1:D8** as the range to print.

   Note that the two individual ranges are separated by a comma. Use commas to separate nonadjacent range specifications.
4. Print the worksheet. Only the range you defined as the print area will print on two pages.

   Before proceeding, let's remove the print area.
5. Choose the **F**ile, Pri**n**t Area command, then select **C**lear Print Area.

   The print area is cleared so that future printouts will not display just the selected ranges.

Keep this workbook open for the following tutorial.

You can also use your mouse to select a part of the worksheet to print.

Defining a Print Area by Using the Mouse

In this tutorial, you print part of your worksheet by doing the following:

1. In C2lp2, select cells A1:B20 by clicking and dragging.

2. From the File menu, choose Print.

   The Print dialog box opens.

3. In the Print What area, click the Selection option.

4. Choose OK.

Objective 6: Add Headers and Footers

You can add headers and/or footers to a printout of your worksheet by using the Header/Footer tab in the Page Setup dialog box (see figure 5.16). A header or footer creates a consistent look across all the pages of a document. You can use a header, for example, to place a title at the top of each page. And you can use a footer to automatically number each page at the bottom. Headers and footers appear one-half inch from the top or bottom of the paper.

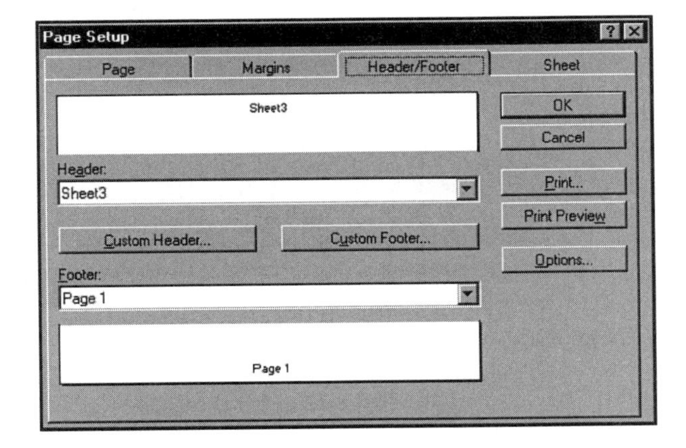

Figure 5.16
The Header/Footer tab of the Page Setup tabbed dialog box.

A header or footer can include such items as text, a page number, the current date and time, and formatting such as boldface and italic. Excel's default header, as you have seen on your printouts, is the name of the file being printed. The default footer is the page number. You can delete both of these if you choose. You change the default header or footer by clicking either the **C**ustomize Header or C**u**stomize Footer button.

When you indicate that you want a custom header or footer by clicking the appropriate button, the Header or the Footer dialog box is displayed (see figure 5.17). The dialog box has three sections in which you enter header (or footer) information that will print on each page. The left section inserts information aligned with the left page margin; the center section inserts information centered on the page; and the right section inserts information aligned with the right margin.

When you select one of these three sections and choose the appropriate button, Excel will include the information specified by the button at the top or bottom of each page and left-aligned, centered, or right-aligned. By choosing the Format

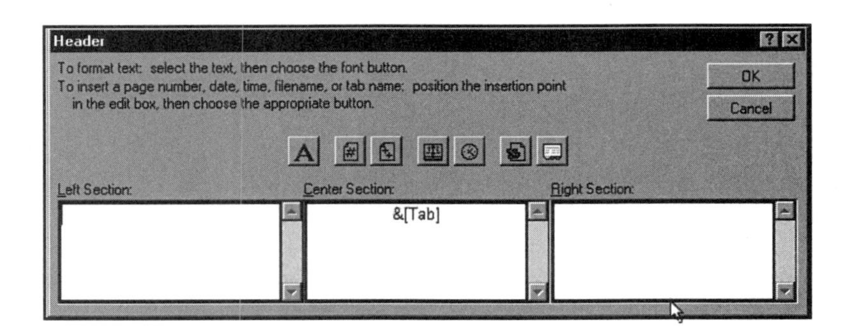

Figure 5.17
The Header dialog box.

Font button in the Header or Footer dialog box, you can format the header or footer in various fonts.

Excel uses codes to assign formatting. When you click the buttons in the Header or Footer dialog box, a code is inserted (and displayed) in the appropriate section. This code tells Excel what to print at that location on the page. All codes begin with an ampersand (&) and are followed by a letter. The default header setting is &[Tab], which prints the sheet name centered at the top of the page. The default footer setting is Page &[Page], which prints the word *Page* followed by the page number centered at the bottom of the page. Table 5.3 shows the other header and footer buttons.

Table 5.3 Header and Footer Buttons

Icon	Description
A	Enables you to choose a font and other formatting options for selected header or footer text.
	Inserts a page number.
	Indicates the total number of pages in the document.
	Inserts the date.
	Inserts the time.
	Inserts the file name.
	Inserts the sheet name from the sheet's workbook tab.

Using the Page Setup Command to Print Headers

In this tutorial, you print your name in the left side of the header of the C2lp2 worksheet, and remove the file name from the header. Follow these steps:

1. Open the File menu, and choose the Page Setup command. The Page Setup tabbed dialog box appears.

2. Click the Header/Footer tab (refer to figure 5.16).
3. Click the Custom Header button. The Header dialog box appears (refer to figure 5.17).
4. Type your name; it will appear in the Left Section window.
5. Double-click in the Center section window to select the default header code.
6. Press Del to remove the code.
7. Choose OK to close the Header dialog box.
8. Choose OK to close the Page Setup dialog box.
9. Print the worksheet, and you will see the header.

Footers are often useful when you print a worksheet. In the next tutorial, you learn how to create a custom footer.

Using the Page Setup Command to Print Footers

In this tutorial, you print the date and time in the right side of the footer in the C2lp2 worksheet and delete the page number from the footer. Follow these steps:

1. Open the File menu, and choose Page Setup. The Page Setup dialog box appears.
2. Click the Header/Footer tab.
3. Click the Custom Footer button. The Footer dialog box appears.
4. Click in the Right Section window.
5. Click the Date button.
6. Click the Time button.
7. Click and drag over `Page &[Page]` in the Center Section window to select this text.
8. Press Del.
9. Choose OK to close the Footer dialog box.
10. Choose OK to close the Page Setup dialog box.
11. Print the worksheet, and you will see the footer.

Objective 7: Use Print Preview

Because a worksheet is actually one large grid of cells, you may have difficulty visualizing what a sheet will look like when you print it. Choose the **F**ile, Print Pre**v**iew command, or click the Print Preview button on the Standard toolbar whenever you want to see what a worksheet will look like when you print it. The sheet will be displayed in the Print Preview window (see figure 5.18). Excel's **F**ile, Print Pre**v**iew command enables you to view and arrange your sheet (or a print area) before you print it.

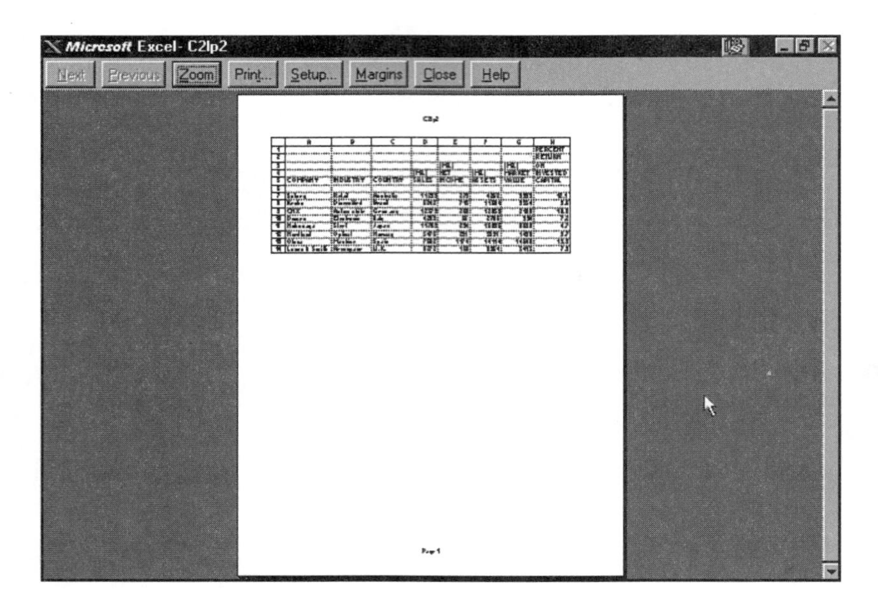

Figure 5.18 The Preview window.

Remember: Defining a print area is necessary only if you choose to print only selected areas of the entire worksheet. In Print Preview, you can see what the document will look like on the page. The Preview feature also includes buttons that enable you to change the margins of the document, change column width, and zoom in on a section of the document to view a section up close. Table 5.4 lists the functions of the buttons displayed at the top of the Preview window.

Table 5.4 The Print Preview Buttons

Button	Function
Next	View the following page (if available).
Previous	View the preceding page (if available).
Zoom	Magnify or reduce the view of the page.
Prin**t**	Display the Print dialog box.
Setup	Display the Page Setup dialog box.
Margins	Display or hide the adjusting handles to change the margins or column widths.
Close	Return to the active sheet.
Help	Obtain help on using Print Preview.

Scrolling

Preview mode
Mode in which you see an overview of the print area showing you what the page will look like when printed.

The **N**ext and **P**revious buttons located at the top of the Preview window enable you to move from one page to the next in *Preview mode*. If you are previewing a one-page document, the **N**ext and **P**revious buttons are dimmed. If you are previewing multiple pages, the **N**ext button is available only if a page follows the page you are viewing. The **P**revious button is available only if a page precedes the page you are viewing.

Zooming

In Preview mode, you may not be able to see the exact detail of your document. If you need a close-up view of the document, you can zoom in and view enlarged sections of it.

Previewing Your Worksheet

In this tutorial, you see what the C2lp2 worksheet will look like before you print. Follow these steps:

1. Choose **F**ile, Print Pre**v**iew. The document appears in the Preview window.
2. Remain in Print Preview mode for the next tutorial.

You can also Zoom when you are in Print Preview, as you learn in the next tutorial.

Zooming in Preview Mode

In this tutorial, you use the Zoom feature on the C2lp2 worksheet in Print Preview mode. If you have not already done so, complete the preceding tutorial before starting this tutorial. Follow these steps:

1. Position the mouse pointer over the section you want to see enlarged, and click once. (The mouse pointer changes to a magnifying glass when positioned over any part of the document.)
2. Use the vertical and horizontal scroll bars to move to other sections while maintaining the enlarged view.
3. Click the left mouse button once to return to the full-page view.
4. Click the **C**lose button to exit Print Preview mode and return to the active document.

You can adjust the top margin on the Print Preview window and see how the new margin will look. This technique is illustrated in the next tutorial.

Adjusting the Top Margin

In this tutorial, you adjust the C2lp2 worksheet's top margin on the Preview window. Follow these steps:

1. Choose File, Print Preview. The document appears in the Preview window.
2. Click the Margins button if the margin lines are not showing on-screen.
3. Place the mouse pointer on the handle (the black square) on the top margin line. The pointer will change shape to a black double-headed arrow (see figure 5.19).

Pointer on top of margin handle

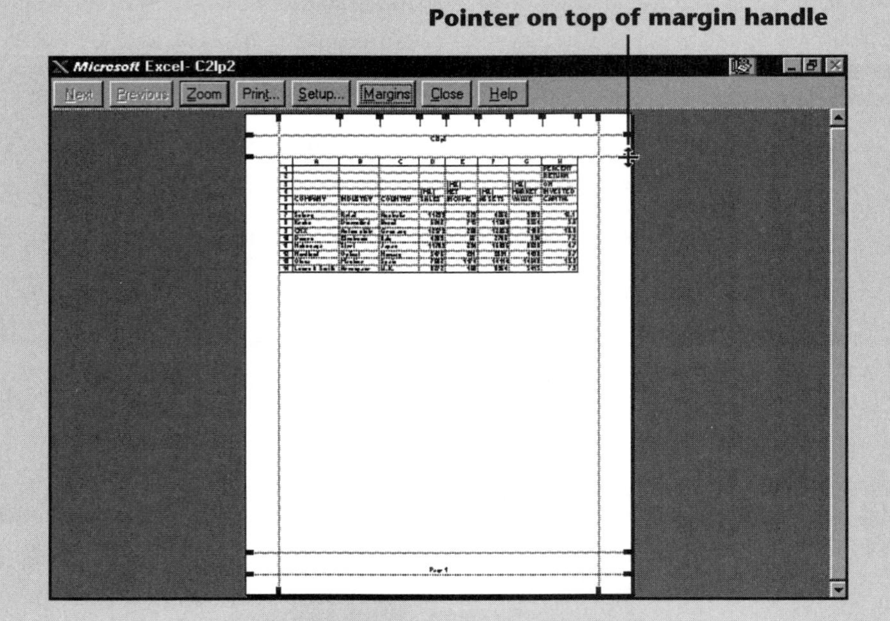

Figure 5.19 The Preview window with the margins turned on and the margin adjusting pointer showing on the top margin.

4. With the mouse pointer on the handle, press and hold down the left mouse button while you drag the handle down two or three inches. Release the mouse button.
5. Click the Print button to see how changing the top margin changes the location of the worksheet on the printout.

Objective 8: Break a Worksheet into Pages by Inserting Manual Page Breaks

Manual page break Determines the end of a page; inserted with a command.

If you select for printing an area that cannot fit on a single page, Excel inserts automatic page breaks to divide the worksheet into separate pages. A page break appears on-screen as a dashed line between the end of one page and the beginning of the next page. If you are not satisfied with the location of the automatic page break, you have the option of inserting manual page breaks. A manual page break enables you to control where a page ends. After you insert a manual page break, the automatic page breaks readjust for the following pages. To insert a page break, you select the cell below and to the right of the location where you want the page to break. The selected cell becomes the upper left corner of a new page. After you choose the **I**nsert, Page **B**reak command, a manual page break appears above and to the left of the active cell. Manual page breaks appear onscreen as boldfaced, dashed lines.

To insert only a horizontal page break, you select the entire row that you want at the top edge of a new page. (Click the row number heading to select the entire row.) The page break is inserted above the selected row. To insert only a vertical page break, you select the entire column that is to the right of where you want to insert the page break. (Click the column letter heading to select the entire column.) The selected column will be placed at the left edge of the next page. In figure 5.20, a manual horizontal page break was inserted above the Expenses section.

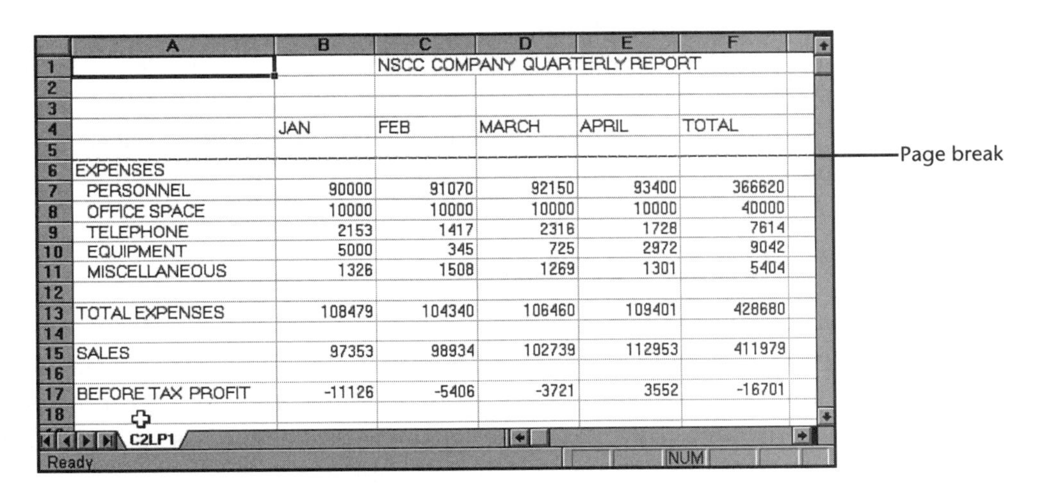

	A	B	C	D	E	F
1			NSCC COMPANY QUARTERLY REPORT			
2						
3						
4		JAN	FEB	MARCH	APRIL	TOTAL
5						
6	EXPENSES					
7	PERSONNEL	90000	91070	92150	93400	366620
8	OFFICE SPACE	10000	10000	10000	10000	40000
9	TELEPHONE	2153	1417	2316	1728	7614
10	EQUIPMENT	5000	345	725	2972	9042
11	MISCELLANEOUS	1326	1508	1269	1301	5404
12						
13	TOTAL EXPENSES	108479	104340	106460	109401	428680
14						
15	SALES	97353	98934	102739	112953	411979
16						
17	BEFORE TAX PROFIT	-11126	-5406	-3721	3552	-16701
18						

Figure 5.20
A manual page break.

You can delete a manual page break by selecting the cell below or to the right of the page break intersection. If the correct cell is selected, the **I**nsert menu displays the Remove Page **B**reak command rather than the Page **B**reak command. An automatic page break cannot be removed.

Inserting a Horizontal Page Break

In this tutorial, you insert a horizontal page break between rows 12 and 13 in the C2lp2 worksheet. Follow these steps:

1. Select the entire row that will be immediately below the inserted page break. (Click the row 13 heading number to select the entire row.)
2. Open the **I**nsert menu, and choose the Page **B**reak command.
3. To remove the horizontal page break, select the entire row below where you inserted the page break. (Click the row number 13 to select the entire row.) Choose the **I**nsert, Remove Page **B**reak command.

5

You insert and remove vertical page breaks using a similar technique.

Inserting a Vertical Page Break

In this tutorial, you insert only a vertical page break between columns B and C in the C2lp2 worksheet. Follow these steps:

1. Select the entire column to the right of where you want to insert the page break. (Click the column C heading to select the entire column.)
2. Choose **I**nsert, Page **B**reak.
3. To remove the vertical page break, select the entire column to the right of where you inserted the page break. (Click the column C heading.) Choose the **I**nsert, Remove Page **B**reak command.

You can remove all manual page breaks in a worksheet after the entire worksheet is selected. Select the entire worksheet by clicking the Select All button, which is located above the row 1 heading and to the left of the column A heading. Open the **I**nsert menu, and choose the Remove Page **B**reak command. All manual page breaks disappear.

Objective 9: Print Worksheets

After setting up the printer and document, you are ready to execute the **F**ile, **P**rint command. This command controls the number of copies you print, the number of pages, and the quality of the printing. The Print dialog box is set up to print one copy of all pages of the worksheet unless you select other options. The Print options are described in Table 5.5.

Table 5.5 Print Options

Option	Description
Selectio**n**	Prints a selected range.
Selecte**d** Sheet(s)	Prints the selected worksheet(s)—usually the worksheet on which you are working.
Entire Workbook	Prints all the sheets in the workbook.
Copies	Specifies the number of copies to print.
All	Prints all the pages indicated in the Print What area (usually what you want to do).
Pages **f**rom and **t**o	Text boxes that enable you to define the first page you want to print (**f**rom) through the last page (**t**o).

A shortcut for printing is the Print button on the Standard toolbar. You can bypass the Print dialog box and print one copy of the active sheet by clicking this button.

Printing Multiple Copies of Your Document

In this tutorial, you print three copies of the C2lp2 worksheet. Follow these steps:

1. Make sure that the C2lp2 worksheet is open.
2. Choose **F**ile, **P**rint. The Print dialog box appears (see figure 5.21).

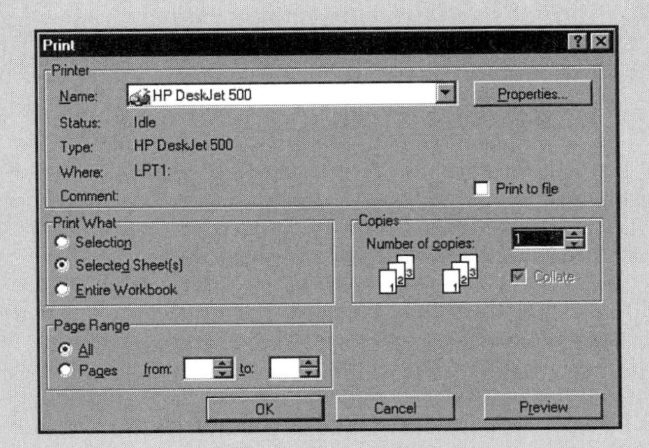

Figure 5.21 The Print dialog box.

3. Click the up-arrow button at the right of the Number of **C**opies text box to change the number in the box to 3.
4. To print, choose OK, or press Enter.

Chapter Summary

In this chapter, you have learned to rename, move, copy, add, and delete worksheets in workbooks. This chapter also introduces you to many aspects of viewing and printing in Excel. You have learned how to view your document in zoomed (magnified or reduced) view; how to control the way a page is set up before you print; and how to insert and remove manual page breaks, define print areas, and add headers and footers to a document. You have also learned about Print Preview and the options included in Preview mode for zooming.

The following chapter introduces you to charting, which is one of Excel's most exciting and powerful features. In Chapter 6, "Charting Data," you learn how to create a chart as a separate document and how to create a chart on a worksheet. You also learn how to change to another chart type, format a chart, and print a chart.

Checking Your Skills

True/False

For each of the following, circle *T* or *F* to indicate whether the statement is true or false.

T F **1.** The **W**indow, **Z**oom command changes the way a worksheet prints.

T F **2.** You cannot have two workbooks open at the same time in Excel.

T F **3.** Before you can print a portion of a worksheet, you must first define that portion as a print area.

T F **4.** A page break in your worksheet appears on-screen as a solid double line.

T F **5.** Manual page breaks cannot be removed.

T F **6.** The **Z**oom command enables you to view a larger area of your worksheet on-screen.

T F **7.** The default print orientation in Excel is **L**andscape.

T F **8.** You cannot delete automatic page breaks.

T F **9.** The **F**ile, Page Set**u**p command enables you to change the default **T**op Margin setting.

T F **10.** Excel can print a worksheet only on standard 8 1/2 by 11-inch paper.

Multiple Choice

In the blank provided, write the letter of the correct answer for each of the following.

_____ **1.** The **P**rint command is found in the _______ menu.

a. **W**indow

b. **O**utput

c. **O**ptions

d. **F**ile

_____ **2.** The button that is located above the row 1 heading and to the left of the column A heading is the _______ button.

a. Insert

b. Select All

c. Row & Column Print

d. none of the above

_____ **3.** The _______ command enables you to specify the number of copies you print.

a. **O**ptions, **O**utput

b. **W**orksheet, **C**opies

c. **F**ile, **P**rint

d. none of the above

_____ **4.** If you cannot print all the columns in your worksheet on one page, you should select _______ orientation.

a. **L**andscape

b. Po**r**trait

c. wrap

d. **5**0% Zoom

_____ **5.** Automatic page breaks cannot be _______.

a. seen on-screen

b. removed

c. defaulted

d. none of the above

_____ **6.** The _______ button in the Page Setup dialog box enables you to specify text to be printed at the top of each page.

a. **O**ptions

b. C**u**stom Footer

c. **C**ustom Header

d. **T**itle

_____ **7.** The command that enables you to set a print area in your worksheet is in the _______ menu.

a. **F**ile

b. **T**ools

c. **P**rint

d. **O**ptions

_____ **8.** The command that enables you to print multiple copies of your worksheet is in the _______ menu.

a. **F**ile

b. **T**ools

c. **P**rint

d. **O**ptions

_____ **9.** Which of the following commands in Print Preview enables you to see your document enlarged?

a. **E**nlarge

b. **M**agnify

c. En**h**ance

d. **Z**oom

_____ **10.** The command that enables you to insert a page break into your document manually is found in the _______ menu.

a. **F**ile

b. **I**nsert

c. Work**s**pace

d. **O**ptions

Completion

In the blank provided, write the correct answer for each of the following.

1. Manually defining a print _______________ is necessary if you want to print only part of a document.

2. A _______________ is information that prints in the top margin of a worksheet printout.

3. To print a worksheet without the horizontal lines between the rows, you choose the _______________ option in the Page Setup dialog box.

4. To see what a worksheet will look like before you print it, you can use the _______________ command.

5. You can move between open workbooks that you have previously saved on disk by clicking their names in the _______________ menu.

6. Before you can print a portion of a worksheet, you must first define that portion as a print _______________.

7. _______________ page breaks cannot be removed.

8. The **P**rint command is found in the _______________ menu.

9. The print orientation that enables you to print the greatest number of columns on one page is the _______________ orientation.

10. The **P**rint, _______________ command enables you to view your document before you print it.

Applying Your Skills

Review Exercises

Exercise 1: Printing a Worksheet with Modified Print Settings

Open the NSCC QUARTERLY REPORT worksheet (C2lp1) that you built in Continuing Project 1 at the end of Chapter 2. Print two copies without gridlines. Print one copy without gridlines and with the column letters and row numbers on the printout. Close without saving revisions to the workbook.

Exercise 2: Printing a Worksheet with Manual Page Breaks

Print the NSCC QUARTERLY REPORT worksheet (C2lp1) with a vertical page break between columns C and D. Remove the vertical page break, and print the worksheet with a page break between the TOTAL EXPENSES row and the SALES row. Then remove the horizontal page break. Close without saving revisions to the workbook.

Exercise 3: Practicing the Worksheet Insert, Delete, Rename, Copy, and Move Commands

Open two new workbooks to use for practice. Name them **W1** and **W2**, and save them on disk. Try inserting, deleting, and renaming the sheets in one of the workbooks. Type your name in cell A1 of Sheet5 in one of the workbooks. Then copy this sheet to another location within the same workbook. Move the copy to the second workbook, and place it between Sheets 8 and 9. Copy the sheet so that it is the only sheet in a new workbook.

Exercise 4: Using the Page Setup Dialog Box

Open the workbook that you created in Review Exercise 2 at the end of Chapter 2 (C2sp2). Print the worksheet.

Then use the **F**ile, Page Set**u**p command to access the Sheet tabbed dialog box. In the Sheet tabbed dialog box, click the Row and Co**l**umn Headings check box. Now print your worksheet.

Increase the width of column E to 20. Using the **T**ools, **O**ptions command, access the View tabbed dialog box. Click the Fo**r**mulas check box, and then click OK. Print the worksheet. Close without saving the workbook.

Exercise 5: Using Zoom in Print Preview

Open the workbook that you created in Review Exercise 2 at the end of Chapter 2 (C2sp2). Use the Zoom feature in Print Preview to change the magnification of your worksheet.

Continuing Projects

Project 1: Printing a Wide Worksheet

Open the NSCC QUARTERLY REPORT worksheet (C2lp1) that you built in Continuing Project 1 at the end of Chapter 2. Rename the sheet with a meaningful tab name. Expand the column widths of columns B, C, D, E, and F to a width of 18. Preview the printout of the worksheet, and then print it.

Try to delete the automatic page breaks Excel inserts—but don't try for too long! Change the print orientation to Landscape. Preview the printout, and then print the worksheet. Close without saving changes to the workbook.

Project 2: Printing a Worksheet with Headers and Footers

Open the NSCC QUARTERLY REPORT worksheet (C2lp1) that you built in Continuing Project 1 at the end of Chapter 2. Create headers and footers that contain information you want on the printout. Then print the worksheet with these headers and footers. Delete the headers and footers, and print the worksheet again. Close without saving changes to the workbook.

Project 3: Changing the Margins of a Worksheet

Open the First workbook. Then choose File, Page Setup to access the Margins tabbed dialog box. In the Margins tabbed dialog box, try moving the worksheet on the printout by using different top and left margin settings. (You can see the results in Print Preview; you do not need to actually print the worksheet.) Experiment with different margin settings until the worksheet prints (approximately) centered on the printout. Close without saving changes to the workbook.

Chapter 6

Charting Data

People can understand and interpret worksheet data much faster if it is represented graphically. A chart provides a graphical format that has a greater visual impact than rows of numbers in a worksheet. A chart can communicate results that people recognize at a glance. Without a chart, the viewer must analyze each piece of data to draw a conclusion. Charts show the "big picture." Because charts are also fun to make in Excel, you're going to enjoy this chapter.

Embedded chart
A chart within the worksheet that supplies data for the chart.

ChartWizard
A charting tool used to guide you through creating, formatting, and modifying a chart.

Charting the data in an Excel worksheet is a simple process, and Excel offers two ways to create a chart. You can create a chart as a separate sheet in your workbook, or you can create a chart that is included on the same sheet (workbook page) as the worksheet that provides data for the chart. Charts within a worksheet are called *embedded charts*. You create and embed them in a worksheet by using Excel's *ChartWizard*, a charting tool that guides you step-by-step through the process.

Excel builds your chart from the worksheet data you select. The chart is a graph of that data and is linked to the selected data in your worksheet. If you change the underlying worksheet data, the chart updates automatically to reflect the change. After you create a chart, Excel offers many capabilities for enhancing and editing the chart. You can choose from among many different chart types, including column, bar, area, line, pie, scatter, radar, and surface charts. Excel also offers three-dimensional chart types. Each chart type has variations in format. This chapter covers the steps involved in creating a chart; selecting a chart type; and enhancing, formatting, modifying, and printing a chart.

Objectives

By the time, you have finished this chapter, you will have learned to

1. Understand the Most Commonly Used Chart Types
2. Create Separate and Embedded Charts
3. Move and Size an Embedded Chart in a Worksheet
4. Create Different Types of Charts
5. Enhance and Format Charts
6. Print a Chart

Objective 1: Understand the Most Commonly Used Chart Types

Charts come in a variety of basic types, and within these types, more variations exist. Excel can produce 15 types of charts with variations. In business, the most commonly used types of charts are line charts, column charts, bar charts, and pie charts. This chapter concentrates on these four types of charts.

Line charts, column charts, and bar charts can show multiple sets of data and usually are used to show trends or cycles over time or to make comparisons between two or more sets of data. For example, you can use line charts to compare monthly sales in two different years or to compare the budgets of three or four departments in an organization. Line charts are best used when you have large amounts of data, such as sales on the New York Stock Exchange. Column charts are good for making comparisons of smaller amounts of data. Bar charts are helpful when the data has both negative and positive values. Pie charts can chart only one set of values, such as monthly sales for one year. Pie charts, however, are especially useful for showing how various parts (shown as "slices of the pie") contribute to a whole.

Identifying the X- and Y-Axes and the Plot Area

X-axis
The horizontal (category) axis on a chart.

Y-axis
The vertical (value) axis on a chart.

Plot area
The area on the chart containing the pie, lines, columns, or bars.

Line, column, and bar charts are charted using two solid lines that are marked off in units. The horizontal axis is called the *x-axis* (or the *category axis*). In business charts, the x-axis usually represents units of time, such as days, months, and years. These units are often referred to as the x-axis labels. The *y-axis* is the vertical (or *value*) axis. It shows measured units, such as dollars, number of employees, or units of a product produced. Three-dimensional charts have a third axis, the z-axis.

The space on a chart where the pie, lines, columns, or bars are drawn or plotted is called the *plot area*. Charts usually have a main chart title, and the x- and y-axes can also have titles. When multiple groups of data are plotted on the same graph—for example, monthly sales in each of the last three years—a *legend* explaining what each set of bars or lines represents is helpful and is usually included. Pie charts are not plotted with x- and y-axes. Pie charts are sometimes

Legend
A guide, displayed near the chart, that identifies the data in the chart.

exploded (one or two slices are "pulled out" of the pie to emphasize them). With Excel, you can create all these charts. Figures 6.1 and 6.2 show a column chart and an exploded pie chart created using Excel.

Figure 6.1
A column chart.

Chart Wizard button
Drawing button
Chart title
Plot area
Legend
Y-axis
Y-axis title
X-axis
X-axis title
X-axis labels

Figure 6.2
An exploded pie chart.

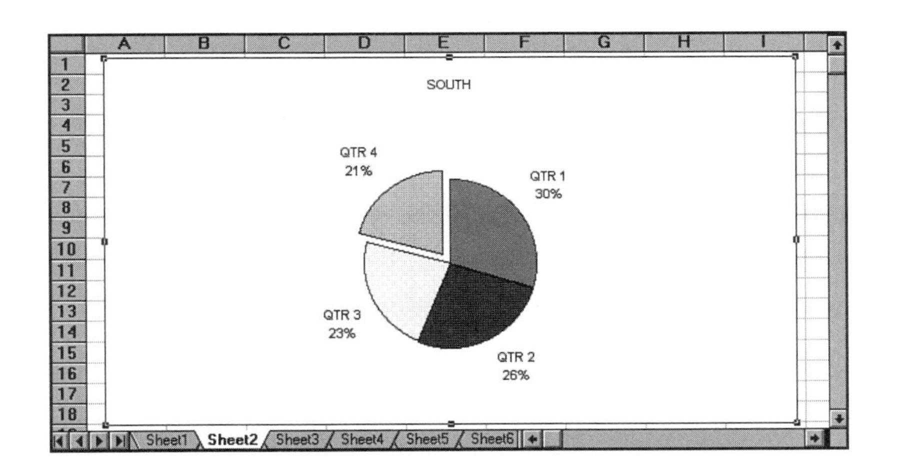

Objective 2: Create Separate and Embedded Charts

Charts are based on selected data in a worksheet. After you select the data, creating a chart in a separate *chart sheet* can be as simple as pressing a single key. Excel displays the selected data in a column chart, the default chart type. Excel automatically "decides" how to plot the chart and how to set up the x- and y-axes. Excel plots the chart based on the size of the numbers in the worksheet and the layout of the selected worksheet data. Later in this chapter, you learn how to change the default chart type and layout and use the *Chart Shortcut Menus* to enhance your chart with formatting. You can keep Excel charts on separate chart sheets in a workbook, or you can embed the chart in the worksheet that contains the data from which the chart was produced.

Saving Charts

Chart shortcut menus
A set of menus, used for editing and formatting charts; they appear when you select a chart and right-click a part of it.

Chart sheet
A workbook sheet that contains a chart but not a worksheet.

A chart embedded in a worksheet gets saved when you save the workbook that contains the worksheet. A separate chart gets saved when you save the related workbook. If you have made changes in the worksheet data on which a chart is based, the chart will be automatically updated (changed) before it is saved.

Entering a Worksheet to Use for Charting Practice

All tutorials in this chapter use the QTRSALES worksheet shown in figure 6.3. Enter the QTRSALES worksheet as shown, and save it in a file on your disk. Name the worksheet's tab QTRSALES. Because the tutorials build on each other, complete them in order. If you cannot complete all the tutorials in one session, be sure to save your work before exiting Excel. Remember, your chart is saved when you save its workbook.

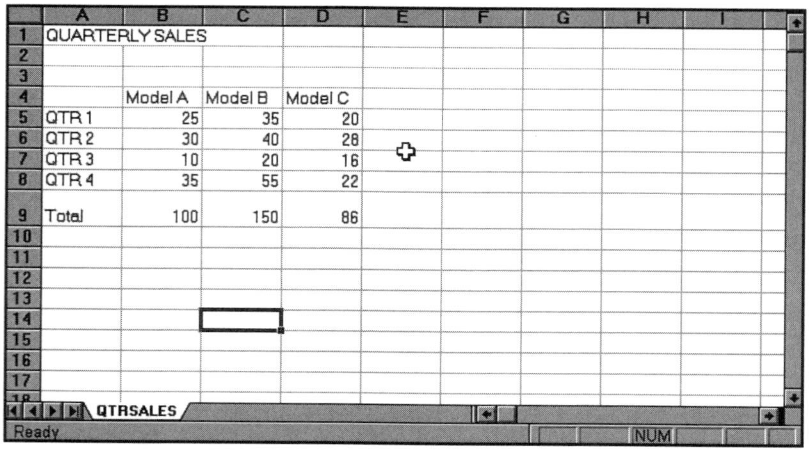

	A	B	C	D
1	QUARTERLY SALES			
2				
3				
4		Model A	Model B	Model C
5	QTR 1	25	35	20
6	QTR 2	30	40	28
7	QTR 3	10	20	16
8	QTR 4	35	55	22
9	Total	100	150	86

QTRSALES

Ready NUM

Figure 6.3
The QTRSALES worksheet.

Understanding the General Procedure for Creating Charts

To create a chart, you always follow these general steps:

1. Select the worksheet data that you want to chart.
2. Decide whether you want the Excel default chart and orientation, or a customized chart (something you learn by experience). Second, decide whether you want an embedded chart or a separate chart sheet.
3. Press F11 if you want Excel to create a chart using the default chart type.

   or

   Click the ChartWizard button on the Standard toolbar (refer to figure 6.1) to create an embedded or a customized chart. Indicate (by clicking and dragging) where in your worksheet you want the chart embedded. When the ChartWizard is displayed, enter your preferences, and then click the ChartWizard Finish button.
4. If you want to change the finished chart, select the chart by clicking it. Then click the right mouse button to access the shortcut menu that enables you to edit and enhance your chart. Where you click determines which

menu appears. Excel displays different shortcut menus when you click a grid line, a chart axis, or a plot area.

Creating Your First Chart Using Excel's Charting Defaults

In this tutorial, you create a default chart from the QTRSALES worksheet. To create the chart on a separate page in your workbook (called a chart sheet), follow these steps:

1. Select the range of cells from A4 to D8.
2. Press F11.

The chart created by using the default settings appears on a new chart sheet, which is inserted into your workbook to the left of the worksheet on which the chart is based (see figure 6.4).

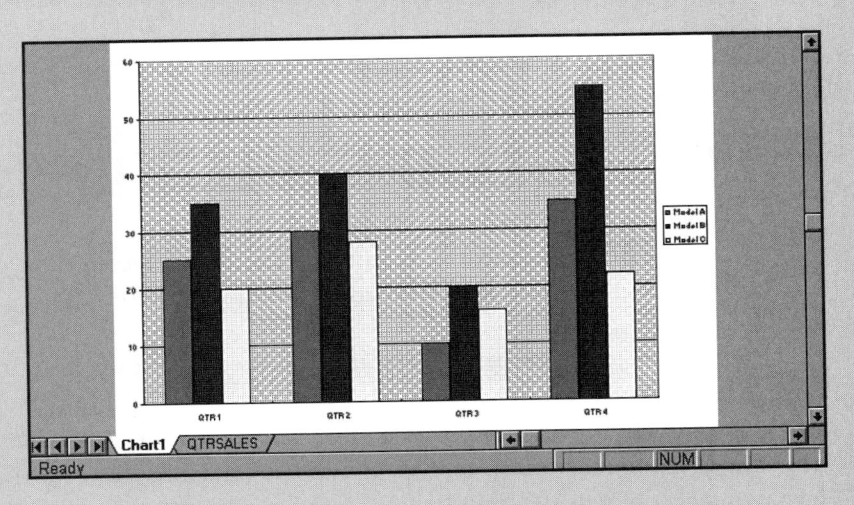

Figure 6.4
The default chart for the selected data.

This new chart is linked to the data it was created from and changes when you change the worksheet data.

If you have problems... Depending on the optional settings in your version of Excel, you may see the small Chart toolbar on your screen. Click the Close button in the upper right corner of the Chart toolbar to close the Chart toolbar.

Understanding Excel's Rules for Creating a Default Chart

Default chart
The chart Excel automatically produces based on the way the data in your selection is organized.

Excel draws a chart for you from the data you select in your worksheet. To draw the chart, Excel uses certain rules based on how the data is laid out (oriented) in the worksheet. These rules produce the *default chart*. The data orientation determines which cells Excel uses for the category axis (the labels along the bottom, or x-axis) and which cells are used for the legend. In most cases, Excel charts come out correctly without intervention from you.

Excel charts the selected data based on the following assumptions:

- The category (x-) axis runs along the longest side of the selection. If your selection is taller than it is wide (more rows than columns), the category labels are taken from the leftmost column in the selection (see figure 6.5). If the selection is wider than it is tall (more columns than rows), the category labels are taken from the first row of the selection.

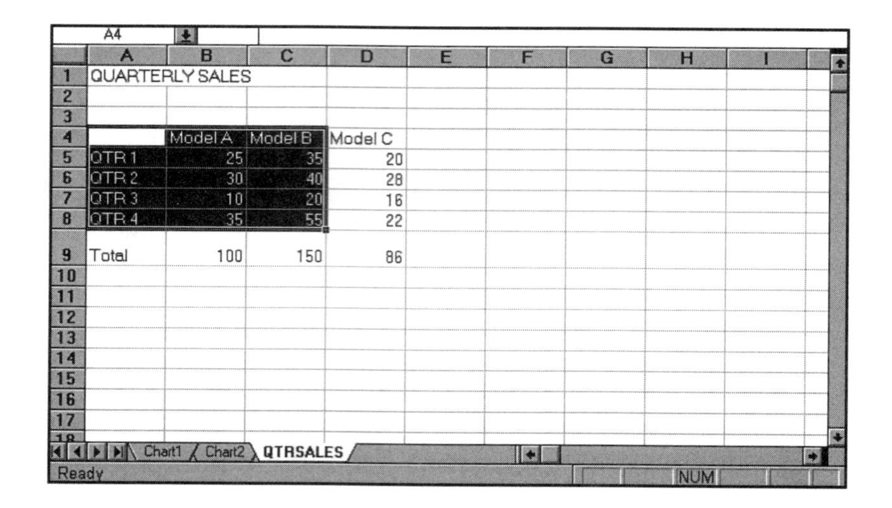

Figure 6.5 A selection that is taller than it is wide, so labels are taken from column A.

- If Excel is not sure how to lay out and plot the selected data, a dialog box appears and requests more information about plotting data.

Because you are just beginning to chart, don't worry about memorizing the rules; they will mean more to you after you have created a few charts. If you don't like the default, just use it as a "first cut" at a chart. You can always modify the default chart with the ChartWizard or the charting shortcut menus. If necessary, you can delete the chart and start over. To delete an embedded chart, click the chart to select it, and press Del. To delete a chart on a separate chart sheet, click the chart sheet tab, right-click, and choose Del from the shortcut menu.

Creating an Embedded Chart on a Worksheet

In the first tutorial, you learned how to create a chart as a separate chart sheet. A chart on a separate page is more suitable for a presentation and can be printed without printing the worksheet data too. Many times, however, you will want to have your worksheet data and its chart on the same page. This way you can show the chart within the context of the worksheet data that it represents. You use the ChartWizard to create embedded charts. When you print the worksheet, the embedded chart also prints. Just as charts on a separate sheet can be any one of Excel's 15 chart types, you have the same options with embedded charts. You can also have many embedded charts in one worksheet.

To remove an embedded chart from a worksheet, click it to select the chart (a border with little black squares appears around the selection), and press Del.

Using the ChartWizard

The ChartWizard button looks like a magic wand inside a chart (refer to figure 6.1). Clicking the ChartWizard button begins the process of creating a chart. The ChartWizard guides you with a series of dialog boxes. When creating a new chart, the ChartWizard uses a five-step method.

Data series
A collection of data from a worksheet; the data your chart represents.

Step 1 shows you the cell range you have selected as the data to chart and allows you to correct the range. (Excel calls this range the *data series*.) In the four remaining steps, ChartWizard prompts you to select a chart type and format it, to change the way the data is plotted, and to add a legend and titles.

If you have problems... When you click the ChartWizard button on the Standard toolbar, the ChartWizard dialog box may not appear. Before the ChartWizard can begin its work, it needs to know the range of cells in your worksheet that will contain the embedded chart. You must first click and drag over this range before the ChartWizard dialog box appears.

The five steps of the ChartWizard are as follows:

1. The ChartWizard displays the range of selected data to chart (see figure 6.6). If necessary, you can correct the range.

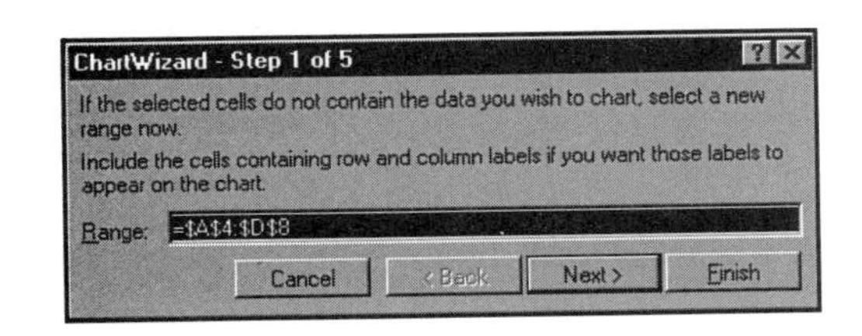

Figure 6.6 Step 1 of the ChartWizard: Specifying the range of data to be charted.

   If you click the **F**inish button, the chart is produced using all the default settings just as if you had pressed F11 except that the chart appears in the worksheet, not in a separate sheet.

2. The ChartWizard prompts you to select the type of chart you want (see figure 6.7).

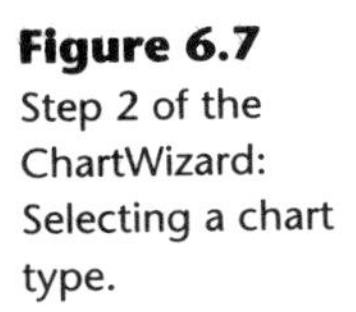

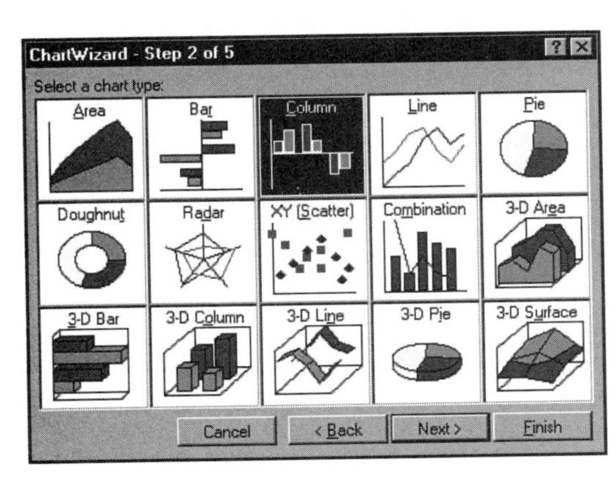

Figure 6.7 Step 2 of the ChartWizard: Selecting a chart type.

3. The ChartWizard prompts you to select from the predefined formats (varieties) available for the chart type you selected in step 2 (see figure 6.8).

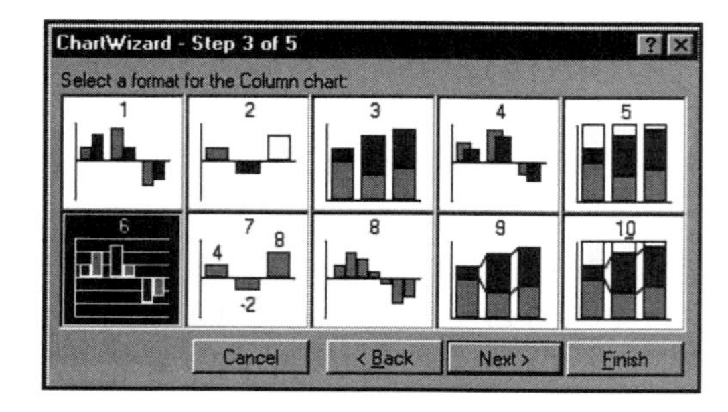

Figure 6.8
Step 3 of the ChartWizard: Selecting a chart type predefined format.

4. The ChartWizard enables you to control the way the data is plotted (see figure 6.9). The left portion of the ChartWizard window displays a sample of the chart as it will appear based on your choices. You should check the sample chart to make sure that the creation process is going according to your plan.

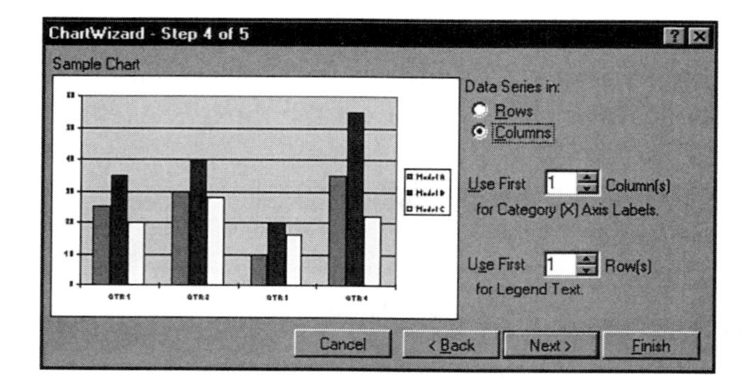

Figure 6.9
Step 4 of the ChartWizard: Selecting how to plot the data.

Attached text
Text on a chart (such as the chart title or axes titles) that cannot be moved.

5. The ChartWizard prompts you to add text to the chart; for example, you may add a chart title and titles as *attached text* to the x- and the y-axes (see figure 6.10). If you want to add a title, click the appropriate text box, and type the title. Again, check the sample chart to be sure that your chart appears as you want it.

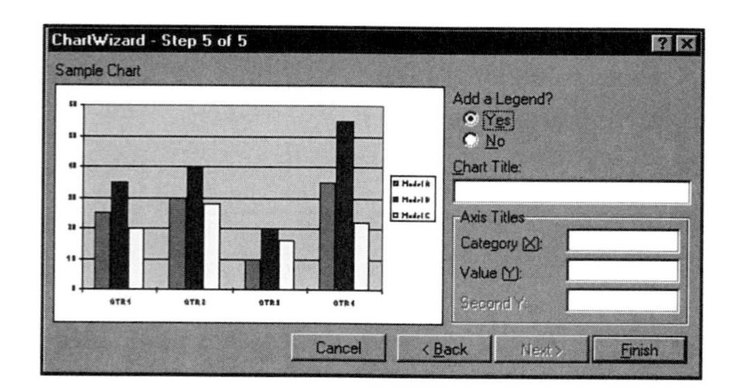

Figure 6.10
Step 5 of the ChartWizard: Entering titles.

When the ChartWizard finishes, the chart is embedded in the worksheet. Later, you learn how to use two of the ChartWizard steps to edit an existing chart.

Each ChartWizard window contains buttons that you can use to move around in the five ChartWizard dialog boxes. Table 6.1 lists the function of each ChartWizard button. The OK button appears only when you use the ChartWizard to modify an existing chart.

Table 6.1 ChartWizard Buttons

Button	Function
Next>	Moves to the next ChartWizard step.
<Back	Returns to the preceding ChartWizard step.
Finish	Creates the chart displayed in the ChartWizard sample area and exits the ChartWizard. (This button, available in each step and in the early steps, creates a chart according to the default or uses any choices that have been selected.)
Cancel	Stops the ChartWizard and returns to your worksheet without creating a chart.

Designating the Chart Area in the Worksheet

As explained, when you create an embedded chart using the ChartWizard, you must first indicate where in the worksheet you want to place (embed) the chart. When you click the ChartWizard, you are prompted in the status bar to click and drag in the worksheet to create a chart (see figure 6.11).

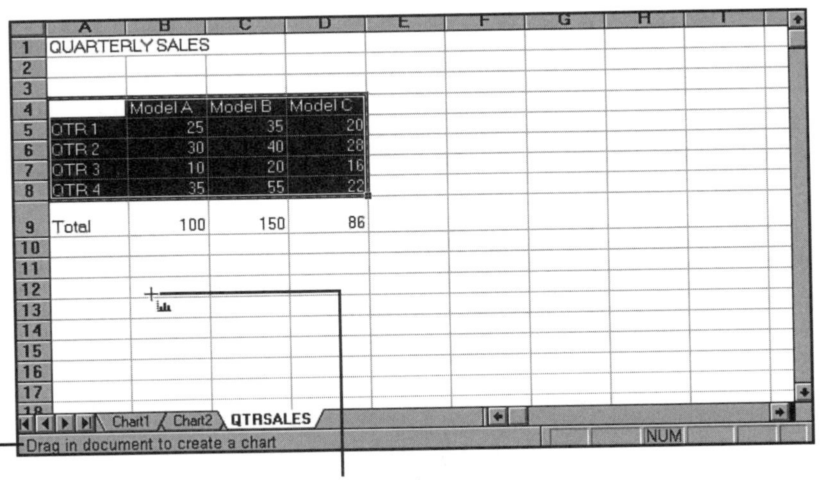

Figure 6.11 The ChartWizard pointer and the Status bar prompt.

You position the mouse pointer (shaped like a cross hair and a tiny chart) on the worksheet cell where you want the upper left corner of the chart to start. Press the left mouse button, hold it down, and drag diagonally toward the lower right corner of the area where you want the chart to appear. A border surrounds the area that the chart will occupy (see figure 6.12). Release the mouse button.

When you release the mouse button after designating the chart area, the first (Step 1 of 5) ChartWizard dialog box appears. When you complete the ChartWizard steps, the chart appears, embedded in the area of the worksheet that you dragged the mouse pointer over (see figure 6.13).

	A	B	C	D	E	F	G	H	I
1	QUARTERLY SALES								
2									
3									
4		Model A	Model B	Model C					
5	QTR 1	25	35	20					
6	QTR 2	30	40	28					
7	QTR 3	10	20	16					
8	QTR 4	35	55	22					
9	Total	100	150	86					

QTRSALES

Drag in document to create a chart NUM

Figure 6.12
Selecting an area in which to place the chart.

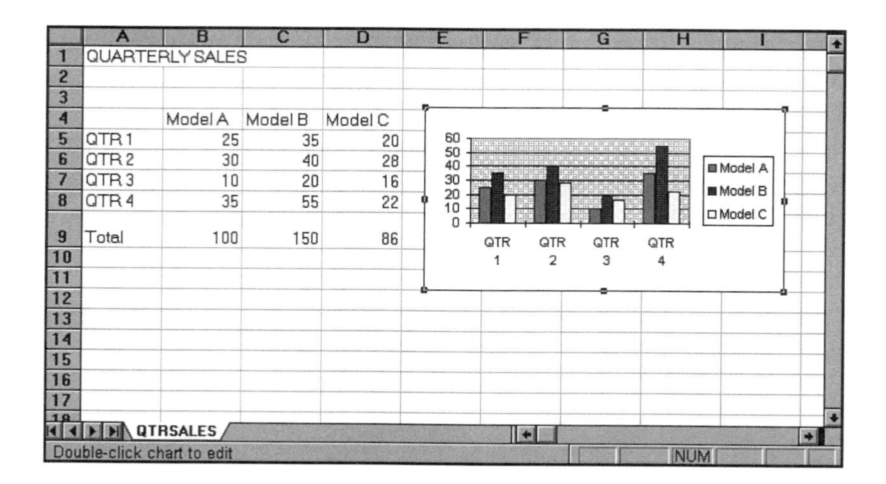

Figure 6.13
The embedded chart.

Creating an Embedded Chart by Using the ChartWizard

In this tutorial, you create a chart from the QTRSALES workbook by using the ChartWizard. Follow these steps:

1. Select the range of cells from A4 to D8.
2. Click the ChartWizard tool on the Standard toolbar.
3. Click and then drag the mouse pointer (looks like a cross hair) over cells A11 to F17 to define the location for the embedded chart. Release the mouse button. Figure 6.14 shows the selected area.

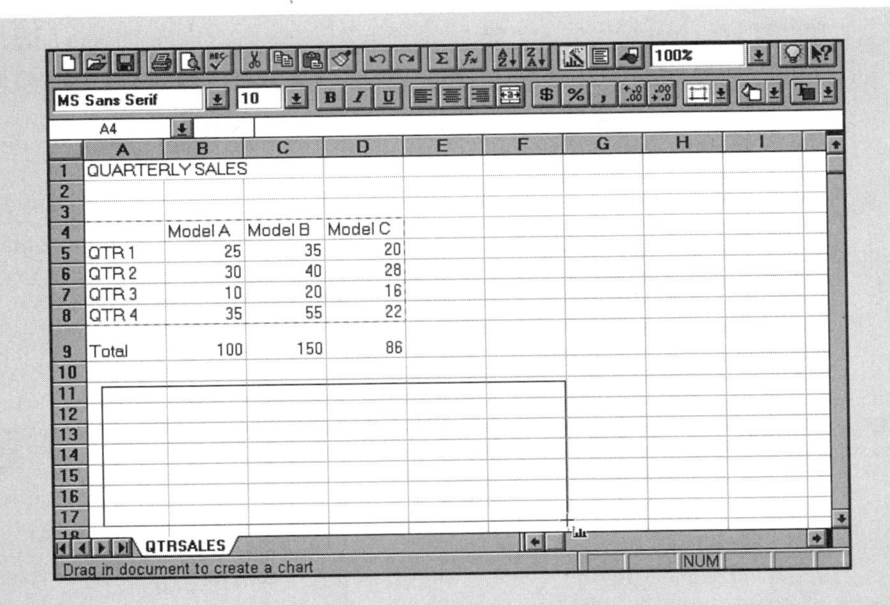

Figure 6.14 The selected area.

The Step 1 of 5 ChartWizard dialog box appears (refer to figure 6.6).

Note: *If you want the chart in a perfectly square area, hold down* Alt *while you drag the mouse. If you want to align the chart with the worksheet's cell grid lines (so it looks better), hold down* Shift *while you drag the mouse. Remember to release the mouse button before you release the* Alt *or* Shift *key.*

4. Choose the Next> button in the Step 1, Step 2, Step 3, and Step 4 windows.

5. Click the Finish button in the Step 5 window.

The chart appears (see figure 6.15). Notice that it is the same chart that you created on a separate chart sheet in the earlier tutorial.

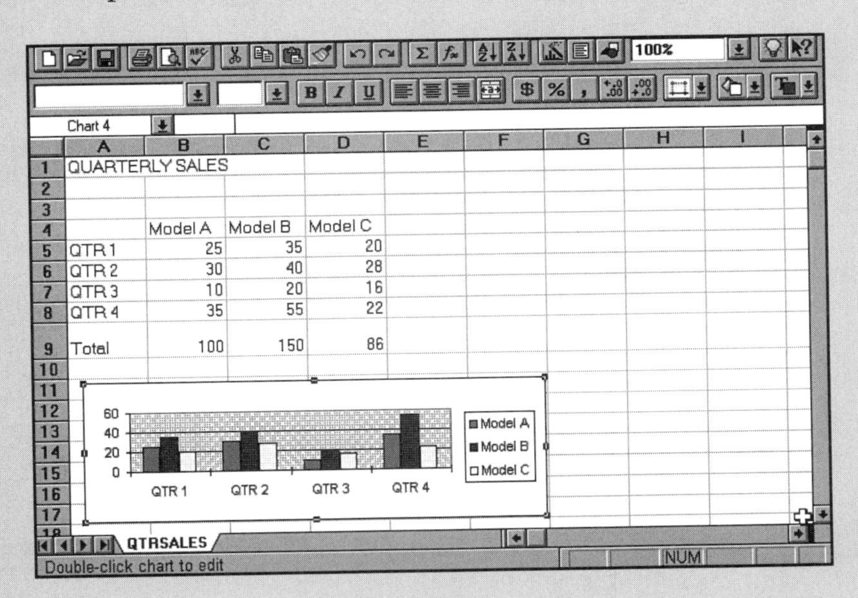

Figure 6.15 The embedded chart.

Keep this workbook open for the following tutorial.

If you have problems... You may find that the y-axis numbers in your embedded chart differ from those in the figures because changing the height of a chart also changes the numbers on the y-axis.

Note: *Because you accepted all the charting defaults, you could have clicked the Finish button in Step 1. Seeing all five of the screens, however, is important.*

Because a chart is a graphical representation of worksheet data, a chart changes when the underlying worksheet data changes. The next tutorial illustrates this concept.

Changing the Worksheet Data on Which a Chart is Based

Charts change as the worksheet data that produces them changes. In this tutorial, you use an embedded chart so that you can immediately see the change. Charts on separate sheets are also linked to their worksheet data and change to reflect changes in their worksheet data.

To watch a chart change as its data changes, follow these steps:

1. Take a good look at your chart. Notice the relative height of the columns and the scale of the y-axis.

2. Type the value **90** in cell B7, and watch the graph as you press Enter.

   Note the change in your chart (see figure 6.16).

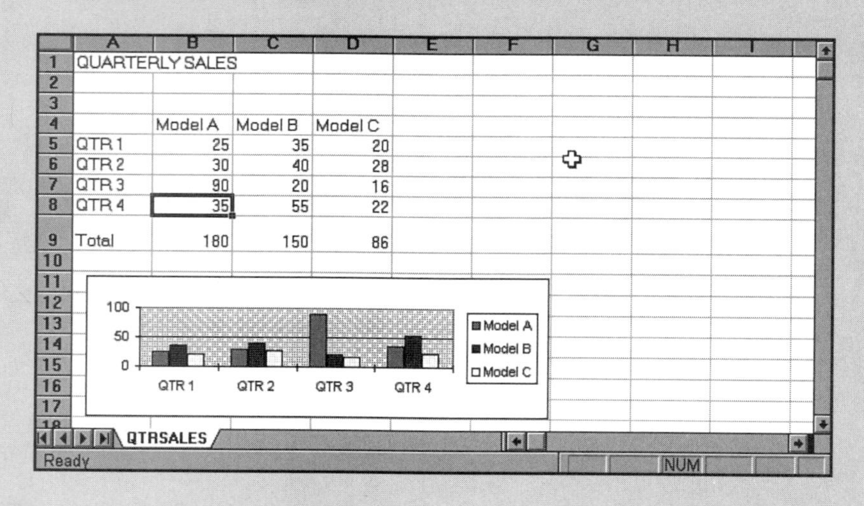

Figure 6.16
The new chart.

3. Change the value in cell B7 back to 10.

   Note the change in your chart.

Keep this workbook open for the following tutorial.

With the ChartWizard you can create embedded charts, as you have already learned. You can also create charts on separate chart sheets, as the following tutorial illustrates.

Creating a Chart on a Separate Sheet by Using the ChartWizard

To create a chart on a separate page of the QTRSALES workbook by using the ChartWizard, follow these steps:

1. Select the range of cells from A4 to D8.
2. Right-click the QTRSALES worksheet tab.
3. From the shortcut menu, choose Insert.
4. Choose Chart.
5. Click OK.

   Steps 1 through 5 of the ChartWizard appear in order.
6. In Step 2, click the Line chart type.
7. In Steps 3 and 4, click the Next> button. In Step 5, click the Finish button.

   A line chart appears in your workbook (see figure 6.17).

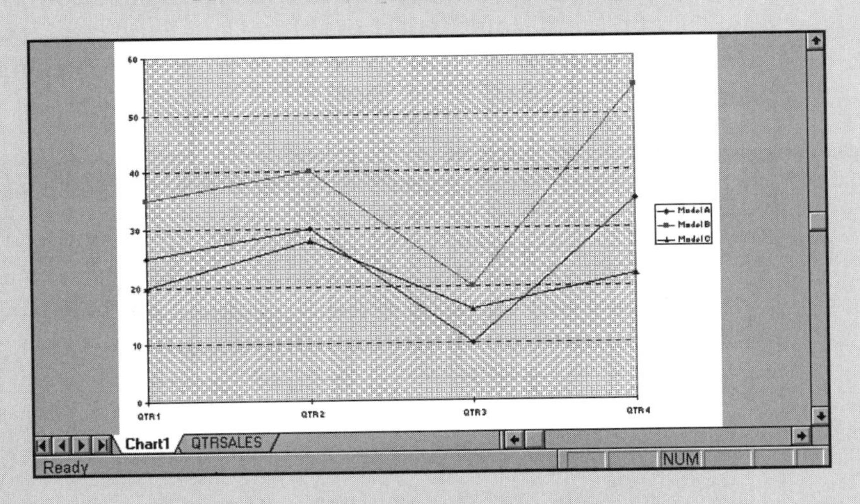

Figure 6.17
The line chart.

8. Click the QTRSALES worksheet tab to return to your worksheet.

Keep this workbook open for the following tutorial.

You can make a chart on a separate sheet using the ChartWizard and edit it using the shortcut menus just as easily as you can make an embedded chart; the techniques are the same. In this book, you learn many of the chart-building techniques using an embedded chart, but you can use the same skills with separate chart sheets.

Copying an Embedded Chart to a Separate Worksheet

To copy the embedded chart from the QTRSALES worksheet to another worksheet, follow these steps:

1. Click the embedded chart to select it.
2. Choose **E**dit, **C**opy (or click the Copy button on the Standard toolbar).
3. Click the tab of Sheet3 (the sheet to which you want to copy the chart).
4. Click any cell in Sheet3, and choose **E**dit, **P**aste (or click the Paste button on the Standard toolbar).

The embedded chart appears in the new worksheet and can be sized and printed if you like.

Keep this workbook open for the following tutorial.

Once you have created a separate chart, you can embed it in a worksheet and vice versa. Excel does not limit you to either embedded or separate charts.

Charting Data Stored in Nonadjoining Areas of a Worksheet

The easiest kind of worksheet data to chart is data in a continuous block of rows and columns. You simply select the block, and Excel creates the chart. But what if you need to graph data that is in two or more nonadjoining ranges on a worksheet?

Selecting Nonadjacent Ranges to Chart

Suppose that you are using the QTRSALES worksheet and you want a column chart of the quarterly sales of Model C. The labels for the columns are in column A. The Model C data in column D is separated from these labels by two columns of data that you don't want in the chart. Follow these steps:

1. Make sure that you select the embedded chart.
2. Clear the embedded chart from the screen by pressing Del.
3. Activate cell D1 to deselect the previously selected range of cells.
4. To select the first set of data, position the cell pointer in cell A4, hold down the left mouse button, and drag to cell A8. Release the mouse button.
5. Select the second set of data by holding down Ctrl as you drag from D4 to cell D8. Then release the mouse button and Ctrl. You should see both blocks of data selected on-screen (see figure 6.18).

Figure 6.18
The selected nonadjacent data.

	A	B	C	D	E	F	G	H	I
1	QUARTERLY SALES								
2									
3									
4		Model A	Model B	Model C					
5	QTR 1	25	35	20					
6	QTR 2	30	40	28					
7	QTR 3	10	20	16					
8	QTR 4	35	55	22					
9	Total	100	150	86					
10									
11									
12									

6 To display the nonadjoining data in a new chart sheet, press F11.

Keep this workbook open for the following tutorial.

Changing the Excel Default Chart Orientation

Earlier in this chapter, you learned that Excel follows several rules to design the layout of your chart. But what do you do if you want to change Excel's default chart orientation? You can easily change a chart orientation when you create the chart using ChartWizard. In the fourth dialog box of the series displayed by ChartWizard (Step 4 of 5), look at the Sample Chart window (see figure 6.19).

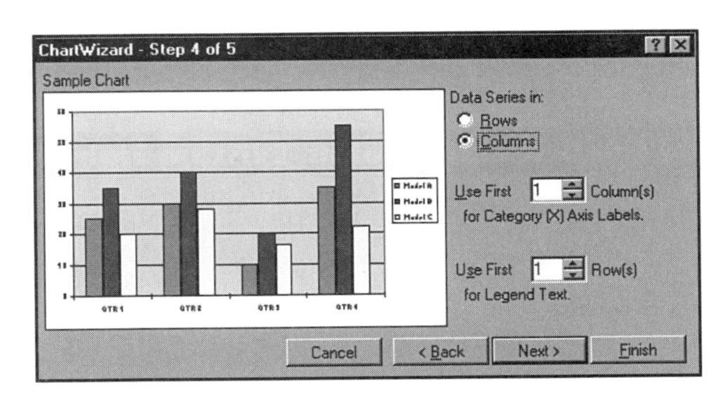

Figure 6.19
The Step 4 dialog box contains the sample chart.

If the default chart from the data is not plotted the way you want, you can easily change to the alternative chart orientation. Click the unselected option button under Data Series in (refer to figure 6.19). You then see Excel's alternative chart displayed in the Sample Chart window. (The data series is the data used to create the chart.) The two option buttons under Data Series control the way the data series is charted. Choose the Next> button to continue creating your chart.

Changing the Excel Default Chart Orientation Using ChartWizard

In this tutorial, you change the default chart orientation when creating a chart in the worksheet. Continue to use the QTRSALES workbook.

Before you begin, clear any embedded chart by selecting the chart and pressing Del. Then select the range of cells from A4 to D8. Follow these steps:

(continues)

6

Changing the Excel Default Chart Orientation Using ChartWizard (continued)

1. Click the ChartWizard tool, and then drag the mouse pointer over cells A11 to F17. The Step 1 of 5 ChartWizard dialog box appears.
2. Choose the Next button in the Step 1, Step 2, and Step 3 dialog boxes.
3. In the Sample Chart window of the Step 4 dialog box, you see the default chart plot.
4. Click the **R**ows option button under Data Series in. The alternative chart appears in the Sample Chart window.

   You may find it helpful to click the **C**olumns option button, study the default chart, and then click the **R**ows option button again so that the differences between the charts become clear to you.
5. Click the **C**olumns option button, and then choose the Next> button.
6. In the Step 5 dialog box, choose **F**inish.

Keep this workbook open for the following tutorial.

Two ChartWizard screens are available to modify an existing embedded chart. The first screen enables you to modify the range of data you want to chart. You use the second screen to change the default orientation of the chart.

Using ChartWizard to Modify the Orientation of an Existing Embedded Chart

Make sure that you open the QTRSALES workbook. To use the two ChartWizard editing screens, follow these steps:

1. Click the chart to select it.
2. Click the ChartWizard button.
3. In the Step 1 box, click Next>.

   Notice that you have only two ChartWizard steps when you edit an existing chart.
4. In the Step 2 box, the Sample Chart area shows the chart as it currently appears in your worksheet.

   Notice that the quarters label the x-axis and the columns represent the different models.
5. Click the **R**ows option in the Data Series in area.

   Notice that the different models now label the x-axis and the quarters are columns in the chart.

6. Click OK to see the modified chart.
7. Perform steps 1 through 4 again.
8. Click Columns option in the Data Series in area, and then click OK.

Keep this workbook open for the following tutorial.

Objective 3: Move and Size an Embedded Chart in a Worksheet

Usually, when you create the chart area for the embedded chart, you are not sure exactly where the chart should appear in your worksheet or how big the chart should be. This situation is not a problem because you can easily select an embedded chart and move it to a new location or change its size. In fact, because you can have many different charts embedded in the same worksheet, you will often want to move or resize charts.

Moving a Chart to a New Location in the Worksheet

You should have the QTRSALES workbook open. The chart you created in the preceding tutorial should still be selected. (The black square handles should appear around the edge of the chart.) If not, select the chart by clicking it. To move the selected chart, follow these steps:

1. Place the mouse pointer in the middle of the selected chart; press and hold down the left mouse button.
2. Drag the chart so that its top edge is in row 3 of the worksheet.
3. Release the mouse button (see figure 6.20).

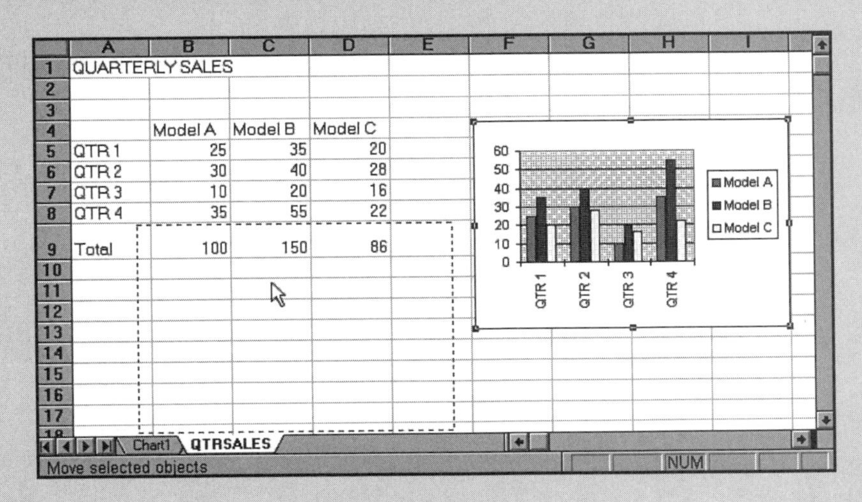

Figure 6.20
Dragging the selected chart.

(continues)

Moving a Chart to a New Location in the Worksheet (continued)

Note: *By using Drag and Drop (selecting an area on the worksheet, dragging it with the mouse, and releasing the mouse button when the selection is in the new location), you can move an embedded chart to any location in the worksheet.*

4. Practice moving the chart to at least two new locations.

Notice that you are moving one chart, not making several copies of the same chart.

Keep this workbook open for the following tutorial.

Sizing a Chart

Handles
The black squares on the boundary enclosing a selected chart.

When an embedded chart is selected, the chart has boundary lines formed by eight small black squares called *handles*. You use the black squares for sizing the chart area. You use the corner handles to size the chart height and width proportionally, and you use the handles in the middle to increase or decrease the chart horizontally or vertically. Changing the chart size often changes the appearance of the chart as well as the display of the labels on the x-axis and the scaling of the y-axis. If labels on the x-axis are vertical or broken into two or more layers ("scrunched together"), expanding the horizontal size (width) of the chart makes the labels more readable.

Changing the Size of a Chart

In this tutorial, you change the size of an embedded chart; you can use the same techniques to size a chart in a separate sheet.

To change the size of your embedded chart, follow these steps:

1. Select the chart by clicking it. The black square selection handles appear.
2. Place the mouse pointer on the handle in the middle of the lower edge of the selected chart. This step requires some careful moving of the mouse; the mouse pointer becomes a double-headed arrow when it is positioned properly on the handle.
3. Press and hold down the left mouse button, and drag the handle to row 16 of the worksheet.
4. Release the mouse button.
5. Place the mouse pointer on the handle at the lower right corner of the selection.
6. Press and hold down the left mouse button, and drag diagonally to the right several columns and down to row 20 of the worksheet.

7. Release the mouse button.

   Notice that both the width and height of the selection change when you drag a corner handle of the selection.

   You will often need to adjust an embedded chart's size until it looks just the way you want it to. When you change the size of a chart, you change the labeling of the x-axis, the scaling of the y-axis, or the amount of worksheet space occupied by the chart.

8. Try making the embedded chart smaller and larger to see how Excel changes the x- and y-axes scaling and labels. Adjust the size of the chart so that it is easy to read but does not blot out too much of your worksheet.

Keep this workbook open for the following tutorial.

Objective 4: Create Different Types of Charts

Excel has the capacity to produce 15 types of charts—either embedded or separate. These 15 types of charts appear in Step 2 of the ChartWizard when you are creating—not editing—a chart. Available variations in the format of the basic type you select in Step 2 appear in Step 3 of the ChartWizard. Not all types of worksheet data can produce all 15 types of charts, but you will find that you always have enough charting power at your fingertips for any Excel worksheet data. You can find an explanation of all 15 chart types in Excel's **H**elp menu.

Selecting a Chart Type

Up to this point, you have created a column chart and a line chart—but column and line charts are not the only types of charts available in Excel. To find out which chart type presents your data best, you should take some time to explore the various types of charts available. In the following tutorials, you will learn to use some new chart types. You will be using the chart shortcut menus.

6

Selecting a Chart Type for an Embedded Chart

You should have the QTRSALES workbook open. In this tutorial, you change the chart type from a column chart to a line chart. Follow these steps:

1. Double-click inside the chart.

   The border becomes thicker and rope-like (see figure 6.21).

(continues)

Selecting a Chart Type for an Embedded Chart (continued)

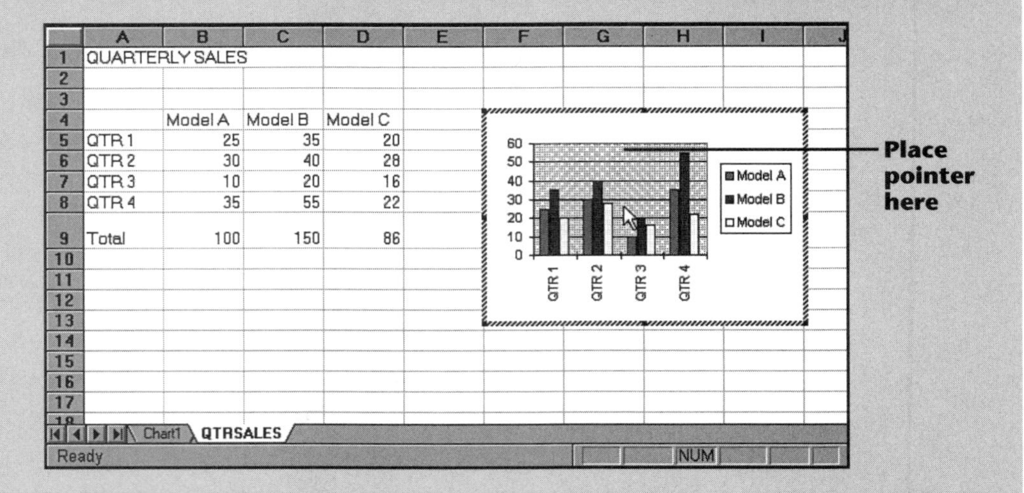

Figure 6.21 The activated chart.

2. Place the mouse pointer on a blank space between the 50 and 60 grid lines (near the top of the chart). Do not place the pointer on a grid line. Use the marked location in figure 6.21 as a guide for placing the pointer.

3. Right-click the chart.

   A chart shortcut menu appears (see figure 6.22).

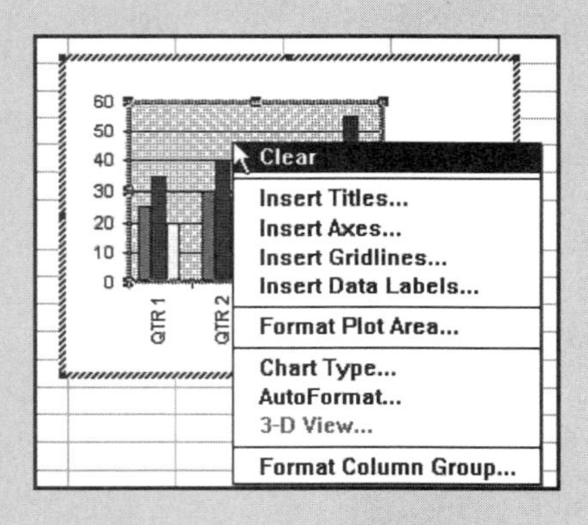

Figure 6.22 The Format Plot Area shortcut menu.

4. Choose Chart Type.

   The Chart Type dialog box appears (see figure 6.23).

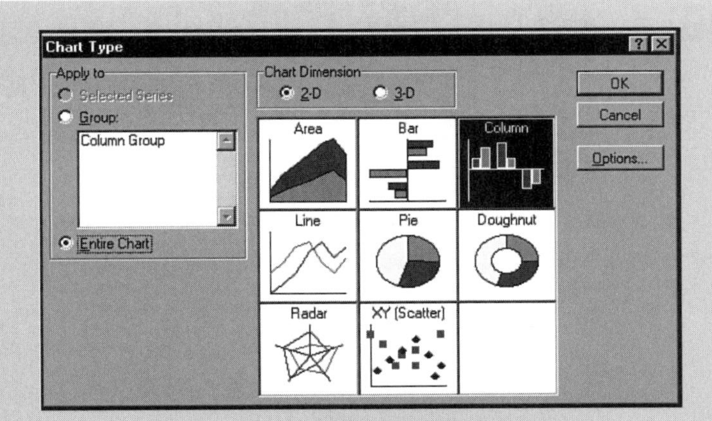

Figure 6.23
The Chart Type dialog box.

❺ Make sure that the **E**ntire Chart option is selected in the Apply to section at the upper left of the dialog box.

❻ Click the picture of the line chart to select a line chart.

❼ Click OK.

The chart changes from a column chart to a line chart; the charted data stays the same—only its representation changes (see figure 6.24).

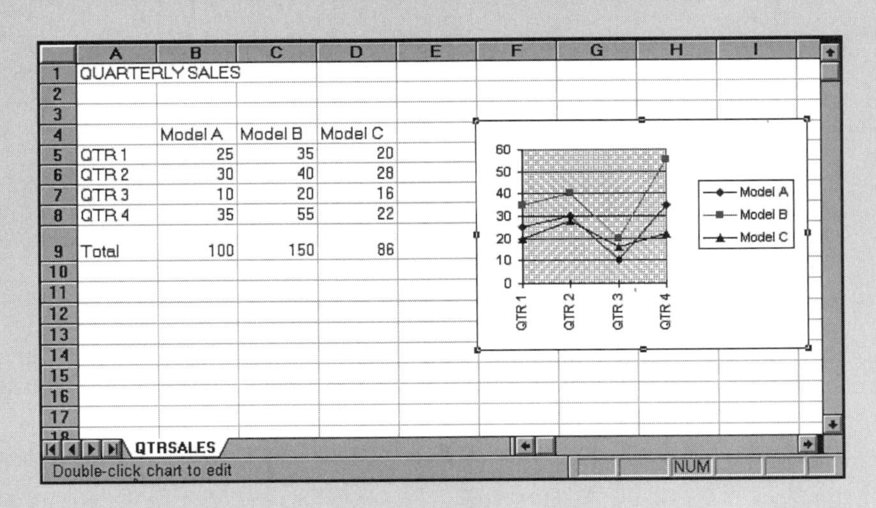

	A	B	C	D
1	QUARTERLY SALES			
2				
3				
4		Model A	Model B	Model C
5	QTR 1	25	35	20
6	QTR 2	30	40	28
7	QTR 3	10	20	16
8	QTR 4	35	55	22
9	Total	100	150	86

Figure 6.24
The new chart.

(continues)

Selecting a Chart Type for an Embedded Chart (continued)

8. Place the mouse pointer in the same location on the chart as you did in step 2 of this tutorial, and right-click.

9. Choose Chart Type.

10. In the Chart Type dialog box, make sure that the **E**ntire Chart option is selected in the Apply To section.

11. In the Chart Type dialog box, click the picture of the bar chart.

12. In the Chart Dimension section of the Chart Type dialog box, click the **3**-D option.

13. Click OK.

    If the chart is too large to be displayed in the chart area, you need to increase the size of the chart area.

14. Place the mouse pointer on the black square sizing handle in the middle of the top border of the selection.

15. Press and hold down the left mouse button, and drag the top of the selection border until it is in row 1 of the worksheet. Release the mouse button.

Now the full chart can be displayed. Your screen should look like figure 6.25.

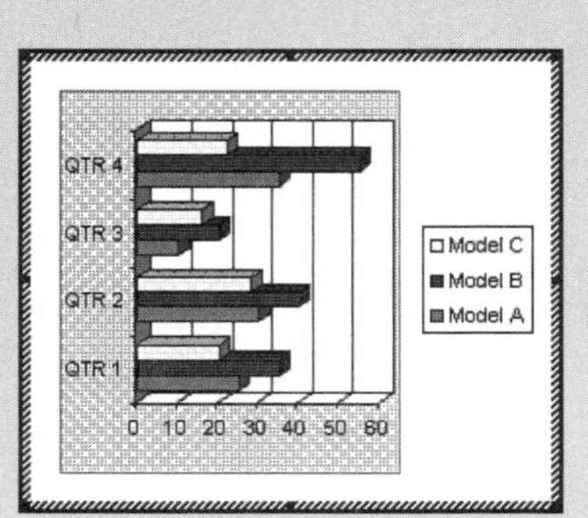

Figure 6.25 The 3-D bar chart.

Keep this workbook open for the following tutorial.

If you have problems... If you click a different part of the chart than is specified in a tutorial, your shortcut menu may be different from the menu shown in a figure. If you get a different shortcut menu, just click outside the shortcut menu to close it. Then place your mouse pointer more carefully, and right-click the mouse button again.

Changing the Type of a Chart on a Separate Sheet

In this tutorial, you use the QTRSALES workbook to create a new 2-D pie chart on a separate sheet. Then you change the chart to a 3-D pie chart. Follow these steps:

1. Select the range of cells from A4 to B8. Note that this smaller range charts only the Model A data because you are creating a pie chart.
2. Right-click the worksheet tab.
3. From the shortcut menu, choose Insert.

The Insert tabbed dialog box appears (see figure 6.26).

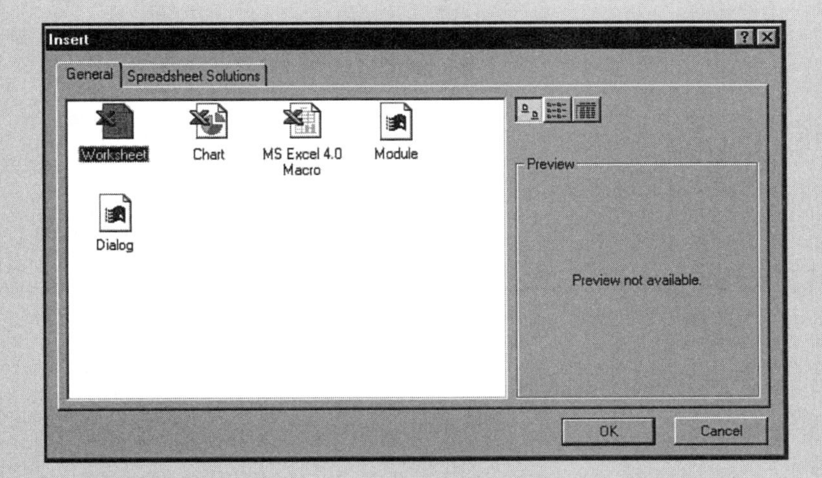

Figure 6.26 The Insert tabbed dialog box.

4. Choose Chart, and then click OK.

   Steps 1 through 5 of the ChartWizard appear in order.
5. In Step 1, click the Next> button.
6. In Step 2, click the Pie chart type, and then click the Next> button.
7. In Steps 3 and 4, click the Next> button; in Step 5 click the Finish button.

   A pie chart appears in your workbook (see figure 6.27).

(continues)

Changing the Type of a Chart on a Separate Sheet (continued)

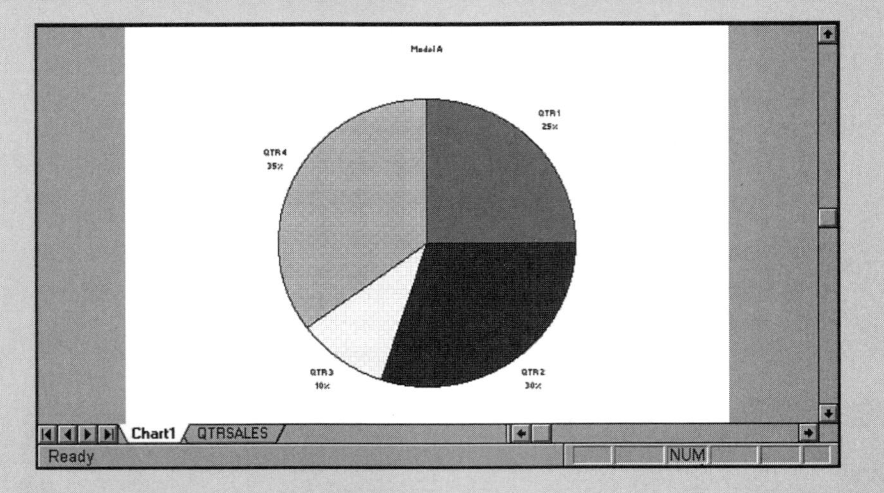

Figure 6.27
The pie chart.

8. Place the mouse pointer in the middle of the QTR1 slice, and click the left mouse button.

   Black square selection handles appear around the outside of the pie.

9. Keep the pointer in the middle of the QTR1 slice, and right-click the mouse button.

   A shortcut menu appears.

10. Choose Chart Type.

11. In the Apply to section of the Chart Type dialog box, choose the **E**ntire Chart option.

12. In the Chart Dimension section of the Chart Type dialog box, click the **3**-D option.

13. Click OK in the Chart Type dialog box.

Note: *The chart becomes a 3-D pie chart; however, the worksheet data that underlies the chart has not changed.*

14. Click the QTRSALES worksheet tab to return to the worksheet.

Objective 5: Enhance and Format Charts

Chart object
An item on a chart (such as an arrow) that you can move, size, and format.

After you have created a chart, you can modify and enhance it. You can insert a new data series into a chart, and you can delete data series from a chart. You can add text notes and *chart objects*, such as arrows, to your chart. You can also format text, change the colors used in the plotting of a chart, and change the color of text in the chart. Start these tutorials with a fresh chart.

Starting a Fresh Chart to Format

To clear any old charts from the QTRSALES worksheet and embed a new chart, follow these steps:

1. Click the old chart; then press Del.
2. Select cells A4:D8.
3. Click the ChartWizard button.
4. Drag the mouse pointer slowly (because of the scrolling) in the worksheet from cell E1 to K18.
5. In the dialog boxes of Steps 1 through 4, click the Next> button.
6. In the Step 5 box, click the Chart Title text box, and type **ABC CORPORATE SALES**.
7. In the Step 5 box, click the X Axis Titles text box, and type **1994**.
8. In the Step 5 box, click the Y Axis Titles text box, and type **Units Sold**.
9. Click the Finish button.

Now your screen should look something like figure 6.28.

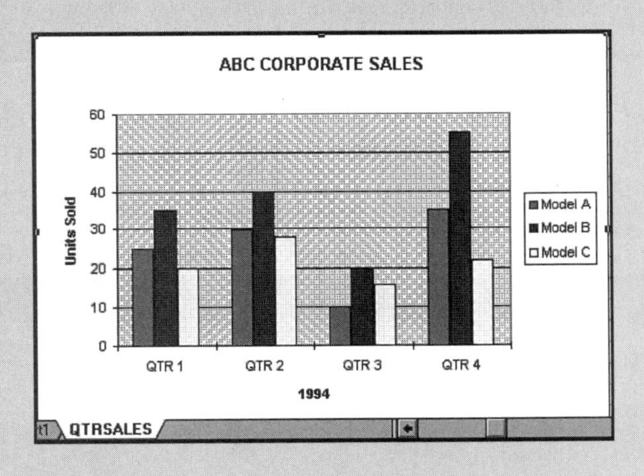

Figure 6.28 The chart with titles.

Keep this workbook open for the following tutorial.

If you decide that your chart contains too much data and looks cluttered, you can easily delete one or more data series from the chart.

Deleting a Data Series from a Chart

To delete a data series directly from the chart you created in the preceding tutorial, follow these steps:

1. Double-click the chart to activate it for editing. The chart border becomes thick and rope-like—ready for you to make changes in the chart.

(continues)

6

Deleting a Data Series from a Chart (continued)

2. Click one of the columns that represents Model C. This step selects all the Model C columns.

3. Press Del.

The entire set of Model C columns is deleted (see figure 6.29).

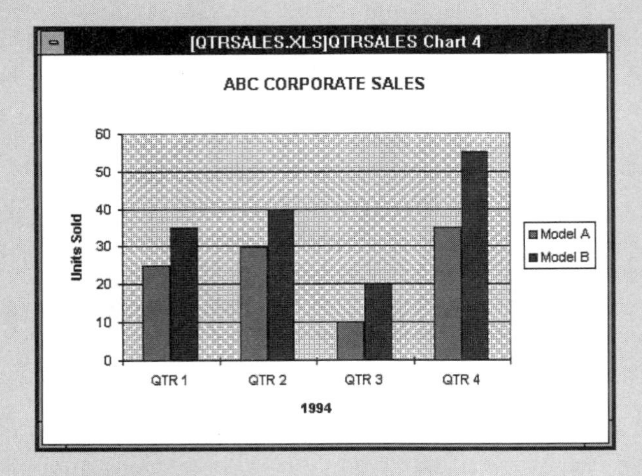

Figure 6.29 The chart with Model C data deleted.

Keep this workbook open for the following tutorial.

After you have created a chart, you may decide that you need to include additional data. You can do this by selecting the worksheet cells that contain the new data and dragging and dropping them onto your chart. The chart will be updated to show the new data.

Adding a Data Series to a Chart

In this tutorial, you add the Model C data back into your chart. Follow these steps:

1. Select the range D4:D8.

2. Place the mouse pointer on the right edge of the selection; then press and hold down the left mouse button, and drag the data over the chart. Release the mouse button when the data is anywhere over the chart.

   This step drops the data onto the chart.

The chart now contains the additional data and looks like the original chart shown in figure 6.28.

Keep this workbook open for the following tutorial.

At some point, you may want to change the color of a set of columns in a chart to emphasize that data series. If you have a color printer, you may find a set of chart colors that looks especially striking in a presentation.

Changing the Color of a Data Series in a Chart

To change the color used for the Model A series, follow these steps:

1. Double-click the chart if you have not activated it for editing.
2. Right-click any Model A column.
3. Click Format Data Series in the shortcut menu.

   The Format Data Series tabbed dialog box appears (see figure 6.30).

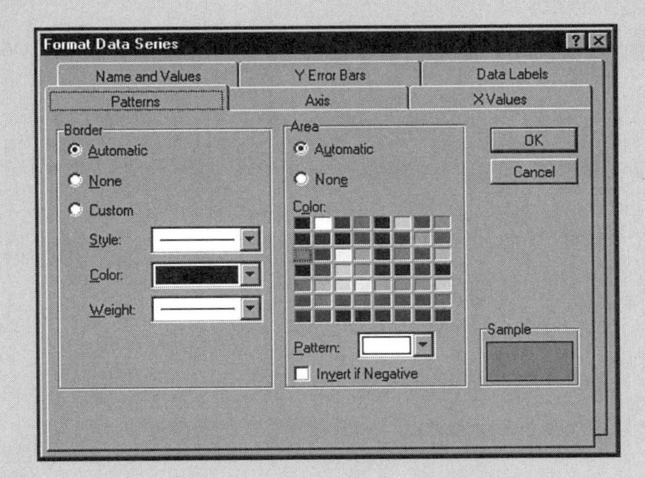

Figure 6.30 The Format Data Series tabbed dialog box.

4. Click the Patterns tab if it does not appear at the front.
5. Click the bright blue square in the upper right corner of the Color palette.
6. Click OK.

The Model A columns should now appear as a bright light blue.

Keep this workbook open for the following tutorial.

Adding Text to a Chart

Unattached text Text in a text box on a chart, which you can select and move to different locations on the chart.

As you have seen, in the ChartWizard, you can add a chart title in your chart, and you can attach titles to the horizontal (x) and vertical (y) axes. You can also include additional explanatory text in an Excel chart. You place explanatory text in a chart by using a text box. The Text Box button is found in the Drawing toolbar.

Note: *You can use the chart spell checker to check the spelling of all text in the chart.*

Some charts may require you to include text that you can move and position on the chart. You enter this text in a text box as *unattached text*. For example, you may want to position text in the form of a brief note or label to explain a specific point on the chart. You can move this text box wherever you like on the chart. To delete the text, you select it by clicking the text and then pressing Del. You can also format, move, and size other chart objects, such as arrows.

Adding Explanatory Text to Your Chart

In this tutorial, you display the Drawing toolbar and add explanatory text to your chart. Follow these steps:

1. Choose **T**oolbars from the **V**iew menu.
2. Click Drawing in the Toolbars dialog box (as shown in figure 6.31).

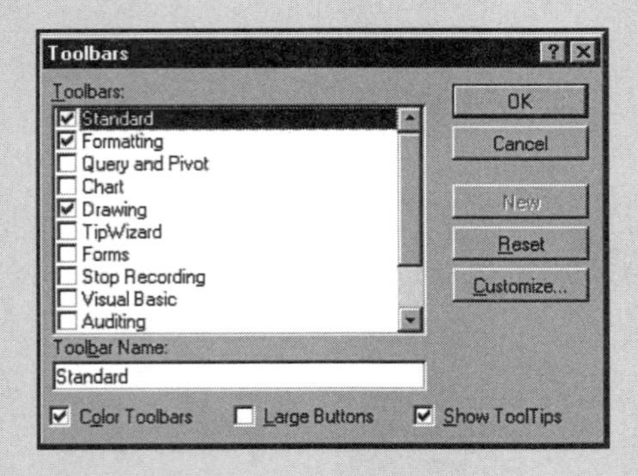

Figure 6.31 To view the Drawing toolbar, click Drawing in the Toolbars dialog box.

3. Click OK. The Drawing toolbar appears on-screen.
4. Click the Text Box button (see Figure 6.32).

   Your pointer changes into a cross hair, which means that you can add a text box.

Figure 6.32 The Drawing toolbar.

5. Place the pointer near the top border of the chart, about one inch to the right of the chart title.
6. Press the left mouse button, and drag down and to the right until you have created a box about 2.5 inches long and 1 inch high. Release the mouse button.
7. Type **Severe Floods**.
8. Click outside the text box.

Keep this workbook open for the following tutorial.

Don't worry about placing the text box in exactly the right location. You can click it and drag the text box to a new location later. If the text box is too small to display all the text, select the text box, and drag the sizing handle to make the box larger. You can delete a text box by clicking it to select the text box and then pressing Del.

Creating an Arrow That Points to Data in Your Chart

To create an arrow pointing from the text box you completed in the preceding tutorial to the chart columns representing the QTR3 data, make sure you have the QTRSALES workbook open, and follow these steps:

1. Double-click the chart to activate the chart for editing, if it is not already activated.
2. Click the black Arrow button on the Drawing toolbar (refer to figure 6.32).

   Your mouse pointer changes to a cross hair, ready for you to draw an arrow.
3. Move the cross hair to a point just below the left end of the text box note *Severe Floods*.
4. Press and hold down the left mouse button. Drag the mouse pointer until it appears just above the QTR3 columns; then release the left mouse button.

   An arrow appears on your chart pointing to the low sales figures for the third quarter (see figure 6.33).

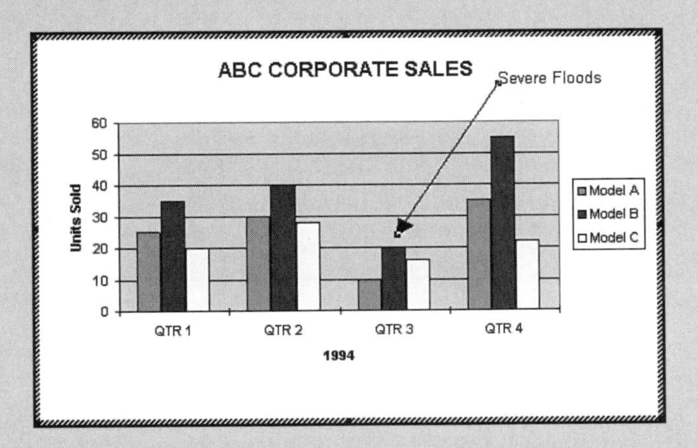

Figure 6.33 The arrow object.

Note: *When the black square selection handles appear on the arrow (click the arrow if it is not selected), you can click and drag a selection handle to size and move the arrow.*

Click outside the chart area to deselect the arrow.

Keep this workbook open for the following tutorial.

Just as you can format the text in a worksheet, you can also format the text in a chart. You can format text by changing the font, point size, or style, or by adding a border, pattern, or color. The shortcut menu choices for formatting begin with the word *Format*. For example, for Text boxes, the menu choice is Format Object; for axis titles, the menu choice Format Axis Title; for the chart title, the choice is Format Chart Title. When you make the choice, a formatting tabbed dialog box enables you to make a variety of formatting changes to the text. The next tutorial illustrates techniques for formatting text.

Formatting Text in Your Chart

In this tutorial, you make some formatting changes to the text in the chart title. Make sure that you have QTRSALES open, and then follow these steps:

1. If necessary, double-click the chart to activate it for editing.
2. Right-click the chart title.
3. From the shortcut menu, choose Format Chart Title.

   The Format Chart Title tabbed dialog box appears.
4. Click the Font tab to bring it to the front.
5. In the Size list, choose a font size of 12.
6. Click the Patterns tab to bring it to the front (see figure 6.34).

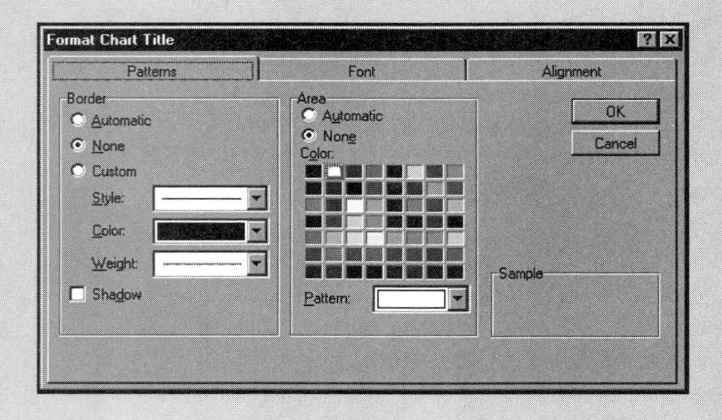

Figure 6.34
The Patterns tab of the Format Chart Title dialog box.

7. Click the down-arrow button next to the Color list, and select the dark blue solid color.
8. Click the Custom Border option button.
9. Click the Shadow check box.
10. Click the yellow square in the top row of the color palette.
11. Click OK.
12. Click off the chart to see the changes.
13. Save the workbook using whatever name you want.

Keep this workbook open for the following tutorial.

Formatting the Plot Area of a Chart

A special Plot Area shortcut menu enables you to make major formatting changes to the plot area and even to change the chart type. In the final tutorial for this objective, you use this shortcut menu to change the column chart to a bar chart.

Using the Plot Area Shortcut Menu

To use the Plot Area shortcut menu, follow these steps:

1. Place the mouse pointer in a blank area between the 50 and 60 grid lines. Double-click the chart to activate it.
2. Keep the mouse pointer in the same position, and right-click the mouse button.

   The Plot Area shortcut menu appears (see figure 6.35).

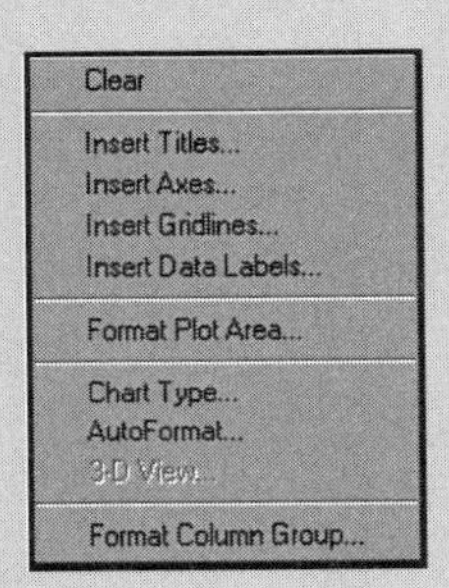

Figure 6.35 The Plot Area shortcut menu.

3. Choose Chart Type.

   The Chart Type dialog box appears.
4. Make sure that the **E**ntire Chart option is selected in the Apply To section.
5. Click the picture of the bar chart.
6. Choose OK.

   The chart type becomes a bar chart.
7. Click off the chart to deselect it.

Keep this workbook open for the following tutorial.

6

Objective 6: Print a Chart

Printing charts operates similarly to printing worksheets. You can print immediately from the Excel workbook screen by clicking the Print button on the toolbar or choosing **F**ile, **P**rint. You can also preview the chart before printing. Previewing a chart gives you a more accurate view of how the chart will appear when printed. By using Print Preview and Page Setup (refer to Chapter 5), you can make adjustments to the page margins that control the size of the chart when it is printed.

Printing Embedded Charts

Charts embedded on worksheets print with the worksheets. To print an embedded chart, simply print the worksheet in which the chart is embedded. You need to remember that if Excel cannot print all of a worksheet on one page, it will print the rest on a second page. This fact may cause part of your chart to print on one page and part to print on a second page. If this happens, move or size the chart so that it all fits on one page. You can also use manual page breaks to control printing (refer to Chapter 5). A useful tip for printing only the embedded chart without the worksheet is to double-click the chart to activate it; then click the Print button.

Printing a Separate Chart

Printing a separate chart doesn't differ much from printing a worksheet. You do not, however, have to define a print area when you print a chart.

In this tutorial, you print your separate chart from the QTRSALES workbook. Follow these steps:

1. Click the chart sheet's tab to make the sheet active.
2. Click the Print button on the Standard toolbar.

Keep this workbook open for the following tutorial.

If you have a color printer, your chart will print in color; otherwise, it will print in black and white.

Printing a Worksheet and Its Embedded Chart

To print your worksheet (in the QTRSALES workbook) with its embedded chart, follow these steps:

1. Click the tab of the worksheet if the worksheet is not active.
2. Move and size the chart so that the chart and worksheet fit on one page. You can use Print Preview to see how your printout will look.
3. Click the Print button.

Your worksheet and chart are printed.

Keep this workbook open for the following tutorial.

You can also print only the embedded chart. In the following tutorial, you print the chart without printing the worksheet.

Printing Only an Embedded Chart

To print only the chart, not the worksheet, follow these steps:

1. Double-click the embedded chart to activate it.
2. Click the Print button.

   Only your chart will print.
3. Close and save the QTRSALES workbook now.

Chapter Summary

In this chapter, you have been introduced to many components of charting. This chapter covers topics related to creating and formatting a chart. You have learned how to create a chart in a separate chart sheet and how to create a chart in a worksheet. This chapter also explains how to add titles, arrows, and text boxes to enhance the appearance of a chart. You have learned how to format all chart objects using the shortcut menus and various dialog boxes. Charting is a major feature in Excel. This chapter has focused primarily on charting basics. If you want to explore charting in more depth and experiment with some of Excel's advanced charting features, you may want to read Que's book, *Special Edition Using Excel for Windows 95*.

Checking Your Skills

True/False

For each of the following, circle *T* or *F* to indicate whether the statement is true or false.

T F **1.** The ChartWizard can create charts that are not embedded in the worksheet.

T F **2.** If your worksheet data selection is taller than it is wide, the labels in the leftmost column of the selection will, by default, appear on a chart's y-axis.

T F **3.** You cannot move an embedded chart around on a worksheet.

T F **4.** When you change the data in a worksheet, a chart embedded in the worksheet also changes to show the new data.

T F **5.** When you have selected an embedded chart, clicking and dragging a black handle changes the size of the chart.

T F **6.** You can create a chart embedded in your worksheet by using the **F**ile, New **C**hart commands.

T F **7.** Excel does not create three-dimensional charts.

T F **8.** Text used as the chart title can be moved on the chart.

T F **9.** You can use a button on the Standard toolbar to place an arrow in your chart.

T F **10.** By default, Excel uses column A of the worksheet to supply labels for the x-axis.

Multiple Choice

In the blank provided, write the letter of the correct answer for each of the following.

_____ **1.** When you right-click a chart object, _____ appears.

a. an arrow

b. a shortcut menu

c. a legend

d. the ChartWizard

_____ **2.** To change the type of chart displayed in a worksheet, you select a new chart type from the _____ menu.

a. Chart

b. Format

c. Gallery

d. none of the above

_____ **3.** The default chart type is a 2-D _____ chart.

a. bar

b. column

c. line

d. pie

_____ **4.** Which of the following is/are example(s) of attached text?

a. a chart title

b. a value axis title

c. a category axis title

d. all the above

_____ **5.** Which dialog box enables you to control the type of border applied to a selected chart object?

a. Format

b. Patterns

c. Text

d. none of the above

_____ **6.** A _____ enables you to identify the data in a chart.

a. legend

b. gallery

c. ChartWizard

d. none of the above

_____ **7.** The vertical axis on a chart is the _____-axis.

a. x

b. y

c. z

d. category

_____ **8.** A collection of data in a worksheet that is used as the basis for a chart is called a(n) _____.

a. data series

b. array

c. A-range

d. none of the above

_____ **9.** If the worksheet data selection you are charting is taller than it is wide, by default the x-axis labels are taken from the _____ of the selection.

a. top row

b. bottom row

c. leftmost column

d. rightmost column

_____ **10.** The title of the y-axis is an example of _____ text.

a. attached

b. unattached

c. nonformattable

d. border

Completion

In the blank provided, write the correct answer for each of the following.

1. By default, Excel uses the data along the ______________ side of your selection as labels for the x-axis.
2. You can format text in a chart text box by using the ______________ command in the shortcut menu.
3. By default, Excel uses data along the short side of the selected data in your worksheet to create the ______________.
4. The two ways to create a chart from selected data in Excel are by pressing the ______________ and using the ______________.
5. To select nonadjoining areas in your worksheet, you use both the mouse and the ______________ key.
6. When an embedded chart is selected on a worksheet, the chart appears enclosed by boundary lines with eight black squares called ______________.
7. To select an embedded chart, place the mouse pointer on the chart, and ______________.
8. The ______________ command displays or hides major and minor gridlines.
9. You can enter unattached text in a chart by using the ______________ button on the Standard toolbar.
10. The arrow that can be used to point to a column in a chart is found on the ______________ toolbar.

Applying Your Skills

Review Exercises

Exercise 1: Creating an Area Chart

Use the QTRSALES workbook to create an area chart that shows sales for Models A, B, and C for the four quarters. Label the x-axis with the data in cells A5 to A8 of the worksheet. Take the data series from columns B, C, and D of the worksheet. Include a text box with your name, and print the chart.

Exercise 2: Creating a Line Chart Using QTRSALES

Create a line chart on a separate chart sheet in your workbook. The chart should chart Model A sales and Model C sales for the year. Include appropriate titles for the chart and the x- and y-axes. Include a text box with your name. Save the chart on disk, and print it.

Exercise 3: Creating a 3-D Pie Chart from Nonadjoining Ranges

Using the ChartWizard and QTRSALES, create a 3-D embedded pie chart that shows the annual sales for Model B. Give the embedded chart a height of 14 rows and a width of 7 columns. Create a text box that contains your name. Select and print the worksheet.

Exercise 4: Creating a Bar Chart

Consult an almanac to obtain the population of the United States for 1900, 1920, 1940, 1960, and 1980. Create a worksheet and a bar chart to show this data. Label the x- and y-axes appropriately, and include a chart title. Add a text box with your name. Save the workbook as **C6sp4**, and print the chart and the worksheet.

Exercise 5: Creating Line Charts

Consult the *Wall Street Journal* to find financial data on the performance of the stock market or the economy. Choose a set of data to chart. For example, you might choose the movement of the Dow Jones Industrial Average for the preceding 12 months or the movement in the interest rate charged on Federal funds for the preceding 18 months. Create a worksheet and a line chart to show this data. Label the x- and y-axes appropriately, and include a chart title. Add a text box with your name. Save the workbook as **C6sp5**, and print the chart and the worksheet. Change to a different line chart format, and print the chart again.

Continuing Projects

Project 1: Creating and Formatting a Chart

Open the NSCC QUARTERLY REPORT workbook (C2lp1) you created in Continuing Project 1 at the end of Chapter 2. Create a column chart with the four month names on the x-axis. Show the Total Expenses data and the Sales data. Add axis and chart titles and a text box containing your name.

Use as many of the different formatting options as you can to change the default text. Include patterns and borders for the text. Spell check your chart. Finally, save the file as **C6lp1** and print your chart.

Project 2: Creating a Chart with the Alternative to Excel's Default Layout

Open the workbook (C2lp2) that you created in Continuing Project 2 at the end of Chapter 2. Delete the blank row 6. Create a column chart using the Sales, Income, and Assets data for all eight companies. Use the company names as labels on the x-axis. This chart is the default chart. Add a formatted title and axes titles. Add your name as a text box. Save the file as **C6lp2a** and print this chart.

Now create a column chart using the same data but use the alternative layout. Label the x-axis SALES, INCOME, and ASSETS. Add a chart title and axes titles. Add your name in a text box. Save the file as **C6lp2b** and print your chart. How are the two charts you printed different?

Project 3: Plotting Large Amounts of Data on a Chart

Open the C2lp3 workbook, which you created in Continuing Project 3 at the end of Chapter 2. Create an embedded line chart that shows the dollar amounts of sales for each district. Include titles for the x-axis and y-axis and a chart title. Format these titles to emphasize them in the chart.

Stretch the chart horizontally and vertically until all the district names are shown on the x-axis. Print the worksheet.

Place the embedded chart sheet on a separate chart sheet in the workbook. Place your name in a text box at the top of the chart in the separate chart sheet. Print the separate chart sheet.

Change the chart type to a pie chart, and print the chart.

Delete the embedded chart from the original C2lp3 worksheet, and save the workbook on disk.

CHAPTER 7

Managing Data

You are probably familiar with lists of information. Maintaining records for inventories of office equipment, sales prospects, plaintiffs in a lawsuit, client billings, or subscribers to a newsletter can become a real headache when you use pencil and paper or a card file. A computer can help you with this record keeping if you set up a database (a List) using Excel. An Excel List works like an automated card file. With Excel, you can easily enter, edit, find, and delete database information. When the information in your worksheet is organized into a List, you can use database commands to locate and extract data that meets certain criteria. You can also sort a database to put the data into a specific order.

This chapter helps you learn skills you can confidently use to manage a corporate database of 600, or even 6,000, records. With databases that large, you cannot just look at the data to find what you need. Nor can you verify that you have sorted or searched the database properly. You simply cannot catch your own errors because of the amount of data.

Here, you practice with a small database so that you can check your results to verify that you have followed the correct procedures. With only a few fields and records, you can immediately see any errors and so perfect your skills. Then you can confidently work with large databases because you will know exactly what to do. Huge amounts of data don't bother Excel. If you issue the right commands, Excel always gives you the correct results.

This chapter explains what a database is and tells you how to create a database using Excel. You learn to enter, edit, delete, and find data using a data form. You sort a database using one or more fields, search for records meeting specified criteria, and extract from database records that meet specific criteria. This chapter also explains how to use the AutoFilter. The AutoFilter enables you to extract (filter out) the records that meet your selection criteria.

Objectives

By the time you have finished this chapter, you will have learned to

1. Understand What a Database Is
2. Build a Database
3. View Database Records Using the Data Form
4. Add New Database Records
5. Delete Records
6. Sort Records
7. Use the Data Form to Search for Records
8. Find Records in a Database by Using AutoFilter

Objective 1: Understand What a Database Is

Database
The area in a worksheet where your List information is kept.

A *database* stores information in an organized way. A telephone directory and the cards in a card file are examples of a database. Each entry in a telephone directory is a record, and each record contains the same items of information. Each record has a person's last name, followed by a first name or initial, followed by an address, followed by a phone number.

Record
A row of cells containing fields of related information in a database.

In Excel, you construct a database from a worksheet. The database is a range of cells in a worksheet and consists of a row of field names followed by rows of data records. A row in a database worksheet represents a *record*, and the worksheet's columns are the fields of the record. A record contains related information. The information on each line in a telephone directory, for example, is related because the information refers to the same person or organization. Excel uses the term List to refer to worksheets organized as databases.

Field
A column in a database; each column contains one type of information.

Field names
Labels (the column headings) that identify the contents of a column in a database.

All the records in a database contain the same fields. Each column represents a *field*. The fields in a database identify the items of information that are required in each record. The first row of a database must contain labels that identify what the database fields are. These labels are referred to as *field names*. Each field name is entered in a separate column in the top row of the database (the column headings). The field names must be different from each other. In a telephone directory database, the field names would be Last Name, First Name, Street, and Phone (see figure 7.1).

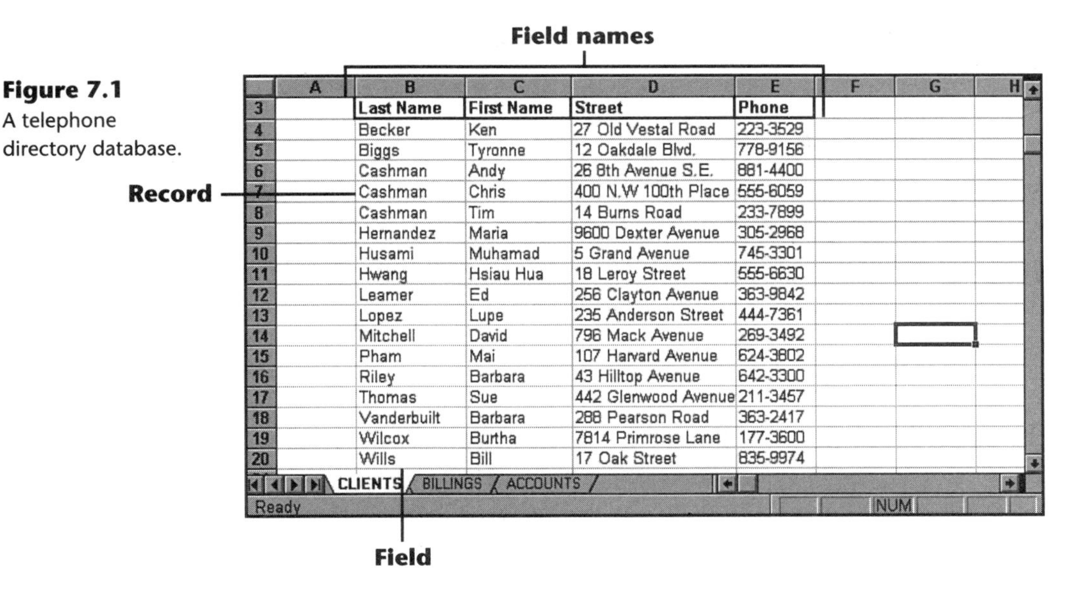

	A	B	C	D	E	F	G	H
3		Last Name	First Name	Street	Phone			
4		Becker	Ken	27 Old Vestal Road	223-3529			
5		Biggs	Tyronne	12 Oakdale Blvd.	778-9156			
6		Cashman	Andy	26 8th Avenue S.E.	881-4400			
7		Cashman	Chris	400 N.W 100th Place	555-6059			
8		Cashman	Tim	14 Burns Road	233-7899			
9		Hernandez	Maria	9600 Dexter Avenue	305-2968			
10		Husami	Muhamad	5 Grand Avenue	745-3301			
11		Hwang	Hsiau Hua	18 Leroy Street	555-6630			
12		Leamer	Ed	256 Clayton Avenue	363-9842			
13		Lopez	Lupe	235 Anderson Street	444-7361			
14		Mitchell	David	796 Mack Avenue	269-3492			
15		Pham	Mai	107 Harvard Avenue	624-3802			
16		Riley	Barbara	43 Hilltop Avenue	642-3300			
17		Thomas	Sue	442 Glenwood Avenue	211-3457			
18		Vanderbuilt	Barbara	288 Pearson Road	363-2417			
19		Wilcox	Burtha	7814 Primrose Lane	177-3600			
20		Wills	Bill	17 Oak Street	835-9974			

Figure 7.1
A telephone directory database.

Data records (data rows) immediately follow the row of field names—no blank rows should appear between the row of field names and the first data record. Do not put a row of dashes (or any other characters) under the row of field names. Usually, you should enter the records into the database one after the other without any blank rows in the database range.

After you have entered all the data records, you select the worksheet range that contains the field names and records and define them as a database. Once you have defined the database, you can use Excel's database commands to add new records; to edit or delete existing records; and to search, sort, and extract the data. Excel Lists (databases) that contain thousands of records are not uncommon. In this chapter, you work with a small database.

Objective 2: Build a Database

When you create a database in an existing worksheet or set up a new worksheet to use as a database, you should follow certain guidelines:

- Consider where you will position the database. If you create a database within an existing worksheet, you must position the database where you can insert and delete additional columns and rows without disturbing the rest of the worksheet. When a column or row is inserted or deleted, that item is inserted or deleted through the entire worksheet.

- The first row of the database must contain field names. Field names can be entered in several rows if the column widths are not wide enough to hold the complete heading. Excel, however, only uses the contents of the cells in the bottom row of the headings as the database field names.

- A field name should describe the field's contents, and it can contain up to 255 characters. As a rule, you should keep field names brief.

- Field names must consist of text, not numbers. (If a field name contains a number, the entire name must be enclosed in quotation marks in order for Excel to interpret the name as text.) A field name can contain spaces (blanks).
- A field name must be unique—you cannot have two fields with the same field name.
- Enter the data records starting in the row immediately below the field names.
- Records can include text, numbers, formulas, and functions.
- Every record must have the same fields, but you do not have to enter data into all the fields for every record. If you don't have the information, you can leave some of the columns in a record empty.

In figure 7.2, the field names in the database—INVOICE, DATE, COMPANY, DUE DATE, and AMOUNT—appear in row 5. Five records have been entered in rows 6 through 10. The data entered in the records includes dates, text, numbers, and formulas. The formula takes the DATE field in column C and adds 30 days to calculate the DUE DATE.

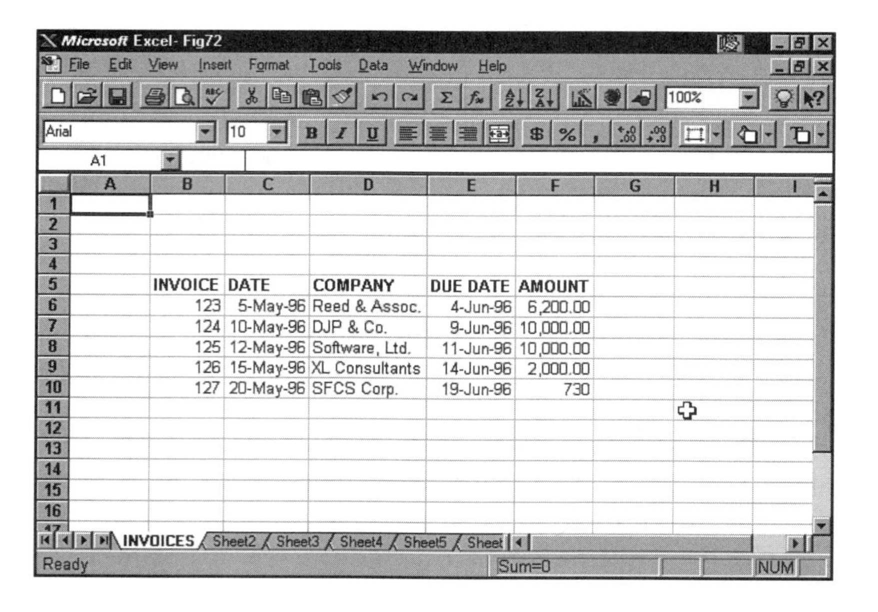

Figure 7.2
A database of outstanding invoices.

Entering Field Names and Records

For the first tutorials in this chapter, you use the data shown in figure 7.2. When you set up a worksheet to be used as a List, you enter the field names and data using the same worksheet entry techniques you learned in earlier chapters.

Close any open workbooks, and start a new workbook. To enter the field names and records, follow these steps:

1. Enter the field names and data into your worksheet (refer to figure 7.2). Enter the contents of the DATE field as shown. For example, type **5/5/96** in cell C6, and press Enter.

2. Format C6:C10 and E6:E10 to the d-mmm-yy format.
3. The DUE DATE field contains a formula that adds 30 days to the corresponding DATE field. In cell E6, enter the formula **=C6+30**.
4. Complete the worksheet and name the sheet (the sheet tab) **INVOICES**.
5. Use the AutoFit Selection feature to set the width of columns B through F.
6. Save the workbook on your disk as **Fig72**.

Keep this workbook open for the following tutorial.

After you have entered the field names and the data records, you define the database (an Excel List). You give the database a name, which Excel uses (refers to) whenever you issue a database command.

Defining Your Database

In this tutorial, you define a range of cells as a database. Use the worksheet you created in the tutorial, "Entering Field Names and Records," and follow these steps:

1. Select the range of cells from B5 to F10 (the entire range of the database).
2. Choose Insert, Name Define.

   The Define Name dialog box appears (see figure 7.3).

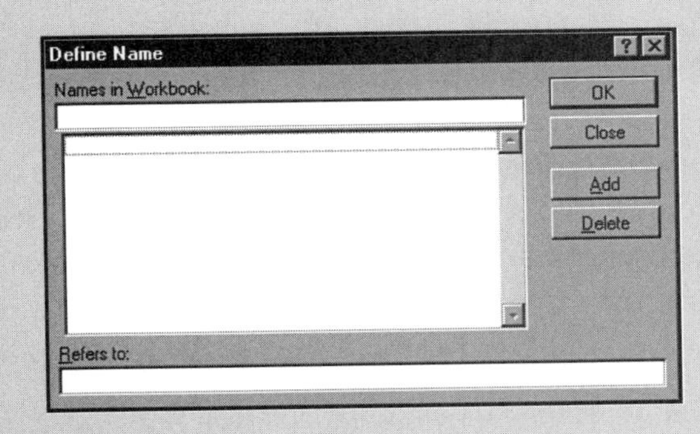

Figure 7.3 The Define Name dialog box.

3. Type **Database**; this name will replace the suggested name (INVOICE) in the Names in Workbook text box.
4. Click OK.

The word `Database` appears in the left side of the formula bar.

Keep this workbook open for the following tutorial.

Objective 3: View Database Records Using the Data Form

Data Form
A form that displays field names, text boxes, and buttons for adding, deleting, and finding records in your database.

Usually, each record in a "real world" database has more fields than your screen can display at one time. Consequently, you constantly have to scroll left and right in a record to see all the information. This scrolling is both inefficient and hard on your eyes. To avoid such problems, you should use Excel's *Data Form*. This on-screen form provides a way for you to see all the fields of a long record at the same time. Using the Data Form is easy. It is a dialog box that shows the contents of all the fields in one data record. The Data Form displays the field names in the database; if the field is not a calculated field, a text box appears to the right of each field name (see figure 7.4).

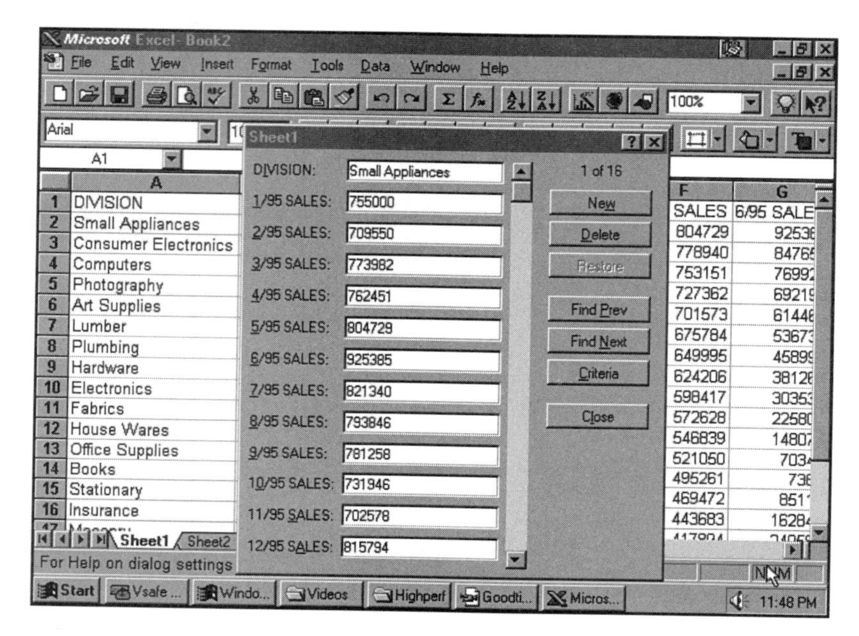

Figure 7.4
A record with many fields viewed in the Data Form.

Using the Data Form also provides an efficient technique for adding, editing, deleting, and searching for records. You use the Data Form frequently in the tutorials in this chapter. Because your sample database is small, the benefits of using the Data Form may not be apparent to you now. When you encounter your first big database, however, you will immediately appreciate the Data Form.

Note: *Before you can begin the following tutorial, you must have completed the tutorial, "Defining Your Database" and have your Fig72 workbook open.*

Viewing Records by Using the Data Form

To view your database records using the Data Form, follow these steps:

1. Open the Data menu; then choose Form.

   The Data Form appears. It displays the contents of the first database record (see figure 7.5). The DATE field is displayed as you entered it (unformatted). Note that the DUE DATE field's contents do not appear in a text box because this field is calculated by Excel, not entered by you.

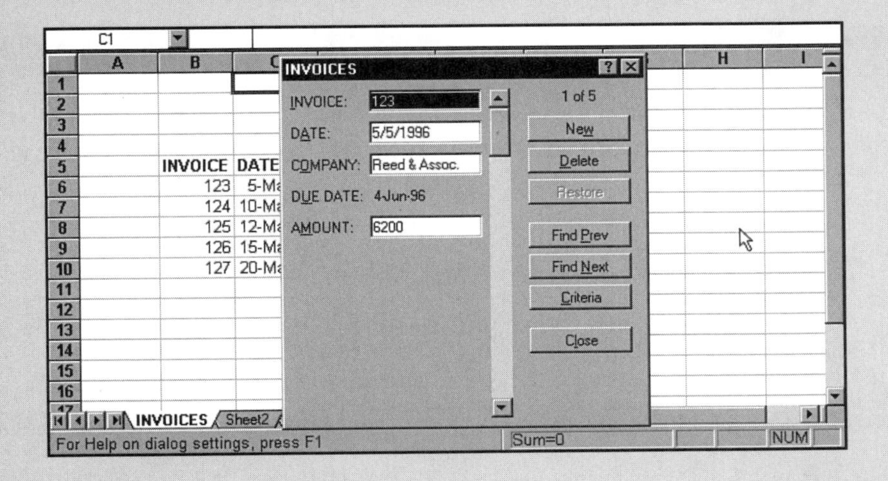

Figure 7.5 The first database record shown in the Data Form.

2. Use the Find Next and the Find Prev buttons, or the scroll bar, to move up and down through the records.

   Note: *Find Next displays the next record in the List unless you are on the last record in the List. Find Prev displays the previous record in the List unless you are on the first record in the List.*

3. Click Close to close the form.

Keep this workbook open for the following tutorial.

7

Objective 4: Add New Database Records

Excel offers two methods for adding records to a database. You can add records in blank cells or rows as you usually do in a worksheet. If you use this method, remember to insert the records within the defined database range. You can also use the Data Form method to enter new records into a defined database. Because the Data Form presents an organized view of the data and makes data entry easier and more accurate, this method is highly recommended. You use the Data Form in this chapter whenever you want to add new records to your database; the database will automatically expand to include the new record(s).

Entering a Formula into a Database

When you use a formula in a database (such as the formula that calculates DUE DATE in the sample database), you must first enter the formula into the worksheet. You cannot use the Data Form to enter or edit a formula. After you set the database and choose the **D**ata, F**o**rm command, any field containing a formula appears in the Data Form as a fixed entry; the field name will not have a text box next to it. When you add a new record to the database using the **D**ata, F**o**rm, Ne**w** command, the field containing the formula is automatically calculated when you enter the new record.

Adding a Record Using the Data Form

In this tutorial, you use the Data Form to add a record to the Fig72 workbook database you defined in the tutorial, "Defining Your Database." Follow these steps:

1. Open the **D**ata menu; then choose F**o**rm. The Data Form containing data for your first record appears (refer to figure 7.5).

2. Choose the Ne**w** button. A New Record Data Form appears (see figure 7.6).

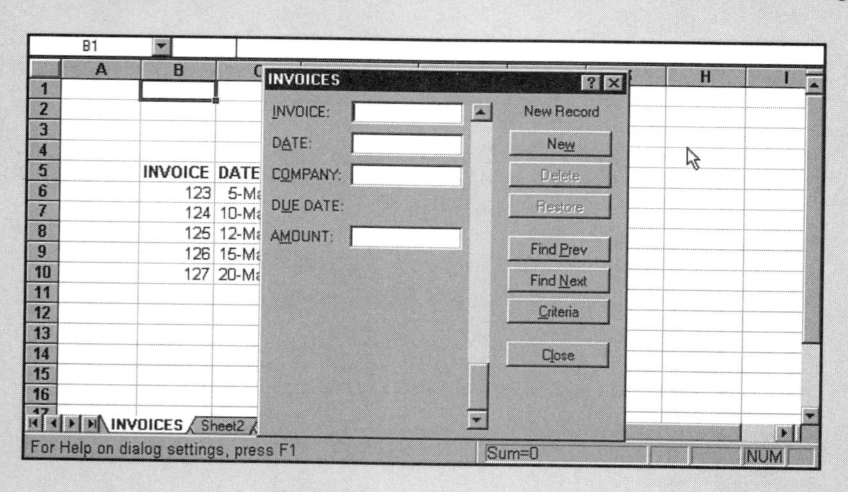

Figure 7.6
The New Record Data Form.

In figure 7.6, the DUE DATE field is a fixed entry on the Data Form because the field contains a formula. Excel enters this result for you.

3. Enter **128** in the INVOICE field, and press Tab to move to the DATE field.

4. Enter **5/25/96** in the DATE field, **Becker's Inc.** in the COMPANY field, and **200** in the AMOUNT field. Press Tab to move down to a new field. Pressing Shift+Tab will move one field up in a form. You can also click in a field to move directly to that field.

Note: *To enter another new record, press Enter when you finish a record. A new blank Data Form is displayed.*

5 Choose Close to clear the form and add the record to your database.

You will use this database in a later tutorial. Save the changed database as **Fig72** on your data disk now.

Keep this workbook open for the following tutorial.

Objective 5: Delete Records

Caution
You cannot "undelete" or recover a deleted record.

You can edit a database using the Data Form, or you can edit directly on the worksheet. When deleting database records, the Data Form is usually the easiest and most accurate method. When you use the form, however, you can delete only one record at a time. The worksheet method (selecting the records and choosing **E**dit, **D**elete) enables you to select more than one record to delete, but you may inadvertently select a record that you do not want to delete. The recommended method is always to use the Data Form when deleting records. The following steps explain how to delete a record using the Data Form.

Deleting a Record Using the Data Form

In this tutorial, you use the Data Form to delete a record. Use the database workbook Fig72, and follow these steps:

1 Open the **D**ata menu, and choose F**o**rm. The Data Form appears (refer to figure 7.5).

2 Click Find **N**ext until the record for INVOICE 126 appears on-screen (see figure 7.7).

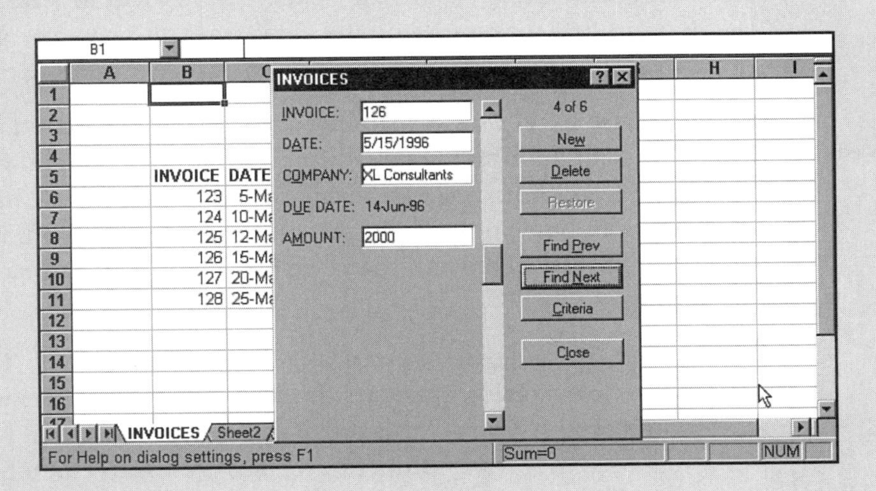

Figure 7.7
The record to be deleted.

3 Choose **D**elete. A dialog box appears to remind you that the displayed record will be permanently deleted (see figure 7.8).

(continues)

7

Deleting a Record Using the Data Form (continued)

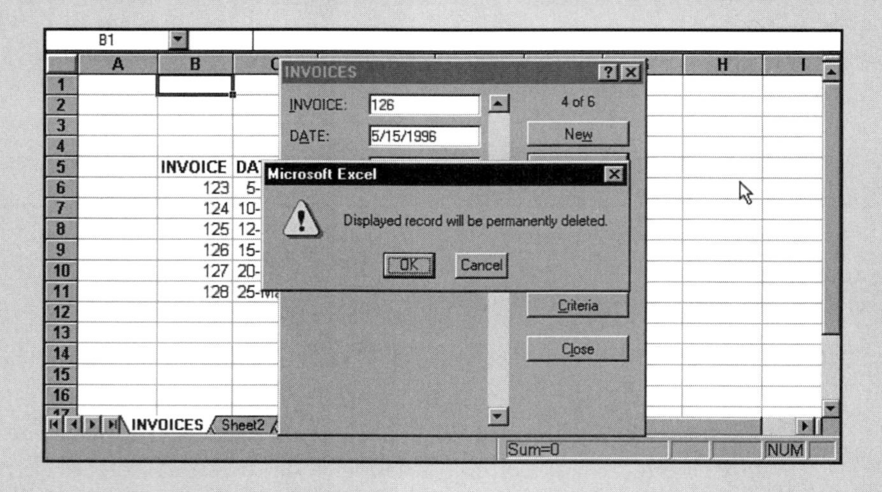

Figure 7.8 The warning box for deleting a record.

4. Choose OK or press Enter to delete the record. The warning dialog box disappears.

   The records below the deleted record renumber to account for the deleted record.

5. Choose Close to return to the worksheet.

When you finish, close the workbook but *do not save the changes.*

Objective 6: Sort Records

Excel sorts databases by using the fields. You can use any field name in the database as a *sort field* for reordering the database. You may, for example, want to sort the records in a telephone directory database according to last name.

Sort field
The field specified to control the reordering of a database.

When you use Excel's sort capability, you can specify second and third sort fields so that you can perform a sort within a sort. If, for example, you are sorting names in a telephone directory database and several people have the same last name, you can base your second sort on the first name field. If several people have the same last name and the same first name, you can base the third sort on the address.

You can sort the database in ascending or descending order. The **A**scending option in the Sort dialog box sorts the rows alphabetically from A to Z. The **D**escending option reverses this order and sorts from Z to A. Numbers are sorted from the lowest negative number to the largest positive number with the **A**scending option, the default selection. Numbers always sort as "less than" (before) letters.

To avoid accidentally messing up your database, always make sure that you use the **F**ile, Save **A**s command to make another copy of the document with another name. You can work with one copy while the other copy remains intact. If you accidentally do something disastrous to your database, you always have that backup copy.

Remember: If you ever perform an incorrect sort, immediately choose the **E**dit, **U**ndo Sort command to reverse the sort and return to the original database List.

If you have problems... One of the most common sorting errors occurs when you are selecting the range in the worksheet to sort. Excel sorts only the selected columns of the records. If you do not select all the records or all the fields within the records, the sort can create a disaster. For example, if you perform a sort and you don't select the last column containing the invoice amount, the sorted data will not align with the correct invoice amounts. The selected data is reorganized when a sort is performed, but the unselected data remains in its original order. Remember to select all fields and all the records.

Sorting Records in Your Database Using One Field

In this tutorial, you sort records in your database. Before you start, use the **F**ile, **O**pen command to open the Fig72 file (the one you saved at the end of the tutorial in Objective 4). To sort the records so that they appear in order of increasing amount, follow these steps:

1. Select the range of cells from B5 to F10. You have to select both the field names and all the records you want to sort.

2. Open the **D**ata menu, and choose **S**ort. The Sort dialog box appears (see figure 7.9).

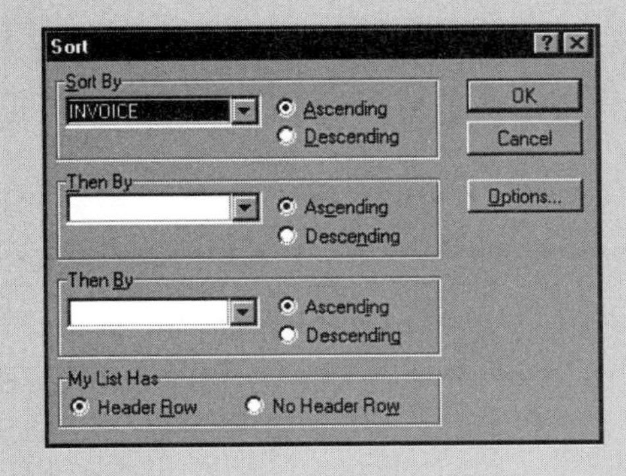

Figure 7.9 The Sort dialog box.

The **S**ort By text box is selected, and the name of the first field appears in the text box.

(continues)

Sorting Records in Your Database Using One Field (continued)

3. Use the options in the My List Has section, at the bottom of the Sort dialog box, to indicate whether you have included the row of field names (a header row) in your selected area (the List of data) to sort. If you have included field names, click the Header Row option. If you have not included field names, click the No Header Row option.

4. Click the down-arrow button next to the Sort By text box.

   The field name list appears (see figure 7.10). You indicate the field that you want to sort by clicking that field's name in the list.

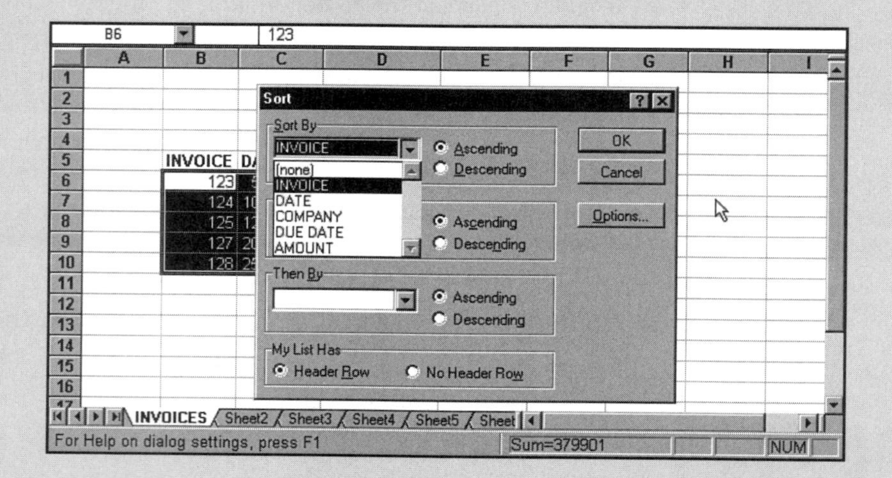

Figure 7.10
The Sort Dialog box showing the field name list.

5. Click AMOUNT in the field name list.

6. Ascending is the default selection, so you don't need to change this option.

7. Because you are sorting only one field, choose OK or press Enter.

   The selected cells are sorted according to the amount.

Keep this workbook open for the following tutorial.

To sort multiple fields, you follow the same procedure you followed in the preceding tutorial except that you also select a second and often a third sort field and indicate whether you want to sort in ascending or descending order.

Sorting Records in Your Database by Using Three Fields

To sort the Fig72 database using three sort fields, follow these steps:

1. Select the range of cells from B5 to F10. You must select both the field names and all the records you want to sort.

2. Open the Data menu, and choose Sort. The Sort dialog box appears (refer to figure 7.9).

3. Click the down-arrow button next to the Sort By text box.
4. Click AMOUNT in the field name list.
5. Click the down-arrow button next to the first Then By text box.
6. Click COMPANY in the field name list.
7. Click the down-arrow button next to the second Then By text box.
8. Click DATE in the field name list.
9. Make sure that the Header Row option button is selected.
10. Click OK to perform the sort.

    The data is sorted in a new order.

Keep this workbook open for the following tutorial.

For the following tutorials, you need to return your database records to their original order. You again practice performing a sort.

Returning Sorted Records to Their Original Order

To return the data to its original order, follow these steps:

1. Make sure that the range of cells from B5 to F10 is selected.
2. Choose Data, Sort. The Sort dialog box appears (refer to figure 7.9).
3. Click the down-arrow button next to the Sort By text box.
4. Click INVOICE in the field name list.
5. Click the down-arrow button next to the first Then By text box.
6. Click (none) in the field name list.
7. Click the down-arrow button to the next Then By text box.
8. Click (none) in the field name list.
9. Make sure that the Header Row option button is selected.
10. Click OK to perform the sort.

Now your database (List) should appear in order of increasing invoice number. Keep this workbook open for the following tutorial.

Objective 7: Use the Data Form to Search for Records

Criteria
Specified tests for the contents of the fields in a record; test conditions used to find records in a database.

Sometimes you will want to search a database for records that meet a specified criterion. *Criteria* provide a pattern or the specific details that help you find certain records. After you establish criteria, you can use Excel commands to locate records that match the criteria. These commands are extremely useful when you are searching a database that contains many records.

Finding Records

You can define the criteria you want a record to match by using either the **D**ata, F**o**rm command or the **D**ata, **F**ilter command. When the selection criteria are simple, using a Data Form provides a quick and easy method for finding and displaying each record that satisfies your selection criteria. In this chapter, you learn how to specify your criteria and find records using a Data Form.

The Criteria Data Form appears when you click a data form's **C**riteria button. The Criteria Data Form gives you several options (see Figure 7.11). To search forward through the List and find the next record that meets the criteria, you choose the Find **N**ext button. To search backward through the List and display the previous record that meets the criteria, you use the Find **P**rev button. To enter new criteria, you choose the **C**riteria button. The **R**estore button cancels any changes you have made to a record. When you finish, you choose the C**l**ose button.

Comparison operators
Symbols used to specify test conditions that involve a range of values.

When you enter numeric selection criteria where you search for a range of values, such as all records with INVOICE field values higher than 125, you use *comparison operators* (special symbols). Table 7.1 lists these operators.

Table 7.1 The Comparison Operators

Operator	Meaning
>	Greater than
<	Less than
>=	Greater than or equal to
<=	Less than or equal to
<>	Not equal to

Finding Records Using the Data Form

To find the records with an AMOUNT field value greater than 2,000 using the Data Form, make sure you have the Fig72 workbook open; then follow these steps:

1. Choose **D**ata, F**o**rm. The Data Form appears.
2. Choose **C**riteria. A blank Criteria Data Form appears (see figure 7.11).

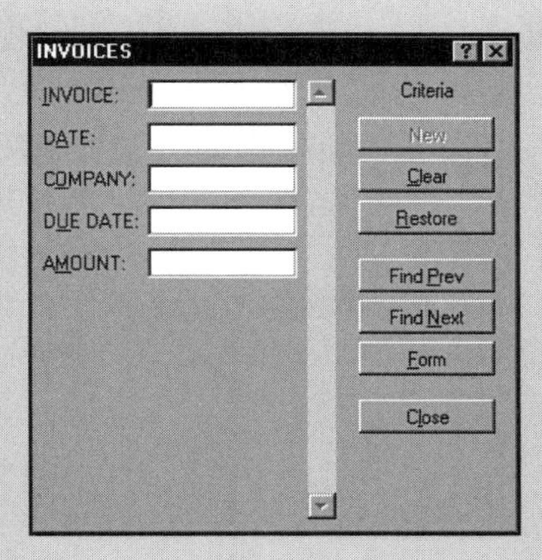

Figure 7.11
A Criteria Data Form.

You select a text box by clicking it. Then you enter the criterion or pattern for which you want to search.

3. Click the AMOUNT text box, and type **>2000**.

Now your Criteria Data Form should look like figure 7.12. The search criterion is an amount greater than 2,000.

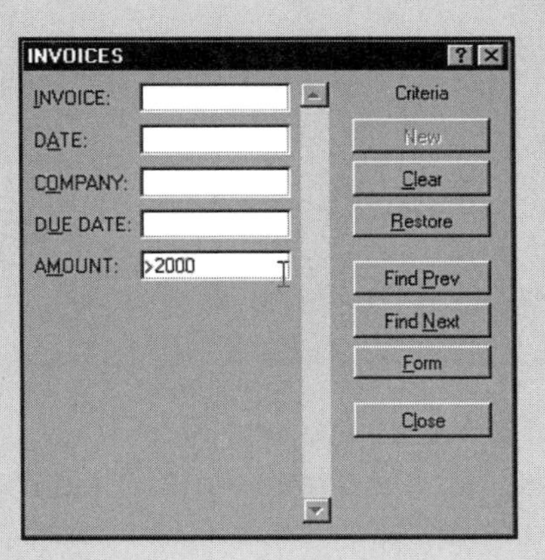

Figure 7.12
A single search criterion.

4. Choose the Find Next button. The next record to match the defined criterion appears on-screen (see figure 7.13). If no matches exist, you hear a beep.

(continues)

Finding Records Using the Data Form (continued)

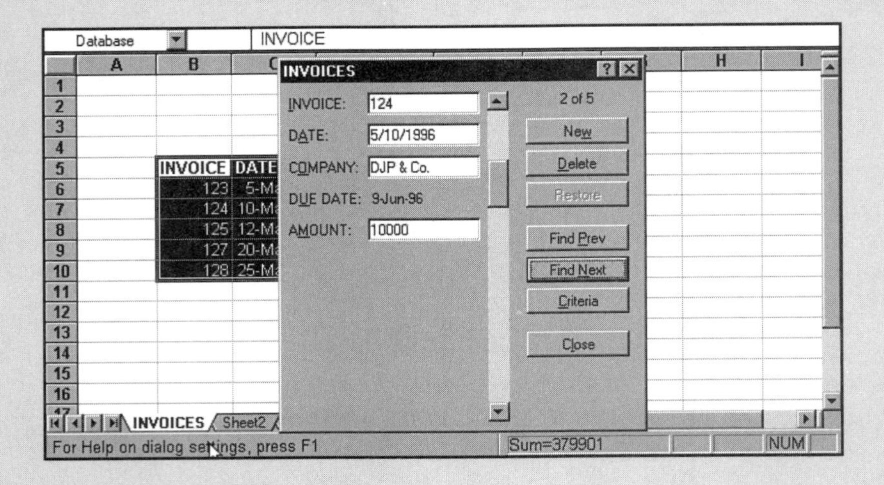

Figure 7.13
The next record matching the search criterion.

Note: *Remember that the search for a record that matches the selection criteria starts from the next record below the record that is current when you first click Find* ***N****ext. You need to click Find* ***P****rev to "find" the current record and any records above the current record that match the criteria.*

5. Choose the Find **P**rev button if you want to search backward through the database to find a match.

6. Choose C**l**ose to clear the dialog box.

Keep this workbook open for the following tutorial.

Key field
A field used to find a particular record in a database because each record contains a unique value in that field.

Searching by Using an Identifier Field

If each record in your database has a unique identifier (sometimes called a *key field*), such as a Social Security number or the invoice number in the sample database, Excel can quickly search even large databases, and find and display the record. Although the sample database doesn't contain many records, the next tutorial illustrates the search technique.

Finding a Specific Record Using the Data Form

In this tutorial, you find the record with an INVOICE number of 126 in the Fig72 database workbook. Follow these steps:

1. Choose **D**ata, F**o**rm. The Data Form appears.

2. Choose **C**riteria. A blank Criteria Data Form appears (refer to figure 7.11.).

3. Type **126** in the **I**NVOICE text box, which already has the blinking insertion point in it.

4. Choose the Find **N**ext button in the Criteria Data Form. The record matching the defined criteria appears on-screen.

5. Choose Close to clear the dialog box.

Keep this workbook open for the following tutorial.

Defining Multiple Selection Criteria

You can specify multiple search criteria. For example, you can search for records that have a specified amount and that have a certain due date. This capability enables you to conduct more specific searches and to find all the records you want in a single search operation.

Note: *A limitation of the Criteria Data Form is that you cannot use the Data Form if you are looking for records that match either one criteria or the other. To find records where one criteria or the other is met, you must use the commands in the Data Filter submenu (discussed under Objective 8).*

Finding Records Using the Data Form and Multiple Criteria in an AND Relationship

In this tutorial, you use multiple criteria to find all records in the Fig72 database workbook that are due after June 7 and have an invoice amount greater than or equal to $2,000. Follow these steps:

1. Choose Data, Form. The Data Form appears.
2. Choose Criteria. A blank Criteria Data Form appears (refer to figure 7.11.).
3. Click the text box to the right of DUE DATE, and type **>6/7/1996**.
4. Click the text box to the right of AMOUNT, and type **>=2000**.

   Figure 7.14 shows the completed Criteria Data Form.

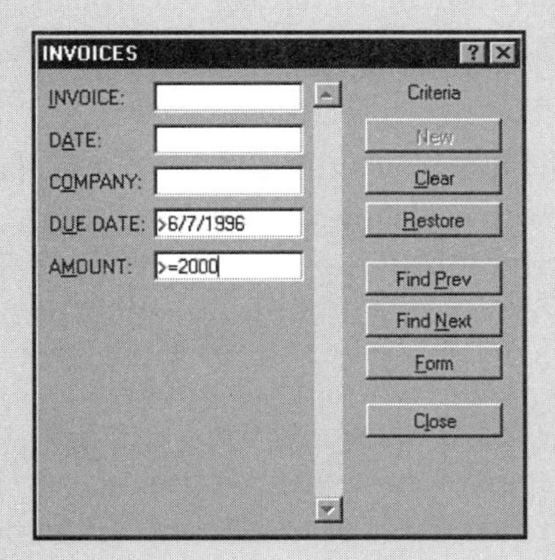

Figure 7.14 Multiple criteria in the Criteria Data Form.

5. Click the Find Next button in the Criteria Data Form.

   The first record that matches the criteria appears (see figure 7.15).

(continues)

7

Finding Records Using the Data Form and Multiple Criteria in an AND Relationship (continued)

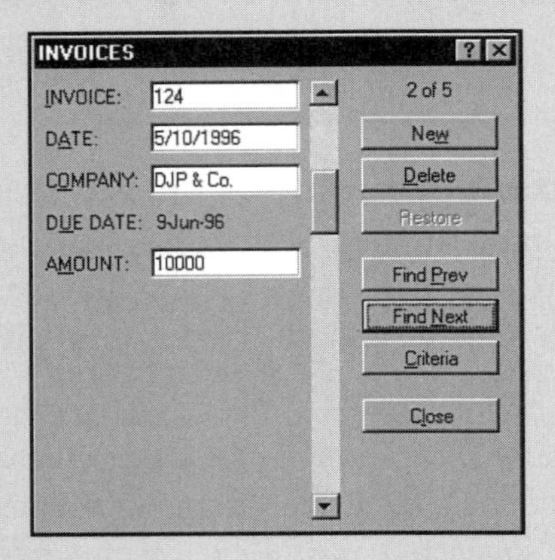

Figure 7.15
The first match.

6. Use the Find **N**ext and Find **P**rev buttons to see all the records that match the multiple criteria.

7. Choose C**l**ose to clear the dialog box.

Keep this workbook open for the following tutorial.

Objective 8: Find Records in a Database by Using AutoFilter

If you want to find records that match more complex criteria or if you want to print the records, you must use the **D**ata, **F**ilter command. This command displays a submenu with two filtering options: Auto**F**ilter and **A**dvanced Filter.

Note: *For specifying very complex criteria, you use the* **A***dvanced Filter command, which is beyond the scope of this text. To learn more about specifying complex selection criteria, read Que's book* Special Edition Using Excel for Windows 95.

Filter
The criteria that tell Excel which database records to display.

In this section, you learn how to specify a *filter* for a List (a database) to show only the data you want to see. To select your List for filtering, click any cell in the List, and the entire List containing the cell gets selected. Then you choose the **D**ata, **F**ilter, Auto**F**ilter command. Filter arrows appear next to the field names in your List (see figure 7.16).

When you click a filter arrow, a list of criteria appears under the arrow (see figure 7.17). Four choices always appear in your list of criteria. Two of the choices, (All) and (Custom), always appear at the top of the list. (All), the default choice, shows all the records without using the field to filter out records. You can choose (All) when you want to remove any filtering criteria you have previously established for a field. (Custom) enables you to specify multiple selection conditions in an AND or OR relationship. When you choose (Custom), you can use the comparison operators (shown in Table 7.1) in your criteria.

Filter arrows

	A	B	C	D	E	F	G
1	Region	District	Dollars	Employee	Increase		
2	Central	Butte	$437,224.00	15	58%		
3	North Central	Minneapolis	$205,433.00	10	14%		
4	North East	Washington	$138,377.00	4	37%		
5	North West	Portland	$101,470.00	2	94%		
6	North West	Seattle	$174,974.00	4	5%		
7	South	Atlanta	$234,923.00	7	11%		
8	South Central	Dallas	$378,452.00	5	19%		
9	South West	San Diego	$123,456.00	3	3%		
10	South	Birmingham	$118,729.00	6	47%		
11	South East	Charleston	$194,632.00	6	21%		
12	North Central	Chicago	$457,291.00	12	72%		
13	South Central	New Orleans	$127,821.00	5	56%		
14	North West	Boise	$117,880.00	2	12%		
15	North East	New York	$141,337.00	5	3%		
16	North East	Philadelphia	$207,485.00	7	38%		

c2lp3

Figure 7.16 The filter arrows provided by the AutoFilter command.

	A	B	C	D	E	F	G
1	Region	District	Dollars	Employee	Increase		
2	Central	(All)	$437,224.00	15	58%		
3	North Central	(Top 10...)	$205,433.00	10	14%		
4	North East	(Custom...) / Atlanta	$138,377.00	4	37%		
5	North West	Birmingham	$101,470.00	2	94%		
6	North West	Boise / Boston	$174,974.00	4	5%		
7	South	Butte	$234,923.00	7	11%		
8	South Central	Dallas	$378,452.00	5	19%		
9	South West	San Diego	$123,456.00	3	3%		
10	South	Birmingham	$118,729.00	6	47%		

Figure 7.17 The options provided by the AutoFilter command.

Two choices always appear at the bottom of the list, (Blanks) and (NonBlanks). (Blanks) shows all records without an entry for a field. (NonBlanks) shows only records that have an entry for a field. The remaining choices in the criteria list are the data values in the field. When you choose a data value as a criterion (a filter), only the records with this value in the field will be displayed—all the other records will not "pass through the filter."

You can use the filter arrows to create selection criteria using as many of the database fields as you want. When a selection criteria exists for a field, its filter arrow is colored blue. To remove a filter condition, click the blue filter arrow, and select the (All) criterion. To turn off the AutoFilter, choose **D**ata, **F**ilter; then choose Auto**F**ilter. The filter arrows next to the field names disappear, and all the data records appear.

For the remaining tutorials in this chapter, use the workbook C2lp3, which you created in Continuing Project #3 at the end of Chapter 2 (see figure 7.18). If you did not complete that project, ask your instructor for the data file. The following tutorials show you how to use AutoFilter to extract from your database the records that meet one or more selection criteria.

Figure 7.18
The C2lp3 database.

Microsoft Excel - C2LP3.xls

File Edit View Insert Format Tools Data Window Help

A1 Region

	A	B	C	D	E	F	G
1	Region	District	Dollars	Employees	Increase		
2	Central	Butte	$437,224.00	15	58%		
3	North Central	Minneapolis	$205,433.00	10	14%		
4	North East	Washington	$138,377.00	4	37%		
5	North West	Portland	$101,470.00	2	94%		
6	North West	Seattle	$174,974.00	4	5%		
7	South	Atlanta	$234,923.00	7	11%		
8	South Central	Dallas	$378,452.00	5	19%		
9	South West	San Diego	$123,456.00	3	3%		
10	South	Birmingham	$118,729.00	6	47%		
11	South East	Charleston	$194,632.00	6	21%		
12	North Central	Chicago	$457,291.00	12	72%		
13	South Central	New Orleans	$127,821.00	5	56%		
14	North West	Boise	$117,880.00	2	12%		
15	North East	New York	$141,337.00	5	3%		
16	North East	Philadelphia	$207,485.00	7	38%		

Chapt7

Ready Sum=0

Filtering Records Using One Filter Criterion

Open the workbook file C2lp3. Name the worksheet tab Chapt7. Your screen should look like figure 7.18. To extract only the records from offices in the North East region, follow these steps:

1. Click cell A1 to select the entire List.

   Only the cell you click appears to be selected, but all the cells in the List are now selected.

2. Choose **D**ata, **F**ilter; then choose Auto**F**ilter.

   The filter arrows appear next to the field names (see figure 7.19).

Figure 7.19
The C2lp3 database when AutoFilter is in use.

A1 Region

Filter arrows

	A	B	C	D	E	F	G
1	Region	District	Dollars	Employee	Increase		
2	Central	Butte	$437,224.00	15	58%		
3	North Central	Minneapolis	$205,433.00	10	14%		
4	North East	Washington	$138,377.00	4	37%		
5	North West	Portland	$101,470.00	2	94%		
6	North West	Seattle	$174,974.00	4	5%		
7	South	Atlanta	$234,923.00	7	11%		
8	South Central	Dallas	$378,452.00	5	19%		
9	South West	San Diego	$123,456.00	3	3%		
10	South	Birmingham	$118,729.00	6	47%		
11	South East	Charleston	$194,632.00	6	21%		
12	North Central	Chicago	$457,291.00	12	72%		
13	South Central	New Orleans	$127,821.00	5	56%		
14	North West	Boise	$117,880.00	2	12%		
15	North East	New York	$141,337.00	5	3%		
16	North East	Philadelphia	$207,485.00	7	38%		

3. Click the filter arrow in cell A1.

4. From the list that drops down, choose North East.

5. Only the records from the North East Region are extracted and displayed on the database screen (see figure 7.20).

Figure 7.20 The extracted database records.

	A	B	C	D	E	F	G
1	Region	District	Dollars	Employee	Increase		
4	North East	Washington	$138,377.00	4	37%		
15	North East	New York	$141,337.00	5	3%		
16	North East	Philadelphia	$207,485.00	7	38%		
19	North East	Boston	$184,862.00	5	15%		
21							
22							
23							

6. If your computer has a printer attached to it, click the Print button to print the extracted records.
7. Click the blue filter arrow in cell A1.
8. Scroll up through the list, and click (All).

This step removes the filtering condition that uses this field. The filter arrow in cell A1 is no longer blue; no records are filtered out.

Keep this workbook open for the following tutorial.

In the next tutorial, you use the Custom AutoFilter to display only those records that meet either one condition or another condition.

Filtering Records Using an OR Relation in One Field

Using a Custom Filter to see only the records of offices in the North East OR the South, follow these steps:

1. Click the filter arrow in cell A1.
2. From the list, click (Custom...).

   The Custom AutoFilter dialog box appears. In this dialog box, you build your selection criteria. The dialog box contains two criterion text boxes so that you can use multiple selection conditions. To the left of each criterion box, you see a down-pointing arrow button that enables you to select an operator (=, >, <, >=, <=, <>). If you set two selection conditions, you can make them work in an AND or an OR relationship by clicking the appropriate option in the dialog box.

3. Select North East from the dialog box's Region drop-down list (see figure 7.21).

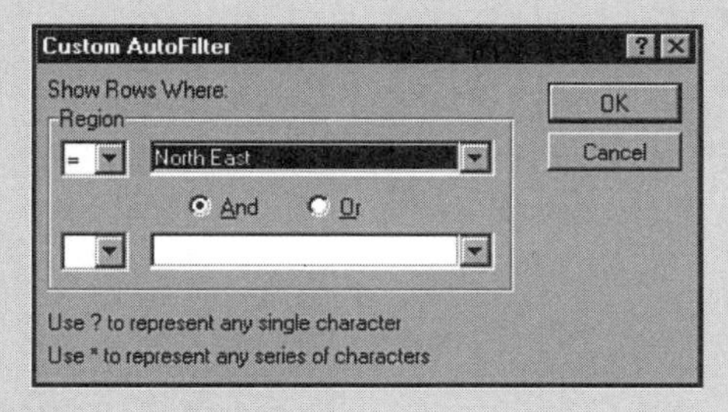

Figure 7.21 The Custom AutoFilter dialog box.

(continues)

7

Filtering Records Using an OR Relation in One Field (continued)

4. Click the **Or** option to make the relationship between the two criteria an OR relationship.

5. Click the down-pointing arrow to the left of the lower criterion box to display the drop-down list of relational operators (see figure 7.22).

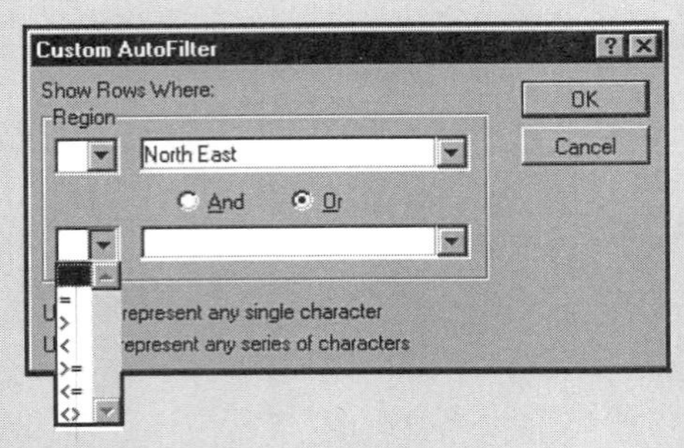

Figure 7.22 The list of relational operators.

6. Click the = operator.

7. Click the down-pointing arrow to the right of the second (the lower) criterion box.

   The list of data values in the field appears (see figure 7.23).

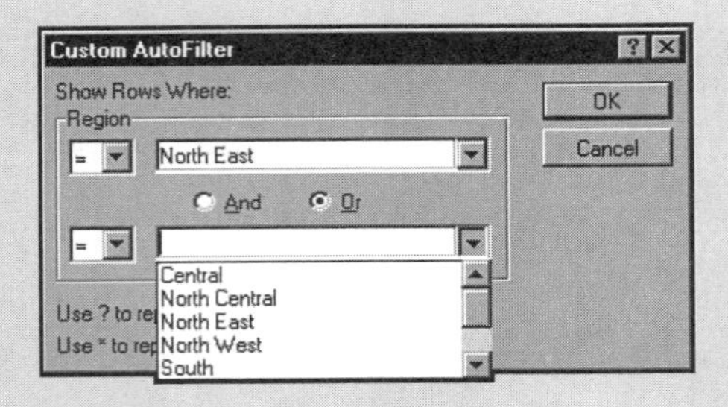

Figure 7.23 The list of the field's data values in the database.

8. Click South in the list of data values.

   Now your dialog box should look like figure 7.24. Make sure that the = relational operator appears in both boxes to the left of the criterion boxes and that the **Or** option is selected.

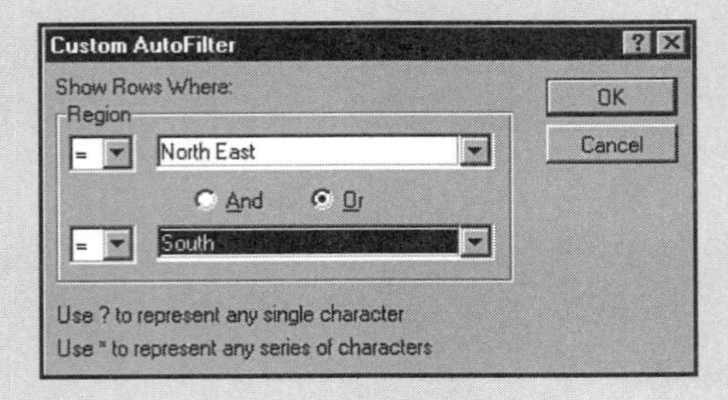

Figure 7.24 The completed Custom Auto-Filter dialog box.

9. Click OK.

   The records of offices in either the North East or in the South are extracted (see figure 7.25).

Figure 7.25
The extracted database records.

	A	B	C	D	E	F	G
1	Region	District	Dollars	Employee	Increase		
4	North East	Washington	$138,377.00	4	37%		
7	South	Atlanta	$234,923.00	7	11%		
10	South	Birmingham	$118,729.00	6	47%		
15	North East	New York	$141,337.00	5	3%		
16	North East	Philadelphia	$207,485.00	7	38%		
19	North East	Boston	$184,862.00	5	15%		
20	South	Miami	$102,382.00	2	27%		
21							
22							

10. Click the filter arrow in cell A1, and choose (All) to remove the filtering condition.

Keep this workbook open for the following tutorial.

Note: *You should remove all old filtering conditions before you set new filtering conditions. Otherwise, you may forget that you have previously set a filtering condition that is still affecting a more recent search.*

Filtering Records Using Two Fields in an AND Relation

To see the records for offices in the North West with only two employees, you do not need a Custom Filter. Just follow these steps:

1. Click the filter arrow in cell A1.
2. In the List, click North West.

   All the North West offices appear. Now you add the additional filter that will filter out all North West records that don't have exactly two employees.

3. Click the filter arrow in cell D1.
4. In the List, click 2.

   Now your screen should look like figure 7.26. Note that two of the filter arrows on your screen are blue because you are using two fields in your criteria. These filters will keep filtering until you remove them or leave the AutoFilter.

Figure 7.26
The extracted database records.

	A	B	C	D	E	F	G
1	Region	District	Dollars	Employee	Increase		
5	North West	Portland	$101,470.00	2	94%		
14	North West	Boise	$117,880.00	2	12%		
21							
22							
23							

(continues)

Filtering Records Using Two Fields in an AND Relation (continued)

5. Remove both filters by clicking each blue filter arrow and clicking (All) in the list.

Now all the records should be displayed because you have removed the filters. Remember to remove old filters that you are not going to use again before you set up new filters.

Keep this workbook open for the following tutorial.

Often, you will need to select those records that contain data that falls within a range of data values. The next exercise shows you how to do this.

Filtering Records Using Filters That Filter Out a Range of Values

To find the offices with sales of more than $120,000.00 AND fewer than 6 employees, follow these steps:

1. Click the filter arrow in cell C1.
2. Click (Custom) in the list.

   The Custom AutoFilter dialog box appears.
3. Click the down-arrow button to the left of the first (the top) criterion text box.
4. In the list, click >.
5. In the first (the top) text box, type **120000**.
6. Click OK.
7. Click the filter arrow in cell D1.
8. Click (Custom).

   The Custom AutoFilter dialog box appears.
9. Click the down-arrow button to the left of the first criterion box; then click < in the list.
10. Click the down-arrow button to the right of the first criterion text box.
11. In the values list, click 6.
12. Click OK.

Now your screen should look like figure 7.27. Notice that all the extracted records have sales of more than $120,000.00 AND fewer than 6 employees.

Figure 7.27
The extracted database records.

	A	B	C	D	E	F	G
1	Region	District	Dollars	Employee	Increase		
4	North East	Washington	$138,377.00	4	37%		
6	North West	Seattle	$174,974.00	4	5%		
8	South Central	Dallas	$378,452.00	5	19%		
9	South West	San Diego	$123,456.00	3	3%		
13	South Central	New Orleans	$127,821.00	5	56%		
15	North East	New York	$141,337.00	5	3%		
19	North East	Boston	$184,862.00	5	15%		
21							
22							
23							

⑬ Choose **D**ata **F**ilter Auto**F**ilter.

All filters and the AutoFilter are turned off, and all your records are displayed. You can now close the workbook and exit from Excel.

Chapter Summary

This chapter introduces you to fundamental database concepts. You have learned what a database is and how you create a database in an Excel worksheet. Other topics in the chapter include entering data into a database, and using the Data Form to add and delete records. You have also learned how to sort your database. Additionally, you have learned how to define criteria and find records that match the criteria by using the Data Form and the AutoFilter.

If you want to explore databases in more depth and experiment with some of Excel's advanced database features, you may want to read Que's book *Special Edition Using Excel for Windows 95*. It includes instructions on how to use Excel's SQL feature, which enables you to access external databases and bring the data into an Excel worksheet.

Checking Your Skills

True/False

For each of the following, circle T or F to indicate whether the statement is true or false.

T F **1.** Each database field name can occupy only one cell.

T F **2.** A record is one column in the database.

T F **3.** A field used as a filter in AutoFilter has a red arrow.

T F **4.** The row of field names should be included in the range of cells you plan to sort.

T F **5.** When you use the Data Form to insert a record into your database, the database range does not expand to include the new record.

T F **6.** Excel can sort data using up to two fields.

T F **7.** You can find records in an Excel database by using the Data Form.

T F **8.** You can sort database records using the Data Form.

T F **9.** An Excel database can be sorted only in ascending order.

T F **10.** When sorting a database, you should select only the fields used to sort the records before selecting the **S**ort command.

Multiple Choice

In the blank provided, write the letter of the correct answer for each of the following.

_____ **1.** Which of the following relationship(s) can be used in Custom AutoFilter criteria?

a. AND

b. OR

c. both AND and OR

d. IF

_____ **2.** Which of the following menus contain the command that enables you to delete a record from a database?

a. **F**ile

b. **D**ata

c. **T**ools

d. F**o**rmat

_____ **3.** Which of the following menus contain the command that enables you to define a criteria?

a. **E**dit

b. **D**ata

c. **S**election

d. none of the above

_____ **4.** Excel enables you to sort up to _____ different fields.

a. two

b. three

c. four

d. five

_____ **5.** Which of the following options in the criteria list, displayed when you click a filter arrow, removes any filters for that field?

a. (Blank)

b. <>

c. (All)

d. none of the above

_____ **6.** Using the Data Form, you can _________ records.

a. add

b. delete

c. find

d. all the above

_____ **7.** The symbol for the criterion "less than" is _____.

a. <

b. >

c. |

d. ~

_____ **8.** The best way to add records to a database is to use the _____ command.

a. **E**dit, **A**dd

b. **E**dit, **I**nsert

c. **D**ata, **I**nsert

d. **D**ata, F**o**rm

_____ **9.** If you perform a sort that is incorrect, choose the _____ command to return to the record order of the original database.

a. **E**dit, **U**ndo Sort

b. **D**ata, **R**esort

c. **D**ata, **U**ndo Sort

d. **D**ata, **R**estore

____ **10.** Which of the following buttons in the Data Form do you click to find the records that match a search condition in the database?

a. **S**earch

b. S**e**ek

c. **C**riteria

d. none of the above

Fill-in-the-Blank

In the blank provided, write the correct answer for each of the following.

1. To establish a filter to search a database for records with a PAYMENT field value of less than 100, the criteria is ______________.
2. The best way to add records to an existing database is by using the Data ______________.
3. When you have finished finding records using the **D**ata, **F**ilter command, you can return to the normal worksheet mode by ______________.
4. To find records in a database where one criteria OR the other is met, you use the ______________.
5. To find a record in the database with an invoice number less than 130, you enter ______________ in the INVOICE field of the Data Form.
6. The ______________ names indicate the information contained in each record.
7. The first row of a database must contain ______________.
8. A ______________ is a pattern or the specific details you are looking for in a database record.
9. In an ascending Excel sort, ______________ will be sorted before letters.
10. An Excel database is also referred to as an Excel ______________.

Applying Your Skills

Review Exercises

Before you start these exercises, make sure you have the Excel window maximized so that you can see all the data in your database.

Exercise 1: Sorting a Database

Open the C2lp2 file, which you created at the end of Chapter 2.

1. Delete row 6 so that the field names are in the row above the data. Save this worksheet on your disk as **C7sp1**.

2. Sort the database worksheet in ascending order on the INDUSTRY field, and print the worksheet. Now sort the database in descending order on the NET INCOME field. Return the records to INDUSTRY order by using the **U**ndo Sort command.

   If, as you work on this exercise, you find that the Sort dialog box appears over the database so that you can't see the rows and columns to use as sort keys, click the title bar of the dialog box, and drag the box to a better position on-screen.

Exercise 2: Adding Records Using the Data Form

Open the C7sp1 file that you saved at the start of Exercise 1.

1. Define cells A5 through H13 as a database. Use the Data Form to add the two records shown in rows 14 and 15 of figure 7.28. Your worksheet should now look like the one in figure 7.28. Save the new worksheet as **C7sp2**.

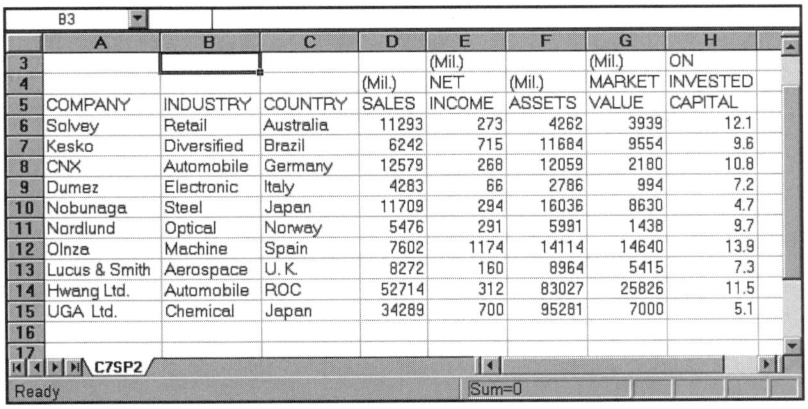

Figure 7.28 The completed Investments database.

B3

	A	B	C	D	E	F	G	H
3					(Mil.)		(Mil.)	ON
4				(Mil.)	NET	(Mil.)	MARKET	INVESTED
5	COMPANY	INDUSTRY	COUNTRY	SALES	INCOME	ASSETS	VALUE	CAPITAL
6	Solvey	Retail	Australia	11293	273	4262	3939	12.1
7	Kesko	Diversified	Brazil	6242	715	11684	9554	9.6
8	CNX	Automobile	Germany	12579	268	12059	2180	10.8
9	Dumez	Electronic	Italy	4283	66	2786	994	7.2
10	Nobunaga	Steel	Japan	11709	294	16036	8630	4.7
11	Nordlund	Optical	Norway	5476	291	5991	1438	9.7
12	Olnza	Machine	Spain	7602	1174	14114	14640	13.9
13	Lucus & Smith	Aerospace	U.K.	8272	160	8964	5415	7.3
14	Hwang Ltd.	Automobile	ROC	52714	312	83027	25826	11.5
15	UGA Ltd.	Chemical	Japan	34289	700	95281	7000	5.1
16								
17								

C7SP2

Ready Sum=0

Exercise 3: Finding Records Using the Data Form
Open the C7sp2 file that you saved at the end of Exercise 2.

Use the Data Form to find all the records of companies in the Automobile industry. Then use the Data Form to find the records of all the companies with a Percent Return on Invested Capital less than 7 percent.

Exercise 4: Entering Records Using the Data Form
Enter the field names shown in figure 7.1 and the data (in figure 7.1) for Ken Becker. Then use the Data Form to enter the remaining records. Enter all the data shown in figure 7.1. Click the Criteria button and enter >L in the Last Name text box in the Criteria form. Use the Find **P**rev and Find **N**ext buttons to find the records of people whose last names begin with the letters L through Z. Save the file as **C7ex4**.

Exercise 5: Sorting Records Using an Address Field
Sort the records in the database you created in Exercise 4 using ascending order and the Street field. Print the result. Use the data form to add your name, street address, and phone. Then sort the database again so that it is in order by Last and First name. Print the result. Save the file again as **C7ex5**.

Continuing Projects

Project 1: Sorting a Database on Multiple Fields and Using Multiple Criteria

1. Open the C7sp2 database. Sort the database in ascending order. Use the following multiple sort keys:

   1st key = COUNTRY
   2nd key = INDUSTRY
   3rd key = VALUE

2. Define the records as a database, and then use the **D**ata, F**o**rm command to find all the records of companies in the Automobile industry.

   Next, use the **D**ata, F**o**rm command to find the records of all the companies with a Percent Return on Invested Capital less than 7 percent.

3. Use AutoFilter to display the records of all the companies with a Percent Return on Invested Capital less than 7 percent.

4. Print the records of all the companies with a Percent Return on Invested Capital less than 7 percent.

Project 2: Setting Up, Sorting, and Searching a Database

1. Create a database of your friends and coworkers. Include (at least) the following fields: Last Name, First Name, Initial, Age, Gender, Phone, and Birthday.
2. Save the worksheet on your disk as **C7cp2**, and then use the Data Form to delete and add records.
3. Sort the database so that it is in alphabetical order using the Last Name, First Name, and Initial fields.
4. Use the Data Form to find records. Set up a criteria using the Data Form to find the records with Smith in the Last Name field AND an Age over 30. (You may need to add some new "coworkers" to your database first.) Then use AutoFilter to extract these records and print them.

Project 3: Sorting and Searching the Regional Offices Database

1. Open the C2lp3 database. In column F, number the records in order from 1 to 19. This numbering will enable you to sort the database in any order and then return the records to their original order by sorting using column F.
2. Sort the data in order from highest Dollars of sales to lowest Dollars of sales. Print the worksheet.
3. Sort the data in order using the Region field. Print the worksheet.
4. Return the data to its original order by sorting the numbers in column F.
5. Use AutoFilter to display the records of any offices in either the North Central or South Central regions with sales of more than $300,000.00. Print the results.
6. Close the C2lp3 workbook without saving your changes.

CHAPTER 8

Using Excel Macros to Automate Repetitive Tasks

Procedure
A macro; a series of Visual Basic statements that you create using the Macro Recorder and store together in a macro sheet.

In the preceding chapters, you learned how to use Excel to perform a variety of tasks. Some tasks, like moving account balances from the 30 Days Overdue area of a worksheet to the 60 Days Overdue area at the end of a month, or entering budget line items and formatting new sheets at the beginning of a new month, are repetitive. Whenever you find yourself performing the same series of actions again and again in Excel, you should consider using Excel's Recorder. When you use the Recorder to record your actions and commands, Excel creates a Visual Basic *procedure* (called a macro in Excel). Once a procedure has been created, you never have to enter the same commands or perform the sequence of mouse actions again; you simply tell Excel to run the recorded procedure.

Visual Basic for Applications
A programming language; the Excel Macro Recorder creates macros consisting of Visual Basic statements.

These procedures function in the same way as the macros you may have used in earlier versions of Excel or in another spreadsheet program, such as Lotus 1-2-3. *Visual Basic for Applications* is the Microsoft programming language used in the newest Microsoft products. You don't, however, have to be a programmer or even understand Visual Basic to create procedures. You just tell Excel to watch what you do and create and save a program to do the same things. In this way, you can automate repetitive tasks. The Visual Basic procedures you record are then stored in workbook sheets called modules.

Macro
A stored list of commands and keystrokes that Excel automatically executes.

A *macro* provides a great time saver for performing a repetitive task in a worksheet. Excel macros can automatically perform such tasks as entering keystrokes, formatting, and issuing commands. Using macros may sound complicated, but it is really easy—as you will see.

Module
One or more Visual Basic macros stored in a separate workbook sheet (a module sheet).

To create a macro, you simply turn on the Excel Macro Recorder, perform the sequence of actions that you want to record, and then turn off the Macro Recorder. As you record your actions, they immediately get translated into a Visual Basic procedure and stored in a separate *module* sheet in your workbook. You can then use the macro in any worksheet in the workbook. The secret to creating these automated procedures is a little planning and some practice.

Objectives

By the time you have finished this chapter, you will have learned to

1. Create a Macro by Using the Macro Recorder
2. Run a Macro
3. Create a Button to Run Your Macro
4. Delete a Macro from a Workbook

Objective 1: Create a Macro by Using the Macro Recorder

Before you start the Recorder, plan exactly what you want to do in the worksheet and the order in which you want to take the actions. Then run through the steps in the procedure to verify that they work exactly as you planned. As a rule, planning and then recording the macro in one session works the best because you will make fewer mistakes. You should also decide on a name, without spaces or periods, for the macro; the name should reflect the actions the macro performs. If the name is more than one word and you want to separate the words, use an underscore (_).

After you have planned the steps in the procedure and decided on a name, you need to prepare to record the macro. Before starting the Macro Recorder, prepare the worksheet by doing everything you do not want included in the macro. This preparation may include such things as opening a new worksheet or scrolling to a specific location.

Once you start the Macro Recorder, everything you do in Excel—every cell you select, every character you type in the worksheet, and every command you choose—gets recorded and becomes part of the Visual Basic procedure. When you run the macro, the results are the same as if you had entered all the keystrokes, formatting, and commands yourself. The macro works faster, however, and you don't have to worry about making a typing error.

Automate
To create a Visual Basic Procedure (a macro) to perform repetitive worksheet tasks automatically.

In this chapter, you first familiarize yourself with using the Excel Recorder by creating a macro that *automates* the creation of a simple worksheet. This worksheet has an input cell and a calculated output cell. You enter a cost in the input cell, and the output cell calculates the discounted cost. The discount rate is displayed in a third cell.

Preparing to Record a Macro

To prepare your worksheet and display the Record New Macro dialog box, follow these steps:

1. Open a new workbook by choosing **F**ile, **N**ew or by clicking the New Workbook button at the left end of the Standard toolbar.

❷ Choose **T**ools, **R**ecord Macro; then choose **R**ecord New Macro (see figure 8.1).

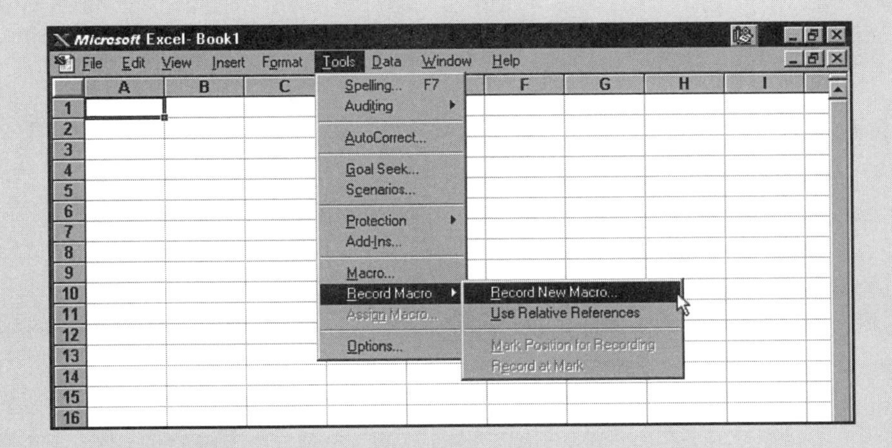

Figure 8.1
The menu choices to begin recording a new macro.

The Record New Macro dialog box, shown in figure 8.2, appears.

Figure 8.2
The Record New Macro dialog box.

Caution
Remember, no spaces are allowed in a macro name.

You enter the first information used by the Macro Recorder in the Record New Macro dialog box. You use the **M**acro Name and **D**escription text boxes to name your macro and add a short description of the purpose of the macro. Including a complete but brief description here is important if you intend to keep this macro for more than a few days. If you do not write a good description, you probably won't remember what the macro does when you want to use it, say, a year from now. Excel usually suggests a description that includes the date and the name of the purchaser of the copy of Excel you are using. Delete this default description, and enter your description.

8

Starting the Macro Recorder

To fill in the Record New Macro dialog box and start the Macro Recorder, follow these steps:

❶ In the **M**acro Name text box, type **DiscountCalculator**.

❷ Click the **D**escription text box, and delete the text now in the box.

(continues)

Starting the Macro Recorder (continued)

3. In the empty Description text box, type **A macro to create a discount calculator**. Always remember to include a clear description.

4. Click OK.

The Stop Recording Macro button appears as the only button in a floating toolbar in the upper right corner of the worksheet, and the word `Recording` appears in the status bar at the bottom of the screen (see figure 8.3). The Macro Recorder now records what you do—all your keystrokes and mouse clicks—until you click the Stop Recording button.

Figure 8.3
The screen when the Macro Recorder is running.

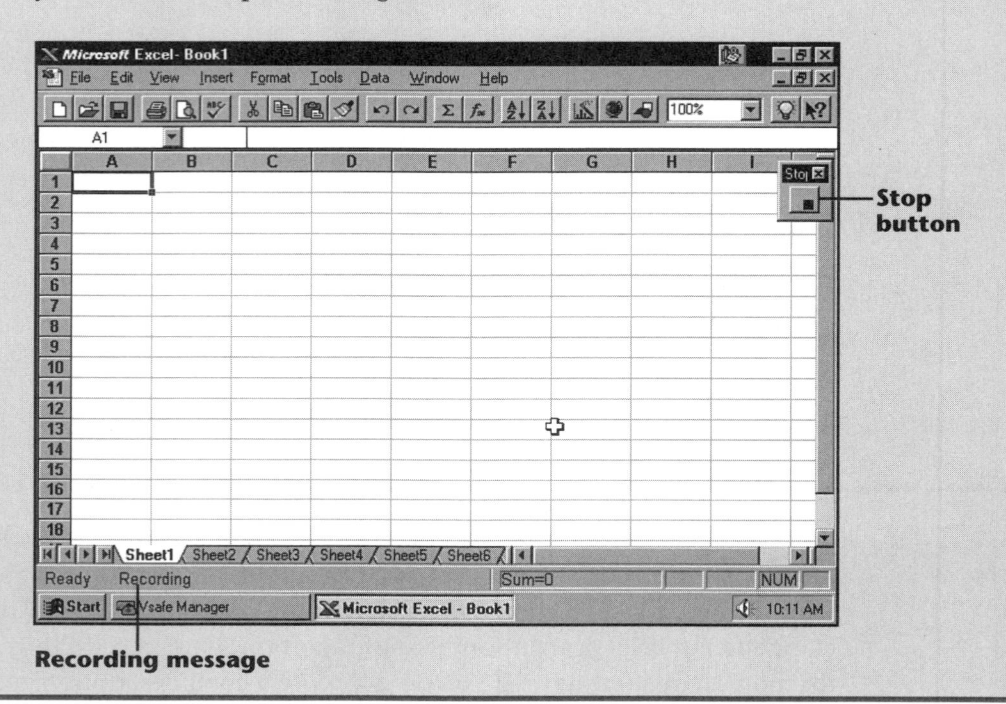

Caution
Work slowly and carefully as you record a macro because the Recorder will record any mistakes.

You now record the macro by simply creating the worksheet as you would normally. Read through the 19 steps in the following tutorial before you start. If you make a mistake, the Recorder will record it, and your macro won't work properly, so work slowly. If you make no mistakes when recording a macro, it will always run correctly regardless of how many complicated steps the macro has.

Recording the Macro

To create the worksheet, follow these steps:

1. Choose the **T**ools, **O**ptions command.

2. Click the View tab, and click the **G**ridlines check box to turn off the gridlines. Then click OK.

3. Type **Retail price** in cell B5, and press Enter.

4. Select cell C5, and choose F**o**rmat, C**e**lls.

5. Select the Protection tab, and deselect the Locked check box.

   This step turns off protection for the cell so that later, when you enable protection for the worksheet, you can still change the value in this cell.

6. Select the Number tab, select the currency format and click OK.

7. Enter **Discounted value:** in cell B7.

8. Enter **Discount rate:** in cell B9.

9. Place the mouse pointer on the vertical bar between the B and C column headings; it becomes a black double-headed arrow. Press and hold down the mouse button, and drag to make column B wide enough for the whole label in cell B7 to fit within the column.

10. Select cells B5:B9, and choose Format, Cells.

11. Click the Alignment tab, and in the Horizontal section, click the Right option button. Then click OK to right-justify the text in the cells.

12. Select cell C7, and choose Format, Cells.

13. Click the Number tab; select the currency format, and then click OK.

14. In cell C7, enter the formula **=(1-C9)*C5**.

15. Select cell C9, and choose Format, Cells.

16. Click the Number tab, select the Percentage format, and click OK.

17. Set a discount rate by entering **.05** in cell C9.

18. To protect the cells in the worksheet so that the user cannot type in them, choose Tools, Protection, Protect Sheet. Then click OK in the Protect Sheet dialog box.

The worksheet should now look like figure 8.4.

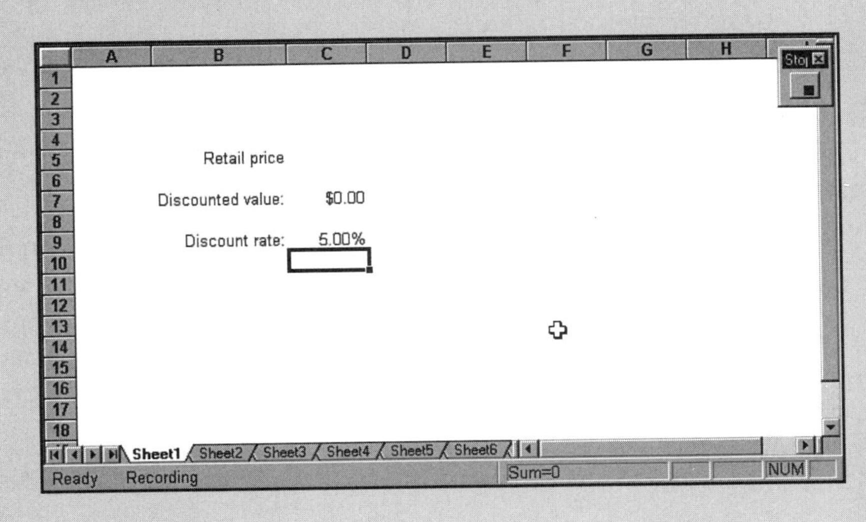

Figure 8.4
The worksheet after you have entered the commands, formatting, and keystrokes.

(continues)

Recording the Macro (continued)

19. You have finished all the steps in the macro. Click the Stop Macro button in the floating toolbar.

You have completed the macro. Excel stores it in the workbook sheet Module1, which is added into your workbook after Sheet16. Your next step is to test the macro to make sure that it works correctly.

Testing the Worksheet Procedure

To verify that you followed the proper steps as you recorded the macro, you can test the worksheet. Follow these steps:

1. Enter **10** in cell C5. The amount `$9.50` should appear in cell C7 (see figure 8.5).

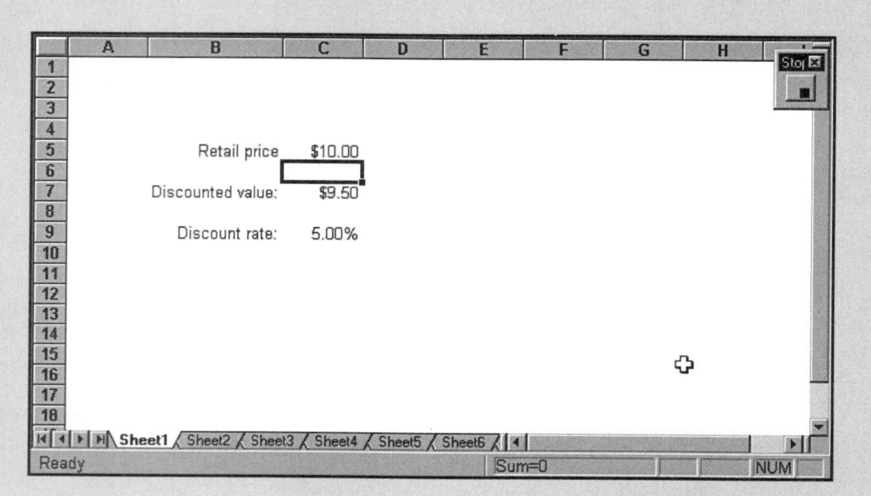

Figure 8.5 The worksheet as you are testing it.

2. Try to type anywhere else on the worksheet. Excel displays a box telling you that you cannot enter anything because the cell is locked. You protected the worksheet cells so that the users can enter data only where they are supposed to—in the input cell.

Viewing the Macro

You don't need to examine the recorded macro (or even understand it) before you use it. You can, however, easily take a look at the macro, but make sure not to change it accidentally. To examine your new procedure, find the Module1 tab at the bottom of the screen (after Sheet16), and click it. Your macro appears onscreen and looks like figure 8.6. (Depending on your program settings, you may not see the Visual Basic toolbar.)

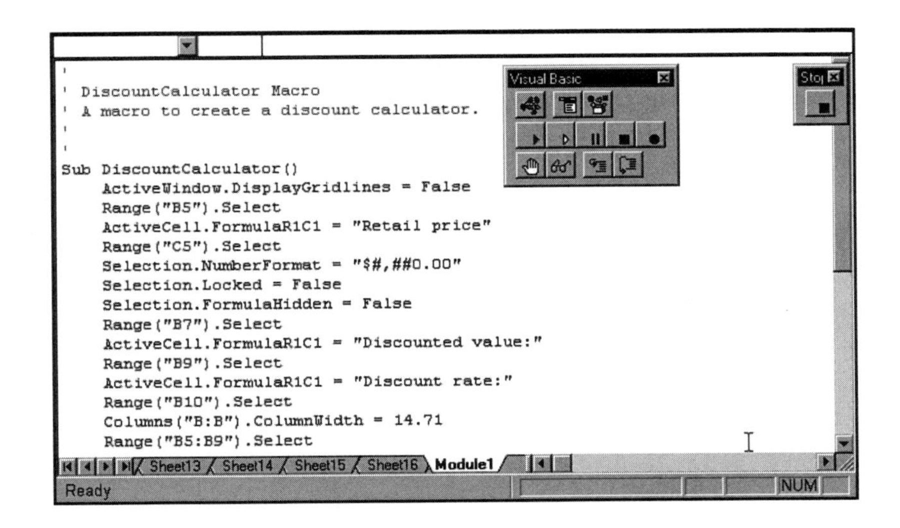

Figure 8.6
The new macro.

Some text in the module appears in green. These green lines are comment lines. Notice that the macro name and the description both appear in green and that each comment line is preceded by an apostrophe. If you use many Visual Basic macros, you can insert your own comments into a macro to document and explain its functions. The beginning and the end of a macro are indicated by blue text. The rest of the macro appears in black text. At the right of the screen is the Visual Basic toolbar, used to alter and test a macro. The alteration of macros is beyond the scope of this text. You probably want to let the Recorder create your macros until you become very familiar with Visual Basic.

Objective 2: Run a Macro

Caution
Be sure to make a backup of your workbook before you run a new macro.

You should save a backup copy of your workbook on disk before you run a macro for the first time. You could have an error in the macro that erases or alters part of your worksheet or file on your disk.

To run the macro you just created, first move to (click the tab of) an unused worksheet in your workbook (Sheet2, for example). Make sure that the sheet has nothing useful in the B5:C9 range because this procedure overwrites that area. If you want to reuse the sheet where you created the DiscountCalculator, make sure to turn off protection before you run the macro because the protected sheet cannot be changed.

Running Your New Macro

To run your new macro, follow these steps:

1. Click the tab of an unused worksheet in the workbook. The macro will create the discount calculations in this worksheet. If the Stop macro recording floating toolbar is not on your screen, choose View, Toolbars and click the check box next to Stop Recording in the Toolbars dialog box. Click OK.

(continues)

8

Running Your New Macro (continued)

2. Choose **T**ools; then choose **M**acro.

   The Macro dialog box appears (see figure 8.7). This dialog box shows all the procedures (macros) available in this workbook and enables you to run or delete a macro.

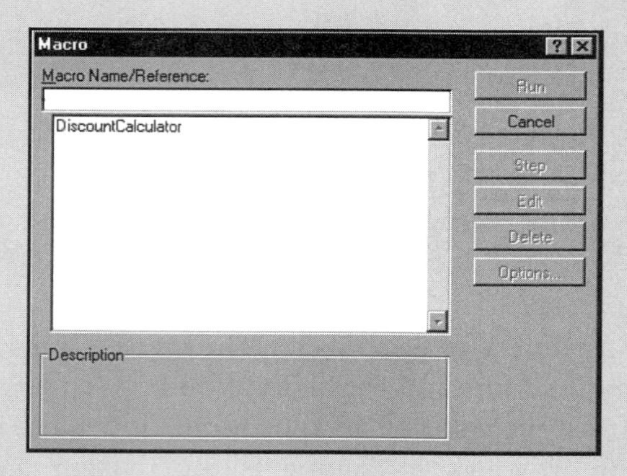

Figure 8.7
The Macro dialog box.

3. In the Macro dialog box, click the DiscountCalculator procedure to select it; then click the Run button.

The worksheet appears, and the macro runs, setting the contents and the formatting of the worksheet cells.

The completed worksheet is identical to the one you created with the Recorder running. And isn't running the macro more efficient than typing all the commands and keystrokes again? That's working smarter—not harder—in Excel 7.0.

If you have problems... Sometimes, a macro may not insert its results in the right place in your worksheet, or a macro may not work at all. Some macros may require you to select a cell (perhaps A1) before you run the macro. When you design a macro, you may want to activate a cell as the first step in the macro itself. Make sure that you make the appropriate cell active before you start the macro.

Objective 3: Create a Button to Run Your Macro

As you have learned, you can run macros by using the **T**ools, **M**acro command. Most people, however, prefer to create a button in their worksheet and attach their macro to the button. The button can then be edited to contain the name of the macro. Then just clicking that button runs the macro. The tool that creates a button for you is in the Drawing toolbar.

In the next tutorial, you create a button in an empty worksheet, attach the DiscountCalculator macro to the button, and then name the button to show which macro it runs. In the second tutorial of this section, you use the button to run the DiscountCalculator macro. Under Objective 4, you learn how to delete a button you no longer need from a worksheet.

Creating a Button to Run a Macro

To draw a button that you can use to run your macro, follow these steps:

1. Click the tab of an empty worksheet (use Sheet3) in the workbook that contains the DiscountCalculator macro. If the Stop macro recording floating toolbar is not on your screen, choose **V**iew, **T**oolbars and click the check box next to Stop Recording in the Toolbars dialog box. Click OK.

2. If the Drawing toolbar is not on your screen, click the Drawing button on the Standard toolbar.

   The Drawing toolbar appears (see figure 8.8). You use this toolbar to draw a button in your worksheet.

Figure 8.8
The Drawing toolbar.

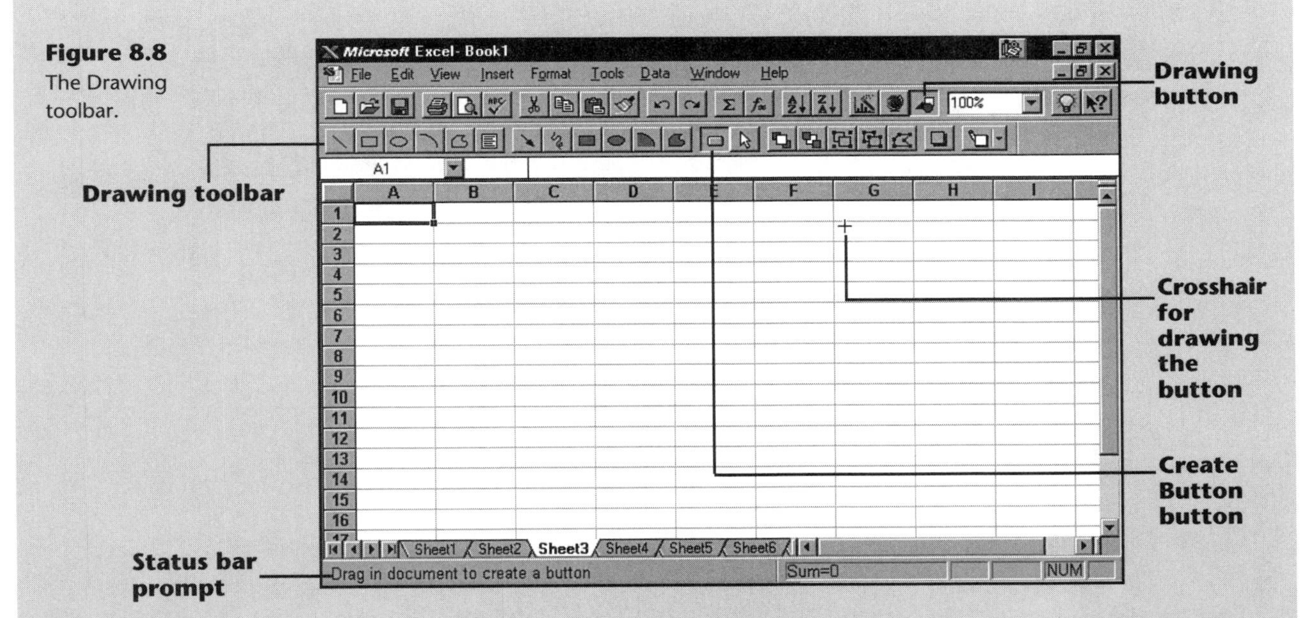

3. Click the Create Button button in the Drawing toolbar (refer to figure 8.8).

   The mouse pointer changes to a crosshair, ready for you to create the button.

4. Click and drag over the range of cells G2:I3.

   When you release the left mouse button, the new worksheet button is created in the range G2:I3. The Assign Macro dialog box appears (see figure 8.9).

(continues)

8

Creating a Button to Run a Macro (continued)

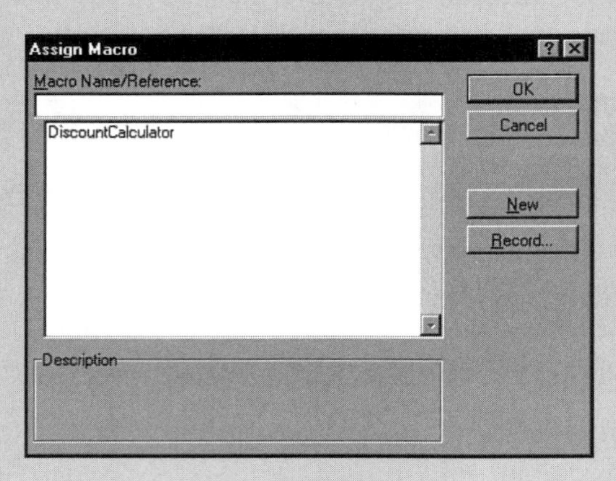

Figure 8.9 The Assign Macro dialog box.

5. In the Macro Name/Reference list box, click DiscountCalculator; then click OK.

Now your screen will look like figure 8.10.

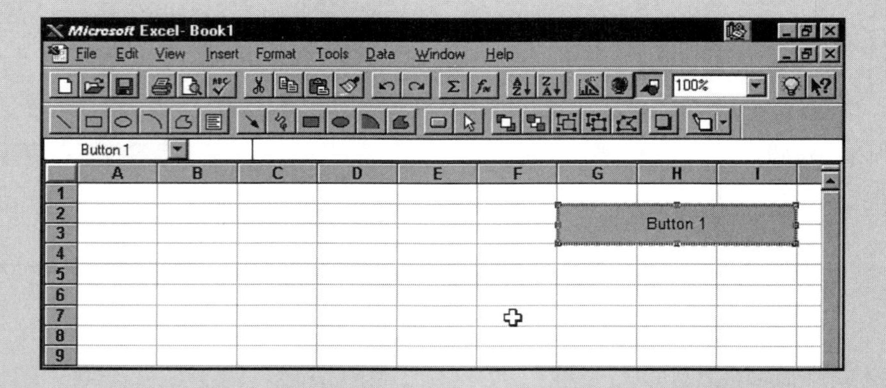

Figure 8.10 The new button, labeled Button1.

Now you need to delete the default text in the button and replace it with the name of your macro.

6. Double-click inside the button to place the blinking insertion point inside the button. Delete the default text in the button.
7. Make sure that the blinking insertion point still appears inside the button; then type **DiscountCalculator**.
8. Click in a cell outside the button to deselect the button.
9. Click the Drawing button on the Standard toolbar.

The Drawing toolbar disappears from your worksheet.

Now your screen should look like figure 8.11.

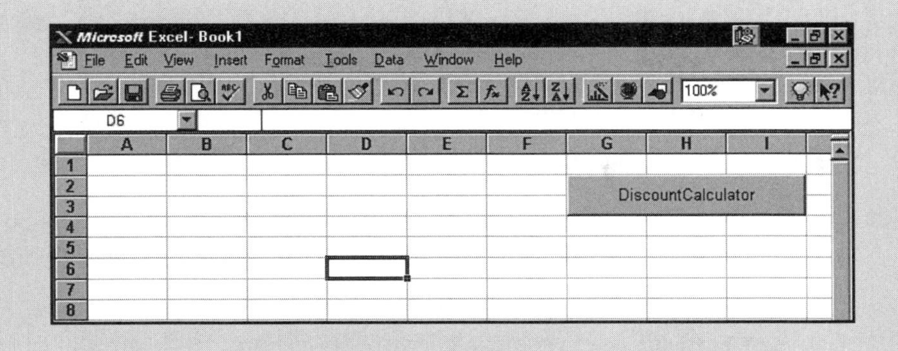

Figure 8.11 The finished worksheet with the macro button.

If you have problems... Suppose that you made a mistake with the button. If the button still has the square selection handles around it, press Del to delete the button. If the button does not have the square selection handles around it, press and hold down Ctrl; then click the button. The button is selected (square handles appear), and pressing Del deletes the button. Remember: To select a button without executing its attached macro, hold down ↵Enter when you click the button.

Running Your Macro by Clicking a Button

To run your macro by clicking the button, follow these steps:

1. Make sure that you have the workbook containing the macro open and that the worksheet (Sheet3) containing the button is selected (click the Sheet3 tab).

2. Click the DiscountCalculator button.

The macro creates the Discount Calculator and protects the worksheet.

Objective 4: Delete a Macro from a Workbook

When you save a workbook, the macros that it contains also get saved. If you want to delete a macro from the open workbook, you use the **T**ools, **M**acro command.

8

Deleting the Discount Calculator Macro

To delete a macro from your open workbook, follow these steps:

1. Choose **T**ools, **M**acro.

   The Macro dialog box appears (refer to figure 8.7).

(continues)

Deleting the Discount Calculator Macro (continued)

2. In the list of macro names, click the name of the macro you want to delete. Click DiscountCalculator.

3. Click the Delete button.

   The macro is deleted from the workbook. Usually, you will also want to delete the button that runs the macro. This button is still in Sheet3.

   In Sheet3, because the macro turned on worksheet protection, you must first turn off worksheet protection; then you can delete the button.

4. Choose Tools, Protection; then choose Unprotect Sheet.

   The worksheet is now unprotected, and you can select and delete the button.

5. Press and hold down Ctrl, then click the DiscountCalculator button.

   The square selection handles appear around the button (see figure 8.12).

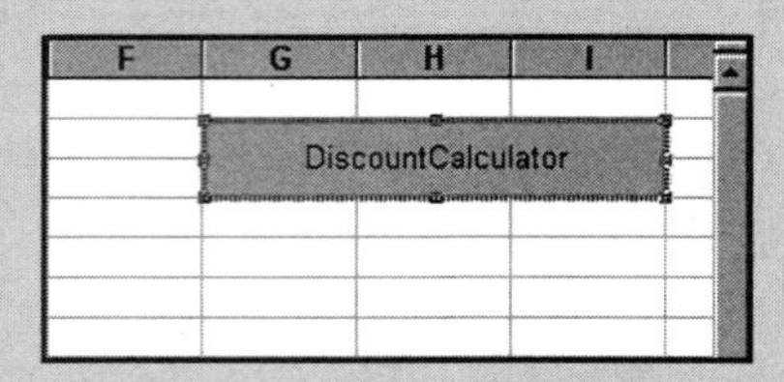

Figure 8.12 The selected macro button.

6. Press Del.

   The button is deleted.

Chapter Summary

This chapter explains what an Excel macro is. You have learned how to create and run a macro. You also learned how to delete a macro and the button that you created to run that macro. In the next chapter, you learn how to link two Excel worksheets and how to link Excel worksheets with other Windows applications.

Checking Your Skills

True/False

For each of the following, circle T or F to indicate whether the statement is true or false.

T F **1.** A macro can be used only in the worksheet in which it was recorded.

T F **2.** Macros are stored by Excel in a sheet that it names Macro1.

T F **3.** You can create macros only by using the Recorder.

T F **4.** When a button that has been created to run a macro is selected, its border has square handles.

T F **5.** The Standard toolbar contains a button to start the Macro Recorder.

T F **6.** The Macro Recorder will not record menu choices.

T F **7.** A macro name cannot contain a space.

T F **8.** A macro name cannot consist of more than eight characters.

T F **9.** The Stop Macro button is found in the Drawing toolbar.

T F **10.** A macro can contain a maximum of 20 statements.

Multiple Choice

In the blank provided, write the letter of the correct answer for each of the following.

_____ **1.** To select a macro button, you first press and hold down the _____ key before you click the button.

a. Alt

b. Ctrl

c. Del

d. Shift

_____ **2.** To begin recording a macro, you first choose _____ in the menu bar.

a. **E**dit

b. **R**ecord

c. **T**ools

d. none of the above

_____ **3.** The command you choose to display the dialog box that enables you to delete a macro is **T**ools, _____.

a. **E**dit

b. **E**rase

c. **M**acro

d. **V**iew

_____ **4.** You signal Excel that you have finished recording a macro by clicking the _____ button.

a. Turn Off Recorder

b. Stop

c. Exit

d. none of the above

_____ **5.** To display the toolbar that enables you to create a button to run a macro, click the _____ button on the Standard toolbar.

a. Drawing

b. Macro

c. Play

d. none of the above

_____ **6.** The **L**ocked check box is found in the tabbed dialog box displayed by the _____ command.

a. F**o**rmat, C**e**lls

b. **T**ools

c. **U**tilities

d. none of the above

_____ **7.** The command that lets you run a macro is found in the _____ menu.

a. **T**ools

b. **F**ile

c. **W**indow

d. none of the above

_____ **8.** The default name that Excel provides inside a button is _____.

a. Run

b. Macro

c. Start

d. none of the above

_____ **9.** You attach a macro to a button by using the _____ Macro dialog box.

a. Assign

b. Attach

c. Create

d. Run

____ **10.** You can enter text in a button when the button is _____.

a. pressed

b. running the macro

c. selected

d. being drawn

Completion

In the blank provided, write the correct answer for each of the following.

1. When you place the mouse pointer on a button, the pointer changes shape to a ______________.
2. A macro is saved on disk when you save its ______________.
3. A macro will work the ______________ way every time you run it.
4. The language in which Excel macros are written is ______________ for Applications.
5. To delete a selected button, press the ______________ key.
6. The command to protect the cells of a worksheet so that a user cannot type in them is found in the ______________ menu.
7. A ______________ is a series of commands stored in a worksheet.
8. Comments in a macro are colored ______________.
9. Before you run a macro, you should ______________ your workbook.
10. The first step in creating a macro is to ______________ the steps in the macro.

Applying Your Skills

Review Exercises

Exercise 1: Recording and Running a Macro

1. Record a macro to place the column heading NAME in cell A1, PHONE in cell B1, and DEPARTMENT in cell C1. Then change the width of column A to 20. Make the headings boldface.
2. Switch to an empty worksheet, and then run the macro. Keep the worksheet open for the next exercise.

Exercise 2: Recording a Macro That Uses a Dialog Box

Record a macro that uses the Format Cells dialog box to outline the border of cells A1:C1. Move to an empty worksheet, and create a button that will run the macro. Run the macro. Keep the worksheet open for the next exercise.

Exercise 3: Recording a Print Macro

1. Record a macro that will print a worksheet. Remember that Excel cannot print an empty worksheet.
2. Move to an empty worksheet, create buttons to run each of the macros you created in the first two exercises. Run the macro from Exercise 1, and then run the macro from Exercise 2. Finally, run the macro to print the worksheet. Keep the worksheet open for the next exercise.

Exercise 4: Recording a Page Setup Macro

1. Record a macro that will change the page orientation to landscape.
2. Create a button to run the macro. Keep the worksheet open for the next exercise.

Exercise 5: Deleting Macros and Their Buttons

1. Delete the macros that you used in Review Exercise 3.
2. Delete the buttons you created to run the macros in Review Exercise 3.

Continuing Projects

Project 1: Recording a Macro to Set Up a Database, Create a Chart, and Print a Worksheet

Open a new workbook. Record a macro to open the C2lp2 workbook and print the worksheet.

Then the macro should delete row 6, name the worksheet data as a database, and display the Data Form. You should be able to view, find, add, and delete records. When you click the Close button in the Data Form, an embedded line chart of sales for the companies should be produced, and the worksheet should be printed. Finally, C2lp2 should be closed without saving the changes.

Attach the macro to a button named LP1. Save the workbook, and then click the button, and run the macro.

Project 2: Recording a Macro to Produce the Performance Report Worksheet

Record a macro that will recreate the worksheet you built in the first Review Exercise 1 at the end of Chapter 2. Run the macro in Sheet3 of the workbook that now contains Review Exercise 1 from Chapter 2. Print the new worksheet.

Project 3: Recording a Macro to Format and Print the NSCC COMPANY QUARTERLY REPORT Workbook

Open the NSCC COMPANY QUARTERLY REPORT workbook, C2lp1, that you created in Continuing Project 1 at the end of Chapter 2.

Record a macro that does the following actions:

a. Changes the font type and increases the size of the text in the title.

b. Centers the title between the left and right edges of the worksheet.

c. Places red borders around the column headings.

d. Selects a pattern to use inside the cells of the column headings.

e. Changes the format so that thick vertical lines are displayed between the cells in rows 4 through 17.

f. Formats all numbers in the worksheet as currency with two decimal places and displays negative numbers in red.

g. Places the date in cell A1.

h. Saves the workbook on disk as C8lp3.

i. Prints the worksheet.

Create a button to run the macro; then test the macro. When the macro is correct, print the module sheet that contains the macro.

CHAPTER 9

Linking Worksheets and Creating Summary Reports

The spreadsheets or databases used by the manager of a retail store have a different level of detail than those used by the regional manager of the retail chain. Generally, at higher levels in an organization, spreadsheets are used to show "the big picture" without providing extraneous detail. At lower levels of the organization, however, what is needed is detailed information on the operation of the office, department, or retail store.

When you build a higher-level summary worksheet, reentering information that is already in a lower-level worksheet is inefficient. The worksheets used by higher-level managers summarize the detailed data in worksheets used by lower-level managers. Quarterly reports summarize the information from three monthly reports. Excel has the capability to extract information (such as sales totals) from multiple detail worksheets in order to create a higher-level summary worksheet.

In this chapter, you learn how to link a cell in one (source) worksheet to a cell in a second (dependent) worksheet. When the data in the source worksheet is changed, the data in the dependent worksheet is instantly updated. You learn how to link information in an Excel worksheet to a document in another Windows application. Then you learn how to create summary reports that contain subtotals and averages for groups of related records in a worksheet. In the final section of this chapter, you learn how to consolidate three annual reports into one summary report.

Objectives

By the time you have finished this chapter, you will have learned to

1. Create Links between Worksheets
2. Change and Restore Links

3. Link Data from a Worksheet to a Windows Application
4. Create a Summary Report with Subtotals
5. Create a Consolidated Report

Objective 1: Create Links between Worksheets

Link
A one-way data connection from the source workbook to the dependent workbook.

Dependent workbook
A workbook containing an external reference (a link) to another (source) workbook and, therefore, dependent on the other workbook for data.

Source workbook
A workbook that supplies data over a link to a dependent workbook.

When you create a worksheet, you will sometimes want to use data stored in a different worksheet or workbook. You can copy and paste the data, but if the data changes, you have to copy and paste again. Creating a *link* gives you the solution to this problem.

You can create a link between a worksheet in a *dependent workbook*, the workbook that receives data, and a worksheet in a *source workbook*, the workbook that contains the original data. The link carries data from the source sheet to the dependent sheet. A link is like a pipeline between the two; the pipeline carries data in one direction only (from the source workbook to the dependent workbook). Links can also be established between a worksheet in an Excel workbook and a document created by another Windows application.

By default, Excel updates the dependent data automatically when the source data changes. As you will see later, you can also tell Excel not to update the dependent data if you want to retain the older data in the dependent worksheet.

You can link one cell or a range of cells. Linked data in a dependent worksheet can be formatted, used in a function or formula, and charted just like the data that is actually entered into the dependent worksheet.

Note: *The terminology used to refer to linked (source and dependent) workbooks differs in Excel textbooks. Sometimes, you will see the terms source workbook (or worksheet) and target workbook, or supporting workbook and dependent workbook.*

Linking enables one workbook to share the data in another workbook. Source workbooks can be on-screen or on disk; the dependent workbook can always get the information it needs through the link. If the source workbook is open when the dependent workbook opens, the target workbook's linked data is automatically updated (read) from the source workbook. If the source workbook is not open when you open the dependent workbook, you have a choice. You can use the data the dependent workbook had when it was saved, or you can have the dependent workbook read in new data from the source workbook on disk.

Linking data enables you to avoid the problems inherent in large, cumbersome workbooks. You can build small worksheets and workbooks to accomplish specific tasks and then link all these components together to form a larger system. Links between workbooks can pass data, numbers, and text to the receiving (dependent) workbook.

In the following tutorials, you will set up a dependent worksheet in a practice workbook. A cell in the dependent worksheet will receive a sales total from an existing source workbook cell. Next, you will display both workbooks side-by-side on-screen. You will then create a link between a cell in the source worksheet and a cell in the dependent worksheet. Finally, you will test the link to see that it works properly.

Creating and Formatting a New Worksheet to be Used as a Dependent Worksheet

In this tutorial, you prepare a new worksheet that will receive data from a source worksheet. You will make the new worksheet the dependent worksheet. Then you open C2lp1, which you created in the first continuing project in Chapter 2. You will use C2lp1 as the source worksheet..

If you have any workbooks open now, close them all; then open a new workbook. We will refer to this new workbook in the following tutorials as the Book1 workbook. You will set this workbook up to be the dependent workbook as you work through the tutorials. Follow these steps:

1. Change the width of column A to 16.
2. Enter **NSCC Company** in cell A1.
3. Enter **Total Sales** in cell A2.
4. Format cell A4 to Currency with two decimal places.

   Now your worksheet should look like figure 9.1. Cell A4 in this worksheet will receive its data from the Total Sales cell in C2lp1. Keep this workbook open for the following step.

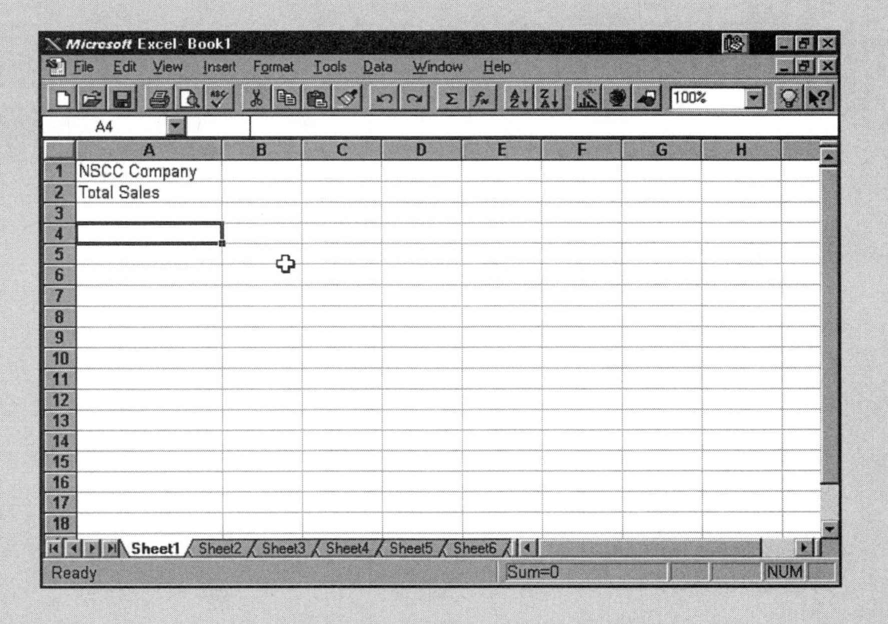

Figure 9.1 The dependent worksheet.

5. Open C2lp1 by using the **F**ile, **O**pen command.
6. Name the sheet tab of the NSCC worksheet **C2lp1**.

Keep these workbooks open for the following tutorial.

Creating links between worksheets is easiest when the worksheets are both visible on-screen at the same time. In the next tutorial, you arrange your screen so that both worksheets (the source worksheet and the dependent worksheet) appear simultaneously.

Displaying the Source and Dependent Worksheets Simultaneously

To display both worksheets simultaneously, follow these steps:

1. Choose **W**indow.
2. Choose **A**rrange. The Arrange Windows dialog box appears (see figure 9.2).

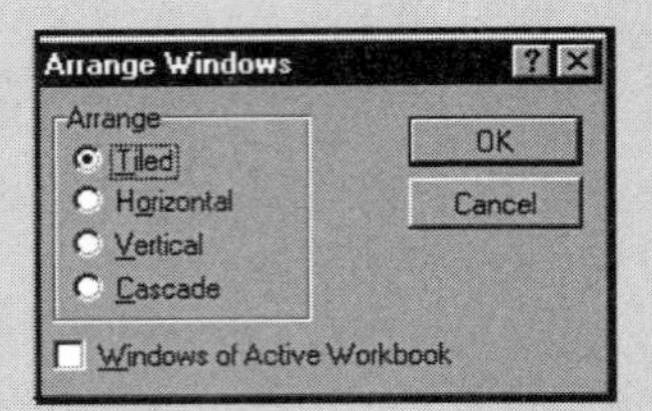

Figure 9.2 The Arrange Windows dialog box.

3. If the **T**iled option is not already selected, click it.
4. Click OK.

Now you should be able to see both workbooks simultaneously (see figure 9.3).

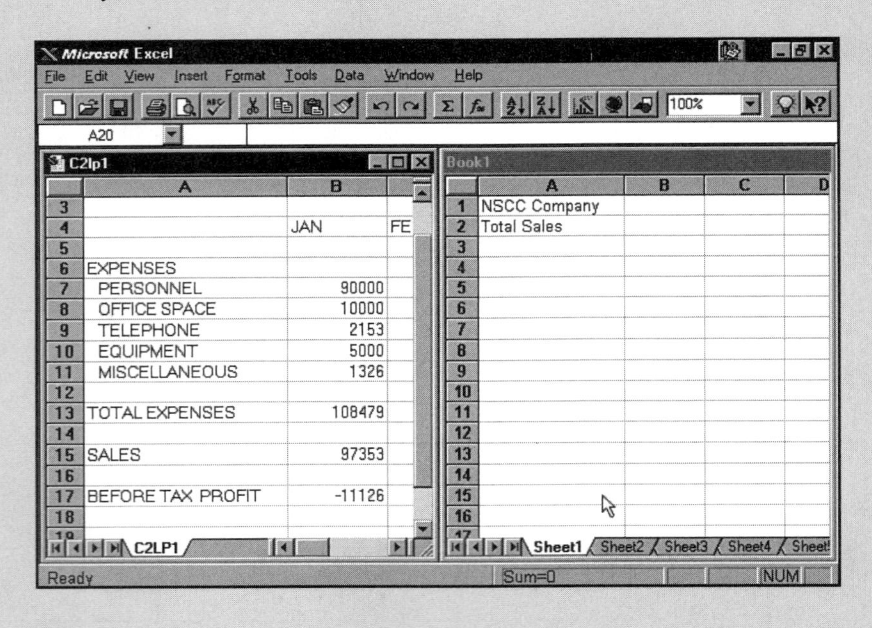

Figure 9.3 Both the source (C2lp1) and dependent workbooks appear on-screen simultaneously.

Keep these workbooks open for the following tutorial.

The C2lp1 workbook is the active workbook, but you can activate a cell in the Book1 workbook by clicking that cell. Notice that the active workbook has scroll bars so that you can move to any cell in the worksheet.

External reference formula
A reference to a cell or range in another Excel workbook.

In the next tutorial, you establish a link between these two worksheets. You create an *external reference formula* in cell A4 of the new workbook. This external reference formula is the link that extracts data from the source workbook (C2lp1) and places that data in the new (dependent) workbook.

Linking the Two Worksheets

To create the link between the two worksheets, follow these steps:

1. Scroll in the C2lp1 worksheet until cell F15, which contains the Total Sales for NSCC, appears.
2. Activate cell F15.
3. Place the mouse pointer on cell F15, and right-click. The shortcut menu appears (see figure 9.4).

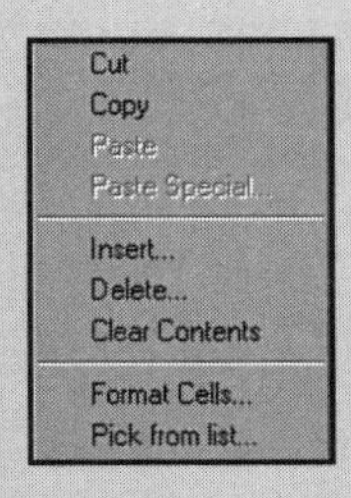

Figure 9.4 The shortcut menu.

4. Choose Copy in the shortcut menu. The moving dashes appear around cell F15.
5. Click cell A4 in the Book1 worksheet.
6. Right-click in cell A4. The shortcut menu appears again (see figure 9.5).

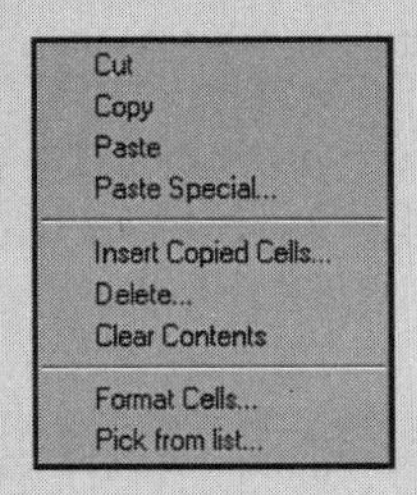

Figure 9.5 The second shortcut menu.

7. Choose Paste Special. The Paste Special dialog box appears (see figure 9.6).

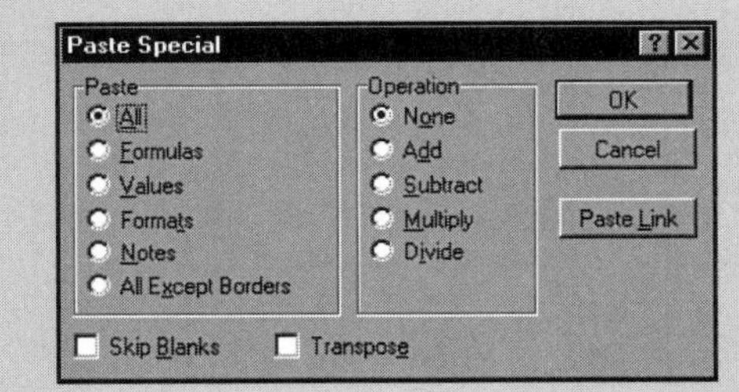

Figure 9.6 The Paste Special dialog box.

(continues)

9

Linking the Two Worksheets (continued)

8. Click **All** in the Paste options list if this option does not already have a dot in the circle.

9. Click the Paste **Link** button.

Keep both workbooks open for the following tutorial.

Now the external reference formula `='[C2LP1.XLS]C2LP1'!$F$15` is placed in cell A4 and displayed in the formula bar. This formula brings data into cell A4 of the dependent workbook from cell F15 of the C2lp1 worksheet in the source workbook (C2lp1). The value, $411,979.00, from C2lp1 appears in cell A4 (see figure 9.7).

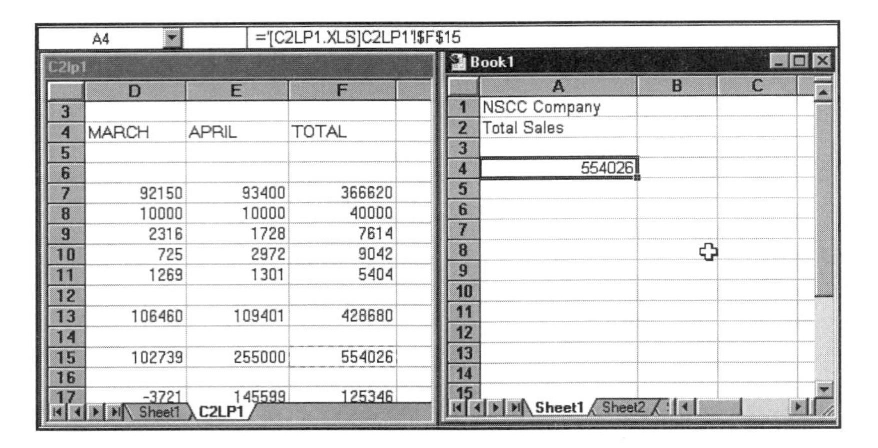

Figure 9.7
The linked worksheets.

Now that you have established the link, you can test it. If cell F15 did not contain a formula, you could just type a value in cell F15, and cell A4 in Book1 would immediately change to display the new value. When a cell contains a formula, you must change a value in a cell that is used in the formula to test the link.

Testing the New Link

To test whether you have a link between cell F15 in C2lp1 and cell A4 in Book1, follow these steps:

1. Click cell F15 in C2lp1.

2. Press Esc to return to the Ready mode (and stop the moving dashes).

   The formula in cell F15 sums cells B15:E15. When you change cell E15, the contents of both F15 and cell A4 in the dependent worksheet will change.

❸ Click cell E15, and type **2000**. Then press Enter. Now your screen should look like figure 9.8.

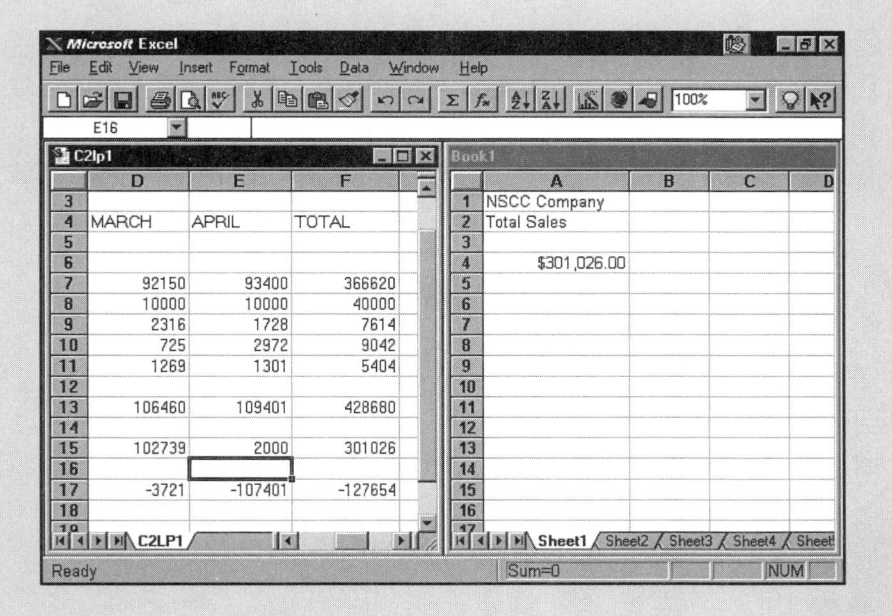

Figure 9.8
The altered worksheets.

Notice that a new total has been calculated and that it also appears in cell A4.

Keep these workbooks open for the following tutorial.

In the next tutorial, you save the new workbook (currently Book1) as C9ex6 and again change the value in cell E15 of C2lp1. What will happen to the contents of cell A4 in the dependent workbook? Actually, the results depend on what you do the next time you open the dependent workbook. Before Excel opens a dependent workbook, Excel gives you the option of updating any links. If you choose not to update the dependent workbook, the dependent workbook retains the values it had when last saved.

Testing the Link Further

In this tutorial, you will save (as C9ex6) and then close the dependent workbook. Then you will change C2lp1 and save it. Finally, you open the dependent workbook (C9ex6) and update the link. Follow these steps:

❶ Click a cell in the new workbook to make the workbook active.

❷ Save the new workbook as **C9ex6.**

❸ Close C9ex6 by clicking the Close button. If you are prompted to save changes, click **Yes**.

(continues)

Testing the Link Further (continued)

4. Maximize C2lp1 by clicking its Maximize button.
5. Change cell E15 in the C2lp1 worksheet to **255000**. The new sales total in cell F15 becomes 554026.
6. Close C2lp1.
7. When prompted to save changes, click **Y**es.
8. Open C9ex6. The alert box appears (see figure 9.9).

Microsoft Excel

This document contains links. Re-establish links?

Yes No Help

Figure 9.9
The Alert box prompting you to update the dependent workbook by reestablishing links.

9. Click the **Y**es button.

Notice that cell A4 is immediately updated (see figure 9.10). Note also that the external formula in cell A4 is changed to reflect that the source workbook is now stored on disk. Your external formula will look different because the formula depends on where the source workbook is stored on your disk.

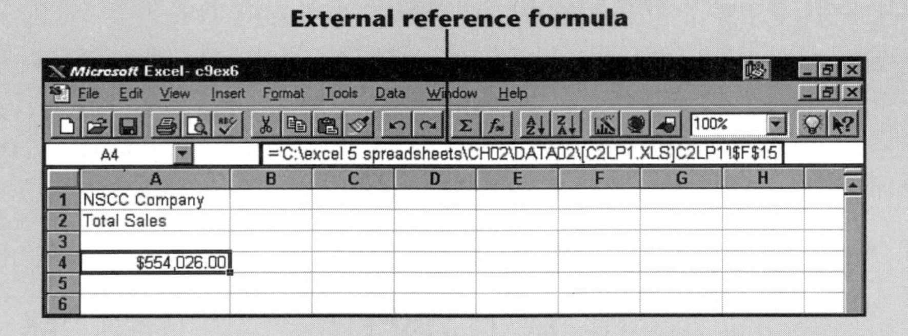

Figure 9.10
Cell A4 is updated.

As you have seen in the previous tutorials, creating links enables you to use the same data for more than one worksheet. Also, when the original (source) data changes, the linked data in other worksheets is updated.

Saving Linked Workbooks

You should save any open source workbooks before you save the open dependent workbooks linked to them. Then you can be sure that the formulas in a source workbook have been calculated and that any changed workbook and worksheet names used in the external reference formulas of the dependent workbook are updated.

If you name or rename a source workbook with the **S**ave or Save **A**s command, the dependent workbook must be open for the names in the external reference formula to get updated. Save the source workbook; then resave the dependent workbooks. This procedure ensures that the dependent workbooks record the new path and file names of their source workbooks.

If you move the source workbook to another directory, remember to delete or rename it because when you close the dependent workbook, the links to your data will be broken.

In the next section, you learn how to restore a dependent workbook's broken link using the **E**dit, Lin**k**s command.

Objective 2: Change and Restore Links

External reference formulas are the mechanisms through which a dependent workbook receives data from its source workbook. The actual link between two sheets is created by the external reference formula in the dependent workbook. The formula that links the data from the source sheet to the dependent sheet consists of an equal sign and the external cell reference

='[C2LP1.XLS]C2LP1'!$F$15.

The linking formula contains an absolute cell address preceded by an exclamation point. The formula also includes the file name and sheet name of the source worksheet. The path name, if the source workbook is in a different directory from the dependent workbook, is also included in the formula. For external cell references, workbook names are always enclosed by square brackets [ ]. If source workbooks get renamed or moved to other directories, dependent workbooks cannot find the needed data. These links are lost and must be reestablished.

Changing and Updating Links

To reestablish links to a workbook or to link a dependent workbook to a different source workbook, follow these steps:

1. Open the dependent workbook.
2. Choose the **E**dit, Lin**k**s command to display the Links dialog box; then select the file links to change or update (see figure 9.11).

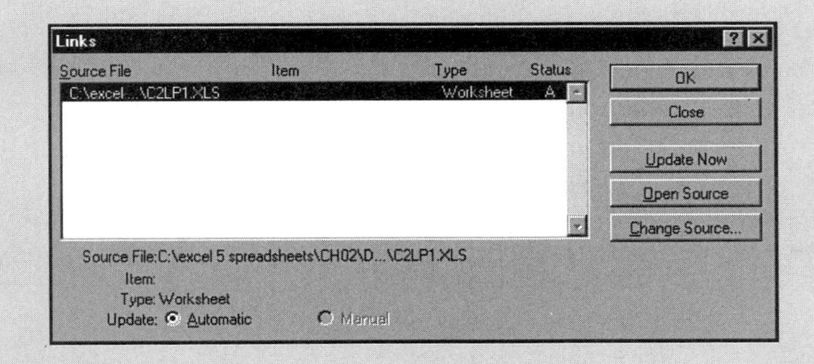

Figure 9.11
The Links dialog box and selected file for which you want to reestablish or change the links.

(continues)

Changing and Updating Links (continued)

❸ Click the Change Source button to display the Change Links dialog box. The current link appears at the top of the dialog box (see figure 9.12).

Figure 9.12
The Change Links dialog box.

Current source in link

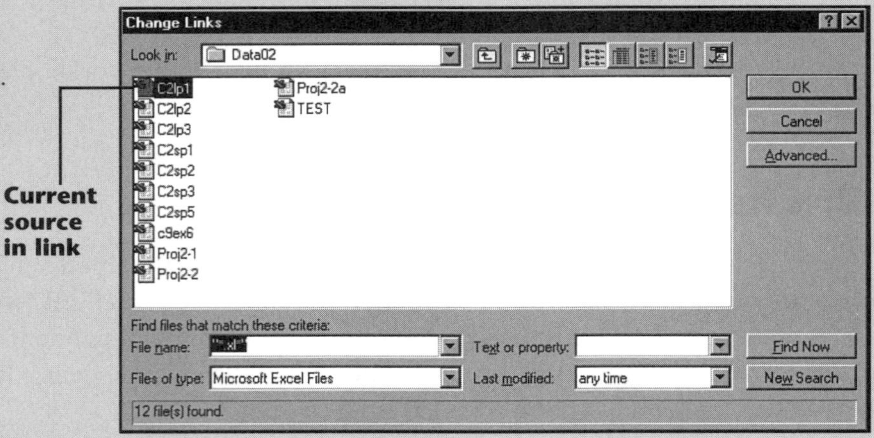

You reestablish the link by typing a folder and file name to indicate the folder and file name of the new supporting workbook that you want to establish as the source.

❹ The current link in this tutorial is the one you want to keep. Click OK.

❺ In the Links dialog box, click OK.

Keep C2lp1 open for the next tutorial.

Restoring Links

If you move the source workbook file to another directory, rename it, or delete it, the links to your data will be broken. If you have a backup copy of your source file, or if your file is in another directory, you can easily change the link so that your data will appear in the dependent workbook as before. If you need to move a file into a new directory, also make sure to move any files linked to the moved file to the same directory.

Note: *If you want to delete a source file and remove any links to it, you can select the linked cells on the dependent worksheet and clear the linking formulas. If you want to retain the information, but not the link, you can copy the cells on the dependent worksheet that contain the linked information, and then use the Paste* ***S****pecial command to paste only the values in place of the links.*

Breaking a Link

In this tutorial, you deliberately break the link between C2lp1 and C9ex6. Make sure that you have both workbooks open. You can shift between open workbooks by using the **W**indow menu. If the workbook you want to see is open but not on-screen, click its name in the list of open workbooks at the bottom of the **W**indows menu.

When you have opened both workbooks, follow these steps:

1. After opening C2lp1, use the **F**ile, Save **A**s command to save C2lp1 as **C2lp1bak**.

   Switch to C9ex6 and verify that the external reference formula in cell A4 now shows C2lp1bak as the source workbook. *Remember:* the actual formula appears in the formula bar.

2. Save C9ex6.
3. Exit from Excel.
4. Use the Windows Explorer program to delete C2lp1bak.

   Now the source workbook in the link to C9ex6 is deleted, and the link no longer exists. However, the external reference formula is still in cell A4 of C9ex6.

5. Close Windows Explorer.

If you break a link between a source and dependent file, you can restore the link. Whether you want to restore a link to a source workbook that was moved to another directory or change a link to point to a new source workbook, the steps are similar.

Reestablishing a Lost Link

To reestablish the link using C2lp1 as the source, follow these steps:

1. Start Excel, and open C9ex6.

   A message box appears to remind you that this document contains links (see figure 9.13).

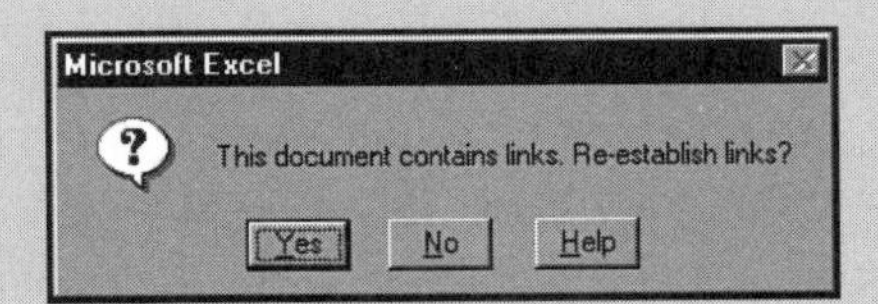

Figure 9.13 The message box.

2. Click the **N**o button.
3. From the **E**dit menu, choose Lin**k**s.

   The Links dialog box appears (see figure 9.14).

(continues)

Reestablishing a Lost Link (continued)

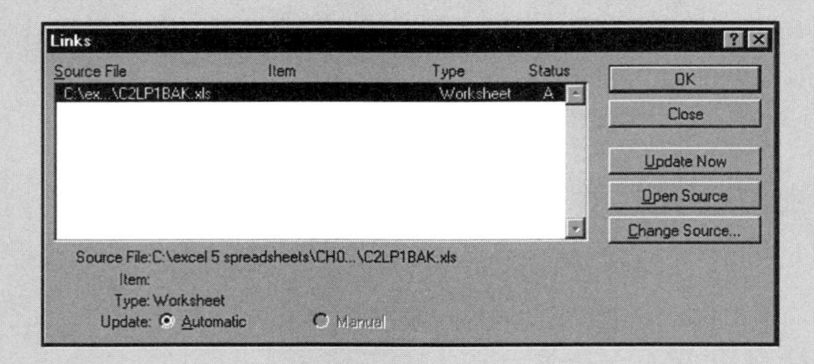

Figure 9.14 The Links dialog box.

4. Click the Change Source button.

   The Change Links dialog box appears (see figure 9.15). (The list of files on your disk will differ from those in the figure.)

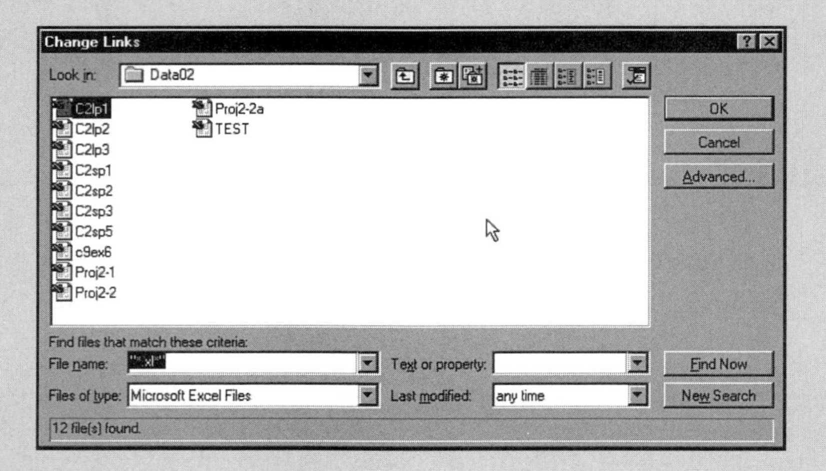

Figure 9.15 The Change Links dialog box.

5. Click the file name of the new source workbook, C2lp1.
6. Click OK.
7. Click the OK button in the Links dialog box.

The new source workbook is now included in the external reference formula in cell A4 of the dependent workbook C9ex6 (see figure 9.16). The link will now update automatically. Keep C9ex6 open for the next tutorial.

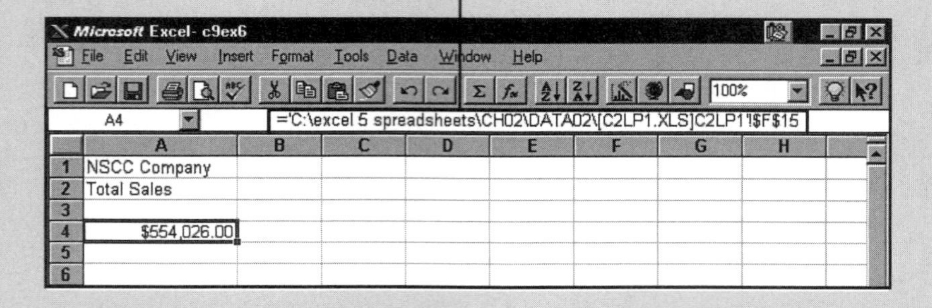

Figure 9.16 The new external reference formula.

When you no longer want a cell in a dependent workbook to be updated automatically from a source workbook, you can remove the link. Usually, you will want the dependent workbook to retain the most recently updated value from the source workbook. The next tutorial shows you how to remove the link and save the updated value.

Removing a Link

First, make sure that you have both C2lp1 and C9ex6 open. Tile the windows, as you learned how to do in "Displaying the Source and Dependent Workbooks Simultaneously." To remove the link and save the most recently updated value in cell A4, follow these steps:

1. Click cell A4 in the C9ex6 window to activate it.
2. Choose **E**dit, **C**opy.
3. Choose **E**dit, Paste **S**pecial.
4. In the Paste Special dialog box's Paste section, select the **V**alues option button.
5. Click OK.
6. Press ↵Enter.

The Paste Special, Values combination places the most recently updated value (not formula) in cell A4. Cell A4 no longer contains an external reference formula.

Verify that the link is broken by making a change in the expenses in C2lp1 and checking to see whether cell A4 in the dependent workbook C9ex6 is updated.

Save and close C9ex6. Close C2lp1 without saving it.

Objective 3: Link Data from a Workbook to a Windows Application

You can copy information from one Windows application into another by using the Clipboard and the **C**opy and **P**aste commands. Often, workers preparing reports copy Excel worksheets or Excel charts into word processing documents. Many word processing programs don't have the capability to lay out a grid of numbers or to create a chart, but Excel can do these tasks easily.

When you use the **C**opy and **P**aste commands, the current worksheet or the chart is copied into the word processing document. If the data in the worksheet changes, however, the worksheet or chart in the word processing document is not updated. You may not want updating, for example, if you want your report to reflect your organization's data at one point in time, and you are sure that you will know about any last-minute updates to the worksheet. Sometimes, however, you will want to create a link between the (dependent) word processing document and the (source) Excel worksheet.

In the following tutorials, you create a link between a practice word processing document and your Excel worksheet. When you have a link to another Windows application, it functions and is updated just like a link between two Excel workbooks. You use Windows 95 WordPad in these tutorials because it is supplied with Windows 95. You will, however, use the same techniques with any Windows word processor. If you are not familiar with WordPad, check with your instructor before beginning the next tutorial.

Creating a Link to Display a Worksheet in a WordPad Document

In this tutorial, you create a link between part of your C2lp1 worksheet and a WordPad document. Follow these steps:

1. Open the C2lp1 workbook (the one used in previous tutorials) if it is not already open.
2. Select cells A4 to E11.
3. Choose **E**dit, **C**opy (or click the Copy button on the Standard toolbar) to place these cells in the Clipboard.
4. Use the Windows 95 Start button to start the WordPad program. (Wordpad is in the Accessories group.)
5. In WordPad, type **These are our expenses:**, and press Enter twice.
6. Choose **E**dit, Paste **S**pecial.

   The Paste Special dialog box appears (see figure 9.17).

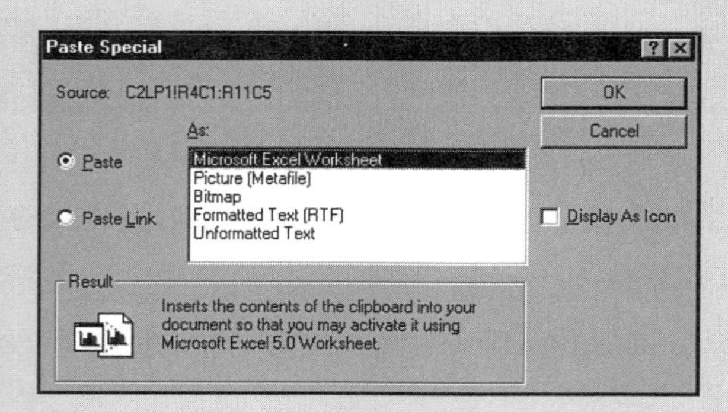

Figure 9.17
The Paste Special dialog box.

7. Click the Paste **L**ink option button.
8. Click OK.

   The range of selected worksheet cells is pasted into the document and linked to the C2lp1 worksheet.

   Now your worksheet should look like figure 9.18.

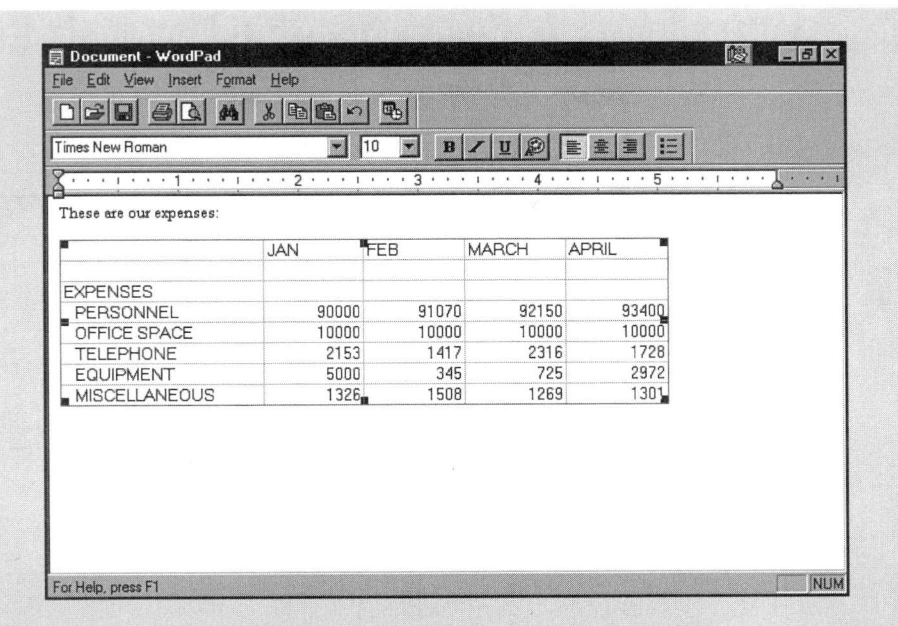

	JAN	FEB	MARCH	APRIL
EXPENSES				
PERSONNEL	90000	91070	92150	93400
OFFICE SPACE	10000	10000	10000	10000
TELEPHONE	2153	1417	2316	1728
EQUIPMENT	5000	345	725	2972
MISCELLANEOUS	1326	1508	1269	1301

Figure 9.18 The worksheet cells in the WordPad document.

9. Press the down cursor movement key on your keyboard until the blinking cursor appears just to the right of the right-most cell in the bottom row of the spreadsheet. This cell contains the number *1301*.

10. Press ↵Enter twice to insert several blank rows to prepare for the next tutorial.

Keep your workbook and your WordPad document open for the next tutorial.

You can also create a chart in Excel and copy it to a word processing document. Charts help your readers see comparisons more easily and give your reports a professional appearance.

Creating a Link to Display a Chart in a WordPad Document

To create a chart in the C2lp1 worksheet and paste the linked chart into your WordPad document, follow these steps:

1. Switch to Excel, which still has the C2lp1 workbook open. Press Esc to stop the moving dashes.

2. Use the ChartWizard to create an embedded column chart (in the C2lp1 worksheet) that shows the Personnel expenses for January through April. (If you need a review of charting non-contiguous ranges, see Chapter 6.)

   Your chart should be about 6 columns wide and about 12 rows high (see figure 9.19).

(continues)

Creating a Link to Display a Chart in a WordPad Document (continued)

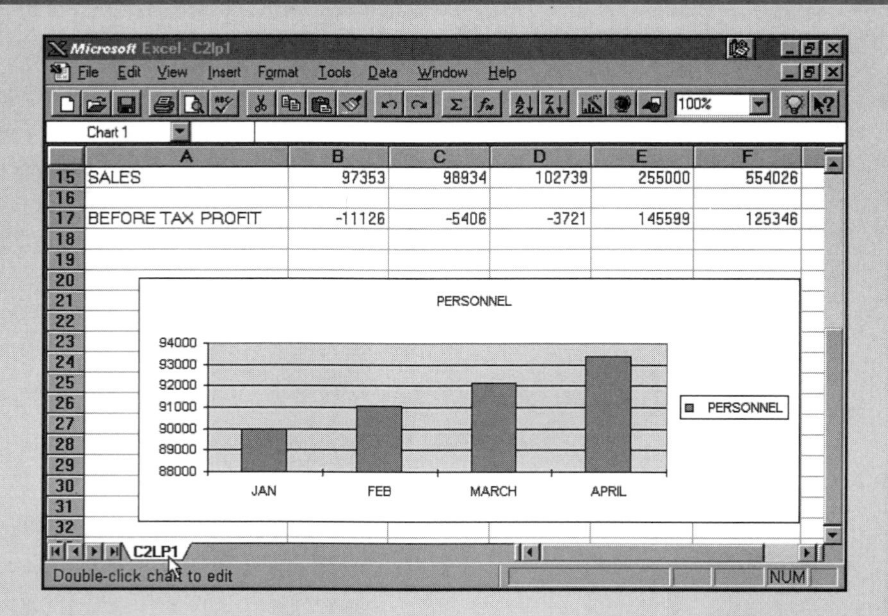

Figure 9.19 The ChartWizard chart in Excel.

3. If the chart is not already selected, click the chart to select it.

4. Choose **E**dit, **C**opy.

5. Switch to the WordPad document.

6. Choose **E**dit, Paste **S**pecial.

   The Paste Special dialog box appears.

7. Click the Paste **L**ink option button, and then click OK.

   The chart is inserted into the WordPad document (see figure 9.20).

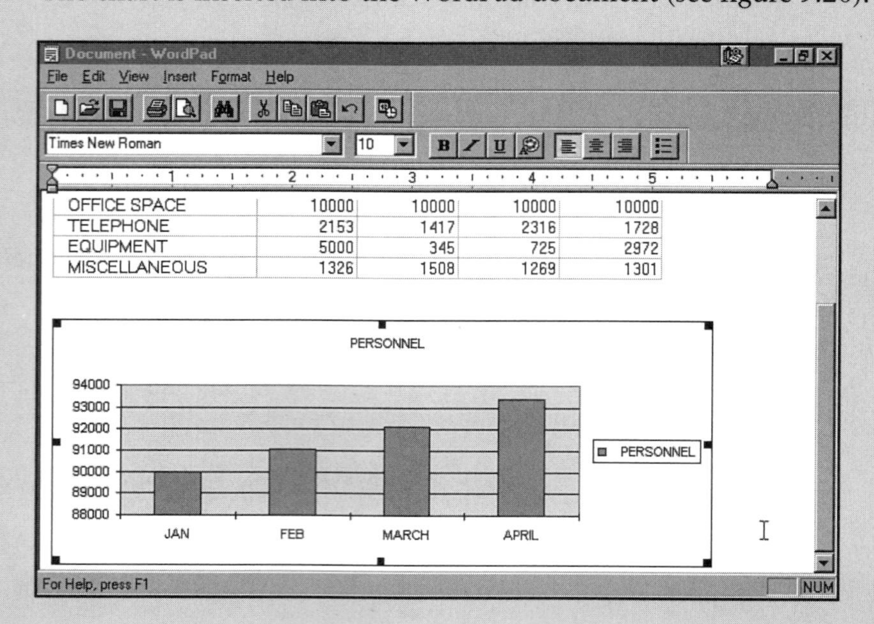

Figure 9.20 The ChartWizard chart in your WordPad document.

8. If you have a printer attached to your computer, print the WordPad document.

Note: *If you are not familiar with WordPad, you first choose the **F**ile, **P**rint command to display the Print dialog box. In the Print dialog box, click OK to print your document. You can click the Print button if the WordPad Toolbar appears on your screen.*

Keep both your workbook and your WordPad document open for the next tutorial.

Testing the links between applications is always a good idea. When you have verified the proper functioning of the link, you can be sure of your results. This test becomes especially important when you have multiple links between applications.

Testing the Link

In this tutorial, you test the link to see whether changing the source (C2lp1) will update the dependent WordPad document. Follow these steps:

1. Switch back to Excel.
2. Change the January Personnel expenses in cell B7 to **99000**, and press Enter.
3. Switch back to the WordPad document.

   If your link was established properly, the chart in your WordPad document should now look like figure 9.21. Compare figure 9.21 to figure 9.20. Scroll to the top and then back to the bottom of your WordPad document. Note that both the (dependent) worksheet selection and chart have been updated through the link. The chart stayed the same size, but the y-axis labels have changed.

(continues)

9

Testing the Link (continued)

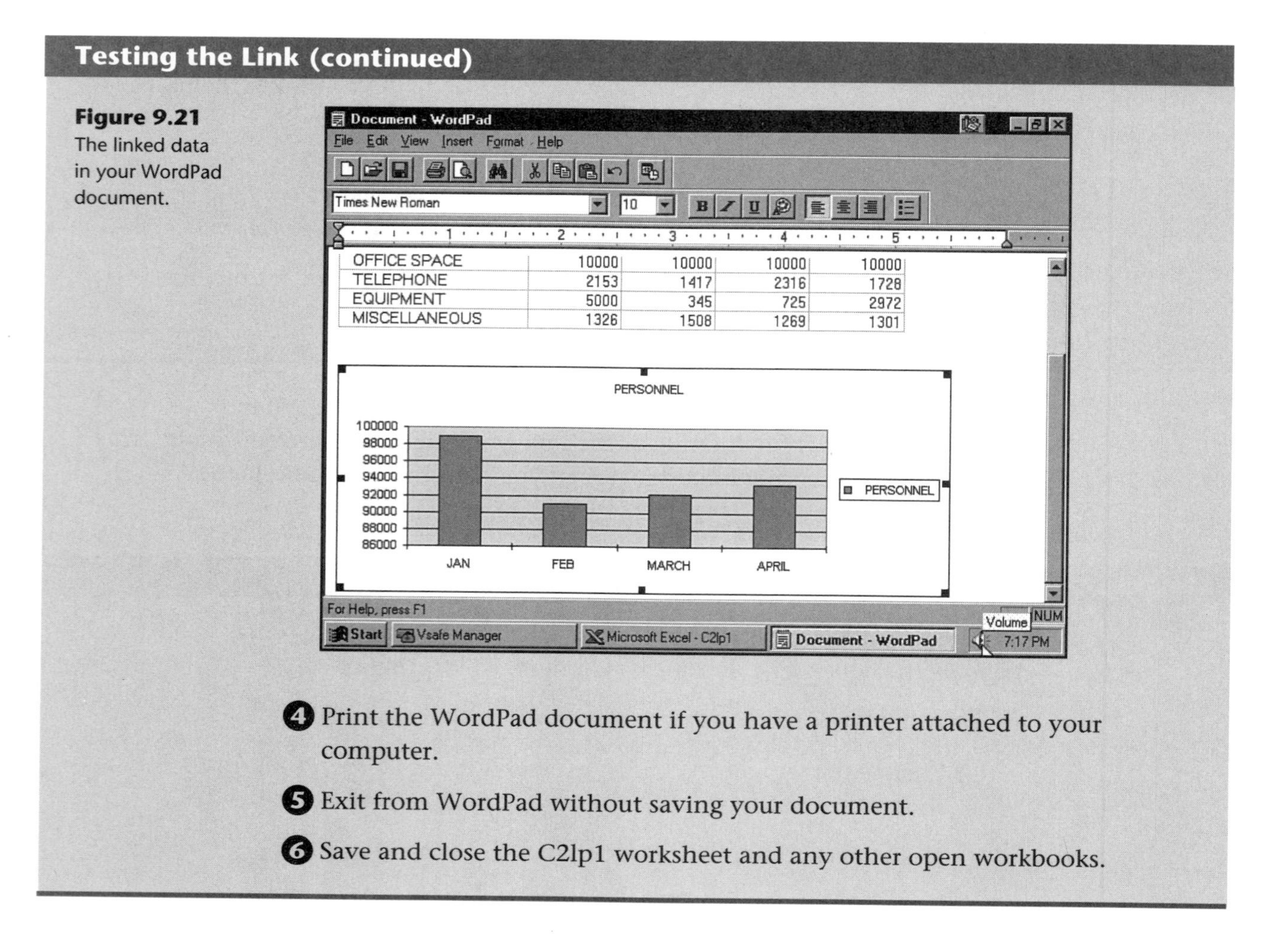

Figure 9.21
The linked data in your WordPad document.

4. Print the WordPad document if you have a printer attached to your computer.

5. Exit from WordPad without saving your document.

6. Save and close the C2lp1 worksheet and any other open workbooks.

Objective 4: Create a Summary Report with Subtotals

Summary report
Report in which data is broken into groups and summarized by group subtotals with an overall total given at the bottom of the list.

When you use Excel in an office, you will usually need to share the information in your worksheets. When you prepare a report, or even organize your data for your own use, you often need to prepare a *summary report* of your information. As you learned in Chapter 7, large amounts of data are stored as records in an Excel list. Subtotals are the standard way of summarizing information in lists of sales, payrolls, expenses, inventories, and other kinds of data. You can easily and quickly summarize the data in a list by creating subtotals in Excel.

Creating a summary report is a two-step process. First, you sort your data into groups; then you use the **D**ata, Su**b**totals command to produce subtotals, averages, and counts for each group. Excel will label the subtotals, averages, and counts with the appropriate group names. By using this method, you keep the details (the supporting information) in the worksheet and also produce a "bottom line" that managers can use. In the following tutorials, you learn how to create automatic subtotals that summarize the information in a list. For these tutorials, use the C2lp3 workbook you completed in Continuing Project 3 at the end of Chapter 2.

Creating Subtotals of Sales for Each Region

To create subtotals for dollars of sales for each region and a grand total, follow these steps:

1. Open the C2lp3 workbook.
2. Sort the data by Region in ascending order.

   This sort groups the data into regions so that Excel can create subtotals.
3. Click any cell in the list to activate the list for Excel. (For example, click cell A2.)
4. Choose **D**ata, Su**b**totals.

   The Subtotal dialog box appears (see figure 9.22).

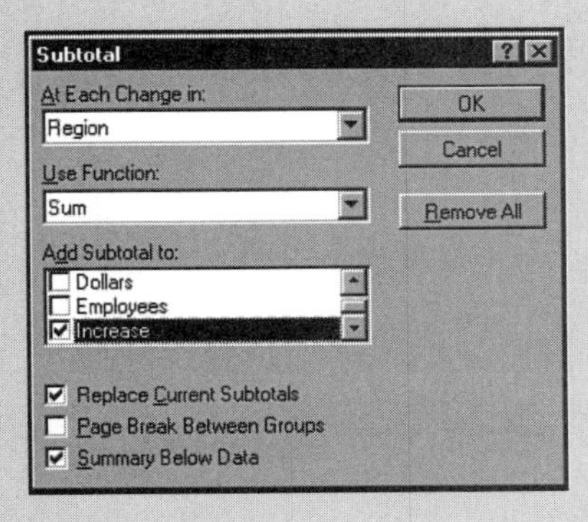

Figure 9.22
The Subtotal dialog box.

5. Click the arrow at the right of the **U**se Function drop-down list box.
6. Click Sum in the drop-down list.

   This step tells Excel to use the SUM function to create subtotals at the end of each group and then to create a grand total at the end of the summary report.
7. In the A**d**d Subtotal To text box, click any field name's check box that contains a check mark. This step removes any preexisting subtotal settings for a field.
8. Click the Dollars check box so that it is the only field with a check mark in its check box.

   Now your screen should look like figure 9.23.

(continues)

Creating Subtotals of Sales for Each Region (continued)

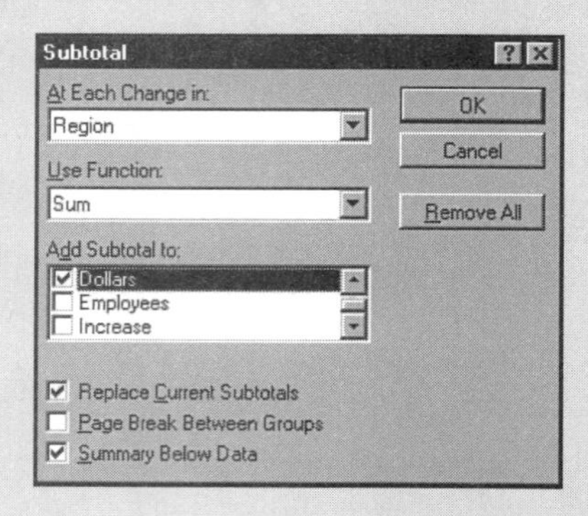

Figure 9.23 The completed Subtotal dialog box.

9 Click OK.

Now your screen should look like figure 9.24. Notice that the subtotals for each region are calculated and labeled with the appropriate region. (When a regional grouping ends, Excel automatically calculates a subtotal.)

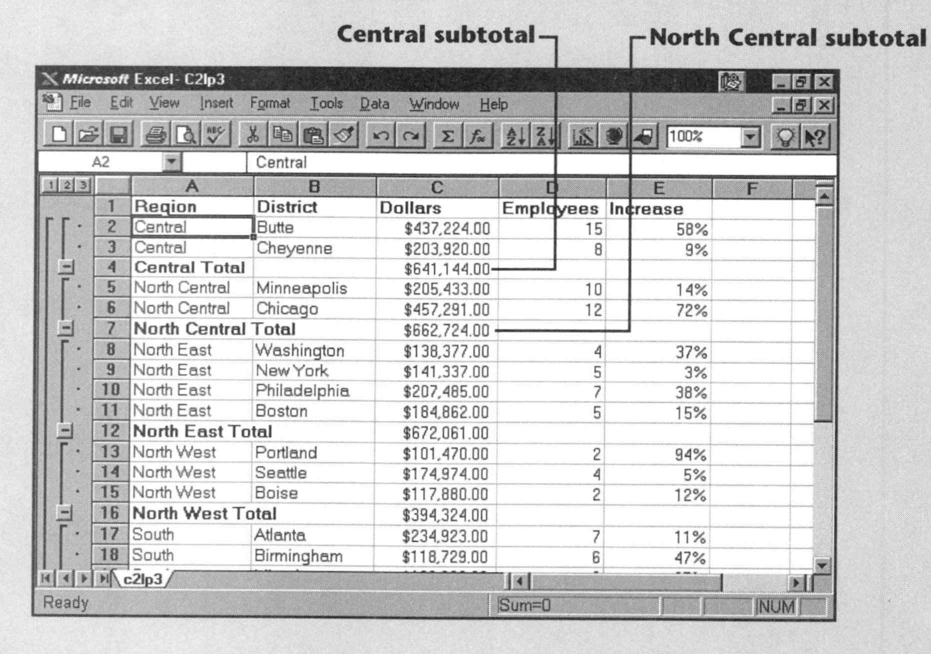

	A	B	C	D	E	F
1	Region	District	Dollars	Employees	Increase	
2	Central	Butte	$437,224.00	15	58%	
3	Central	Cheyenne	$203,920.00	8	9%	
4	Central Total		$641,144.00			
5	North Central	Minneapolis	$205,433.00	10	14%	
6	North Central	Chicago	$457,291.00	12	72%	
7	North Central Total		$662,724.00			
8	North East	Washington	$138,377.00	4	37%	
9	North East	New York	$141,337.00	5	3%	
10	North East	Philadelphia	$207,485.00	7	38%	
11	North East	Boston	$184,862.00	5	15%	
12	North East Total		$672,061.00			
13	North West	Portland	$101,470.00	2	94%	
14	North West	Seattle	$174,974.00	4	5%	
15	North West	Boise	$117,880.00	2	12%	
16	North West Total		$394,324.00			
17	South	Atlanta	$234,923.00	7	11%	
18	South	Birmingham	$118,729.00	6	47%	

Figure 9.24 The Summary subtotals.

10 Scroll down your screen to see the rest of the records and the grand total.

11 If you have a printer attached to your computer, print the worksheet.

Keep your workbook open for the following tutorial.

When you calculate a series of different subtotals, you must remove the old subtotals before producing the next set of subtotals.

Removing Subtotals

To remove the subtotals in the list, follow these steps:

1. Choose Data, Subtotals.
2. In the Subtotal dialog box, click the Remove All button.

The subtotals are removed, and you see the original sorted list on your screen.

Keep your workbook open for the following tutorial.

Excel can also calculate averages for subgroups of your data. This capability is useful for many kinds of reports.

Summarizing by Using Averages for Each Region

To find the average dollars of sales, the number of employees, and the increase for each region, follow these steps:

1. Click cell A2 to activate the list.
2. Choose Data, Subtotals.
3. Click the arrow to the right of the Use Function drop-down box.
4. In the drop-down list, click Average to use the AVERAGE function to produce averages for each group.
5. Use the scroll bar in the Add Subtotal To list box to see the available fields.
6. Click the Employees and the Increase check boxes. Check to make sure that the Dollars check box also has a check mark in it. Only the check boxes for these three fields should contain a check mark (see figure 9.25).

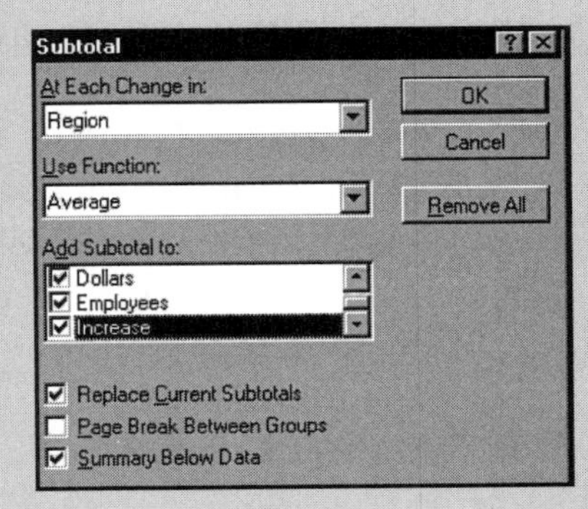

Figure 9.25
The Subtotals dialog box for averages.

(continues)

9

Summarizing by Using Averages for Each Region (continued)

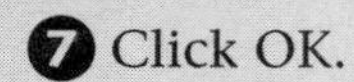
7. Click OK.

Now your screen should look like figure 9.26. Note that the averages are calculated for Dollars of Sales, Employees, and Increase.

Figure 9.26
The Summary Report using averages.

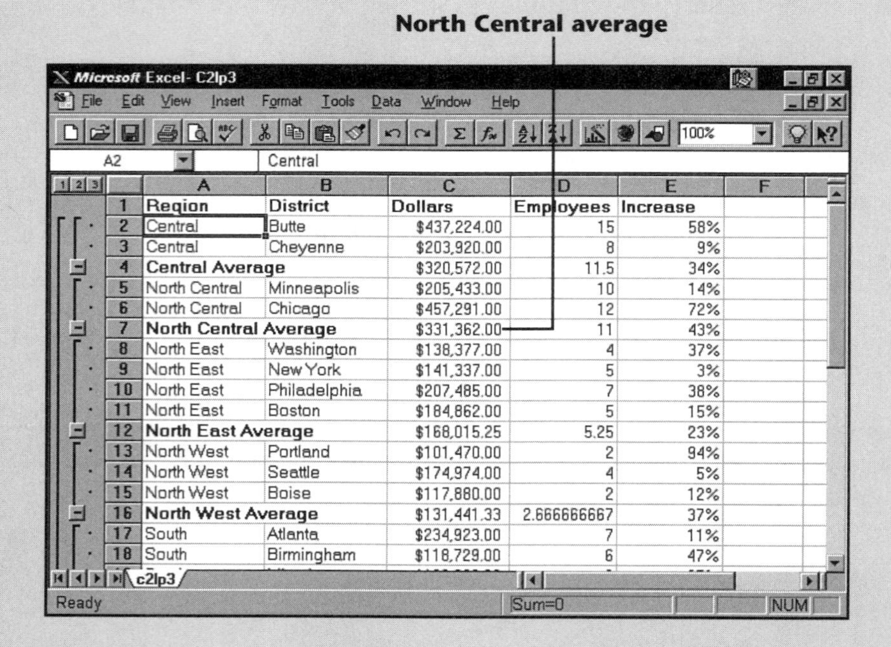

	A	B	C	D	E
1	Region	District	Dollars	Employees	Increase
2	Central	Butte	$437,224.00	15	58%
3	Central	Cheyenne	$203,920.00	8	9%
4	Central Average		$320,572.00	11.5	34%
5	North Central	Minneapolis	$205,433.00	10	14%
6	North Central	Chicago	$457,291.00	12	72%
7	North Central Average		$331,362.00	11	43%
8	North East	Washington	$138,377.00	4	37%
9	North East	New York	$141,337.00	5	3%
10	North East	Philadelphia	$207,485.00	7	38%
11	North East	Boston	$184,862.00	5	15%
12	North East Average		$168,015.25	5.25	23%
13	North West	Portland	$101,470.00	2	94%
14	North West	Seattle	$174,974.00	4	5%
15	North West	Boise	$117,880.00	2	12%
16	North West Average		$131,441.33	2.666666667	37%
17	South	Atlanta	$234,923.00	7	11%
18	South	Birmingham	$118,729.00	6	47%

8. If you have a printer attached to your computer, print the worksheet.

Now you remove all subtotals from your list.

9. Choose **D**ata, Su**b**totals.

10. In the Subtotal dialog box, click the **R**emove All button.

11. Close the C2lp3 workbook without saving it.

Objective 5: Create a Consolidated Report

Consolidated report
A report in which data from multiple source areas (usually different worksheets) is gathered into one worksheet.

Suppose that you have three worksheets of sales data and you need to print a report that summarizes them all. When you create a *consolidated report*, you pull all the data together from the three sheets and place the combined data on one sheet. Then you can print your report from that sheet. Excel can create this kind of consolidated worksheet automatically for you by performing calculations on similar data across multiple worksheets and workbooks and placing the results of the calculations in a consolidation worksheet. Excel uses *consolidation functions* to create these reports.

For example, each month you could use the SUM function to consolidate department budgets into one division budget; then you could consolidate the division

Consolidation function
The function (like SUM or AVERAGE) that Excel uses when it consolidates your data.

budgets into one corporate budget. You create the consolidated worksheets from existing data; no additional work is necessary. The consolidation is easiest for Excel if all the worksheets have the same physical layout, as is often the case with budget worksheets. If the layouts differ, Excel can usually figure out what you want it to consolidate by examining the worksheets' row and column headings.

Source area
The cell ranges from which the Consolidate command draws data.

Destination area
The range of cells you select to hold data summarized by the Consolidate command.

The worksheets (or the ranges in worksheets) that will be consolidated are called the *source area*. You can specify up to 255 source areas to consolidate. The area of the worksheet into which the source areas are consolidated is called the *destination area*. When you consolidate worksheets, you have the option of creating a link between the source area and the destination area. If you choose to create links to the source data, the destination area data gets updated when the source area data changes.

In the following tutorial, you consolidate three annual sales reports. The consolidation function that you use is the SUM function. The sheets for these tutorials are available from your instructor as C9ex5.

Selecting a Destination Sheet and a Consolidation Function

To select a destination sheet and a consolidation function, follow these steps:

1. Open C9ex5.

   The three sheets in this workbook contain data that is laid out similarly. You will consolidate the data in these three sheets into a fourth sheet.

2. Switch to the CONSOLIDATED sheet by clicking its tab.

3. In cell A1, type **TOTAL SALES BY QUARTER 1993 - 1995**.

4. Select cell A3.

5. Choose **D**ata, Co**n**solidate.

   The Consolidate dialog box appears (see figure 9.27).

Figure 9.27
The Consolidate dialog box.

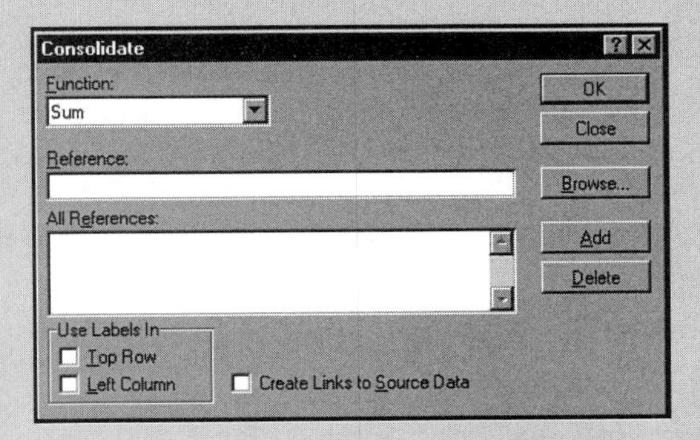

6. In the **F**unction drop-down list box, make sure that Sum is the function selected.

Keep the Consolidate dialog box open for the following tutorial.

In the next tutorial, you use the Consolidate dialog box to specify the consolidation function, the source areas to consolidate, and the row and column labels you want Excel to use in the consolidated report.

Selecting the Information to Consolidate

To select the sheets to be consolidated, follow these steps:

1. In the Consolidate dialog box, click the **R**eference text box (refer to figure 9.27).

2. At the bottom of your screen, click the QTRSALES 1995 sheet tab.

3. Drag the Consolidate dialog box out of the way (if necessary); then click and drag to select cells A4:D9 in the 1995 Quarterly Sales sheet.

4. Click the **A**dd button in the Consolidate dialog box.

   Now your dialog box should look like figure 9.28. The **R**eference text box contains the sheet name and the cell references of the selection.

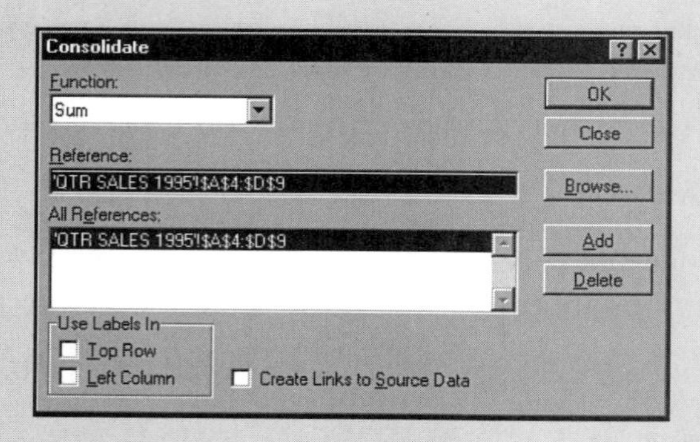

Figure 9.28 The partially completed Consolidate dialog box.

5. Click the QTRSALES 1994 sheet tab. (Use the scroll buttons at the left of the sheet tabs to move to a sheet.)

6. The corresponding cells, A4:D9, are already selected. Click the **A**dd button.

7. Click the QTRSALES 1993 sheet tab. The range A4:D9 is already selected. Click the **A**dd button.

   Now the three consolidation ranges appear in the All R**e**ferences list of the Consolidate dialog box (see figure 9.29).

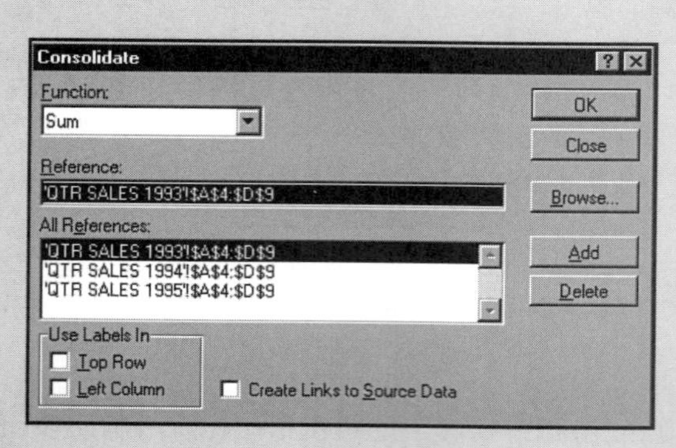

Figure 9.29 The Consolidate dialog box listing all three ranges.

8. At the lower left corner of the Consolidate dialog box is a Use Labels In area that contains two check boxes, Top Row and Left Column. Check both of these boxes.

   These labels will provide the column (top row) and row (left column) headings on the consolidated report. The column labels come from the top row of the source areas. The row headings come from the left column of the source areas.

9. Click OK, and the three sheets are consolidated in your worksheet (see figure 9.30).

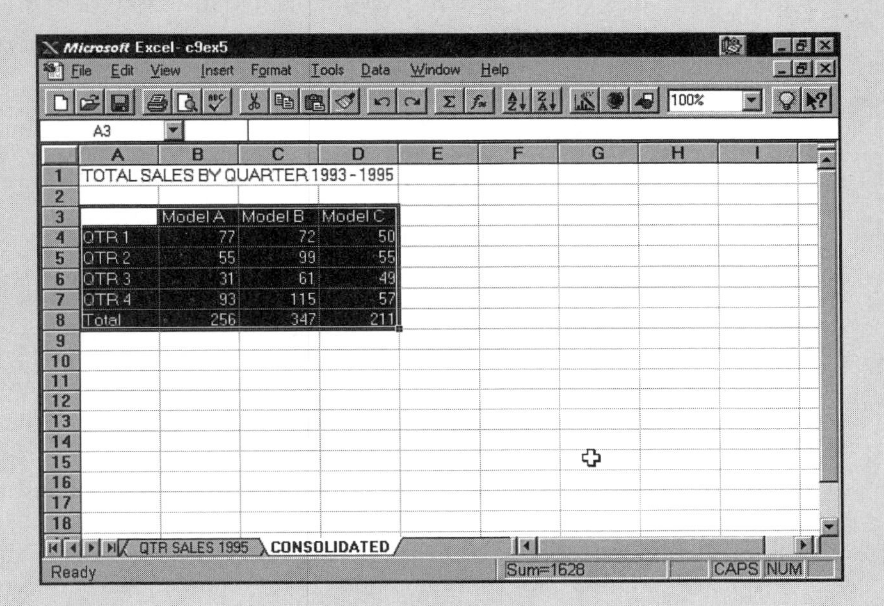

Figure 9.30
The consolidated worksheet.

Chapter Summary

In this chapter, you have learned how to link two Excel worksheets and how to repair a link that has been destroyed. You have learned how to link an Excel worksheet or chart into another application. You also learned how to produce a summary report with subtotals and how to consolidate multiple worksheets into one overall report.

In the next chapter, you learn how to perform a what-if analysis by creating scenarios with the Scenario Manager.

Checking Your Skills

True/False

For each of the following, circle *T* or *F* to indicate whether the statement is true or false.

T F **1.** Managers at higher levels in an organization need more details in a worksheet.

T F **2.** A source workbook is the workbook that supplies the data that is sent on a link.

T F **3.** A link carries data in two directions: source to dependent and dependent back to source.

T F **4.** By default, Excel always automatically updates the linked data in a dependent workbook.

T F **5.** Dependent worksheets are also called target worksheets.

T F **6.** You can link one cell or a range of cells.

T F **7.** Source workbooks in a link must be on-screen for the link to update the dependent workbook properly.

T F **8.** You cannot format linked data in a dependent workbook.

T F **9.** Once a link has been lost, you cannot reestablish it.

T F **10.** A link between a source workbook and another Windows application will not update automatically.

Multiple Choice

In the blank provided, write the letter of the correct answer for each of the following.

_____ **1.** Which of the following can be passed over a link between workbooks?

a. numbers

b. text

c. ranges of cells

d. all the above

_____ **2.** Between which of the following can you establish links?

a. worksheets

b. workbooks

c. Excel and another Windows application

d. all the above

_____ **3.** To display two worksheets simultaneously on your screen, you use the **W**indow, _____ command.

a. **A**rrange

b. **S**plit

c. **D**ouble

d. none of the above

_____ **4.** To create a link between the source and the dependent worksheets, you use the _____ command.

a. **P**aste

b. Paste **O**bject

c. Paste **L**ink

d. none of the above

_____ **5.** The actual cell reference in an external reference formula is always preceded by _____.

a. {

b. [

c. @

d. !

_____ **6.** Worksheets that will be consolidated are called the _____ area.

a. input

b. source

c. target

d. consolidation

_____ **7.** When you consolidate worksheets, you have the option of creating a _____.

a. link

b. destination

c. function

d. none of the above

_____ **8.** When you select the information to consolidate, you use the _____ dialog box.

a. Consolidate

b. Select

c. Source

d. Summarize

_____ **9.** You can specify up to _____ source areas to consolidate.

a. 10

b. 124

c. 142

d. 255

____ **10.** To remove summary subtotals from a list you use the _____, Su**b**totals command.

a. **D**ata

b. **R**emove

c. **T**ools

d. none of the above

Completion

In the blank provided, write the correct answer for each of the following.

1. The part of the link that actually extracts the data from the source workbook and places it into the dependent workbook is the ______________.

2. You should usually save the link's ______________ workbook before you save the link's ______________ workbook.

3. The command that you use to restore broken links is the ______________ command.

4. To remove a link between two sheets, you must delete the ______________ from the linked cells in the dependent worksheet.

5. The ______________ command enables you to create subtotals.

6. A link is a ______________-way connection between the source worksheet and the dependent worksheet.

7. A dependent workbook contains a(n) ______________ reference to another workbook.

8. If a source workbook is ______________ when the dependent workbook opens, the dependent workbook's linked data is automatically updated from the source workbook.

9. A(n) _____________ report is a worksheet in which list data is broken into groups and summarized by group subtotals with an overall total at the bottom.

10. A(n) _____________ report is one in which data from multiple source areas is gathered into one worksheet.

Applying Your Skills

Review Exercises

Exercise 1: Linking the C2lp1 Worksheet to a Dependent Worksheet

Open a new workbook (the dependent workbook), and link cell A10 of the new workbook to cell B17 of the C2lp1 workbook (the source workbook). The Before Tax Profit for January should appear in cell A10 of the new workbook. Test the link by changing the sales in cell B15 of C2lp1. Does cell A10 in the new workbook change?

Exercise 2: Removing a Link between Two Linked Workbooks

Remove the link that you established in Review Exercise 1. Test to see that you removed the link by entering a new sales value in cell B15; cell A10 in the new workbook should not change.

Exercise 3: Linking an Excel Worksheet Chart into a WordPad Document

Create a chart using the data in the C2lp2 worksheet. Insert the chart into a WordPad document, and verify that when you change data in C2lp2, the chart in the WordPad document gets updated.

Exercise 4: Creating Subtotals by Using the SUM Function

For this exercise, use the workbook C9ex45, available from your instructor. Create LOCATION subtotals (use the SUM function) for the PRICE field. Print the worksheet with the subtotals.

Exercise 5: Creating Subtotals by Using the AVERAGE Function

For this exercise, use the workbook C9ex45, available from your instructor. Create LOCATION subtotals (use the AVERAGE function) for the ROOMS field. Print the worksheet with the subtotals.

Continuing Projects

Project 1: Establishing a Link and then Restoring the Link

Use the International Investments Worksheet C2lp2, which you created in Chapter 2. At the foot of the Sales, Income, Assets, Value, and Capital columns, calculate the average for each column. Then create a new linked worksheet that contains these averages in cells A5 through E5.

Change the Sales, Income, Assets, Value, and Capital values for the Solvey Company in the C2lp2 worksheet. Verify that the linked averages in cells A5 through E5 also change. Save the new workbook as **C9lp1**, and then close it. Save C2lp2 as **Sourcewb**, and then close it. Using Windows Explorer, delete C2lp2. Then return to Excel, open C9lp1, and reestablish the link to Sourcewb. Print C9lp1 and Sourcewb.

Project 2: Consolidating a Weekly Budget

Open a new workbook. In Sheet1, enter your weekly income and fixed expenses for the first week of the month. Enter your income and fixed expenses for week 2 in Sheet2, week 3 in Sheet3, and week 4 in Sheet4. In Sheet5, consolidate your weekly budgets into a monthly budget. Save the workbook as **C9lcp2**. Print the workbook.

Project 3: Producing Subtotals

Using C2lp3, create a report that shows subtotals for the average Dollars of sales and average Increase. The subtotals should be grouped by number of employees. Print the report. Check the **P**age Break Between Groups check box in the Subtotal dialog box. Uncheck the **S**ummary Below Data check box in the Subtotal dialog box. Print the report using the new settings. Compare the results of the two reports.

CHAPTER 10

What-If Analysis and the Scenario Manager

What-if analysis
A form of data analysis, used in spreadsheets, in which you change key variables to see the effects on the results of the computation.

It's a tough job making good decisions in business. You have many factors to consider and many options to examine and compare. You also need to understand the implications of selecting one alternative over another and the effects of changing business conditions on the desirability of an alternative. Analyzing the effect of alternatives is known as "What-If" analysis. Excel can help with this problem because it has the built-in capabilities to compare alternatives and perform *what-if analyses* quickly and accurately.

In this chapter, you learn to use one-input and two-input data tables to compare alternatives. Then you learn how to set up a forecasting model in a worksheet in order to examine more complex business situations. Forecasting worksheets enable you to "play out" various business scenarios to see the future implications of decisions you make now. In the last section of this chapter, you learn how to use Excel's Scenario Manager to create and organize business scenarios.

Objectives

By the time you have finished this chapter, you will have learned to

1. Use a One-Input Table
2. Use a Two-Input Table
3. Set Up a Forecasting Worksheet
4. Use the Scenario Manager

Objective 1: Use a One-Input Table

Excel makes possible rapid what-if analysis. Worksheets provide immediate feedback to such questions as "What if we reduce costs by 5 percent?" and "What if we sell 11 percent more?" Sometimes, however, you want to see the results of calculating a formula for a whole series of input values. For example, "What would be the results of this formula for interest rates from 5 percent to 7 percent in increments of .10 percent?" Answering that question would require you to enter 21 different values. If you also wanted a printout of the results for each value, you would soon start looking for a better way to find the answers you need.

One-input table
A table produced when a series of different values is used in place of one variable in a formula.

Whenever you need to substitute (plug in) a series of values into a cell in one or more formulas, Excel's data tables provide the best solution. When you need to substitute values for only one variable (one cell) in a formula, you use a *one-input table*. Excel can create a table that shows the inputs you want to test and the test results, which means you don't need to enter all the possible inputs at the keyboard. You can have more than one data table in a worksheet, enabling you to analyze different variables in different areas of the worksheet.

Calculating a Table Using One Input Cell and One or More Formulas

One of the most frequently used examples of a one-input data table is a table that calculates the loan payments for a series of different interest rates. The single-input data table described in this section creates a List (a table) of monthly payments, given a range of different loan interest rates. The series of different interest rates is the "one input" that produces the table of results.

Before you create a data table, you need to build a worksheet that solves your what-if problem. For example, a worksheet that calculates a payment on a house or car loan must use the principal, interest rate, and term of the loan. Then in the worksheet, you use the PMT function to produce the amount of the monthly payment for the loan (see Chapter 4 for a review of the PMT function).

Tip

Drag the AutoFill handle (at the lower right corner of the selected cell or range) across a series to fill in incremental numbers for input values.

In the first tutorial, you create the worksheet that calculates the loan amount for one input value. In the second tutorial, you set up a one-input data table to produce payment results for a series of interest rates.

Creating the Loan Calculator Worksheet

Start Excel and open a new workbook. To build the worksheet used as the basis for the data table, follow these steps:

1. Enter the worksheet shown in figure 10.1. Cells D3:D5 contain numbers. The formula in cell D7 is `=PMT(D4/12,D5*12,D3)`.

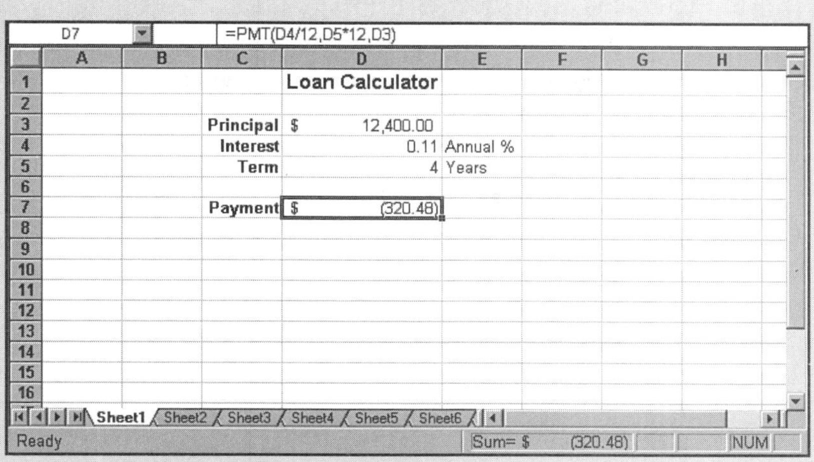

Figure 10.1
The Loan Calculator worksheet.

D7 =PMT(D4/12,D5*12,D3)

	A	B	C	D	E	F	G	H
1				Loan Calculator				
2								
3			Principal	$ 12,400.00				
4			Interest	0.11	Annual %			
5			Term	4	Years			
6								
7			Payment	$ (320.48)				

Sheet1 Sheet2 Sheet3 Sheet4 Sheet5 Sheet6
Ready Sum= $ (320.48) NUM

The PMT function arguments are explained in Chapter 4. The first argument is the monthly interest rate, the second is the number of monthly payments, and the third argument is the amount of the loan.

2. Format cells D3 and D7 to Currency.

Note: *Payments are negative numbers in this worksheet because the cash is going out.*

3. Save the workbook (but don't close it) as **Table1**.

Keep this workbook open for the next tutorial.

Next, you enter the series of different values you want to use as inputs (plugged in) to the formula. You can enter the series of inputs in either a row or a column.

Creating the Loan Data Table

To create the data table in Table1 (the Loan Calculator spreadsheet), follow these steps:

1. In cell C10, enter **Interest**.

2. In cell D10, enter **=D7**. Cell D7 contains the formula that will produce your result. You can also type a formula rather than reference a formula located elsewhere.

   Cells C11:C17 will contain the interest rates (10 percent to 13 percent) you will use as the one input variable.

3. In cell C11, enter **.10**.

4. In cell C12, enter **.105**.

(continues)

Creating the Loan Data Table (continued)

5. Select cells C11:C12.

6. Drag the fill handle down to cell C17.

7. Format cells C11:C17 to Percent with two decimal places.

8. Format cells D10:D17 to Currency.

Now your worksheet should look like figure 10.2.

Figure 10.2 The Loan Calculator worksheet ready for the Data Table command.

	A	B	C	D	E	F	G	H
1				Loan Calculator				
2								
3			Principal	$ 12,400.00				
4			Interest	0.11	Annual %			
5			Term	4	Years			
6								
7			Payment	$ (320.48)				
8								
9								
10			Interest	$ (320.48)				
11			10.00%					
12			10.50%					
13			11.00%					
14			11.50%					
15			12.00%					
16			12.50%					
17			13.00%					
18								

Sheet1 / Sheet2 / Sheet3 / Sheet4 / Sheet5 / Sheet6
Ready Sum=0 NUM

Note: *To see the results of other formulas in the table, you enter these formulas in other cells across the top of the table. For example, you can enter more formulas in cells E10, F10, and so on.*

9. Select C10:D17, the cells that will make up the table.

10. Choose **D**ata, **T**able to display the Table dialog box (see figure 10.3).

Figure 10.3 The Table dialog box.

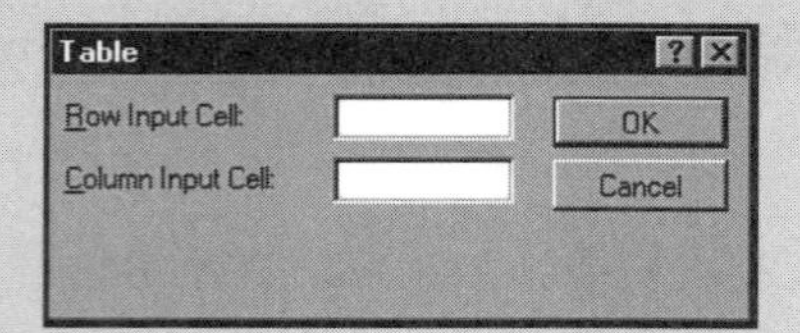

The one-input variable (the values to be substituted in the formula) is interest rate. The series of interest rates are stored in the column of cells C11:C17. The cell in the PMT formula that you want this column of values "plugged into" is D4.

11. Click in the **C**olumn Input Cell text box in the Table dialog box, and enter **$D$4**.

12. Click OK.

The data table fills with the payment amounts that correspond to each interest rate in the table (see figure 10.4).

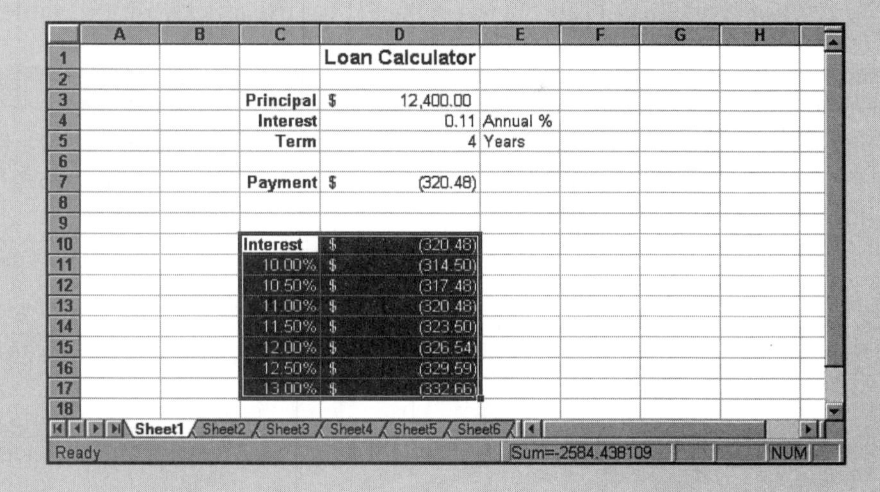

Figure 10.4
The completed table, with results in column D for each value in column C.

13. Save the workbook as **Table1** on your disk, and keep this workbook open for the next tutorial.

14. If you have a printer attached to your computer, print the worksheet.

If you have problems... For most students, deciding which cell to use as the input cell is the most confusing part of setting up a table. Ask yourself, "If I wanted to calculate payment amounts manually, in which cell would I type all the changing values?" That cell is the input cell. In the Loan Calculator worksheet, you type these interest rates into cell D4. By entering $D$4 into the **C**olumn Input Cell, you are telling Excel to test each interest rate in the left column of the table by moving that rate into cell D4. The resulting payment that is calculated for each interest rate (shown in column C) is then placed in the corresponding cell in column D.

Objective 2: Use a Two-Input Table

Two-input table
A table produced when a series of different values are used in place of two variables in a formula.

Sometimes, you will want to see a table that shows the results when two input variables (in two different worksheet cells) are "plugged into" a formula. To do this task, you set up a *two-input table*. In a two-input table, you use both a **R**ow Input Cell *and* a **C**olumn Input Cell. In the following tutorials, you create a data table that changes two input values—interest and principal. The worksheet calculates the result of the PMT function for all combinations of those values. The top row of the table contains the different principal amounts to be substituted for the **R**ow Input Cell, and the left column of the table contains the sequence of interest rates to substitute in the **C**olumn Input Cell.

When you use two different input values, you can test the results from only one formula. The formula, or reference to the formula, must be in the top-left corner of the table. In the first of the following tutorials, you modify the Loan Calculator worksheet (Table1) to prepare it for use as a two-input table.

Modifying the Loan Calculator Worksheet

To modify the Loan Calculator worksheet so that you can use it as a two-input table, follow these steps:

1. Enter **=D7** into cell C10.
2. In cell D9, enter **Principal Amounts**.
3. In cell B11, enter **Interest**.
4. In cell B12, enter **Rates**.
5. Format cells D10:H10 to Currency with two decimal places.
6. Format cells D11:H17 to Currency with negative numbers in parentheses.
7. Enter **10000** in cell D10.
8. Enter **11000** in cell E10.
9. Select cells D10:E10.
10. Drag the fill handle to cell H10.
11. Adjust the column sizes so that the numbers you entered in row 10 can be displayed.

Now your worksheet should look like figure 10.5.

Figure 10.5
Table1 modified for use as a two-input table.

	A	B	C	D	E	F	G	H
1				Loan Calculator				
2								
3			Principal	$12,400.00				
4			Interest	0.11	Annual %			
5			Term	4	Years			
6								
7			Payment	($320.48)				
8								
9				Principal Amounts				
10			($320.48)	$10,000.00	$11,000.00	$12,000.00	$13,000.00	$14,000.00
11		Interest	10.00%	$10,000.00				
12		Rates	10.50%	$10,000.00				
13			11.00%	$10,000.00				
14			11.50%	$10,000.00				
15			12.00%	$10,000.00				
16			12.50%	$10,000.00				
17			13.00%	$10,000.00				
18								

Keep this workbook open for the next tutorial.

In the next tutorial, you create a two-input data table to calculate and display your results when both the interest rate and the principal change.

Creating the Two-Input Loan Data Table

To set up the two-input table, follow these steps:

1. Select cells C10:H17.

2. Choose **D**ata, **T**able to display the Table dialog box (refer to figure 10.3).

   In your table, the principal values are in the row at the top of the table area, and the principal input cell in the worksheet is cell D3. Interest is still in the column at the left of the table area, and the column input cell is D4.

3. Click the **R**ow Input Cell text box in the Table dialog box, and type **$D$3**.

4. Click the **C**olumn Input Cell text box, and type **$D$4**.

5. Click OK.

   Figure 10.6 shows the results of the two-input data table. Each dollar value is the amount you pay on a loan with this principal amount and annual interest rate. Because each monthly payment represents a cash outflow, the results appear in parentheses to show that amounts are negative.

Figure 10.6 The completed data table with the results of combinations from two input values (interest and principal).

C10 =D7

	A	B	C	D	E	F	G	H
1				**Loan Calculator**				
2								
3			**Principal**	$12,400.00				
4			**Interest**	0.11	Annual %			
5			**Term**	4	Years			
6								
7			**Payment**	($320.48)				
8								
9				Principal Amounts				
10			($320.48)	$10,000.00	$11,000.00	$12,000.00	$13,000.00	$14,000.00
11		Interest	10.00%	($253.63)	($278.99)	($304.35)	($329.71)	($355.08)
12		Rates	10.50%	($256.03)	($281.64)	($307.24)	($332.84)	($358.45)
13			11.00%	($258.46)	($284.30)	($310.15)	($335.99)	($361.84)
14			11.50%	($260.89)	($286.98)	($313.07)	($339.16)	($365.25)
15			12.00%	($263.34)	($289.67)	($316.01)	($342.34)	($368.67)
16			12.50%	($265.80)	($292.38)	($318.96)	($345.54)	($372.12)
17			13.00%	($268.27)	($295.10)	($321.93)	($348.76)	($375.58)
18								

6. Save the workbook as **Table2**.

7. If you have a printer attached to your computer, print the worksheet.

8. Close the Table2 workbook.

After you complete the data table, you can change any worksheet values on which the data table depends. Excel recalculates the table using the new values. In Table2, typing a new term amount in cell D5 causes new payment amounts to reappear. You can also change the numbers in the rows and columns of input values and see the resulting change in the data table. In the example worksheet, you can type new numbers or use **E**dit, F**i**ll, **S**eries to replace the numbers in C11:C17 or in D10:H10. The table will be automatically updated.

Objective 3: Set Up a Forecasting Worksheet

Excel's worksheets are most frequently used for budgeting, as you have already experienced. The second most frequent use of Excel worksheets is forecasting. In business, you need to have a good feel for the influence of key financial factors. Because these factors will mean the future success or failure for your business, you must be able to project changes in these factors.

Worksheet model
A worksheet with formulas that represent real-world business operations; can be used to create scenarios.

With a worksheet, you can create a financial model of your business. This *worksheet model* will contain certain facts about your business. The worksheet will also contain assumptions you make about how your business functions financially now and in the future. These assumptions are represented by formulas in the worksheet.

A model, whether it be financial or weather, uses certain key inputs to produce outputs (results). As the inputs change, the results change. Weather models require inputs like temperature, humidity, and wind direction. Financial models use such inputs as tax rates, interest rates, costs of goods sold, and advertising costs. Just as the accuracy of weather forecasts depends on the validity of the weather model used, the accuracy of your financial forecasts depends on the validity (in terms of realism) of your model.

Because a business is never affected by just one factor, financial models have multiple inputs. The interaction of these inputs can be complicated and difficult to keep in mind when you think about your business. For this reason, Excel worksheets are often used to perform what-if analyses, answering such questions as "What if sales increase by 5 percent, costs of goods sold increase by 2.5 percent, personnel costs are reduced 6 percent, and marketing costs jump 3 percent? What will the bottom line look like then?"

Scenario
A projected sequence of possible future events; a set of changing input values and their results.

Changing cells
The input worksheet cells in a scenario.

Financial projections are often called *scenarios*. To make financial projections in Excel, you set up a model of your business situation. The input cells of the model are called the *changing cells*. Each set of changing cells represents a set of what-if assumptions you use with the worksheet model. Then you can "play out" a set of different business what-if scenarios to see which one gives you the best result.

In this section, you use a financial model workbook (Forecast) that produces a projection of sales, expenses, and net income to test the effects of changing sales and costs on your net income "bottom line."

Examining the Forecast Worksheet

Your instructor will give you a copy of the Forecast workbook, which contains an example of a modeling worksheet that could be used by the NSCC Company in what-if scenarios (see figure 10.7). The worksheet uses growth percentage estimates for Sales, Cost of Goods Sold (COGS), General and Administrative Costs (G&A), and Marketing Costs (Mktg). These four percentages are the changing cells in NSCC's scenario. By changing the values in these cells, which are the key inputs to NSCC's business model, you change the results of the model. These results are for a period of five years. Annual Net Income and Total Income are the results that would be of most interest to NSCC's management.

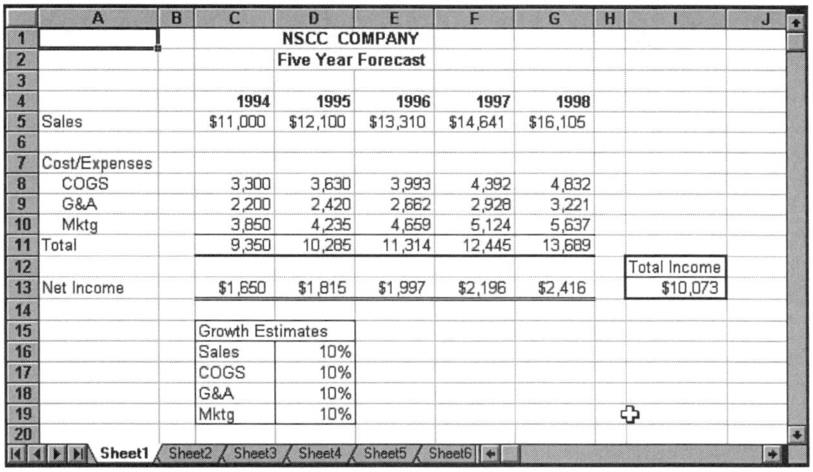

Figure 10.7
A simple financial modeling worksheet.

	A	B	C	D	E	F	G	H	I	J
1				NSCC COMPANY						
2				Five Year Forecast						
3										
4			1994	1995	1996	1997	1998			
5	Sales		$11,000	$12,100	$13,310	$14,641	$16,105			
6										
7	Cost/Expenses									
8	COGS		3,300	3,630	3,993	4,392	4,832			
9	G&A		2,200	2,420	2,662	2,928	3,221			
10	Mktg		3,850	4,235	4,659	5,124	5,637			
11	Total		9,350	10,285	11,314	12,445	13,689			
12									Total Income	
13	Net Income		$1,650	$1,815	$1,997	$2,196	$2,416		$10,073	
14										
15			Growth Estimates							
16			Sales	10%						
17			COGS	10%						
18			G&A	10%						
19			Mktg	10%						
20										

Sheet1 / Sheet2 / Sheet3 / Sheet4 / Sheet5 / Sheet6

The projections used in forecasting model worksheets usually start with known data for the first time period. This data is used as the starting value to estimate the projected value for the next time period. In this example, NSCC knows its values for 1994. The annual growth rate estimates in cells D16:D19 are then used to calculate the results for the next time period. For example, 1995's sales are estimated by multiplying 1994's sales by 110 percent (1 + $D$16) to give a 10 percent growth in sales. Sales for 1996 are estimated in the same way using the 1995 value. Take a moment to look at the formulas in cells D5:G10 so that you can understand how the model estimates growth.

This worksheet is, of course, a very simple model, and the growth estimates may not be realistic. The worksheet does, however, illustrate the principles and the techniques used in creating financial forecasting models. In the next tutorial, you will enter new values (growth estimates) in the input cells (the changing cells) and see the results.

Entering New Input Values for the Model

To enter new values in the NSCC Company worksheet's changing cells, follow these steps:

1. Change the sales growth estimate in cell D16 to **20** percent.

   Note the change in the results of the forecast.

2. Change the G&A costs growth rate to **12** percent (see figure 10.8).

(continues)

Entering New Input Values for the Model (continued)

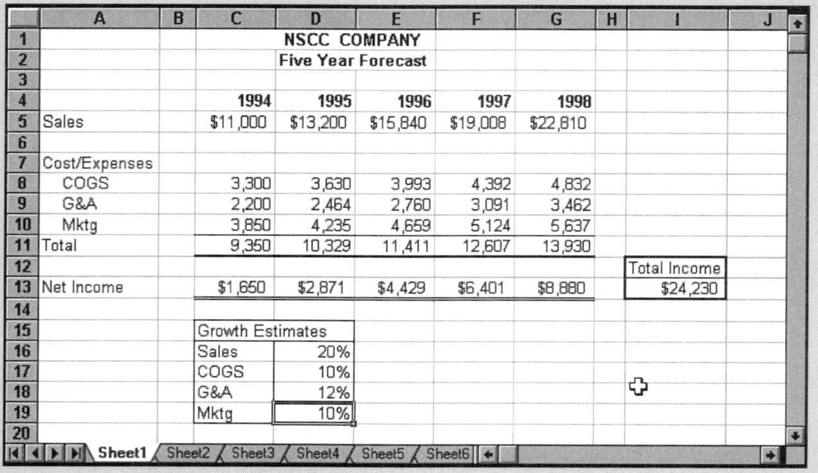

Figure 10.8 The worksheet with the new values entered.

	A	B	C	D	E	F	G	H	I	J
1				NSCC COMPANY						
2				Five Year Forecast						
3										
4			1994	1995	1996	1997	1998			
5	Sales		$11,000	$13,200	$15,840	$19,008	$22,810			
6										
7	Cost/Expenses									
8	COGS		3,300	3,630	3,993	4,392	4,832			
9	G&A		2,200	2,464	2,760	3,091	3,462			
10	Mktg		3,850	4,235	4,659	5,124	5,637			
11	Total		9,350	10,329	11,411	12,607	13,930			
12									Total Income	
13	Net Income		$1,650	$2,871	$4,429	$6,401	$8,880		$24,230	
14										
15			Growth Estimates							
16			Sales	20%						
17			COGS	10%						
18			G&A	12%						
19			Mktg	10%						
20										

Sheet1 / Sheet2 / Sheet3 / Sheet4 / Sheet5 / Sheet6

3. If you have a printer attached to your computer, print your worksheet.

Keep this workbook open for the next tutorial.

Now, you are ready to do some simple what-if analyses yourself. Notice closely the results of the changes you make in the following tutorial.

Playing What-If

To do your own what-if analysis, follow these steps:

1. Change the growth rate estimates to see the effects on the results of the model.

2. After you have tried three or four different combinations of growth percentage estimates and have seen the results, close the worksheet *without* saving it.

3. Open the original version of Forecast that you were given by your instructor so that you will be ready to work through the tutorials under the following objective.

Objective 4: Use the Scenario Manager

Rather than use just one set of input values in the model to see what the results will be, most managers like to try out a range of different input values. This practice is called "testing a range of different scenarios." Looking at the results of the scenarios gives managers a better feel for what is likely to happen over the next few months or years. With many different input values being run through a financial forecasting worksheet, however, keeping the different scenarios organized can be

Scenario Manager
An Excel feature that creates and saves different sets of data as separate scenarios.

difficult. Excel's *Scenario Manager*, a dialog box available through the **S**cenarios command in the **T**ools menu, is designed to make this task easier. The Scenario Manager helps you create, save, and run multiple scenarios.

In this section, you use Excel's Scenario Manager to input a set of what-if assumptions into your worksheet model and see how the results of the model are affected. The Scenario Manager enables you to define changing cells for your worksheet. You then create different scenarios using these changing cells. The Scenario Manager enables you to store multiple scenarios in the worksheet so that you don't need to save multiple copies of your data.

10

Testing Multiple Solutions with Scenarios

Worksheets are ideally suited for what-if analysis. You enter values into key cells and watch what happens to the results. Although this procedure enables you to enter new alternatives easily, reentering previous sets of values is often tedious. In many situations, you need to look at many alternatives, a need that requires entering many different sets of input values (changing cells).

Excel's Scenario Manager can manage multiple scenarios by storing different values for input data cells in scenarios to which you assign different names. These values are stored in the worksheet and saved when you save the worksheet. You can keep many versions—or scenarios—of input values and easily switch among them. When you want to view the results from a different scenario of input values, you just choose a different named scenario from the Scenario Manager dialog box.

A model with named scenarios should have a clear set of one or more key input values and a clear set of one or more result values that change based on the inputs. The Forecast worksheet meets both of these criteria. When you type new numbers for the growth estimates in cells D16:D19, the Net Income figures adjust automatically, and you see the new Total Income in cell I13. You have a clear set of input values as well as a clear result value. You use Forecast to create scenarios with the Scenario Manager by saving different named sets of input values for the changing cells. These values are the input values saved by the Scenario Manager (see figure 10.9).

Figure 10.9
The changing cells in the worksheet hold the input values for the scenario.

	A	B	C	D	E	F	G	H	I	J
1				NSCC COMPANY						
2				Five Year Forecast						
3										
4			1994	1995	1996	1997	1998			
5	Sales		$11,000	$12,100	$13,310	$14,641	$16,105			
6										
7	Cost/Expenses									
8	COGS		3,300	3,630	3,993	4,392	4,832			
9	G&A		2,200	2,420	2,662	2,928	3,221			
10	Mktg		3,850	4,235	4,659	5,124	5,637			
11	Total		9,350	10,285	11,314	12,445	13,689			
12									Total Income	
13	Net Income		$1,650	$1,815	$1,997	$2,196	$2,416		$10,073	
14										
15			Growth Estimates							
16			Sales	10%						
17			COGS	10%						
18			G&A	10%						
19			Mktg	10%						
20										

Sheet1 / Sheet2 / Sheet3 / Sheet4 / Sheet5 / Sheet6

The changing cells

Before running a what-if scenario with the Scenario Manager, you should give names to the input cells. Excel does not require that the input cells have names, but if they do, the dialog boxes and reports in the Scenario Manager will display the names rather than the difficult-to-understand cell addresses.

Naming the Input and Result Cells

To name the input and result cells for the Forecast worksheet, follow these steps:

1. Select cells C16:D19.
2. Choose Insert, Name, Create, and select the Left Column check box.
3. Click OK.
4. Select cells I12:I13.
5. Choose Insert, Name, Create, and select the Top Row check box.
6. Click OK.

This process uses the labels in the left column (column C) to create names for the cells in the right column (column D). Steps 4 and 5 name the final result cell Total_Income by using the label in cell I12.

Note: *The Scenario Manager uses a name instead of a cell reference if a name applies specifically to just that cell. If a name applies to more than the single cell, the Scenario Manager ignores the name. To determine whether a cell has a name, select the cell. If a name has been assigned, it will appear in the name box at the extreme left of the formula bar. Otherwise, the name box will display the cell reference. To display a list of names in the worksheet, click the arrow adjacent to the name box in the formula bar.*

Displaying the Scenario Manager Dialog Box

To open the Scenario Manager dialog box, follow these steps:

1. Select the input cells (the changing cells), C16:D19.

   Keep these cells selected. When you create your scenario, Excel uses the currently selected cells with their current values as the default changing cells.

2. Choose Tools, Scenarios.

   The Scenario Manager dialog box appears (see figure 10.10). No scenarios have been stored yet.

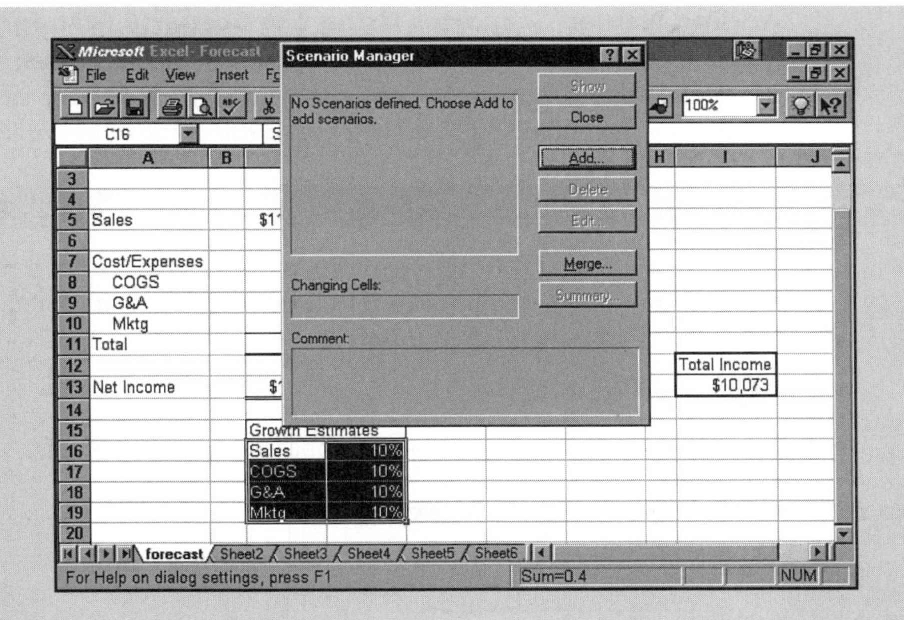

Figure 10.10 The Scenario Manager dialog box.

3. Drag the Scenario Manager dialog box up over the menu bar so that you can see the input cells and the result cell (refer to figure 10.10). Excel will remember where you want the dialog box displayed whenever you use the worksheet.

The Scenario Manager dialog box offers you many options for dealing with your scenarios. Table 10.1 explains the functions of the elements of Scenario Manager dialog box.

Table 10.1 Elements of the Scenario Manager Dialog Box

Element	Function
Boxes	
Scenarios	Lists the names of any defined scenarios in the active worksheet; if there are no scenarios, the box is empty.
Changing Cells	Displays the cells containing the data that is to change in each named scenario.
Comment	Displays the date a scenario was created or edited, the name of the individual who created or modified the scenario, and any text you type as a comment.
Buttons	
Show	Displays in the worksheet the changing cell values for the scenario selected in the Scenarios box. The worksheet is recalculated to reflect the new values.
Close	Closes the Scenario Manager dialog box.
Add	Enables you to add a new named scenario.
Delete	Immediately deletes the scenario you have selected in the Scenarios box.
Edit	Displays the Edit Scenario dialog box, enabling you to edit a scenario.

Adding Named Scenarios Using the Scenario Manager

Suppose that you need to create four scenarios for this model: the original values, a most-likely estimate, a best-case estimate, and a worst-case estimate. These estimates will enable you to get a sense of the range of options for the future.

Adding Your First Named Scenario

To create a scenario with the Scenario Manager, make sure that you have the correct input cells selected (C16:D19) and that the Scenario Manager dialog box is displayed on-screen. Then follow these steps:

1. Click **Add**.

   The Add Scenarios dialog box appears (see figure 10.11).

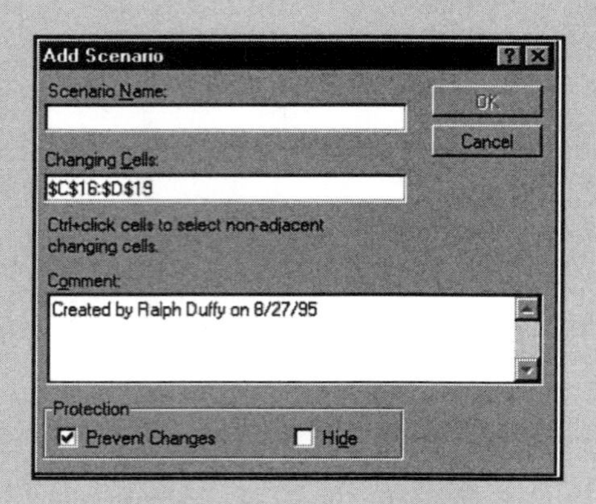

Figure 10.11 The Add Scenarios dialog box.

2. Type the name of the scenario, **Original**, in the Scenario **N**ame text box.

   Scenario names can have up to 255 characters and can contain spaces and numbers.

3. Click OK.

4. The Scenario Values dialog box appears with a listing of the values in the changing cells (see figure 10.12).

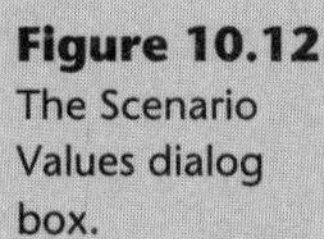

Figure 10.12 The Scenario Values dialog box.

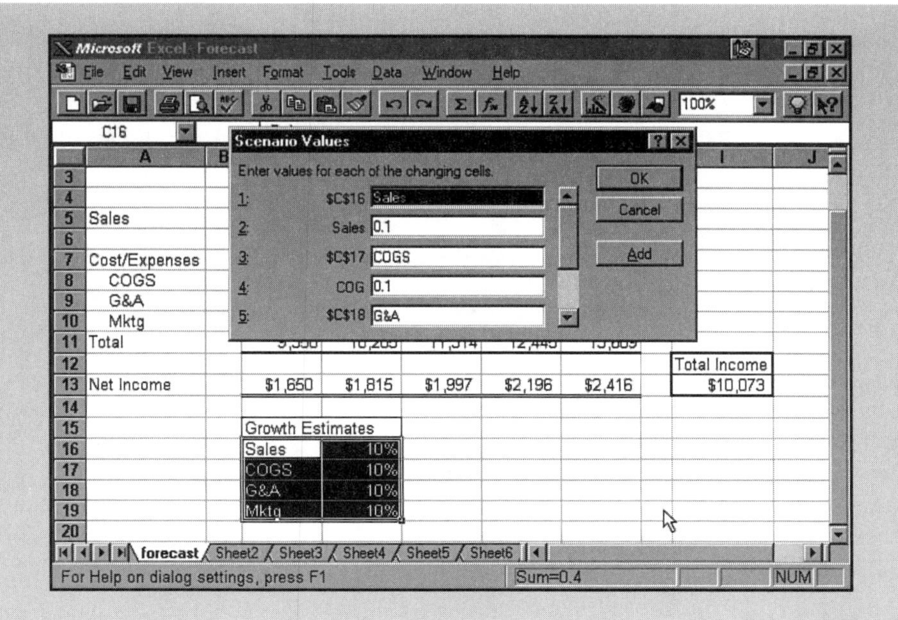

5. Click OK.

   The Scenario Manager dialog box appears.

6. Click Close.

You now have a single scenario stored in the worksheet. Behind the scenes, Excel saves the set of values in the input cells as the Original scenario.

Adding the Other Named Scenarios

To add the Most-likely, Best-case, and Worst-case scenarios to your worksheet using the Scenario Manager, follow these steps:

1. Enter the following Most-likely scenario numbers into the Forecast worksheet's input (changing) cells: **15** percent for Sales, **15** for COGS, **12** for G&A, and **17** for Mktg.

2. After changing the input values, select the input cells C16:D19.

   Keep these cells selected. When you create your scenario, Excel uses the currently selected cells with their current values as the default changing cells. If you forget to do this, you can always enter the changing cells in the Scenario Manager's Changing Cells text box.

3. Now you can use the Scenario Manager to add the new scenario. Follow the same steps you followed in the preceding tutorial except type **Most-likely**, the name of the scenario, in the Scenario Name text box.

(continues)

Adding the Other Named Scenarios (continued)

4. Now add the Best-case, and then the Worst-case scenarios.

   Use the following values for the input cells (D16:D19) in the worksheet:

   Best-case scenario: **20** for Sales, **18** for COGS, **18** for G&A, **19** for Mktg

   Worst-case scenario: **12** for Sales, **14** for COGS, **18** for G&A, **20** for Mktg

5. After you have chosen OK to accept the Worst-case scenario. The Scenario Manager dialog box reappears—this time, with all four named scenarios listed (see figure 10.13).

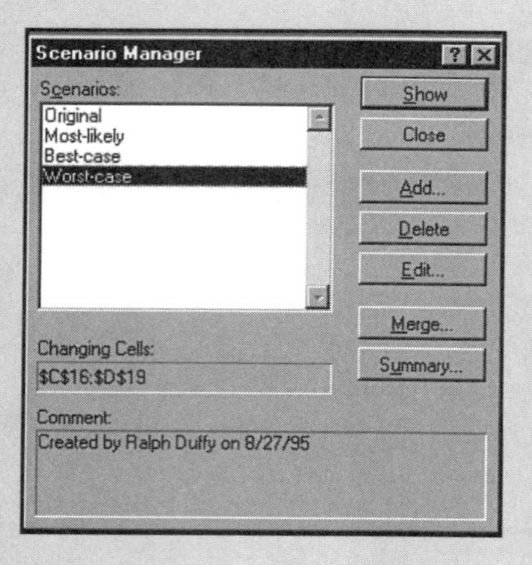

Figure 10.13 The Scenario Manager after adding the four scenarios.

6. Click Close to close the Scenario Manager dialog box.

   You now have all four scenarios on the worksheet ready to review.

7. Save the updated workbook to disk as Forecast2.

Keep this workbook open for the following tutorials.

Because the named scenarios are stored in hidden names in the worksheet, when you save the workbook, you save the scenarios you have just created. Saving the workbooks helps prevent you from losing your scenarios if you accidentally make a mistake. When you save the workbook, the input (changing) cells for the scenarios, as well as the scenario names and values, are stored with the worksheet.

Now that you have some named scenarios in the worksheet, you can quickly switch the model from one scenario to another. Simply choose a different scenario from the Scenario Manager dialog box. The values for the scenario you choose appear in the changing cells, and the worksheet is recalculated.

Switching between Named Scenarios

To switch between scenarios using the Scenario Manager, follow these steps:

1. Choose **T**ools, **S**cenarios to display the Scenario Manager dialog box.

   The current scenario (the one from which you are making the switch) is selected.

2. If necessary, drag the dialog box up over the Excel menu bar to reveal more of the screen so that the input and result cells are visible.

3. Double-click the name of a different scenario in the Scenarios list box.

   (Alternatively, you can select a scenario from the **S**cenarios list box, and choose Show.)

   The values for the scenario you choose appear in the changing cells, and the worksheet is recalculated.

4. When you have finished examining the scenarios, select the scenario you want to display, and then choose Close.

After you have named scenarios in your worksheet, you can go back and change the values for any given scenario. With this capability, you can have a great many scenarios without the tedious work of reentering spreadsheet figures.

Editing a Scenario

To edit the scenario with the Scenario Manager, make sure that the Forecast2 workbook is open, then follow these steps:

1. Choose **T**ools, **S**cenarios to display the Scenario Manager dialog box (refer to figure 10.13).

2. Select the scenario that you want to change from the Scenarios list box.

3. Click the **E**dit button. The Edit Scenario dialog box appears (see figure 10.14).

Figure 10.14
The Edit Scenario dialog box.

Edit Scenario
Scenario Name: Best-case
Changing Cells: $C$16:$D$19
Ctrl+click cells to select non-adjacent changing cells.
Comment:
Created by Ralph Duffy on 8/27/95
Modified by Ralph Duffy on 8/27/95
Protection
Prevent Changes
Hide
OK
Cancel

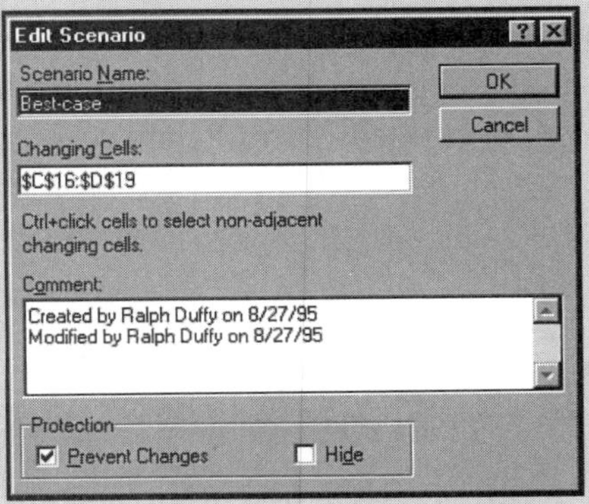

(continues)

Editing a Scenario (continued)

4. To specify different changing cells, edit the contents of the Changing Cells text box.
5. Choose OK. The Scenario Values dialog box appears (refer to figure 10.12).
6. Make changes in the appropriate text box(es), and then choose OK.
7. In the Scenario Manager, choose Show to make the worksheet reflect the changes.
8. Choose Close to close the dialog box.

Do not save the changes. Keep this workbook open for the next tutorial.

Eventually, you will finish exploring a particular named scenario. And usually, you will not want to keep the scenarios you no longer use. You can easily delete a named scenario by using the Scenario Manager.

Deleting Named Scenarios

To delete a named scenario, follow these steps:

1. Choose Tools, Scenarios to display the Scenario Manager dialog box.
2. Click the name of the scenario you want to delete in the Scenarios list box.
3. Click the Delete button.

   The scenario is immediately deleted.
4. Close your workbook without saving the changes.

Chapter Summary

In this chapter, you have learned to use a worksheet in a new way. You have also learned how to do a simple comparison of alternatives using one-input and two-input tables. You have learned how to set up a worksheet to run financial projections and test what-if alternatives. Finally, you have learned how to use the Scenario Manager to create, run, edit, and delete scenarios.

Checking Your Skills

True/False

For each of the following, circle *T* or *F* to indicate whether the statement is true or false.

T F **1.** The changing cells in an Excel scenario are the result cells.

T F **2.** Clicking the **D**elete button in the Scenario Manager displays the Delete Scenario dialog box.

T F **3.** The command that enables you to name one or more cells is found in the **T**ools menu.

T F **4.** The top row of a one-input data table consists of one or more formulas or references to formulas.

T F **5.** A forecasting worksheet contains a model of an aspect of your business.

T F **6.** A scenario name cannot contain spaces.

T F **7.** You can have a maximum of three scenarios in a worksheet.

T F **8.** You can use formulas when setting up a one-input data table, but you cannot use functions.

T F **9.** The input variables to a two-input table must appear in two adjacent columns.

T F **10.** When you use two different input values in a two-input table, you can test the results from only one formula in the table.

Multiple Choice

In the blank provided, write the letter of the correct answer for each of the following.

_____ **1.** To display the changing cell values on a worksheet for the selected scenario, click the _____ button in the Scenario Manager.

a. **C**alculate

b. **D**isplay

c. **E**dit

d. none of the above

_____ **2.** To leave the Scenario Manager and return to the active worksheet, click the _____ button.

a. Close

b. Exit

c. Quit

d. none of the above

_____ **3.** You can access the Scenario Manager through the _____ menu.

a. **E**dit

b. **T**ools

c. **V**iew

d. none of the above

_____ **4.** A _____ table is produced when you use a series of different values in place of one variable in one or more formulas.

a. one-way table

b. two-way table

c. both a and b

d. none of the above

_____ **5.** A worksheet _____ is a worksheet with formulas that represent real-world business operations.

a. data table

b. Result Area

c. model

d. none of the above

_____ **6.** The command that enables you to edit a scenario is available through the _____ menu.

a. **A**lter Scenario

b. **E**dit

c. **W**indows

d. none of the above

_____ **7.** A scenario name can consist of up to _____ characters.

a. 8

b. 20

c. 33

d. 255

_____ **8.** The command to create a name for a range of cells is accessed through the _____ menu.

a. **I**nsert

b. **E**dit

c. **F**ile

d. **T**ools

_____ **9.** The _____ button in the Scenario Manager dialog box enables you to add a new named scenario.

a. **A**dd

b. **I**nclude

c. **E**dit

d. none of the above

_____ **10.** Excel saves the set of values in the _____ cells as a scenario.

a. input

b. changing

c. data

d. both a and b

Completion

In the blank provided, write the correct answer for each of the following.

1. A(n) ______________ table is produced when you use a series of different values in place of two variables in a formula.

2. The command that enables you to create tables of results is found in the ______________ menu.

3. An Excel ______________ is a named set of input values that you can substitute in a worksheet model.

4. You should give a(n) ______________ to the input cells in a scenario.

5. To create a scenario in the Scenario Manager, you click the ______________ button.

6. ______________ analysis is a form of data analysis in which you change key variables to see the effects on the results of the computation.

7. The dark square at the lower right-hand corner of a selected cell or range is called the ______________ handle.

8. The Excel function that is used to calculate the amount of the monthly payments on a loan is the ______________ function.

9. For most students, deciding which cell to use as the ______________ cell is the most confusing part of setting up a data table.

10. Financial projections are often called ______________.

Applying Your Skills

Review Exercises

Exercise 1: Using a One-Way Loan Analysis Table

Set up a one-way loan analysis table that calculates the monthly payments on a principal of $10,000.00 for interest rates of 5 percent through 9 percent in increments of 0.5 percent. The loan must be paid off in 5 years. Print your worksheet. Save the workbook as **C10sp1**.

Exercise 2: Using a Two-Way Loan Analysis Table

Set up a two-way loan analysis table that calculates the monthly payments for principals of $10,000.00, $12,000.00, $14,000.00, and $16,000.00. The interest rates are 7 percent through 12 percent in increments of 0.5 percent. The term of the loan is 6 years. Print your worksheet. Save the workbook as **C10sp2**.

Exercise 3: Setting Up a One-Input Depreciation Schedule

Set up a one-way table that prints a depreciation schedule using the double-declining balance method (use Excel's DDB function). Assume that the new piece of equipment costs $5,000.00 and has a lifetime of 7 years. The salvage value of the machine is $600.00. Print your worksheet. Save the workbook as **C10sp3**.

Exercise 4: Setting Up a Two-Input Depreciation Schedule

Modify the C10sp3 worksheet you created in Review Exercise 3 so that the table shows a depreciation schedule for a new piece of equipment if the cost ranges from $5,000.00 to $6,000.00 in increments of $100.00. Use a lifetime of 7 years and a salvage value of $600.00. Print your worksheet. Save the workbook as **C10sp4**.

Exercise 5: Setting Up a One-Input Data Table

Go to the library, and look up the per capita national debt. Calculate the average percent increase in the per capita national debt over the last four years. Using this value, print what the estimated per capita national debt will be in each of the next ten years. Save the workbook as **C10sp5**, and print the worksheet.

Continuing Projects

Project 1: Forecasting the Future for the Munch Mart Sandwich Shop

The owner of the Munch Mart has asked you to set up some best-guess, best-case, and worst-case five-year scenarios for her business. You have met with her and have a copy of her (very much simplified) income statement for 1994 (see figure 10.15).

Using the information shown in figure 10.15, set up a workbook to project the statement over five more years. Assume that the percent increases will be consistent for all five years of the projection. Use the Scenario Manager to produce your own percent increases for all three scenarios. You should include as inputs Percent Increases for Sales, Cost of Sales, Payroll, Supplies, Advertising, Rent, and Other. Save the workbook as **C10lp1**. Print the three worksheets (the best-guess worksheet, the best-case worksheet, and the worst-case worksheet) that result from these scenarios.

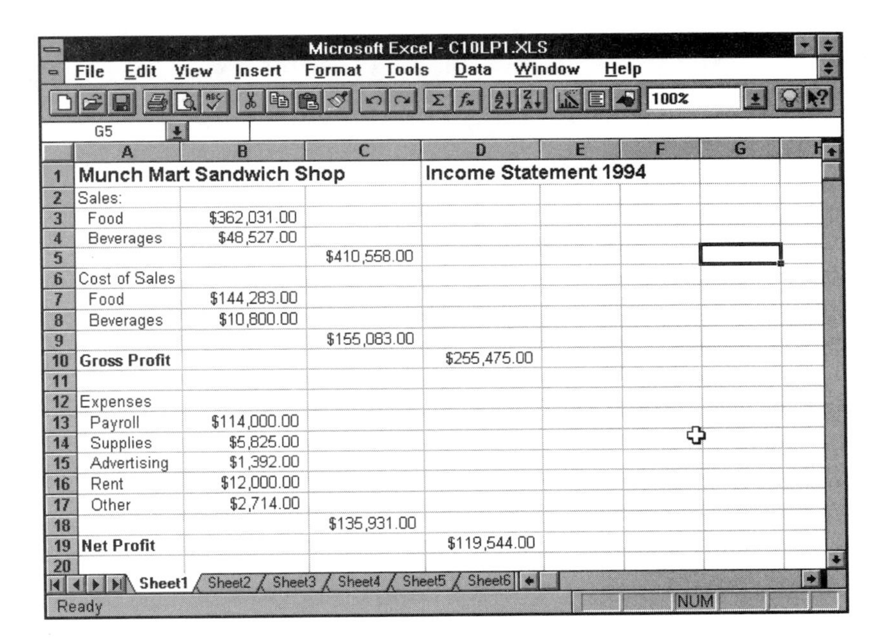

	A	B	C	D
1	Munch Mart Sandwich Shop			Income Statement 1994
2	Sales:			
3	Food	$362,031.00		
4	Beverages	$48,527.00		
5			$410,558.00	
6	Cost of Sales			
7	Food	$144,283.00		
8	Beverages	$10,800.00		
9			$155,083.00	
10	Gross Profit			$255,475.00
11				
12	Expenses			
13	Payroll	$114,000.00		
14	Supplies	$5,825.00		
15	Advertising	$1,392.00		
16	Rent	$12,000.00		
17	Other	$2,714.00		
18			$135,931.00	
19	Net Profit			$119,544.00
20				

Figure 10.15 The Income Statement from the Munch Mart.

Project 2: Setting Up a Forecasting Worksheet Using Your Personal Budget

Although your favorite personal scenario may be winning the lottery, the odds are against you. A more reasonable forecast might involve a 7 percent yearly increase in salary, a 5 percent reduction in expenses for entertainment, a 10 percent reduction in the interest you are paying, and possibly a 1 percent reduction in taxes. Using your own personal budget and a little imagination, set up a forecasting worksheet to represent your annual cash flow for the next four years. Include budget items for rent, food, and clothing, but assume that these expenses will remain constant over the four years. Save your workbook as **C10lp2**, and then print your worksheet.

Project 3: Creating Scenarios Using Your Personal Budget

Modify the C10lp2 forecasting worksheet so that you can create scenarios using this worksheet. Set up three scenarios, and name them Worst Case (the percent changes in your budget are the worst you anticipate), Best Case (the percent changes are the best that you can hope for), and Most Likely (the percent changes are what you reasonably anticipate). Run each of the three scenarios, and print the three worksheets that result from the scenarios. Save the workbook containing the scenarios as **C10lp3**.

APPENDIX A

Working with Windows 95

Graphical user interface (GUI)
A computer application that uses pictures, graphics, menus, and commands to help users communicate with their computers.

Microsoft Windows 95 is a powerful operating environment that enables you to access the power of DOS without memorizing DOS commands and syntax. Windows uses a *graphical user interface* (GUI) so that you can easily see on-screen the tools you need to complete specific file and program management tasks.

This appendix, an overview of the Windows 95 environment, is designed to help you learn the basics of Windows 95.

Objectives

By the time you finish this appendix, you will have learned to

- Start Windows 95
- Use the Mouse
- Identify the Elements of a Window
- Understand the Start menu
- Manipulate Windows
- Exit the Windows 95 Program

Desktop
The background of the Windows screen, on which windows, icons, and dialog boxes appear.

Objective 1: Start Windows 95

Icon
A picture that represents an application, a file, or a system resource.

Shortcut
A shortcut gives you quick access to frequently used objects so you don't have to look through menus each time you need to use that object.

The first thing you need to know about Windows is how to start the software, and in this lesson, you learn just that. Before you can start Windows 95, however, it must be installed on your computer. If you need to install Windows 95, refer to your Windows 95 manual or ask your instructor for assistance.

In most cases, Windows 95 starts automatically when you turn on your computer. If your system is set up differently, you must start Windows 95 from the DOS prompt (such as `C:\>`). Try starting the Windows 95 program now.

Starting Windows

1. Turn on your computer and monitor.

   Most computers display technical information about the computer and the operating software installed on it. It is likely that the computer then displays a DOS prompt (`C:\>`) in the upper-left corner of the screen.

2. At the DOS prompt `C:\>`, type **win** and then press Enter.

   When you start the Windows 95 program, a Microsoft Windows 95 banner displays for a few seconds; then the *desktop* appears (see Figure A.1).

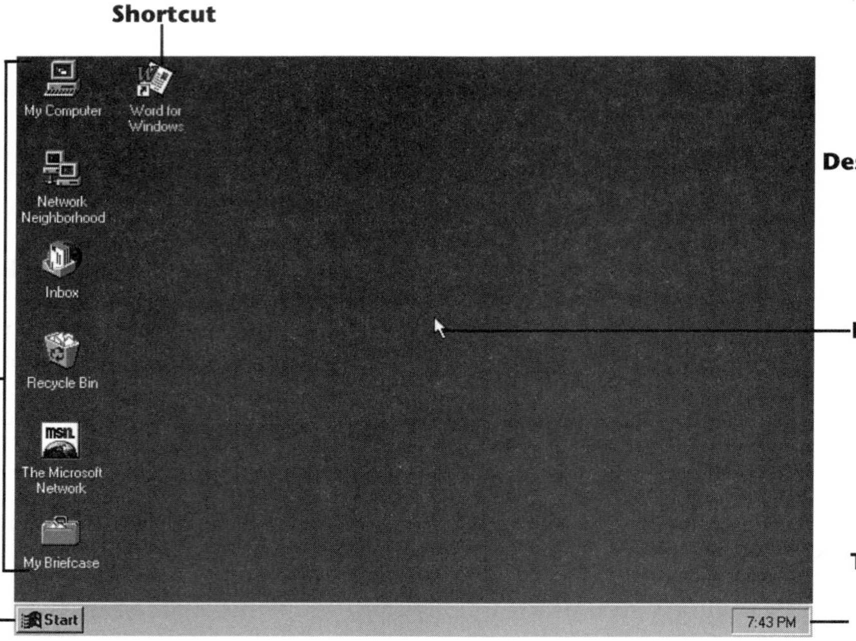

Figure A.1
The Windows 95 desktop appears a few seconds after a Windows 95 banner.

Taskbar
Contains the Start button, buttons for each open window and the current time.

Program *icons* that were created during installation (My Computer, Recycle Bin, Network Neighborhood) are displayed on the desktop. Other icons may also appear, depending on how your system is set up. *Shortcuts* to frequently used objects (such as documents, printers, and network drives) can be placed on the desktop. The *Taskbar* appears along the bottom edge of the desktop. The *Start button* appears at the left end of the taskbar.

Objective 2: Use the Mouse

Start button
A click on the Start button opens the Start menu.

Mouse
A pointing device used in many programs to make choices, select data, and otherwise communicate with the computer.

Windows is designed to be used with a *mouse*, so it's important that you learn how to use a mouse correctly. With a little practice, using a mouse is as easy as pointing to something with your finger. You can use the mouse to select icons, to make selections from *pull-down menus* and *dialog boxes*, and to select objects that you want to move or resize.

In the Windows desktop, you can use a mouse to

- Open windows
- Close windows
- Open menus
- Choose menu commands
- Rearrange on-screen items, such as icons and windows

Pull-down menus
Menus that cascade downward into the screen whenever you select a command from the menu bar.

Dialog box
A window that opens on-screen to provide information about the current action or to ask the user to provide additional information to complete the action.

Mouse pointer
A symbol that appears on-screen to indicate the current location of the mouse.

Mouse pad
A pad that provides a uniform surface for a mouse to slide on.

The position of the mouse is indicated on-screen by a *mouse pointer*. Usually, the mouse pointer is an arrow, but it sometimes changes shape depending on the current action.

On-screen the mouse pointer moves according to the movements of the mouse on your desk or on a *mouse pad*. To move the mouse pointer, simply move the mouse.

There are four basic mouse actions:

- *Click*. Point to an item, and then press and quickly release the left mouse button. You click to select an item, such as an option on a menu. To cancel a selection, click an empty area of the desktop. Unless otherwise specified, you use the left mouse button for all mouse actions.
- *Double-click*. Point to an item, and then press and release the left mouse button twice, as quickly as possible. You double-click to open or close windows and to start applications from icons.
- *Right-click*. Point to an item, and then press and release the right mouse button. This opens a Context menu, which gives you a shortcut to frequently used commands. To cancel a Context menu, click the left mouse button outside of the menu.
- *Drag*. Point to an item, and then press and hold down the left mouse button as you move the pointer to another location, and then release the mouse button. You drag to resize windows, move icons, and scroll.

If you have problems... If you try to double-click but nothing happens, you may not be clicking fast enough. Try again.

Objective 3: Understand the Start Menu

Program folder
Represented by an icon of a file folder with an application window in front of it, program folders contain shortcut icons and other program folders.

The Start button on the taskbar gives you access to your applications, settings, recently opened documents, the Find utility, the Run command, the Help system, and the Shut Down command. Clicking the Start button opens the Start menu. Choosing the Programs option at the top of the Start menu displays the Programs menu, which lists the *program folders* on your system. Program folders are listed first, followed by shortcuts (see Figure A.2).

When the Start menu is open, moving the mouse pointer moves a selection bar through the menu options. When the selection bar highlights a menu command with a right-facing triangle, a submenu opens. Click the shortcut icon to start an application. If a menu command is followed by an ellipsis, clicking that command opens a dialog box.

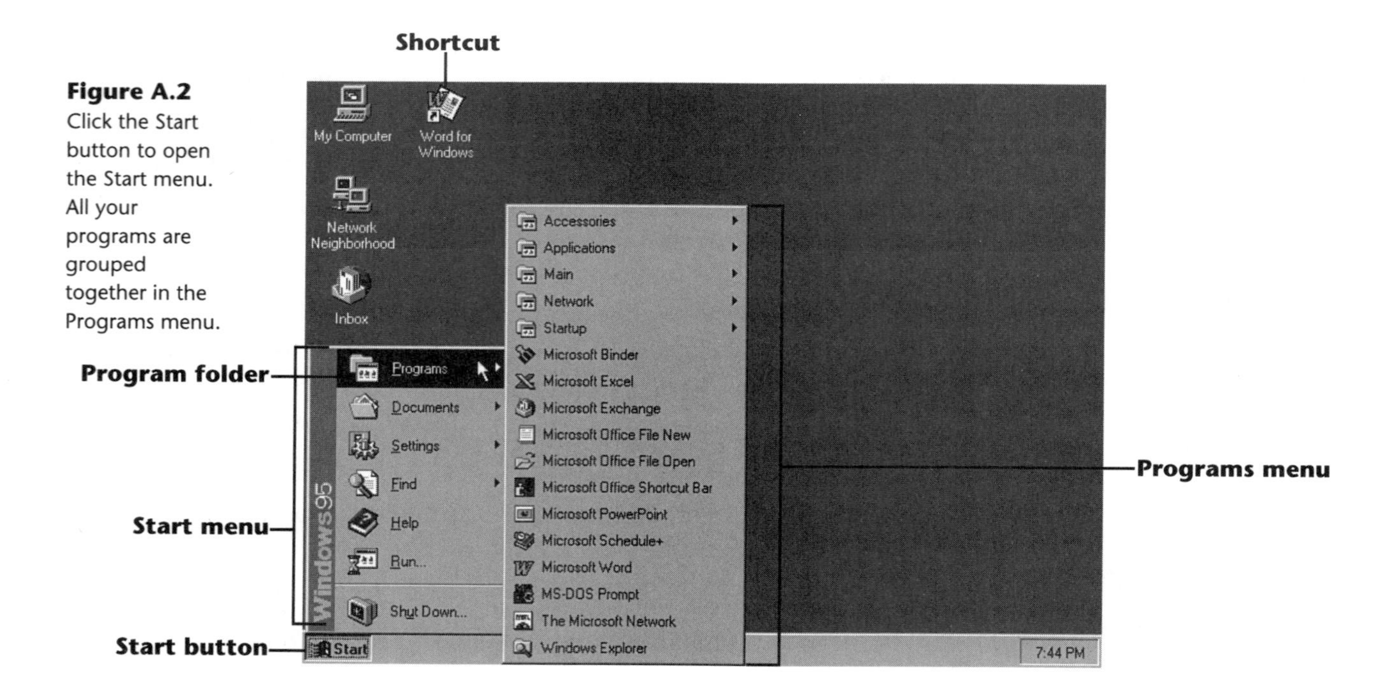

Figure A.2 Click the Start button to open the Start menu. All your programs are grouped together in the Programs menu.

Objective 4: Identify the Elements of a Window

In the Windows program, everything opens in a window. Applications open in windows, documents open in windows, and dialog boxes open in windows. For example, double-clicking the My Computer icon opens the My Computer application into a window. Because window elements stay the same for all Windows applications, this section uses the My Computer window for illustration.

Title Bar

Across the top of each window is its title bar. A title bar contains the name of the open window as well as three buttons to manipulate windows. The Minimize button is for reducing windows to a button on the taskbar. The Maximize button is for expanding windows to fill the desktop. The Close button is for closing the window.

Menu Bar

The menu bar gives you access to the application's menus. Menus enable you to select options that perform functions or carry out commands (see Figure A.3). The File menu in My Computer, for example, enables you to open, save and print files.

Some menu options require you to enter additional information. When you select one of these options, a dialog box opens (see Figure A.4). You either type the additional information, select from a list of options, or select a button. Most dialog boxes have a Cancel button, which closes the dialog box without saving the changes; an OK button, which closes the dialog box and saves the changes; and a Help button, which opens a Help window.

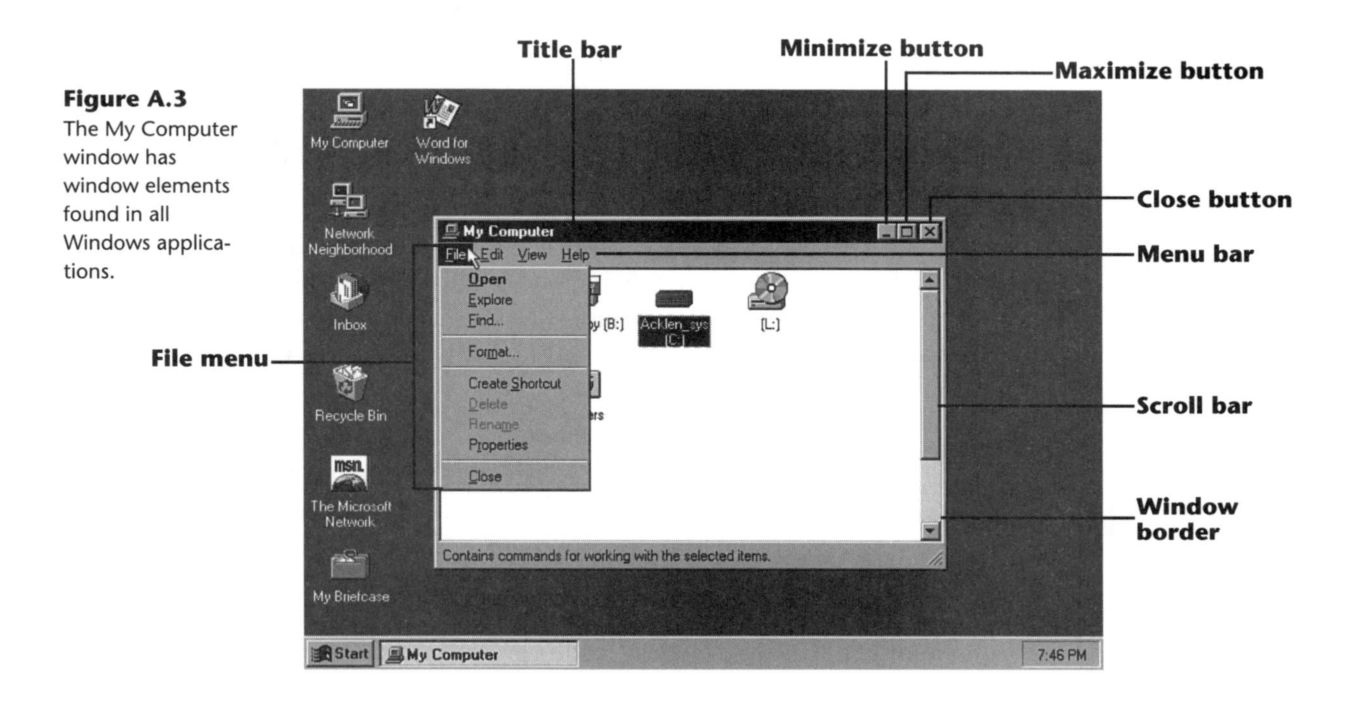

Figure A.3
The My Computer window has window elements found in all Windows applications.

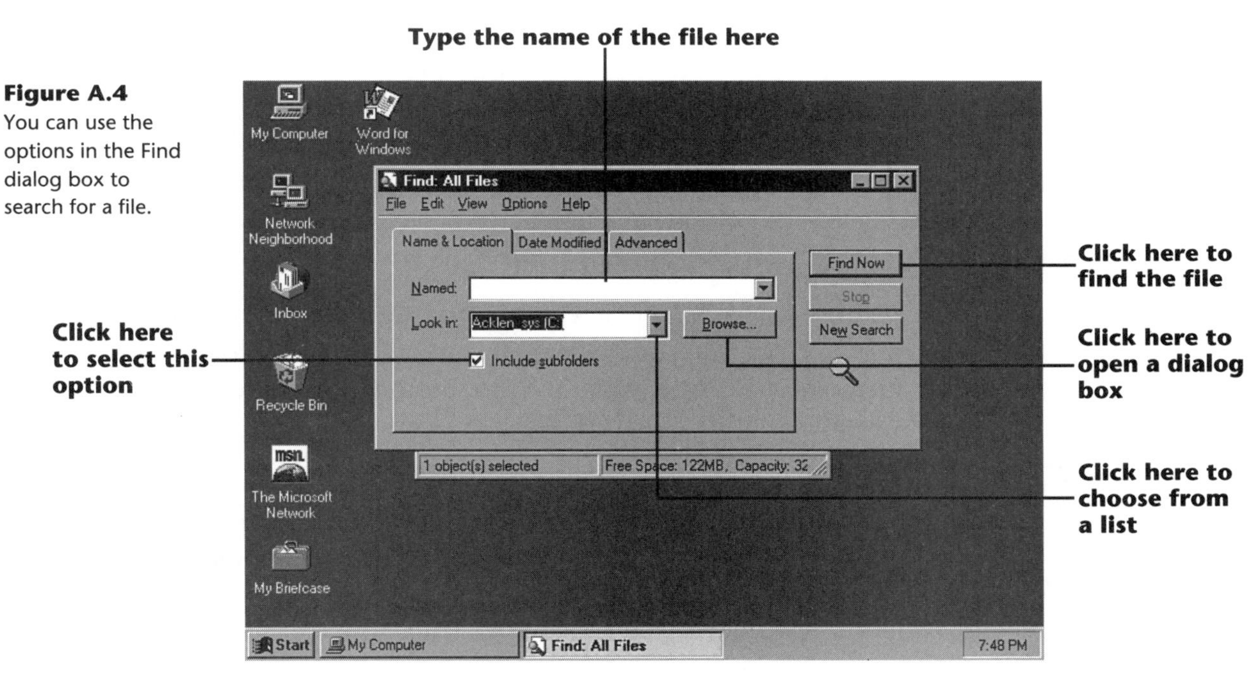

Figure A.4
You can use the options in the Find dialog box to search for a file.

Scroll Bars

Scroll bars appear when you have more information in a window than is currently displayed on-screen. A horizontal scroll bar appears along the bottom of a window and a vertical scroll bar appears along the right side of a window.

Window Border

The window border identifies the edge of the window. In most windows, it can be used to change the size of a window. The window corner is used to resize a window on two sides at the same time.

Objective 5: Manipulate Windows

When you work with windows, you need to know how to arrange them. You can shrink the window into a button or enlarge the window to fill the desktop. You can stack windows together or give them each an equal slice of the desktop.

Changing the size and position of a window enables you to see more than one application window, which makes copying and pasting data between programs much easier. You can also move a window to any location on the desktop. By moving application windows, you can arrange your work on the Windows desktop just as you arrange papers on your desk.

Maximizing a Window

Maximize
To increase the size of a window so that it fills the entire screen.

You can *maximize* a window so it fills the desktop. Maximizing a window gives you more space to work in. To maximize a window, click the Maximize button on the title bar.

Minimizing a Window

Minimize
To reduce a window to an button.

When you *minimize* a window, it shrinks the window to a button on the taskbar. Even though you can't see the window anymore, the application stays loaded in the computer's memory. To minimize a window, click the Minimize button on the title bar.

Restoring a Window

When a window is maximized, the Maximize button changes into a Restore button. Clicking the Restore button restores the window back to the original size and position before the window was maximized.

Closing a Window

When you are finished working in a window, you can close the window by clicking the Close button. Closing an application window exits the program, removing it from memory. When you click the Close button, the window (on the desktop) and the window button (on the taskbar) disappear.

Arranging Windows

Tile
To arrange open windows on the desktop so that they do not overlap.

Cascade
To arrange open windows on the desktop so that they overlap, with only the title bar of each window (behind the top window) displayed.

Changing the size and position of a window enables you to see more than one application window, which makes copying and pasting data between programs much easier. You can also move a window to any location on the desktop. By moving application windows, you can arrange your work on the Windows desktop just as you arrange papers on your desk.

Use one of the following options to arrange windows:

- Right-click the Taskbar and choose Tile **H**orizontally.
- Right-click the Taskbar and choose Tile **V**ertically. See Figure A.5 for an example.
- Right-click the Taskbar and choose **C**ascade. See Figure A.6 for an example.

- Click and drag the window's title bar to move to the window around on the desktop.
- Click and drag a window border (or corner) to increase or decrease the size of the window.

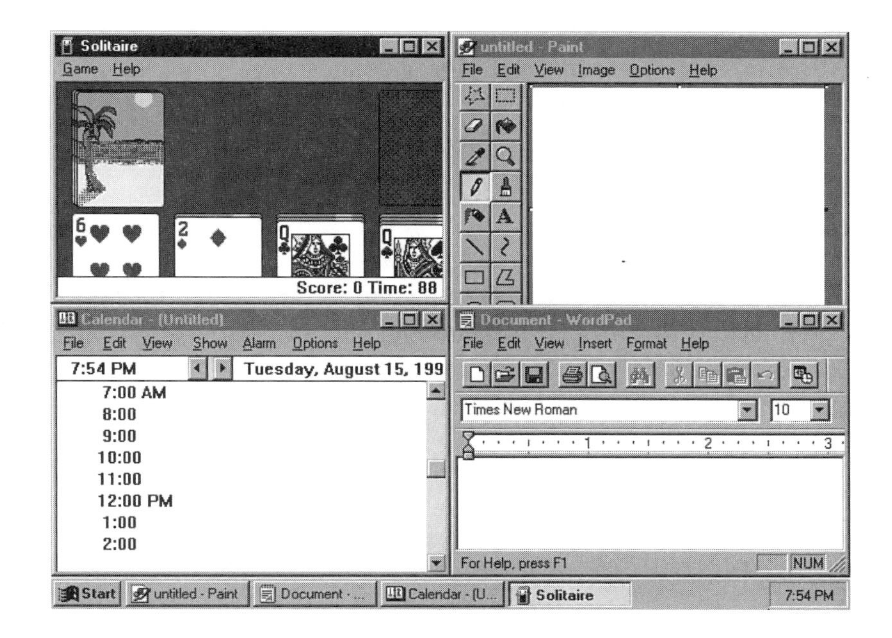

Figure A.5
The windows are tiled vertically across the desktop.

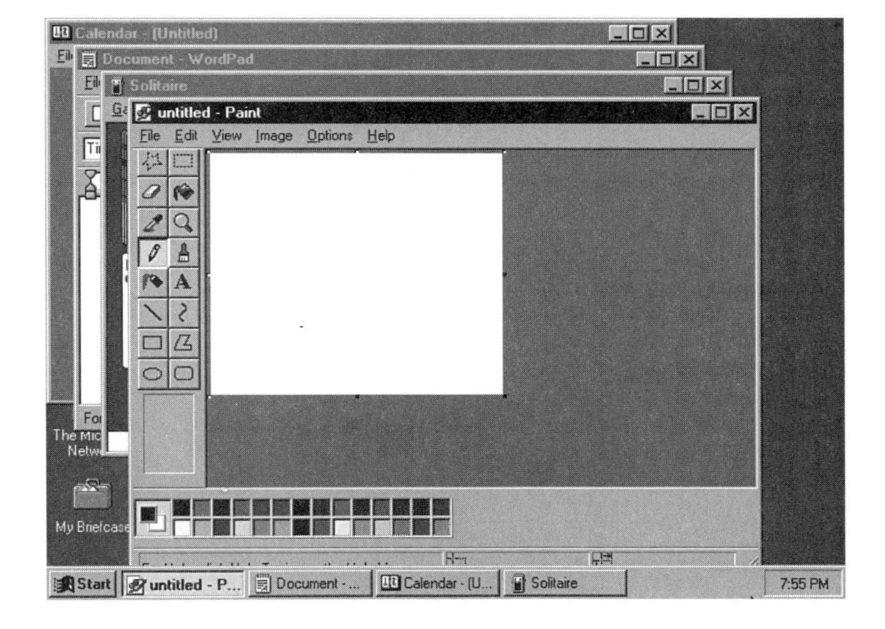

Figure A.6
The windows are cascaded on the desktop.

Objective 6: Exit the Windows 95 Program

In Windows 95, you use the Shut Down command to exit the Windows program. You should always use this command, which closes all open applications and files, before you turn off the computer. If you haven't saved your work in an application when you choose this command, you'll be prompted to save your changes before Windows shuts down.

Exiting Windows

You should always exit Windows before turning off your computer. To exit Windows, follow these steps:

1. Click the Start button on the taskbar.
2. Choose Shut Down.
3. Choose Shut down the computer.
4. Choose Yes.

Windows displays a message asking you to wait while the computer is shutting down. When this process is complete, a message appears telling you that you can safely turn off your computer now.

Index

A

B

C

D

E

F-G

H

I-K

L

M

N

O

P-Q

R

S

T

U-V

W

X-Z